Why Parzival?

An Epic of Our Age with Global Reach and Its Secret Connections to Waldorf Education

ALSO BY ERIC G. MÜLLER

- The Waldorf Main Lesson
- Do You Love Your Teachers? Memoir of a Waldorf Teacher
- Life Poems for my Students
- Rounding the Cape of Good Hope
- The Invisible Boat (Volume I)
- The Invisible Boat and the Molten Dragon (Volume II)
- Tiny Tin Elf — (illustrations: Ella Manor Lapointe)
- The Mermaid of Amarvin Island (illustrations: Martina A. Müller)

- Fringe Locations
- Drops on the Water: Stories of Growing Up from a Father and Son (Coauthor: Matthew Zanoni Müller)

- Rites of Rock
- Meet Me at the Met
- The Black Madonna and the Young Sculptor

- Coffee on the Piano for You
- Frogs, Frags, & Kisses
- Pilgrim Poet — Roaming Rebel
- Truth, Lies, & Light (published under Elryn Westerfield)

Why Parzival?

An Epic of Our Age with Global Reach and Its Secret Connections to Waldorf Education

By
Eric G. Müller

Printed with the support of the Fern Hill Fund
and The Foundation for Rudolf Steiner Books

ISBN:
Paperback: 978-1-7366829-8-2
Hardback: 978-1-7366829-9-9

Printed in the USA

Published in 2023
by Alkion Press
14 Old Wagon Road, Ghent, NY 12075
alkion-press.com

Title: Why Parzival? An Epic of Our Age with Global Reach
and Its Secret Connections to Waldorf Education

Author: Eric G. Müller
Layout and Design: Ella Manor Lapointe
Cover Design: Ella Manor Lapointe
Cover Art and Title Page Illustration: Violet Middlebrook
Back Cover Art: Lila Porcelly, Solomon Bergquist, Alexander Madey

CONTENTS

1 ~ AN EPIC OF OUR AGE WITH GLOBAL REACH

An Introduction

15 ~ CREATING CONTEXT

Zooming In

Parzival between the Ancients and the Present

The Rise of the Grail Stories

Grail Motif

45 ~ BOOK ONE

Inheritance and Heritage

Black and White

Gahmuret

Belacane

75 ~ BOOK TWO

Herzeloyde

Who Is Herzeloyde?

89 ~ BOOK THREE

Nature Boy

Encounter with the Birds

"Oh Mother, What Is God?"

Knights in the Forest

Advice, Grief, Departure

Jeschute

Sigune

Fisherman

The Red Knight

King Arthur's Court

Lady Cunneware

The Fight

Gurnemanz

147 ~ **BOOK FOUR**

Belrepeire
Condwiramurs
Mystical Midnight Meeting
Victory, Wedding, Justice
Who is Parzival?

169 ~ **BOOK FIVE**

The Angler
Parzival's Welcome
The Grail Ceremony
Sigune in the Linden Tree
Jeschute and Orilus Reunited
Who Are Sigune and Schionatulander?

197 ~ **BOOK SIX**

Three Drops of Blood
Cundrie, the Sorceress
Ekuba, Queen of Janfuse
Doubt and Departure

225 ~ **BOOK SEVEN**

Pure Knight
Weighing the Options
Obie and Obilot
Battle for Bearosche

239 ~ **BOOK EIGHT**

Antikonie
Chess Gambits
Conflict Resolution

251 ~ **BOOK NINE**

The Return
Sigune the Anchoress

Grail Horse
The Grey Knight
Trevrizent

285 ~ **BOOK TEN**

One Year Later
Orgeluse
Malcreature and Urjans

299 ~ **BOOK ELEVEN**

Gawain's Questions
Terre Marveile, Lit Marveile, Schastel Marveile

311 ~ **BOOK TWELVE**

The Pillar
The Leap
Gramoflanz
Orgeluse Divulges

329 ~ **BOOK THIRTEEN**

Secrecy and Sorting Out
Clinschor
Greetings and Meetings

339 ~ **BOOK FOURTEEN**

Parzival Revealed
Reconciliation

349 ~ **BOOK FIFTEEN**

The Strange Knight
Welcoming Feirefiz
Induction to the Table Round

369 ~ **BOOK SIXTEEN**

The Suffering of Anfortas

Parzival Asks the Question
Reunions: Trevrizent, Condwiramurs, Sigune
Grail Ceremony
Baptism
Departure and New Beginnings
Prester John
Who Is Titurel?

413 ~ ROUNDING OUT THE CIRCLE

Suggested Activities and Assignments

427 ~ Bibliography

431 ~ Acknowledgments

432 ~ About the Author

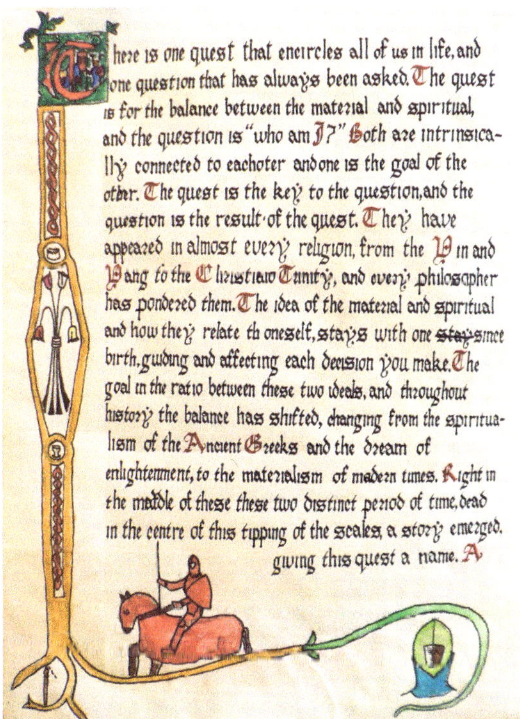

AN EPIC OF OUR AGE WITH GLOBAL REACH

An Introduction

"An artist's duty, as far as I'm concerned, is to reflect the times. . . . That, to me, is my duty. And at this crucial time in our lives, when everything is so desperate, when every day is a matter of survival, I don't think you can help but be involved. . . . We will shape and mold this country or it will not be molded and shaped at all anymore. . . . How can you be an artist and NOT reflect the times? That to me is the definition of an artist." ~ Nina Simone

The study of Wolfram von Eschenbach's *Parzival* in the 11th grade has been a staple of Waldorf education since its inception a hundred years ago in mid-January 1923—a mere fortnight after the burning of the first Goetheanum—when Walter Johannes Stein, after numerous discussions with Rudolf Steiner, taught that first inaugural block. From then on it has held a prominent position in the curriculum. For my part, I have taught

Parzival for the last twenty five years at the Hawthorne Valley Waldorf High School in upstate New York. It continues to be one of my favorite blocks to teach for a multiple reasons: it's a great and profound story that has proved the test of time and relates to where the 11th graders are in their development; it addresses the challenges we, as modern human beings, are forced to face, and illustrates the path of development we all share, while providing answers and solutions to almost every challenge imaginable; it clarifies the different layers of love and life from an outer and inner perspective; Parzival's journey is the prototype of each person's evolving journey into the world and into the soul, offering endless opportunities for in-depth discussions; indeed, there is something for everybody through its all-encompassing and all-inclusive nature, for the thematic content provides us with the means to harmonize the multifaceted polarities of the world, especially in regard to the dichotomy between spirit and matter, the seen and unseen, the good and the bad. *Parzival* bolsters the inner life and wakes us up to the needs of the world and our fellow human beings, and through awakening we become more aware and willing to take action where it is needed and necessary. The layers of deep mythical content are expressed through an abundance of archetypal imagery, which makes working with this tale unforgettable and can leave a lifelong impact.

Only recently have some high schools begun to drop this medieval romance from the curriculum, especially here in the USA. This surprised me, given the unique standing of *Parzival* in Waldorf schools, which, however, spurred me on to take a new and fresh look at why Rudolf Steiner deemed this particular Grail poem to be of such profound importance, expressly for our modern age and the students in the 11th grade. Though convinced of its validity, I nevertheless found myself questioning my core values and reasons for teaching this block year after year. In *The Kingdom of Childhood*, Steiner states:

> It is essential that you have some understanding of the real essence of every subject that you teach, so that you do not use things in your teaching that are remote from life itself. Everything that is

> intimately connected with life can be understood. I could even say that whatever one really understands has this intimate connection with life.[1]

During my reevaluation and thorough scrutiny, I asked myself: Has my teaching of *Parzival* "become remote from life?" How successful have I been in connecting the contents with life? Is it still relevant to the students? To what extent does it meet them? Is it too Eurocentric? Have I unwittingly become abstract and intellectual? I questioned the penetration of my own understanding of this complex and deeply arcane literary work. In truth, who can ever plumb its depths? Anybody who has ever studied or taught *Parzival* knows that it's a never-ending venture, with new questions constantly arising. Still, have I been able to reflect clearly enough how Parzival portrays the times we live in? Are my elucidations and guidance enough to satisfy the wide range of contemporary students who come from all walks of life, races, and cultures? Does it truly reach beyond the here and now into the future? If yes, have I been effective enough in conveying that? Have I been conscious enough of how this "intimate connection with life" changes with the times, as it does and must? At least I've tried. The endeavor to persevere I call "*Parzivalling*."

The impulse to write about my experiences as a teacher happened to correspond with the centennial of the first *Parzival* block—an appropriate moment to honor Wolfram's epic and to give thanks to the tremendous work rendered by scholars, fellow teachers, and students all around the world. Moreover, I wanted to uncover and track numerous unanswered questions that still lingered (and will continue to do so), even after all these years. In my pursuit of the ever-growing number of questions, Parzival's overriding validity revealed and confirmed itself with newfound freshness. The more I entered into the work and themes, the more I was convinced, all over again, of their relevance, not only for adolescents but for anybody who is interested in Eschenbach's *Parzival,*" for they carry a prophetic dimension

1 Rudolf Steiner, *The Kingdom of Childhood*, Torquay, August 16, 1924, (Anthroposophic Press, 1995), p. 72.

which makes them as valid now as when they were first composed."[2] The thematic content speaks directly to 11th graders as they begin to venture into their own interior, asking deeper life questions about love, life, death, destiny, and the spirit. At this age they often feel like outsiders, and Parzival, to a large extent, is the ultimate outsider who struggles through his imperfections to find his true self. The students know that anyone who has deeper questions and seeks the truth will automatically feel somewhat severed from the crowd. *Parzival* offers a roadmap to an authentic life.

Parzival is more like a living plant than a book—a tree bearing new and ever-changing fruit, depending on the times, for each age demands something different. And each page is like a leaf that grows and wilts, germinates and buds. Moreover, the epic's groundwork is strewn with seeds that sprout when the time is at hand. It is not a finished product, but constantly in the making. The storyteller, the listener, and the reader, they all become cocreators. Alternatively, one could compare *Parzival* to the fabulous phoenix that cyclically rekindles itself, rising from the ashes in each successive age. And the age we are living in now is another one of these nodal moments of renewal.

Over the years I have had numerous deeply moving moments with my students. These successes, failures, and insights are worth sharing to some degree, as they go hand in hand with my emerging and evolving understanding of the material. As mentioned, students connect most readily to the thematic content if it feels real and relevant to their own lives and to our contemporary circumstances. More recently, I've noticed, the students are especially interested to hear how *Parzival* might relate to other cultures and their respective worldviews—in other words, its *global reach*, socially, politically, and culturally. And surprisingly, I have found an ever-greater openness to the spiritual underpinnings of *Parzival* and life as such, and how the divine or mystical aspects are portrayed—or not—in society. The students generally do not know much about the world's various religions but are eager to find out more, especially since increased focus and

2 René Querido, *The Mystery of the Holy Grail: A Modern Path of Initiation*, (Rudolf Steiner Publication, 1991), p. V.

respect has been given to the indigenous people and their respective points of view in recent years, all of which embrace a vast and complex sacred cosmology. Adolescents are, after all, in pursuit of meaning, truth, and the highest ideals. They stand midway between the senses and the spirit, and there is a fresh desire to know more about this invisible world in a non-judgmental and objective manner. Mere ideology is anathema to most students, as is anything that has a moralizing tone. They readily respond to open-minded discussions, empirical evidence, and probing questions, in contrast to theory or intellectual notions. Moreover, they cherish a deep reverence for the spirituality, beliefs, and experiences of non-Western cultures, which they want to see reflected in the classroom. In *Why Parzival?* I include parallels from other countries and cultures that mirror and relate to the multilayered themes of the book. The quest for the Holy Grail is, in essence, Love in the making and the wish to embrace all worldviews within the splendor of diversity while simultaneously recognizing the overarching commonality. However, everybody has to arrive at the unifying goals out of themselves—a journey decided upon in freedom.

René Querido, in his book *The Mystery of the Holy Grail*, offers seven steps that can help in the understanding and experience of *Parzival* (some of which can be well used in teaching literature as such). They are as follows: *Step 1.* The plot—the action—the story. *Step 2.* The poetry—the language—the form. *Step 3.* The psychological significance (the interplay of the characters). *Step 4.* The portrayal of individualities in the course of successive incarnations. *Step 5.* The historical background: the time of Christ, the ninth century, the thirteenth century. *Step 6.* The symbolic significance. *Step 7.* The esoteric level: The quest for the Grail as a path of initiation.[3]

All of the above-mentioned steps are included in this book, and I expect most people reading these pages will be somewhat familiar with the Anthroposophical and Theosophical underpinnings. Although the esoteric aspects live within me—to the best of my understanding—I am circum-

3 Querido, p. 22.

spect in how I convey the content to the students. One has to keep it real, objective, and appropriate to the moment. Most of the esoteric content is left unsaid.

It is surprising to what extent *Parzival* and the Grail themes have directly influenced countless facets of contemporary life and popular culture. Of the numerous movies made, some stand out: There's the poignant and heartbreaking film *The Fisher King*, starring Robin Williams and Jeff Bridges, which is a modern rendering of the Grail story set in Manhattan. Or Steven Spielberg's sci-fi movie *Ready Player One*, set in the year 2045, which one of my students brought to my attention a few years back. The movie is based on Ernest Cline's bestseller of the same name, where humans find their salvation in OASIS, a virtual reality universe. In keeping with the quest theme, the hero's virtual name is Parzival—Wade Owen Watts' OASIS avatar. Other popular films that depict the Grail story are *Monty Python and the Holy Grail, Indiana Jones and the Last Crusade, The Silver Chalice, Excalibur, The Da Vinci Code, Captain Thunder, Blood of the Templars*, and many more. Films closely related to the theme of Parzival's quest or aspects thereof include *Good Will Hunting, Forrest Gump, The Natural, Heart of Darkness, Apocalypse Now, Siddhartha, Lord of the Rings, Harry Potter,*[4] and most prominently the blockbuster: *Star Wars*, episodes 4, 5, and 6.[5]

Depending on the context, I sometimes tell the students about the closer connection between *Star Wars*, Waldorf education, and anthroposophy. All students know about the *Star Wars* franchise, most have seen at least one of the films, and there are always some diehard *Star Wars* devotees in every class who know every detail. The Star Wars fandom runs deep and is found in every corner of the world. Nevertheless, there are some unknown aspects of the origin story.

---

4 See J. K. Rowling's *Harry Potter and the Philosopher's Stone.*

5 For more information about some of these last-mentioned films, see *Healing the Fisher King* by Shelly Durrell, (Art Tao Press, 2002).

In the article "Source of the Force,"[6] Douglas Gabriel writes how he and a few other anthroposophists collaborated with Marcia Lucas on the *Star Wars* script, which affected some key aspects of the storyline. Douglas and his colleagues from the Waldorf Institute in Michigan spent three days with Marcia Lucas (nee Griffin) to transform the story, conceived by George Lucas, into a modern fairy tale. Marcia, who was well acquainted with anthroposophy and the works of Rudolf Steiner, had gone to Werner Glass[7] to make the story "more Waldorf-inspired," as Werner said: "so it will have good merit as both a movie and a spiritual story."[8] Marcia wanted their help because it lacked the element of spirituality. Through their collaboration the storyline expanded, became more archetypal, and most importantly, worked on character development. It was Douglas Gabriel, for instance, who suggested that the name Lukas Starkiller be changed to Lukas Skywalker—representing the archetypal human being—in accord with Native American and Tibetan traditions. He also came up with the "light saber." Marcia and Douglas, in developing Luke Skywalker, took into account that every person has to deal with polarities within their souls—the extremes—and that it's best for every Jedi to follow the middle path, the "Force." Finding the middle between the extremes is central to *Star Wars*, as it is to *Parzival*. Following the middle path is also central to Buddhism.

In 1977, just before the launch of *Star Wars* (the first of the Star Wars movies, later subtitled *Episode IV, A New Hope*), Marcia and George Lucas, grateful for all the help they had received, offered all Waldorf schools in the US an advanced screening of the film as a fundraiser. Most schools, however, declined the generous offer, including the school in Eugene, where I later taught, due to the general opposition to technology, and the adverse effects of TV and movies on little children. It is slightly ironic, since most

---

6 Douglas Gabriel, "*The Source of the Force*: Secret Behind Star Wars Inspiration." https://neoanthroposophy.com/2017/02/05/source-of-the-force-secret-behind-star-wars-inspiration/

7 Founder of the "Waldorf Institute" in Detroit, a Waldorf teacher education institution.

8 Gabriel, "*The Source of the Force*:"

Waldorf schools and teacher education programs embraced online teaching so readily during the pandemic, and still do, in many instances.

Douglas Gabriel was also consulted on the films, *Indiana Jones and the Raiders of the Lost Ark,* and *Indiana Jones and the Last Crusade*, directed by Steven Spielberg. In the latter, he was able to convey the esoteric background especially related to the Holy Grail, as well as the basic storyline that includes crusaders, Grail knights, archeologists, the CIA, Nubian temples, and Nazis.[9] However, Douglas was disappointed in the outcome of both movies, as it diluted and trivialized the esoteric content, reducing it to sheer entertainment. Yet, it has prodded some people to delve deeper and to search for greater truths behind the meaning of the Grail.

Many of the films mentioned above were based on books, such as *Ready Player One, Siddhartha, The Da Vinci Code,* to mention only a few, which were also bestsellers. They address, directly and indirectly, qualities that Parzival had to develop within himself through failure, suffering, and disciplined perseverance. Eileen Hutchins, in her *Parzival: An Introduction*, gives two pertinent examples of other notable books, one from the East and the other from the West: Solzhenitsyn's *Gulag Archipelago* and Saul Bellow's *Humbold's Gift*. Solzhenitsyn describes his personal experiences in the awful conditions of the Siberian concentration camp, which consequently led to a whole new outlook on life. While suffering through a near-fatal illness, a camp doctor came to care for him, telling him that all suffering and punishment that humans have to endure are deserved. Next morning that Jewish doctor was found murdered. The last words of the doctor had made a deep impression on Solzhenitsyn, and he recognized his own failings. But more importantly, he realized that disasters and suffering could *awaken new faculties*. Similarly, the protagonist of *Humbold's Gift*, Charlie Citrine, suffers disastrous setbacks and misfortunes. As the situation spins out of control, a friend introduces him to the works of Rudolf Steiner, which puts him onto a path of active thinking and meditation, and he realizes that the qualities he was gaining were worth far more than

---

9 For a detailed account see: https://neoanthroposophy.com/2017/02/05/the-enduring-legacy-of-hans-solo-and-indian-jones/

anything material. In both books, the central characters go through major setbacks and hardships, which help them to wake up to themselves. Their profound soul development could not have happened without the timely intervention of other people. At a nodal moment of their lives, when they needed it most, they received insights that prompted and guided them to enter into a path of self-development, which ultimately led to new faculties and changed the course of their lives. They could never have attained higher consciousness and a new-found compassionate understanding for other human beings without outside help. Both these Noble Prize winners exemplify a Parzivalian path of self-development, appropriate and fitting for our modern age.[10]

A while back I took part in a reading together with an African-American author, Neil J. Smith, a former boxer and member of the Black Panther Party. In his novel, *On the Ropes,*[11] he writes of his experiences. I was intrigued that he'd named the protagonist of his semibiographical novel, Perceval—a young black boxer growing up in the socio-political turbulent 60s. I asked Neil why he chose the name Perceval, and he reminded me that JFK was often compared to King Arthur, and that his administration and presidency was likened to the mythical time of Camelot. He went on to explain that Perceval is the mythic hero who has to overcome almost insurmountable obstacles while searching for the Grail, which is the riddle and mystery of his own destiny. "It's a tale of Perceval Jones finding himself, his selfhood," I recall him saying with a twinkle in his eye.

The Grail theme lives deeply in the modern mindset, made expressly evident after the release of Dan Brown's *The Da Vinci Code*, which subsequently spurred the publication of hundreds of books dealing with the Holy Grail. It's a powerful undercurrent of the present global consciousness.

All these examples let the student know how deeply Parzival's journey is connected to our own time, to the problems facing our age, and to the manifold challenges each individual has to face and contend with in their respective lives.

10 Eileen Hutchins, *Parzival: An Introduction* (Temple Lodge, 1992).

11 Neil J. Smith, *On the Ropes* (Austin Macauley, 2020).

Schools have vastly varied approaches to teaching this block, depending on the teacher, the school, and the region. They all have their merits. My friend Norman Skillen, who taught the *Parzival* block in the Constantia Waldorf School in Cape Town, South Africa, for many years, described to me the tradition that they had developed over the years. The core idea was that the story should be *told* rather than read, in conjunction with a challenging and demanding journey. The scenery in the Cape is, of course, stunning, offering an abundance of mountains, valleys, kloofs, wild rocky terrain, plateaus, spectacular ocean views, and botanical wonders. On any given day the students would not know their daily destination and had no clue what awaited them (on one occasion the students were even blindfolded). In the evenings they usually stayed at a rustic hostel, of which there are a number dotted throughout the landscape. The "Parzival Journey" was a communal event in that there was substantial parental involvement, including delivering food to each venue ahead of time, to make it appear as if it was "provided by the Grail." The story was narrated in the bardic tradition on the trail or indoors at the respective hostels. Every day, time was set aside for the students to work on their journals. These Parzival Journeys, no matter what form they took, served as a community bonding experience, as well as an individual journey of self-discovery, interspersed with moments of courage in the face of the unknown. Apart from the daily journal entries, most of the reading, artwork, discussions, essays, and creative writing was completed back in the classroom after their return, having heard the whole story. A key element to the success of the Parzival Journey was that all cell phones were left at home. In the interim, I have heard of a growing number of other schools that also take students on a comparable retreat or journey.

An exchange student from Chile, South America, gushed about her *Parzival* block in which they did something similar, except that they camped out on a farm. The students were not required to read the book but were given the opportunity to live into the medieval experience through listening. Hearing the story narrated in a vibrant and immediate manner lets the imaginations rise up more vividly than merely reading the medieval text, which to a modern reader might appear long winded and confusing. It certainly is demanding (luckily, most Waldorf teachers become good storytellers over time). Naturally, not all schools are able to organize such substantial trips. However, they might still choose to follow an equivalent format, retelling the story, rather than having the students read the text. More and more teachers, I've discovered, prefer retelling the story than having the students read Eschenbach.

Alternatively, some teachers ask the students to read the entire epic, followed up by academic papers on assigned topics, with sparse artistic activities. This does train close reading and critical thinking, but there is the danger that students will experience this approach as one-sided, intellectual, wearisome, and off-putting.

Several schools focus only on the chapters dealing directly with Parzival, without covering the sections on Gawain, due to time constraints, which is understandable, since every Parzival block feels like it is too short. That said, Gawain's adventures are essential to Parzival's development and should be included in some form or other. It is not a subplot of *Parzival* as some scholars or teachers maintain, but essential to the whole. Each teacher will emphasize different aspects of the story, depending on any number of factors. A school in Germany might, for instance, focus more on the influences of Middle High German on the German language, or the historical background, as it applies to Central Europe.

In regard to the teaching style, I have chosen the middle path. Not being able to go on a journey with the students for a number of reasons, I require the students to read some of the chapters, leaving others optional. I make a point of retelling certain imaginations in a vivid and creative manner, while summarizing other segments. Or we sit in a circle, each student reading a few paragraphs, followed by comments and discussions. For the Gawain part, I have the students report individually on the respective chapters.

Teaching *Parzival* has also found footing in the Far East. The Lei Chuang Waldorf School in Taichung, Taiwan, after developing the main lesson block in the 11th grade for a number of years, staged a full-scale theatrical production of Parzival in the city's theater—approved and subsidized by the state school authority. "Project *Parzival*" became a collaborative event. Apart from a set designer, costume designer, composer, and playwright working on the project, the entire high school was involved. The 9th, 10th, and 11th grade made up the orchestra and the chorus, supporting the 12th grade in their senior play, which included sundry backstage duties. The universality of the medieval Parzival story shone through with all of its poignant power.[12] This grand production, performed in Chinese, had a Wagnerian feel to it, and underscored the global reach of the story and the all-encompassing themes of human development.

Steiner recommended that one should treat the *Parzival* main lesson differently to any other block. What is most important is that the students receive the imaginations of this epic as richly and vibrantly as possible. It is the pictorial content that has the greatest effect. Nevertheless, the discussions, the reading, the reports, the writing of essays, the poetry, the illustrations and drawings or paintings, and the pursuit of meaning remain essential.

---

12 From discussions with Jörg Peter Schmidt, who also wrote about the performance: https://www.sophiainstitute.us/blog/parsifal-in-taiwan,

A few schools—mostly in the French-speaking countries—choose to study Chrétien de Troyes' *Le Conte du Graal*, over Eschenbach's version. It has also become increasingly customary to use abridged versions, though the subtleties and deliciously provocative aspects tend to get lost, especially for the students—and there always are some—who choose and want to read the entire book. They should not be denied that opportunity. That said, there are many pros to using abridged versions, especially for exchange students or students who struggle with reading.

As teachers we learn from one another, and it is always an enriching and satisfying experience to discuss different modes of teaching and to share assignments, projects, and activities with colleagues. In this book I include some of what I've learned from numerous teachers and authors, but mostly from the work with the students right in front of me. At the end of the chapters, I include "Discussion Topics and Questions" for teachers. And at the end of the book, I include suggestions for assignments. These discussion topics, questions, and assignments often arose spontaneously over the years, and only some of them are covered in every block. Each year something new arises.

What is conveyed in these pages is my personal understanding of *Parzival*—and I have taken liberties with some of the interpretations. That said, I am deeply indebted to the writers and scholars who have written and spoken on the subject, most of all Rudolf Steiner. I owe many of my insights to them. Of course, one can never do justice to the far-reaching contents of *Parzival*. It is a work in progress. How we convey the content within the changing times—that's what counts—each in our own way. In all the many exchanges, in and out of the classroom, I have at least reconfirmed my own reasons for why I teach *Parzival*. I know of no other literary work that expresses activism in such an all-encompassing manner, though it demands reading between the lines and having a sense for the imponderables. The answers to many of the world's problems can be found within the pages of *Parzival*, but we need to gain the faculties and capacities to inwardly grow so we can thoroughly wash our eyes to see and read the ever-evolving script. We have to become the Grail to understand the Grail, and that entails a lifelong quest. May others find something worthwhile in these pages. It is my ardent wish that this book will serve those who want to broaden and deepen their understanding of *Parzival*, and that it will be of value to Waldorf teachers and the Waldorf school movement as a whole.

Illustrations:

1. Opening page from a *Parzival* main lesson book (Solomon Berquist).
2. From a *Parzival* performance at the Lei Chuang Waldorf School in Taichung, Taiwan (photo by Jörg Peter Schmidt).

CREATING CONTEXT

Zooming In

"Look at how a single candle can both defy and define darkness."
~ Anne Frank

AT THE OUTSET of the pandemic, I inwardly rebelled against teaching the first *Parzival* lesson remotely, though I readily complied, understanding the need. Waldorf teachers are generally in agreement that the initial lesson of any course or block sets the tone and tenor of all subsequent classes. Care and conscious effort are put into any introductory class with the aim of getting the ball rolling, setting a mood, giving an overview, and establishing a rhythm (a bit like novelists obsessing over their first line or paragraph). One tries to capture the attention of the students, get them enthused, excited, and engaged by stimulating their curiosity for the rest of the three- or four-week block. The seedling class ought to evoke feelings of profundity and significance that will hold the students in good stead for the rest of their lives in one way or another. As Steiner says in *Practical Advice to Teachers*: "You must regard the first lesson you have with your students in every class as extremely significant. In a certain sense a far more important element emanates from this first lesson than from all the others."[1] It's a challenging task at the best of times, but now made more difficult by having to utilize the cyber world of online learning. During the first weeks of the pandemic, I said to myself: I won't wear a mask while teaching, I won't teach outside, I won't get tested nor vaccinated, and I most certainly won't succumb to teaching via Zoom. Of course, I ended up doing all of those no-no-*noes*. And now it forced me to rethink my first class.

Every year I anyway review and reimagine my approach to teaching based on the students in front of me and my own inner development, but this year felt like a pivotal year, not only because of the pandemic but also due to the Black Lives Matter movement and the subsequent growth of DEI programs implemented in institutions and schools all around the country that compelled people to reflect on social injustices in the Western world, especially in the USA. In many ways that first Zoom class on *Parzival* became a seminal moment, prodding me to remember, reexamine, and review my reasons for teaching *Parzival*. I had to come up with a different approach for my inauguratory lesson via Zoom. I couldn't simply rely on my normal rhythm for this four-week block. I admired other teachers who seemed to be faring so much better, who felt comfortable with the remote format and took pride in having mastered this new technocratic frontier.

One by one the students Zoomed in until I had them all, though some had their cameras turned off for one reason or another—unreliable connections in our rural area or an unwillingness to expose their home situation. Others only showed a fraction of themselves. All muted. Impossible to gauge their communal mood, I endeavored to set the pace by an upbeat approach, going through the announcements, but dispensing with the communal Morning Verse, poetry, and singing, mainly because of the impossibility of reciting

1 Rudolf Steiner, *Practical Advice to Teachers*, Lecture Four (Anthroposophic Press, 2000), p. 47.

and singing in unison. That attunement to the day would have to fall away. Other teachers did not give up so easily and I applaud them for that. Be that as it may, I came up with a different introduction, straightforward and simple, which, in retrospect, proved to be effective.

I asked them the following question: *What are the most important and crucial questions facing us today?* It's not that I hadn't asked this kind of question in other classes before, but the context had shifted. Now, I consciously placed the question in front of them like an initiatory inscription on the gateway of our *Parzival* block—similar to the "Know Thyself" (*Gnothi Seauton*) inscribed above the forecourt of the Temple of Apollo at Delphi. Mostly, I'd asked that kind of question at the end of a *Parzival* block. My hope was to get everyone involved, get them thinking, and let the question serve as a stepping-stone to the thematic content of *Parzival*.

I was pleasantly surprised at the response. Every student not only answered my question, but backed up their answers, elucidated them, and posed further questions. Below is a brief summary of their input to which we referred throughout the rest of the block whenever the opportunity arose.

The first student, Kelani,[2] talked about the pandemic, and how humanity around the globe has been influenced, some more than others; the dire consequences of the virus and the resultant domino effect. Initially, she spoke in a quiet and objective manner, until she posed her own question, her voice animated and infused with passion: "What is really going on? Who really knows what this pandemic is all about, and what is really happening?" She paused. Even though we were reduced to ten pixelated Zoom rectangles (eleven with me), something had ignited. I could almost feel the other students leaning in. "What and who can we trust? People say different things, have opposing opinions, and there are so many extremes and different viewpoints; what is trustworthy?" For emphasis she repeated the word *trustworthy*, before adding, "How can we get to the *truth* of something? Who is worthy of trust?"

2 Not their real names.

Vivy spoke next: "How can we get people to treat each other with *kindness* and *respect?*" She sat cross-legged on her bed at home. "I mean, not only to each other, but our surroundings. The environment is disrespected and nature as such is abused. Just look at all the pollution around us. We don't treat the earth with much kindness. What needs to happen to change that?" I almost saw the simultaneous answer enter her mind when she flicked her long blonde hair back, adding, "I think it means that we have to *work on ourselves* in order to treat each other kindlier. Seriously, why do we *show* so little respect to others or to each other? But I have one more thought," she hastened to insert. "We have to *examine* and *reassess* the structure of how our Government operates. Not only the Government but the structure of our economy—this I consider to be extremely important, especially in the light of the storming of the United States Capitol five days ago on January 6. How could things have deteriorated to such an extent as to cause an unruly and riled up mob to march to the Capitol in an infantile and futile attempt to 'stop the steal?' Really, I don't get it. How?" Heads nodded. I was taking furious notes in my own shorthand, trying to keep up with what she was saying.

"I'd like to respond and add to a point that Vivy made," Sariah said, lifting her hand. "You know, when she talked about the structure of the economy. I think it is extremely important that we close the gaps of inequality. So much of that depends on the way economy is structured. My question would be: How can one get everybody on board to work toward closing the economic gaps, so that we don't have such a huge gap between the rich and the poor?" I could see that she wanted to say more, but she leaned back and muted herself.

Quintin, who always thinks before he speaks, posed the question, "What are the most important things to know and to learn? I know it sounds vague, but what determines the choices that we make? Isn't that what's important: the choices that we make—that *are* made? Come to think of it, how *do* we know and learn things? You, know, really know?" He paused. "One more thing, which I think that our time needs to face," he continued, "is that our society is *losing touch* with reality; not only that, we're losing touch with one another. Yes, we're constantly losing touch—with everything. What can we do about that? We live in a fragmented society. If we don't become whole, we're lost. But how to fix it—that's the question."

For a while nobody spoke. Those are the pregnant silences, which feel alive in the schoolroom, but can be experienced as a vacuum in the remote classroom. I prodded Leyton, the philosopher of the class. He took a sip from a white mug. "Coffee. Helps me think," and he smiled self-consciously. "Well, okay . . . we should not only look at the immediate future, but at the long-term results of our actions. We try to have quick fixes. Our age is reactionary. That's not going to help in the long run. We need to bear in mind the *big picture*—that which will be effective far into the future. But how do we get that overview? How can we determine what the big picture is? Who determines that picture? Actually," and he hesitated, staring beyond the screen, "it's a bit like having a vision. We have to envision what we want for the future. In a way, we need to become *visionaries*. The big vision needs to be acknowledged by all, otherwise it remains narrow, small, and as Quintin said, fragmented."

"Yes, the big picture, that is exactly what our age needs," I agreed. "To arrive at a common vision. That takes work. And that's what education should be about." I nodded. "So, who's next?"

Kelani, who is an African American and who'd spoken first, interjected. "No offence, but a crucial challenge facing us today is the school curriculum, not just out there in the mainstream but also in the Waldorf Schools." I could feel the others wondering how I might respond. "It needs to change; it needs to be improved. I am grateful for my Waldorf education, but parts of it need to be updated because some aspects are outdated. And we have to keep the minorities in mind." She spoke fast and passionately, every word well-articulated. "We have to keep moving forward. Always remember, we, the minorities, are important. We are equal."

I agreed with her. If we as teachers, do not strive to improve our lessons on a daily basis, then we start to slide; we fall into a rut, especially when we are so-called experts in our respective subjects. We always need to be open to change and be on a journey of becoming, which includes reading the signs of the times, what they call for and from us; just like I was forced to reevaluate how to present this year's inaugural *Parzival* class via the remote-learning platform. We constantly have to be awake to the Zeitgeist. "At any time during this block I am going to call on you and the others about how I am doing in that regard, and to all the other points that have been mentioned." There was much more I wanted to say on this subject, especially in relation to race, but the story of Parzival would offer numerous opportunities to address questions of diversity.

Deion, also African American, who joined the class half way through 10th grade, elaborated on Kelani's points. "Our entire system is based on white colonialism. Propaganda dominates the educational system—especially the American educational system. There is a false sense of white superiority. We've got to *want* to change." Although none of us saw him because he had his camera switched off, I could imagine him, the way he said *want*. "For example, the storming of the Capitol last week, that really *is* America—stemming from a superiority complex; the 'right wing' mentality in America needs to change. And we have to start here and now."

"Indeed," I responded, "and that is what we are endeavoring to do at this very moment, and it's not just the 'right wing' that needs changing, it's extremism. We cannot lose sight of your point. It's all about entering into a dialogue; coming to agreements together. We will have opportunities during this block to discuss this subject. The key phrase you mentioned is, *we've got to want to change*."

Deion, however, wasn't done yet. "I was also referring to the 'Big Picture' that Leyton mentioned. However, we consciously have to see *ourselves* in that big picture. We cannot separate ourselves off from it. We are part of that big picture. We play a role in it and we need to realize what *impact* we have and can have. If there is going to be change and improvement, we have to be part of it—it's a *shared* responsibility. We can't only rely on others to change. We need to be the change we wish to see in the world, as Mahatma Gandhi said—or something like that. At least, I think it was him."

"You're right, the quote is attributed to Ghandi. It's a good one," I responded.

By now, all but three had contributed.

Gerson, possibly the quietest student of the class, who always listened with a slight smile hovering around the corners of his lips, spoke up "I wonder how we can meet the needs of all the people on this overpopulated earth of ours. So many are starving. How can we stop world hunger? How can we spread the wealth around? How can we stop the suffering?" For a moment, his smile slipped from his lips. "We need to come to some form of balance. But how?" He broke into a coy smile again, as if he was embarrassed about his words.

"What's really important is that we start thinking for ourselves," Akino stated. "People are way too much influenced by our leaders. We shouldn't be. Just because they are leaders does not mean they are right. So, my question is: What are the qualities of a good leader? And related to that—why do so many people fall for someone who is obviously corrupt and keeps on lying and breaking his promises?" She was referring to the hero worship of Trump, and how people are misled and influenced by his incendiary and seditious rhetoric, as witnessed during the insurrection a few days earlier. "I think that we need to question leadership. Leadership, how can we be worthy of true leadership?"

"And what about sexism?" Lyra asked. "There are gender inequalities all across the board that need to be addressed. There's the "#MeToo" and the LGBTQ movement, that are starting to wake people up. But things are so entrenched that we don't even notice how our society manipulates people. What about *fast fashions* and the cultural environment? Capitalism furthers sexism and fascism. How can we get a handle on that? I guess, in the end, it's about the rights of each individual, isn't it? But some people suffer more than others. Some are more privileged." And she ended with, "All animals are equal, but some animals are more equal," quoting George Orwell from *Animal Farm*.

Now that everybody had spoken, the discussion continued, mainly based on what had already been mentioned. I promised to bear in mind their essential points and refer back to them during the block, and I already pictured where I could weave in the different themes in order to address the most *pertinent questions we face today*. No matter what one teaches, it always needs to remain relevant to the here and now, our modern age. That also holds true to other classics such as Homer's *Odyssey*, Dante's *Divine Comedy*, or Goethe's *Faust*. If we do teach the classics, then we need to contemporize them—now more than ever.

In summary we distilled the thoughts and questions into the following themes and concepts: trust, kindness, respect, love, relationships, leadership, environment, nature, tolerance, racism, sexism, gender equality, responsibility, education, knowledge, truth / lies, "big picture" or visionary thinking, community and the individual, interconnectedness versus disconnectedness, violence, economy, agreements, hunger, rulership / governance, socio-political structures, evil, self-development, self-reliance, consequences, freedom, right envisioning, dialogue, keeping current, and, of course, diversity and inclusion.

"Now let's see if we can find some insights, clarifications, revelations, and solutions to the above, as we delve into this medieval epic," I said, once we'd gathered the essential thoughts. "Let's see if it truly has something to offer us. I, for one, am looking forward to going on this voyage of discovery with you over the course of the next few weeks. As you can see, we are dealing with the human condition. Whatever we do and cover in this class needs to remain relevant, in one way or another, to you, me, and the times we live in. Thus, as we begin this journey together, let's keep that question in mind throughout the block: *Why Parzival?*"

Parzival between the Ancients and the Present

"But some day you will be old enough to start reading fairy tales again."[3]
~ C.S. Lewis

The following three questions serve as a backdrop to all of my teaching: *Where are we? Where have we come from? Where are we going?* They are implicitly embedded in almost every sentence I speak. They help

3 From the dedication to Lucy Barfield in *The Lion, the Witch and the Wardrobe.*

to put things in context. It's prudent to start from where we are, however briefly. But in order to understand how we have come to the *present* moment, we need to understand the *past*, which in turn can serve as a directive, informing us how we might want to shape the *future* with a greater sense of responsibility and consciousness.

A number of years ago, I was struck by an article in the *National Geographic* on the Hadron Collider.[4] The title alone is telling: "The God Particle." Although it is devoted utterly to science and deals with matter, it still reverts to quasi-spiritual and almost esoteric language. The subtitle reads, "At the heart of all matter." Interesting that they included the word *heart.* The entire article continues in likewise manner. "[I]ts purpose is simple but ambitious: to crack the code of the physical world; to figure out what the universe is made of; in other words, to get to the very bottom of things." And, as the article admits, "a century of particle physics has given us a fundamental truth: Reality doesn't reveal its secrets easily," or "The universe is a tough nut to crack."[5]

The Hadron Collider—the world's largest particle accelerator—is situated hundreds of feet below the Swiss and French border, and it's somewhat like entering a "subterranean lair of one of those James Bond villains."[6] And, indeed, Dan Brown included the European Council for Nuclear Research (CERN) in his mystery thriller *Angels & Demons*, which was later made into a film. It's easy to understand the allusions to something fantastical and *otherworldly* when one sees pictures of this unbelievable place. Joel Frei, in an article in the "Swiss Review" about the Nuclear Research Center in Geneva, describes it in the following way: "It's a bit like a Harry Potter film here—you never really know where these winding paths will lead." And a bit further: "Answers to the big questions are sought here—Where do we come from? Why this world and not another one? How did the

4 Joel Achenbach, "The God Particle," *National Geographic* (March 2008), p. 90.

5 Ibid., p. 96.

6 Ibid., p. 95.

universe develop?"[7] This global scientific village and their research has distinct similarities to the quest for the Holy Grail of medieval times. I find it droll that the *National Geographic* article referred to the universe and its secrets as a "tough nut," which is a little bit like a vessel. Whether its spiritual truth or material truth, the pursuit is *truth*, which is a most fundamental human aspiration. In this instance the scientists are trying to get to the heart of *matter,* to gain the truth. And though they made and make all sorts of interesting discoveries along the way, the elusiveness of the Truth remains—the search for the Grail.

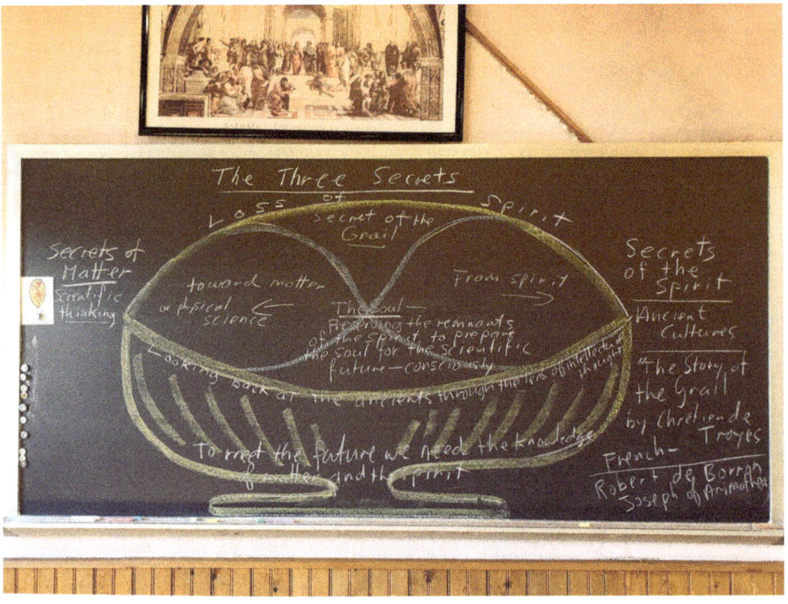

For the ancients around the world, truth was found and experienced in the invisible realms inhabited by goddesses and gods. In ancient India, as we know, the physical world was considered *maya*—illusion. In our modern scientific times, the spiritual world is considered *maya*—it has no reality or is simply dismissed. At best, any talk of the spirit has been relegated to religion. During the thick of the pandemic, we constantly heard the phrase,

7 Joel Frei, "The Unparalleled Experiment," in "Swiss Review: The Magazine for the Swiss Abroad," 2011, p. 12.

"I stand for science," or "follow the science." For the ancients, science, religion, and art were one. Now they have been severed from one another, barely intersecting.

With time, the ancients began to lose direct experience of the spirit. In its place emerged Mystery Centers or their equivalents, such as secret societies in Africa, or the ancient Temple Schools of the Americas, into which the select few were initiated after undergoing severe training and years of strict schooling. Mythologies—the secrets of the universe clothed in stories—were given to the people by the initiated. Kofi Edusei, in his book about the culture of the Akan people in Ghana, calls them *"separation myths"* that explain the reasons behind the gradual separation between humans and the divine order.[8] Many fairy tales from around the world also refer to this separation. Some of the famous Grimms' fairy tales, inspired by initiates of the highest order, belong to the most powerful of these "separation tales," though this overarching aspect has largely gone unrecognized.

Great secrecy surrounded the Mysteries and secret societies, not unlike the well-guarded secrecy around major scientific research centers. It is only relatively recently that these esoteric secrets have begun to be made public, available for all to study. The time is at hand. However, there is a great risk that they will be misunderstood, taken the wrong way, misused and abused—and indeed, they are. Yet, in our age of the consciousness soul they can no longer be kept hidden. And all those who reveal these secrets are in danger, accused of betrayal or of spreading falsehoods. It happened to Rudolf Steiner in Europe, to Vusamazulu Credo Mutwa in Africa, to Hyemeyohsts in America, to name only a few. Just like the relatively recent discoveries of sacred texts, such as the Dead Sea Scrolls or the writings of Mani, more will be found and disseminated accordingly. It is unstoppable and these spiritual secrets will eventually merge with the secrets of matter. What links the ancients and the moderns is the ongoing search to understand the essential truth behind everything: the ancients turned to the *spirit* for truth and the scientists investigate *matter* to find

---

8 Kofi Edusei, *Für uns ist Religion die Erde, auf der wir leben: Ein Afrikaner erzählt von der Kultur der Akan* (Urachhaus, 1985), p. 38.

truth. Charles Kovacs, in his book, *Parsifal and the Search for the Grail,*[9] outlines two such events that underscore this dualism.

The first event that Kovacs describes deals with a story written by Cleve Cartmill called "Deadline," which was published in the magazine *Astounding Science Fiction* in 1944 (Kovacs does not mention any of the names and details). Essentially, the story explains in quite some detail the construction and building of the atomic bomb. At the time, however, this super bomb was being developed in the utmost secrecy at Los Alamos, causing quite a stir amongst the scientists there. The FBI took notice and began to investigate. The investigation into Cartmill even extended to other science fiction writers such as the famous Isaac Asimov. The short of it was that Cartmill received a visit by the FBI, and was questioned on how he came up with the story, especially the main principles of making a nuclear fission device with such accuracy. Eventually, he could clear his name by proving that the story was an imaginative work of fiction, that he only used unclassified scientific journals for his research, and that he was utterly ignorant of the research taking place at Los Alamos. Never having received any intel from anybody, he could prove that he had not betrayed any of the classified *secrets*. He could have been charged with high treason and imprisoned. Nevertheless, he was sworn to silence for many years.

The other event that Kovacs describes goes back to Greek antiquity, to the playwright Aeschylus, approximately 2,500 years ago, who we usually cover during the Comedy & Tragedy block in the 9th grade. It's an apt anecdote to relate, both in 9th and 11th grade, though in a different context. It goes as follows: During one of the performances at the *Great Dionysia*, in which the best playwrights compete against one another, Aeschylus, who is acting in his own play, hears an audience member shout out and accuse him of treason—that he's betraying the secrets of the Mysteries. Aeschylus, realizing the gravity of the situation, runs from the amphitheater at the foot of the Acropolis below the Parthenon in Athens, and seeks sanctuary in the temple of Dionysus, with soldiers in hot pursuit, swords drawn. Aeschylus

9 Charles Kovacs, *Parsifal and the Search for the Grail* (Floris Books), 2002.

demands a proper trial, which is granted, where he is able to prove that he has not been initiated into the mysteries, and that he had no knowledge of those secrets, arguing that the contents of the play are the results of his own insights and creative imagination. Having proven his innocence before the judges, he is allowed to go free.

There is an impressive parallel between these two stories, as Kovacs points out. They were both accused of betrayal for revealing *secrets*. Yet, these secrets are diametrically opposed to one another. The students relate deeply to these two examples, for it validates the creative power of the imagination, substantiating the innate genius withing every person. For the students it can feel like a confirmation of their own dormant genius—the ability to come up with something vital themselves out of their own inventiveness or resourcefulness. It is empowering. What is essential is that the students get an idea of these two diametrically opposed secrets, which will help to put the study of *Parzival* into context.

We live in the age of the consciousness soul, which means that as modern human beings we endeavor to penetrate everything scientifically and rationally. There is no going back. We see and experience it everywhere. Everything is interpreted and analyzed from a materialistic and scientific point of view. The two events discussed above throw light on the two secrets: the secrets of *matter*, on the one hand, and the secrets of the *spirit*, on the other.

As mentioned, secret societies, mystery centers, temple schools, sages, and initiates the world over kept the secrets alive, albeit in strict safekeeping. But times change and humanity's journey is forever evolving. Humanity as such has become increasingly material, entering ever more deeply into the earthly realm. And this is where the *third* secret, as Kovacs says, comes into play. It takes place more or less at the halfway point between ancient Greece and our present age. This third secret is the secret of the *Grail*. What is this secret? In the person of Parzival, we have a *soul* who searches for something, though he does not really know what it is, but he devotes all his energies in the pursuit of that something, which is called the Grail. And the soul of Parzival is the soul of the human being that no longer has such direct access to the spiritual world, not even through the mystery centers or the once powerful sybils, for they too gradually succumbed to corruption, their powers fading. Yet, for the health of humanity, some spiritual essence had to be *preserved*, and it is this divine core which is reflected in the Grail imaginations. This time period—the Middle Ages—stands in the middle between a spiritual past and a material future. And now the human being, through the strength of their own soul powers, must find the power and resilience to hold on to the last vestiges of the spiritual essence, while *preparing* themselves for the scientific/material age to come. And the story of Parzival is an archetype of the human being's striving to find the *truth* that has sustained humanity for eons—the *spirit*—and the truth into which humanity is entering—the depths of *matter*. The darkness of matter contains the light of the spirit, for matter is "frozen spirit." The story of Parzival answers the dual question: How can the knowledge of the spirit be preserved, and how can humanity prepare for the material age to come? The cosmic wisdom of the past meets the earthly wisdom of the future. Parzival—the seminal modern human being—has to traverse through different stages of development in order to not only survive but thrive in

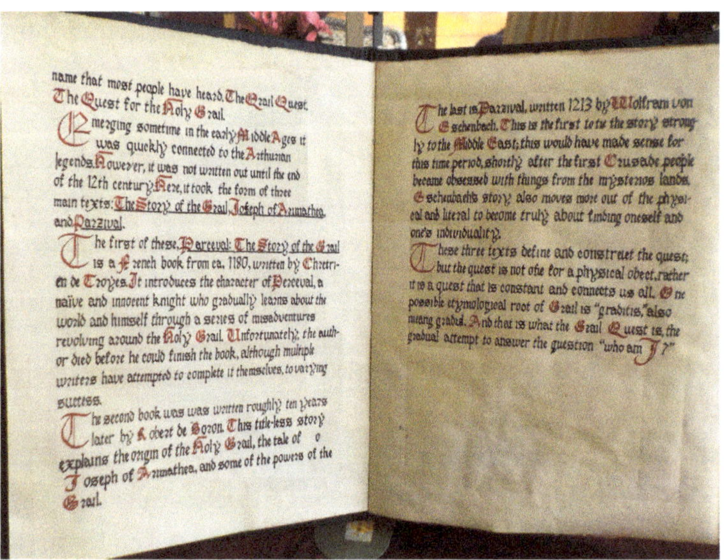
name that most people have heard. The Grail Quest. The Quest for the Holy Grail.

Emerging sometime in the early Middle Ages it was quickly connected to the Arthurian legends. However, it was not written out until the end of the 12th century. Here, it took the form of three main texts: The Story of the Grail, Joseph of Arimathea, and Parzival.

The first of these, Perceval: The Story of the Grail is a French book from ca. 1180, written by Chretien de Troyes. It introduces the character of Perceval, a naïve and innocent knight who gradually learns about the world and himself through a series of misadventures revolving around the Holy Grail. Unfortunately, the author died before he could finish the book, although multiple writers have attempted to complete it themselves, to varying success.

The second book was was written roughly ten years later by Robert de Boron. This title-less story explains the origin of the Holy Grail, the tale of Joseph of Arimathea, and some of the powers of the Grail.

The last is Parzival, written 1213 by Wolfram von Eschenbach. This is the first to tie the story strongly to the Middle East; this would have made sense for this time period, shortly after the first Crusade people became obsessed with things from the mysterious lands. Eschenbach's story also moves more out of the physical and literal to become truly about finding oneself and one's individuality.

These three texts define and construct the quest; but the quest is not one for a physical obect, rather it is a quest that is constant and connects us all. One possible etymological root of Grail is "graditis," also meang gradual. And that is what the Grail Quest is, the gradual attempt to answer the question "who am I?"

the modern world. Parzival "stands at the threshold between two worlds."[10] And by standing at this threshold, the human is wishing to *reconnect* to something higher, to the *invisible* world of the gods and goddesses, to the divine, while grounded here on earth. It is the calling of our time, felt as a deep yearning for something more, consciously and subconsciously. For this reason, Steiner sometimes called the consciousness soul the spiritual soul, especially when he lectured in England. It is true for all cultures around the globe, for all have lost that direct connection to some extent, as mirrored in the diverse mythologies. Kofi Edusei, trained and initiated as a traditional healer, says that these myths express the one constant wish, which is to be reunited once more with the Great Creator.[11]

The Rise of the Grail Stories

"Faith is the bird that feels the light and sings when the dawn is still dark."
— Rabindranath Tagore

The emergence of the Grail stories in the Middle Ages remains a mystery. They first circulated through the oral tradition till they began to be written down in the twelfth and thirteenth centuries, the most famous story involving Parzival's untiring quest for that elusive "thing" ("*dinc*") called the Grail. The earliest surviving text is Chrétien de Troyes' *Le Conte du Graal, (The Story of the Grail),* which appeared approximately around 1180, but remained unfinished. Circa 1190, Robert de Boron wrote *Joseph of Arimathea: A Romance of the Grail*, which recounts how Joseph brought the Grail west to Britain. He identifies the Grail as a cup or vessel that caught the blood of Christ at the crucifixion. The text was intended to be the first part of a trilogy, though *Merlin* remained a fragment and *Perceval* was lost entirely. He drew heavily on the apocryphal *Gospel of Nicodemus*, also known as the *Acts of Pilate*. His writings are seminal to the Arthurian tales.

10 Kovacs, p. 13.

11 Edusei, p. 41.

The most significant of these three early Grail texts is *Parzival* by Wolfram von Eschenbach, which appeared somewhere between 1207 and 1213, and brought the story to a conclusion. It is Eschenbach's *Parzival* that Walter Johannes Stein chose to teach in the 11th grade of the first Waldorf school in Stuttgart. Other books soon followed due to the popularity of these Grail stories, which often elaborated on scenes from *Parzival*, such as Albrecht von Scharfenberg's *The Younger Titurel*, completed around 1270. The most famous of the Arthurian and Grail tales appeared in Thomas Malory's *Le Morte d'Arthur,* completed in 1470.

Not much is known about Wolfram von Eschenbach. He came from Eschenbach, Germany, south of Nuremberg, where they still have a statue of the famous bard in the town square. It is a riddle that we know so little about Wolfram, and it is assumed that the Catholic Church did everything in its power to eliminate and remove all remaining information about him, in line with their thorough eradication of the heretics such as the Cathars and Albigenses. His grave was intact until the 1700s, when that too disappeared. One presumes he lived between 1170 and 1220. Already during his lifetime, he was recognized as the greatest German poet, making it even more improbable that so few details of his life have survived. His contemporaries were Hartmann von Aue, Gottfried von Strassburg, and Walter von der Vogelweide. What we do know comes from the actual *Parzival* text. The Church would have purged them as well, but due to its immediate popularity, many copies were made, up to eighty five transcripts in the thirteenth and fourteenth centuries alone (first printed in 1477).[12] Interestingly enough, *Parzival* was one of the first books to be published after the printing press was invented by Gutenberg. In the beautiful illuminations of the Codex Manesse, containing about 135 miniatures of late medieval German poets, Wolfram is depicted as a knight with his squire. The coat of arms in the Manesse depicts four pairs of black axes, which symbolize service, duty, and strength (three of them on a red background). The double axe depicts balance, which fits well with the

12 Ueli Seiler-Hugova, *Das Grosse Parzivalbuch* (SchneiderEditionen, 2014), p. 452.

theme of duality and polarity, associated with Parzival, especially in regard to following the middle path. It is an imaginative depiction of Wolfram and has no relationship to his actual crest.

Wolfram was a self-described "poor knight" and a Minnesänger, which is the German equivalent of a bard or troubadour. These bards spread the Arthurian and Grail stories throughout Europe, traveling from town to town, from court to court, telling and singing stories of love and adventure. Bard is derived from the Celtic word Bardos, meaning singer, poet, or one who gives praise. The troubadours or trouvéres arose in France during the later Middle Ages, and many were Rosicrucians, which influenced their songs. The name comes from the Old Provencal, "trobar," which means "to find," as in finding or inventing songs and poems. In trouvéres, who followed the troubadours, the French word "trouver" (to find) is clearly stated. "Minne" is the Middle High German word for love or remembering love: hence, "love-singer." Thus, in the bards, troubadours/trouvéres, and Minnesänger, we have three ideals exemplified: praise, finding (or seeking), and love.

At this point, I might relate to the students an anecdote about Walt Disney's connection to *Parzival*, and how it subsequently entered the American psyche (and the world's) in a small but memorable manner. Walt Disney, while traveling through Germany, visited Ludwig II's fairy tale castle of Neuschwanstein in Bavaria, about an hour from Munich. Touring the castle, he entered the room dedicated to the German Minnesänger, called "The Minstrels' Hall," which contains stunning paintings depicting the story of *Parzival*, (or to be more precise, *Parsifal*, since they portray Wagner's interpretation of the story—Ludwig II being a patron of Wagner), which left an indelible impression on him. Disney was so taken by this experience that he based the castles in his theme parks on the unique architectural features of Neuschwanstein. Furthermore, he found the perfect name for Micky Mouse's sweetheart, Minnie Mouse—"Love" Mouse, based on the medieval ideal of Minne—love.[13]

---

13 Shelley Durrel, *Healing the Fisher King: Spiritual Lessons with Parzival, Gump, the Grail, Tao, and Star Wars* (Art Tao Press, Miami, Florida, 2002), p. 159.

Grail Motif

"If you want to talk to God, tell it to the wind." ~ Akan saying

Everybody has heard of the Grail, but most students know nothing or very little about its meaning, significance, or origin, though there are always a few who can connect it to the cup from the Last Supper, which was used to catch the blood of Christ when he was crucified on Golgotha. And inevitably someone mentions *Monty Python and the Holy Grail,* a British comedy from the 70s, that gets more heads nodding and immediate smiles. They know that the term "Grail" indicates an ideal—something important, valuable, and sought after. The Grail is associated with the pursuit of perfection, which nowadays includes all sorts of worldly things: The Holy Grail of facial crèmes, surfboards, coffee, bread, wine, batteries, technology, medicine, card magic, even shipwrecks. Anything. Indeed, just yesterday (as of this writing), The *Washington Post,* in regard to manufacturing fusion machinery that would eliminate the carbon footprint, wrote, "It is the 'Holy Grail' of carbon free-power that scientists have been chasing since the 1950s."[14] The term "Holy Grail" connotes quality and has become a marketing tool that is firmly entrenched in the secular world.

So, what could the "Holy Grail of the human being" mean? What qualities, capacities, and faculties must such a human possess? What would it entail to become the Holy Grail of humanhood? Kofi Edusei writes, "Human beings would not need religion if they were in themselves complete. But since humans are not, they use religion out of a yearning to recreate the original harmony and unity that once existed between them and the Creator."[15] The story of *Parzival* and his quest for the Grail outlines the stages of development that could satisfy just such a yearning and lead humans *forward* to reconnect with that unifying source, mentioned by Edusei—the source that has been lost. What does it mean to be "complete"? These are Grail questions.

---

14 https://www.washingtonpost.com/business/2022/12/11/fusion-nuclear-energy-breakthrough/

15 Edusei, p. 41 (translated by the author).

Dan Brown's *The da Vinci Code*, which deals with the Holy Grail, became a global super-bestseller in 2003, selling tens of millions of copies and translated into fourty plus languages. While teaching *Parzival* during the year of its publication, I asked the class of eighteen students how many had read or heard of the book. All but three students had either read the book or were in the process of reading it. Brown's controversial book spawned hundreds of spinoff books. The "Grail" had become topical again, and remained so for a number of years. Now, when I ask, it's rare to find anybody who has read it, though they've heard of it and some have seen the movie.

The students realize that, although the Grail might seem like a medieval imaginative construct, it nevertheless has staying power and speaks to something deep within the inner soul life of human beings, no matter who you are or where you are from, because it ultimately transcends all that divides us. Joseph Campbell went so far as to suggest that the Grail is the founding myth of Western culture. I would take it a step further and say that it will become the Foundation Myth of all cultures—and to some extent it already has, though it moves just below the surface of consciousness. The Grail can be seen as a "call" to global equality, where all cultures, all people are recognized, and treated with dignified respect. The Grail cannot be owned or possessed. It is always an action for others, because the Grail's heart is love. But the way to this phoenix heart is long and convoluted, and needs to be consciously traveled and acquired—an inner Camino to Santiago de Compostela.

In *Parzival*, Wolfram deliberately waits until chapter nine before elucidating on the Grail theme through the words of the hermit Trevrizent. In my introductory classes of the *Parzival* block, I give a short overview of the Grail—and the epic as such—and its various meanings, which we can then deepen and develop during the block, and especially when covering Book Nine. There has always been an elusive element associated with the Grail. Its meaning changes as we change, mature, and develop. It cannot be fixed through labels and definitions, but only characterized. It eludes discovery, and changes its location periodically. The Grail calls to all seekers but remains a mystery. Like truth and love, we sense the Grail's essence, though it remains fleeting, indefinable.

The Grail is generally considered to be a vessel. Vessels have always played an important role in cultures and religions around the world. The various chalices, of course, play an important role in Christianity's liturgical celebrations, such as holding the wine for the holy sacrament, or the paten that holds the host of the Eucharist. Temple Tanks play a significant role in Hindu temples, the cleansing water within them considered holy, aiding in the purifying ritual of the participants. And the Poorna Khumba (full pitcher) in Hinduism is a pitcher that symbolizes God—the water within considered to be alive with divine spirit. It also addresses the water motif that plays such an important role throughout the story of Parzival, and in religious rituals and mythologies around the world. Similarly, the Ashanti from Ghana erect a forked Onyamedua tree at the entryway of respective structures on which they place a calabash, filled with rainwater—Nyankonsua, water of God—used to bless and purify the people entering the building.[16] Other shrine vessels found all over Africa were used for sacred purposes, and helped to ward off evil spirits and misfortunes. Then there are the various Celtic cauldrons, such as Branwen's Cauldron that had the power to resuscitate dead heroes—a cauldron that overcomes death and rejuvenates. Cerridwen's cauldron has similar powers. In that Welsh legend, the potion is a source of wisdom. And, as most students know, there's the cauldron into which Obelix fell, filled with magic potion which gave him superhuman strength. All these vessels have to do with some sort of new life, rejuvenation, wisdom, strength, or purification, allowing for transformation or transubstantiation. Older versions of the receptacles are often bigger in size, such as tubs, tanks, and cauldrons in which people can bathe or be dipped. The biggest and most archetypal vessel is Mother Earth, Gaia. Smaller containers, ritual cup or chalices, are often made for ceremonial consumption of food or drink. Spiritual sustenance is the common theme of these diverse vessels. They belong to the Yin element.

The Grail is also referred to as a stone, as in Wolfram's epic. Stones as such

---

16 Edusei, p. 50.

play a prominent role throughout Parzival, culminating in the "Thing" called the Grail. Stones have had ritual and mystical significance for eons. One only has to think of the menhirs, the standing stones and cromlechs, the Ka'hba, the Singing Stone of the Native Americans, ancestral stones, the sacred stones from Ethiopia, the Mystic and Wish Stone in Ghana, or the metaphysical Philosopher's Stone of the alchemists (also called "universal medicine"), to name only a few. These respective stones are known to have specific powers and qualities. Depending on the stone, they heal, impart wisdom, listen, absorb or radiate energies, cast significant shadows, radiate warmth or cool down, serve as reminders, have calming and balancing effects, tell stories, serve as a place of safekeeping, bless—and most importantly—function as a link between heaven and earth—the seen and the unseen. In that sense, they have similar properties to the holy vessels.

The Native American story about the Singing Stone encapsulates the ever elusive and Grail-like mystical qualities—as told through the oral tradition in many different forms. Though much longer versions exist, it can be reduced to a basic framework:

> Far in the north, a young son of a chief has a dream about a Singing Stone. He does not understand its significance and asks his mother the meaning of the Singing Stone. She does not know, nor does anybody else. He forgets about it, but a few years later the dream returns, calling to him. Wanting to find out its meaning, he sets off to the east. He is welcomed by the people, but none of them have heard of the Singing Stone. He settles down and forgets about it. A few years later, the dream comes to him once more. Responding to the call, he leaves, hoping to find its meaning in the south. Arriving in the south, he again asks if anybody has heard of the Singing Stone. Nobody has. He settles down once more, even marries and has children. He is happy, but after his children have grown up the dream of the Singing Stone returns, which causes him to leave and seek answers to the Singing Stone in the west. However, they too do not know. He

> stays with them for a number of years, till the call of the Singing Stone enters his ears and heart. By now he is a very old man. Once more he sets out, traveling to the northern territories from where he first set out. He hears singing as he approaches a village. Coming closer he hears them sing, "Welcome home, Singing Stone, welcome home." [17]

The seeker in the above story hears the call to find out the truth behind "The Singing Stone." He sets out numerous times, meets many people and has important life experiences, until finally he discovers that he is what he is searching for—his true and complete self. He has discovered his eternal name. He has found the world in himself, and found himself in the world. Comparable to Singing Stone, when Parzival reaches the Grail, he has arrived home. Maybe, the correct question to ask is not what but "*Who is the Grail?*" It is the very question Parsifal asks in Richard Wagner's opera *Parsifal.*

The quest for the divine is the quest for the Grail, and we find ourselves when we become ONE with the universal song—the harmony of the spheres—or the sounding creative force, encapsulated in the *Aum* or *Om* of the Indians. Many of the world's creation myths relate how the world came into being through music. The Grail, depicted as a vessel or a stone, can also be conceived of as a "tone." In Chinese culture, for instance, the search for the celestial One Tone was ongoing throughout the dynasties, over millennia. Living in accord to the inaudible "primal sound," the "perfect

17 A condensed account by the author using a number of different versions of the story. For a more extended version see *Seven Arrows* by Hyemeyohsts Storm (Ballantine Books, NY, 1972), pp. 21-24.

pitch," the "cosmic vibration," or the "divine will," was fulfilling the highest ideal, which would ensure that society would live in harmony with the universe. Finding the earthly equivalent, the "foundation tone," can be seen as the ultimate quest for the Chinese, depicted most succinctly in the legend of Ling Lun. Sent by the Chinese Emperor, Huang Di (Yellow Emperor), Ling Lun set out, much like a medieval knight, to find the perfect earthly pitch. After a lengthy search, he heard the divine pitch in the love song of the Phoenix, and he captured the foundation tone in a carefully made bamboo pipe. The earthly equivalent of the divine "overtone" is called *Huang Chung*, "yellow bell." Yellow represents the color of wisdom in China. From the earthly *Huang Chung*, Ling Lun developed eleven more pipes to create all twelve tones of the zodiac, which set the standard pitch for all of China. It also became the standard of all measurement: volume, weight, length, mass. Thus, the earth was aligned with the heavens. Each dynasty, however, had to search for the perfect pitch again and again, for relationships change with the passing of time. It truly became the Chinese quest for the Grail to ensure social and political stability. However, the one big difference is that since the Middle Ages, every person has to go in search of inner harmony themselves, through their own resources. The search for the Grail refers to an *individual quest*. That was not possible in ancient times, except for initiates. Nowadays, the search has to be undertaken freely by every person out of their own initiative, and when they feel ready. In this respect, Parzival was the great trailblazer.

The knights of King Arthur were knights of the sword. The knights of the Grail became the knights of the word. As John the Evangelist said: "In the beginning was the word." The "word" is the new "sword." Similarly, the "tone" gives levity to the "stone." We are all Singing Stones, a place where the word, that was in the beginning, will resound again in song, sung from our hearts.

One day, as we were talking about the Grail and its significance, a student raised his hand and mentioned that our discussion had reminded him of something that he had experienced during a survival camp that summer. He related how they had sat around a large fire one evening, when the camp leader asked them to choose a piece of hot coal and carefully place it in a "vessel," which was a piece of bark. With their glowing treasure they then had to leave the group, find their own sleeping place in the dark, and light their own fire using their own personal hot ember. Over the next twenty-four hours, they were charged to tend to the fire, after which they again had to choose a piece of coal from their fire, place it in the vessel of bark, and bring it back to the big communal fire. He mentioned how "sacred" it felt walking to his own camp with his piece of smoldering ember resting in the bark-vessel, separated from the others, and having to build a fire from scratch, making sure to keep the flames going throughout the night and day—and how much care and effort it took. Furthermore, they had to fast during the whole episode, only allowed to drink some water. He experienced it as a time of trusting, fasting, and finding the truth. "It was a bit like receiving something valuable from the big spirit-fire, keeping it alive within ourselves, and then returning it to the communal Grail, bringing something of ourselves with glowing coal to share with the others." He ended by saying that all of the camp participants felt that they had changed as people, that they'd accomplished something unique. That piece of burning coal became their treasured inner fire—and how vulnerable it is, how easily it can be extinguished. His story moved us all, and a moment of silence followed.

Depending on the class, I sometimes lead the students in a "rice bowl meditation," as I call it, loosely inspired by Tich Naht Hanh. For the Buddhists, the rice bowl is a sacred object of meditation. We were lucky enough to have Tich Naht Hanh and some of his close followers, including a couple who had graduated from our school, to give a presentation to our students about mindfulness and meditation. Inspired by their indications, I developed a modified version of one of their meditations. The students are not obligated to participate in the guided meditation. It's up to them, but over the years I have found that they mostly do. The students are often tired in the morning and they appreciate the opportunity to close their eyes and follow my prompts—if they so choose. I switch off the lights, and after a short silence, ask them to empty their minds of all extraneous thought before proceeding somewhat as follows.

"Imagine you are holding a little rice bowl in your hands. It is empty—clean and empty like your minds. Only the image of the empty rice bowl rests in front of you. Give yourself over to that clean bowl of humble emptiness. No more thoughts, no emotions. Maybe something upset you this morning and those feelings are lingering still. Let them evaporate and dissolve like mist in the morning sun. Whatever they were, even the slightest emotional residue—let it go. Let calmness take the place of anger, hurt feelings, annoyance, melancholy, depression, even feelings of excitement or delight—release them all. Learn from your empty rice bowl as it patiently waits. Find the stillness of inner equilibrium. Quieten your bodies too. Maybe there's a tightness in your shoulders, your neck and back, a nervousness in your arms, fingers, foot, or toes. Rest in yourselves. Relax. Full relaxation is a form of emptiness. You are and have become the empty little rice bowl that looks up at you without judgement, like a chaste flower."

I speak slowly, softly, with even pauses in between. They are holding their imaginary bowls and the mood slowly alters—peaceful, quiet, and settled. "Each one of you is carrying a different bowl... your own bowl. All thoughts, feelings, and bodily movement have come to rest. What size is your bowl? How heavy? Cool or warm to the touch? What is it made out of? Wood, porcelain, enamel? How long have you had it? Has it been passed down to you, or was it a gift from someone special? How many meals has it held for you? The bowl is a vessel. It is not flat, but hollowed out. It has a hollow that defines a space. An empty space. Something is missing, like a hole that wants filling. Once filled it needs emptying, which fills and fulfills something else that needs filling; from vessel to vessel. Filling the bowl makes it whole. The hole becomes whole, becomes holy. The ideal of this sacred filling is nourishment: bodily, emotionally, spiritually. What meals, apart from rice, has it embraced? What drinks has it given you? Do you fill it yourself or is it filled for you? What else has it been filled with? In what situations have you used it? Give gratitude for all the times the bowl has served you and will continue to serve you. Is it decorated—painted, engraved, or plain? Did you make your own bowl? Who made the bowl? What kind of wood, if it's wood? What did the tree look like from which it was made? Imagine every detail of its history. If it is ceramic, where did it come from?"

I continue for a while with these types of questions, which vary slightly each time, adding or leaving out this or that detail, but always aiming to keep it pictorial. Then I bring in a change.

"Ever so slowly the empty rice bowl begins to grow, and as it grows, it fills with warmth, like the warmth of a friendly handshake or a smile. As it warms it fills with light, pure and gentle light, like the light within a sun-dipped dewdrop. It keeps on growing, and added to the warmth and light, you smell your favorite fragrance, whatever it may be: the scent of a rose or Jasmine—unique and different for each one of you. Though the bowl grows, it does not weigh you down. Your glowing vessel is growing beyond you, until you are entirely engulfed by it. Now it holds you in its warm embrace. You are filling the bowl, your whole being. Still, it waxes, as do you, reaching into the sky and beyond. You merge with the living bowl that has a life of its own. And still it grows. The little rice bowl has expanded into the firmament, filling with the light of the stars, brightening with every second till the seconds dissolve into eternity. The light never blinds, but embraces and gives. And with the light, colors, and aromas you begin to hear tones, barely audible at first, pulsing as they expand and differentiate, the emerging melodies weaving together, soaring, floating through and around you, joined by a host of voices singing the songs of planets, suns, and stars—the harmony of the spheres."

From this lofty radiant vantage point, I slowly bring them back, letting the grand vessel wane, gradually, carefully, gently, all the way down, till they again imagine the tiny rice bowl empty in front of them, till that too disappears and they are left with a sense of self. I let them sit in silence for a little while, before I switch on the lights, and we get on with the lesson. I have had students come to me much later and refer back to that meditation and how much it had moved them.

During the 11th grade the students also have a block on medieval history, which preferably should precede the *Parzival* block, as it gives them a thorough background to the times. However, if my course is scheduled first, I usually cover the basics of knighthood and chivalry, as it is essential for the students to understand feudalism, chivalry, and other customs and traditions of the Middle Ages. They are mostly quite knowledgeable, having covered the contents in middle school. It's more a matter of bringing it back to consciousness and to compare and contrast these traditions with other forms around the world, such as the Zulu impis, the Samurai, the Native American warriors.

In German, a knight is called a *Ritter* (one who rides), and the French equivalent is *Chevalier*, both referring to mounted knights, horsemen of noble birth, and I point out the close connection between chivalry and chevalier. Furthermore, I remind them that the word "knight" is spelled with a silent "k," which refers to the German word "Knecht", which means servant, and that the ideal of the knight was to serve and to protect, hence the rigorous training in seven-year cycles to become a knight: from page to squire to a knight. The graduation to knighthood began to include a dubbing, which still continues to this day. To be dubbed a knight was called an "accolade" (from Latin "collum" meaning neck), where the knight was struck to the neck or cheek with the sword—a hard blow so they would not forget. To receive the "accolade" is to receive praise. Of course, the students have all seen or heard about the knighting ceremonies and know of a number of celebrities who have received that honor. It brings the medieval world into our time, and sometimes I include a bit of trivia into the class. Some might know that Paul McCartney and Ringo Starr of the Beatles were knighted, or Mick Jagger from the Rolling Stones, and most recently, Brian May from the British rock band Queen. However, they are surprised to hear that the likes of Ronald Reagan, Sidney Portier, Steven Spielberg, and Charlie Chaplin were knighted by Queen Elizabeth.

Though the first Parzival tales were written down in the late twelfth century, early thirteenth, the actual story took place in the ninth century. It is a point that is missed by some scholars, though it is clearly mentioned in Wolfram's text: "Alas, that we no longer have her kindred with us to the eleventh remove! For lack of them all too many are debased today" (p 76). If we go back eleven generations from Wolfram's time, we come to about 870 in the ninth century. This small but significant point has given rise to many false and misleading interpretations of *Parzival*. Similarly, Homer's *Iliad* and *Odyssey* took place in the twelfth or eleventh century but were written down approximately in the mid eighth century BCE.

The medieval ninth century was a nodal point of change, and these changing times, especially in the consciousness of the people, play a significant role in the understanding *Parzival*. What was changing and stirring during this pivotal time helped to shape Europe as we know it, and ultimately the rest of the world. At the core of the changing streams of culture was the drive and urge toward *freedom*; a struggle that played itself out on many levels, and also expressed itself in the well-documented bloodlust of that time, where life meant little, and a tremendous amount of blood was spilled, (shamelessly exploited and milked to the full in the television series *Game of Thrones*, and more recently in *House of Dragons*). However, it also led to the gradual refinement of the people, the reason why the knights had to undergo such severe training and discipline to overcome their own bloodlust. It was a preparatory time that flowered in the twelfth and thirteenth century (sometimes known as the "little Renaissance") and the Renaissance between the fourteenth and seventeenth centuries. A highly significant event also occurred in 869 CE when the spirit was abolished during the Ecumenical Council in Constantinople by the Catholic Church. From then on, the spirit was seen as another aspect of the soul, which contributed to the ensuing materialistic worldview in which we are still entrenched. The emergence of the Grail stream counteracted this materialistic impulse, ensuring that the spirit will not be entirely lost to humanity.

However, soul refinement is a slow and gradual process. The inception of what later led to the breakthrough ages (late Middle Ages and Renaissance) took place in the ninth century and the forces of freedom ruminated in the womb of that century—the time of Parzival, whose destiny epitomizes the age. Parzival was not simply foreshadowing the Renaissance but the modern consciousness soul as such, anticipating today's soul condition and those yet to come. *Parzival* offers guidelines for the inner development needed to meet the challenges of our times and far into the future.

Parzival consists of Sixteen Books or chapters, almost equally divided between the adventures of Parzival and those covering Gawain. Its astonishing mathematical construction can be compared to the architectural complexity of a Gothic cathedral, such as Chartres, built during the twelfth and thirteenth centuries, or the development of polyphony and complex isorhythms in the realm of music. Numbers and their symbolic significance are used consciously throughout the epic, and its structure supports the contents in equal measure. Consequential social, cultural, and political changes took place, well prepared during the eighth and ninth centuries. The period from the late eleventh century to the mid-thirteenth century is also referred to as *the long twelfth century*, which rings true if one considers the flourishing of the troubadours and trouvéres, the writings of the various Grail texts, the musical developments, the architectural achievements, and the growth of secular power. It is an expression of humanity's crossing the threshold into the increasingly material, earthly, and scientific age, culminating in the Renaissance.

Discussion Topics and Questions

- To what extent do scientific innovations influence people's worldviews?
- Is "scientism" the best method to provide truth about the world and reality?
- Compare and contrast science and religion.
- Discuss what the students understand under the term "Holy Grail."

- Examine the symbolism of the Grail in contrast to the sword, lance, or spear.
- To what extent can the imagination be a source of insight and knowledge?
- Do you feel like an outsider or stranger in your own time?
- Find examples of traditions that have fallen into disrepute.
- What is the difference between soul and spirit?

Illustrations:

1. Painting of Wolfram von Eschenbach, based on the *Codex Manesse* 1305-1315 (Rosabel Mongan)
2. Blackboard notes and diagram from a *Parzival* main lesson
3. Pages from a *Parzival* main lesson book (Solomon Bergquist)
4. Personalized crest or coat of arms

BOOK ONE

Inheritance and Heritage

"The heritage of the past is the seed that brings forth the harvest that is the future." — Wendell Philips

There are times in our lives when we take stock, reexamine what has come before in order to determine the future, when we are moved to "think outside the box," when life seems to have come to a dead end or no longer feels applicable, when the trails of glory have dissipated and we need a new lease on life to get recharged. These turning points are true for the individual and for humanity as a whole. What takes the place of the things that have run their course? A new beginning is called for. It is inevitable and observable on all levels of society and nature—great and small. No matter how grand: "things fall apart; the center cannot hold," as Yeats gravely declared. And Parzival is the literary human representative of the imperative need to *start over*. And starting over means pushing through dark dullness into the light. It means being cut off from everything that has come before. Starting fresh. It means taking risks, which takes courage. We're thrust into new adventures out of necessity for our own good. Starting over from scratch, that's what life demands, what evolution commands, what leads us upward and on, lest we fall further into the depths and deadends of darkness. A New Age calls for a New Beginning along the long and winding road toward freedom, guided by Love. And the journey of Parzival—a riveting adventure in itself—traverses the outer to reach the inner.

Whereas Homer's *Odyssey* begins with Odysseus' son, Telemachus, Wolfram's *Parzival* begins with Parzival's father: Gahmuret. Both serve to introduce the respective main characters, highlighting their thematic importance. Eschenbach purportedly composed the first two books, dealing with Parzival's parents after he had completed the epic.[1] In what way do they contribute to the thematic content of *Parzival?*

I ask the students what a conversation might look like when they first meet a person, for instance on a date. "What questions might be asked? What would you want to know? What would they want to know about you? Think back on pivotal meetings you've had." Very quickly it becomes clear that they would ask about each other's background—what they've done, like to do, what music they listen to (always gets mentioned), places they've been, people they know, number of siblings . . . and maybe last, but not necessarily least: a picture of their *parents*—what they do, how many, divorced, stepparents, guardians, rich, poor, vocation. I ask the students why it's relevant, not only to them, but generally in society and from a historical perspective. The comments to the last question are diverse, and often surprising. But they all agree: it is integral to who they are and it puts things into context.

These questions disclose a great deal about their respective backgrounds, how it has influenced them—where they've come from, who they are, who they've become, and what it might mean for their future. Lately, as of this

1 Chrétien de Troyes begins his epic directly with Perceval.

writing, there has been a lot of talk about white privilege. It forces us to think more closely about our own lives, what we've been exposed to, what we have received, and how it might differ radically from minority groups, people of color, or the disenfranchised. It leads to interesting—and not always comfortable—discussions in the classroom, for most classes include people from disparate backgrounds, racially, socially, culturally, economically, etc.

The study of literature is not only to exercise one's ability to analyze and school one's critical thinking, or even to gain an appreciation of the literary work one studies, but to learn something essential about oneself—to help the students navigate the ship of themselves through the world—the ups and downs of life. Knowing ourselves helps us know others, and vice versa. We can gain a deeper and broader understanding of Parzival by knowing something about his parents and his lineage.

One of the assignments I've given students over the years is to write about what they have "inherited," and how their heritage has shaped their lives. It has undergone various iterations over the years. Initially, we only talked about it or included it in journal entries. Once, during this early stage, an exchange student from Germany who came from a monied, privileged, and blue-blooded background decided to do some more in-depth research about his family lineage. A few days later, clearly troubled, he wanted to speak to me in private. He confessed that he came across numerous articles, easily available on the internet that blatantly associated his family with the Nazis. It was plainly laid out, with names of his relatives and their association and actions in the party. I do not remember any of the details, and he did not want to include the information in the main lesson book. He told me that he confronted his parents, who verified his findings. It left a deep and painful impression on him, and made me wonder about the moral responsibility of the assignment.

However, many students relate enthusiastically to the assignment. Since then, I have given the personal essay clear and improved guidelines, based on helpful suggestion from Betty Staley's outstanding book, *Adolescence:*

The Sacred Passage: Inspired by the Legend of Parzival.[2] Personally, I have always accepted my own past with the greatest of gratitude, even though it has included some painful aspects. Having spent my formative years in in apartheid-ridden South Africa, I was well aware of my privileged status, even then as a child, and especially later in high school and university. However, like anything in life, it's what you do with it that counts, be it wealth, power, strength, health, good looks, or talents.

Heritage has many aspects, some of which might be taken for granted, such as the country of birth, the parents, the language or languages one speaks, all the things one has been exposed to. It's not always straight forward and easy. There is much to be proud of, but also ashamed. I want them to examine all of that. Of course, they are free to include or leave out whatever they want. One student, who wrote a lengthy essay on his heritage and inheritance, showed it to me, but also did not want to include it in his main lesson book. The contents were too personal. But he thanked me for the opportunity to come to terms with some uncomfortable aspects, especially the death of his mother. Another student was very open about his past, willingly sharing the uncomfortable aspects. His first words were, "I know nothing of my past, except that both my parents were drug addicts and I was born with drugs in my system." His life had been tough, getting into drugs himself and dealing at an early age, ending up in an institution for a while. Yet, he could acknowledge the gifts he'd received: all that his adoptive parents had done for him, keeping him out of trouble as best they could, sending him to good schools, and caring for his well-being.

The essays on this topic have been some of the most moving, interesting, and diverse I've read. Although I stress gratefulness for what one has received, some students have gone through tragic traumas. One student wrote in a most articulate manner about how he would dearly love to know about his heritage, but because of his African American status, had no clue about his African ancestors, where they came from, who they were, nothing. Yet, the ancestors and their gifts still live on in him, just as they

2 Betty K. Staley, *Adolescence: The Sacred Passage: Inspired by the Legend of Parzival* (Rudolf Steiner College Press, 2006), Chapter 1.

lived on in Parzival, for he too did not initially know anything about his lineage.

Heredity, however, no longer plays such a prevalent role as it had in previous ages. Ayan Hirsi Ali on the first page of the first chapter titled "Bloodlines" of her highly acclaimed book *Infidel*, writes how she had to know and count her forefathers back three hundred years as a five-year-old. In later years her grandmother coaxed and beat her to know her father's ancestry as far as eight hundred years back.

> "Get it right," my grandmother warns, shaking a switch at me. "The names will make you strong. They are your bloodline. If you honor them they will keep you alive. If you dishonor them you will be forsaken. You will be nothing. You will lead a wretched life and die alone. Do it again."[3]

The lineage for a Somali is all important. It is their identity—who they are. For most cultures, ancestors have played a huge role. However, to Ayaan and other contemporary Somalis, the ancestral knowledge seemed pointless, as it does, increasingly so, in the modern global culture.

In the first two chapters, the reader gets introduced to Parzival's bloodline, but when he is born, he is consciously kept from knowing anything whatsoever. It mirrors what is happening to the modern person. The feeling of belonging to the past is increasingly eroding. Now, what matters more is what one does out of one's own resources.

Black and White

"The Tao doesn't take sides; it gives birth to both yin and yang. All is welcome, both light and dark" — Lao Tzu

A brief prologue begins Book One. The polarity of light and dark, white and black is introduced in the first paragraph, a theme we find reflected in most cultures around the globe, most prominently in the yin-yang of

3 Ayaan Hirsi Ali, *Infidel* (Free Press, 2007), p. 3.

describes the dual nature of everything—the living between opposites. The darkness is often denied, and it is largely due to C.G. Jung that it has entered the greater public awareness. He found it essential that we come to terms with our shadow side, giving it a healthy and necessary place in our lives—the area of our subconscious which must be brought to light, to consciousness. This modern concept was highly radical during the Middle Ages, though it has existed for eons in different forms.

The notion of duality is universal, found in Native American and African lore, the ancient texts of India—the East as such—Persia, Egypt, especially amongst the Manichaeans for whom it served as the foundation of their mystical beliefs, based on the works and words of Mani (of whom we shall hear more). The duality between light and dark, black and white, sets the moral and thematic tone of the epic. Colors are used symbolically and great sensitivity is needed in discussing them, especially in regard to black and white. There is no place for prejudice. Dealing with the polarity of light and dark, black and white, has become a modern necessity, even if it feels uncomfortable. There's no transformation without discomfort. Humanity needs to find the right and many-leveled relationship to respective themes. Wolfram, however, does not give "black and white" answers to the theme of polarity. It always depends on the situation. What holds true in one situation cannot necessarily be transferred to another. Hence, his statement: "I have yet to meet a man so wise that he would not gladly know what guidance this story requires."[4] The story is anything but prescriptive. Everything needs to

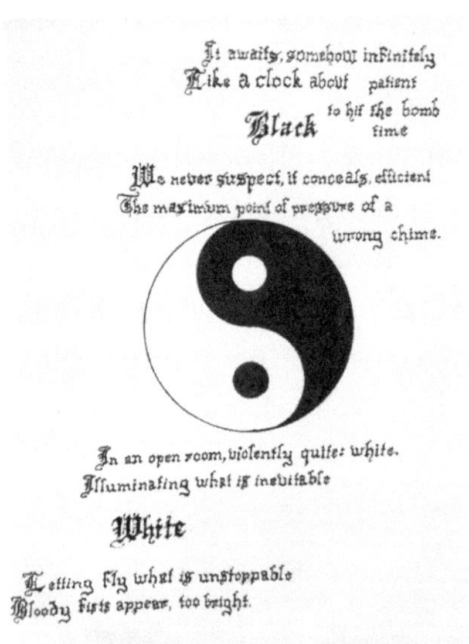

4 Wolfram von Eschenbach, *Parzival*, translated by A.T. Hatto (Penguin Books, 1980), p. 15. From now on all quotes from *Parzival* will be from the Penguin

be viewed from different perspectives. It requires an open mind and heart. Life is polarity in motion.

The following in-class writing prompt helps to stimulate a balanced discussion about color. I ask the students to write about a color of their choice, elucidating the color's positive and negative attributes. It is interesting to note what color they choose and how balanced their interpretations generally turn out between the polar qualities. Color symbolism runs throughout the epic and the writing exercise helps to lay the foundation and facilitate further considerations.

Right from the start, Eschenbach compares our hero, Parzival, to a magpie, a black and white checkered bird. Interestingly enough, the Zulu king, Shaka (or Chaka), had a special relationship to the African magpie, the magpie shrike, with its long tail, which never ceased to catch my eye, whenever I spotted them as a child living in Zululand.[5] I always stopped whatever I was doing to watch these fascinating long-tailed magpies. Shaka saw in the magpie the power to scatter the enemies, and his *impis* would not return from a victorious battle without a long feather from the magpie in their headdress or around their upper arms. The magpie shrike was known as the "one who reigns supreme."[6] If we want to reign supreme over ourselves, then we have to come to terms with our inner magpie. In the Far East, the magpie is considered a good omen, giving joy, especially in marital bliss. It can be seen as happiness through bringing the *opposites* into harmony with one another; opposites within oneself, and the love between two partners,[7] which heralds good news for Parzival. One of the core goals of *Parzival* is to keep the polarities, the dark and light qualities within each human being, in balance—rather than denying them. We have

---

eddition unless otherwise stated.

5 Now KwaZulu-Natal.

6 Londolozi Blog. https://blog.londolozi.com/2017/09/16/african-folklore-the-mystery-of-birds-part-2/#:~:text=Over%20centuries%2C%20the%20African%20people%20started%20to%20see,that%20'all%20shall%20come%20right%20in%20the%20end'.

7 Bird Spot. https://www.birdspot.co.uk/culture/birds-in-chinese-symbolism.

good and evil within us, but instead of denying the shadow side, or the untransformed aspects, we should embrace them, for they are not only part of us, but allow us to develop. As Wolfram says, we "may yet make merry, for heaven and hell have equal part in [us]" (p. 15).

Taoism is all about this duality: black and white. It goes back into prehistoric times. Their entire worldview is based on this polarity, summed up in black and white, light and darkness, though we cannot equate the two in our time, not without making sure we put it into the *right context*. Any kind of bias or perceived prejudice has no place in our time. Too much damage has been done. In-depth discussions with the students on this topic are recommended. Black and white, dark and light, though long recognized as a symbol of good versus evil in Western literature, is really far more universal, the polarities playing a significant role in cultures around the world in one form or another.

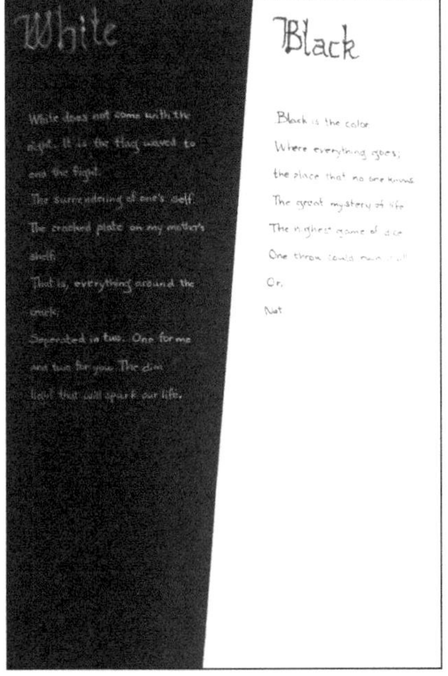

The bald eagle, the most significant bird of the Native Americans, also represents this all-important duality. I remind the students what they have learned about the eagle in 4th grade, and see how much they remember. The duality is highlighted in that it generally lays two eggs—the male and female aspect that expresses itself in life and in ourselves. Studying Native American lore, one can easily see similarities to the Tao. The bald eagle feather, in its division between black and white, light and darkness, represent the dualities of life.

Vuzamazulu Credo Mutwa, the first Zulu High Sanusi (diviner) or Sangoma (traditional healer) to record the history of the Bantu people, starts off his epic *Indaba, My Children* with a creation myth that referrs to the contrasts between light and dark. "Nothing existed but darkness itself—a Darkness everywhere," followed by the birth of "a most tiny invisible spark," which could think and have consciousness of itself, saying "I exist, I am what I am!" as it grew, feeding on itself, until it was so powerful that Nothingness tried "To smother it in darkness which is / The enemy of light / but the spark resisted brighter—and became yet brighter."[8] Light and dark play an important role in African wisdom. As we talk about color, we have to underscore that the symbolism refers to the *inner* life, the soul-spiritual aspect. Yaya Diallo from Mali, West Africa, in his fascinating book *The Healing Drum,* states:

> The person with the white interior has achieved balance between strength and weaknesses. These people know how to share with others . . . They consider the consequences of their actions, not only to themselves but also to their families, the community, the environment. Such people are wise, and it is the greatest of compliments to say a person's interior is white.[9]

On the color black, he writes:

> A dark interior indicates a condition of being closed in upon oneself. Such people are not good for others . . . Someone with a dark interior will undermine a business venture or any group endeavor. Often such people have a way of getting the most important tasks assigned to them, and they bring on failure. They are not bad people, but they are not *conscious* of their actions.[10] (My italics)

The emphasis is on the word "conscious." It is in align with Jung when he

---

8 Credo Mutwa, *Indaba, My Children: African Tribal History, Legends, Customs and Religious Beliefs* (Canongate 1998 [first published in 1964 by Blue Crane Books] pp. 5-6.

9 Yaya Diallo and Mitchell Hall, *The Healing Drum: African Wisdom Teachings* (Destiny Books, 1989), p. 57.

10 Ibid.

expounds on the "shadow side"—the unconscious. When black or dark is mentioned in *Parzival*, it indicates—though not always—a level of inner "dullness" or unconsciousness—in contrast to the spark of consciousness to which Mutwa refers. Furthermore, it suggests the loss of ancient knowledge, the natural clairvoyance, the insight into the invisible worlds which was still readily available.

Orland Bishop, who spent time with Mutwa, writes in his singular book *The Seventh Shrine*:

> The pillar of tradition is the light of awareness in which the ancestral knowledge is transferred from one generation to the next. When tradition is lost, the human seed or spiritual essence enters into the realm of darkness. It creates a beginning for a new expression.... It is a new impulse that enters the human spiritual stream rising out of the dark nature, the cosmic womb.[11]

The theme of spiritual loss can be found in legends, fairy tales, and myths all over the world, as mentioned earlier on in regard to "Separation Tales," that often portray the spiritual and the earthly with light and darkness.

While traveling through Bali, I noticed that countless Hindu statues, trees, boulders, even gongs were dressed in black and white checkered sarongs, called *Saput Poleng* ("Saput" means "blanket"; "Poleng" means "two-toned"). They express the spirit of dualism like the Chinese yin and yang. The *Rwa Bhineda*, which means "two opposites," must be kept in harmonious balance at all times in order to maintain wholeness. White refers to all that is good and joyful, and black to evil, despair, and sorrow. The one supports the other.

Sakokweniónkwas (Tom Porter), in his book on Iroquois teachings, explains with simple straightforward words why the Creator made the sun:

> Because if he didn't, there would be total darkness. And if I walk in total darkness, I can't see. I'll bump into things, and I might

11 Orland Bishop, *The Seventh Shrine: Meditations on the African Spiritual Journey: From the Middle Passage to the Mountaintop* (Lindisfarne Book, 2017), p. 3.

> cut myself, and blood would come. . . . And so because the sun shines all over the world, the Creator wants there to be peace, not war. He wants us to learn how to be in harmony, how to respect the sacred life of all.[12]

And if we find the inner light, we can be in harmony with ourselves, which then radiates out to others.

As stated before, all colors have positive and negative qualities. For instance, though white and light is often associated with "good," it also has associations with temptation, when one is led astray by the light (think *irrlichter*—or the "will-o' the wisps" from fairy tales, also known by other names such "Jack-o-lantern" or—my favorite—the "Giddy Lights"), of which Lucifer, the fallen angel, is the prime example: the *Light Bearer*, who, in his hubris, thought he was better than God.

On the other hand, we have the dark earth in which we plant seeds, the sacred night, the dark womb, dark and quiet caves where hermits find their wisdom. In turn, the seeds strive for light, the baby gets born into the light of life and day, the night revealing the wisdom of the stars, the sages, such as Muhammad stepping out of his cave to reveal his insights. There are countless perspectives to this theme which could fill libraries. What is important is to broaden the topic in order to overcome the ingrained stereotypes associated with the colors. Sometimes I give a brief account of light and darkness according to the prophet Mani, because the Manichaean view is thematically most aligned with *Parzival*. Mani, born in 216 CE, was greatly influenced by the teachings of Zarathustra and the duality between Ahura Mazdao (or Ormuzd), the lord of light and wisdom, and the beings of darkness under Ahriman, the Archontes, the duality of which is reflected in Mani's work.

Mani's creation myth, based on Rudolf Steiner, goes as follows: Due to the tension between Light and Dark, Darkness waged war on Light. Darkness

---

12 Tom Porter (Sakokweniónkwas), Bear Clan Elder of the Mohawk Nation, *And Grandma Said…, Iroquois Teachings as passed down through the oral tradition*, (Xlibris, 2008), p. 20.

(the Archontes) forged right to the frontiers of the light realm in order to conquer it, though failed to pass through. It was decided to punish the dark realm, though the light realm only contained nothing but goodness. The spirits of light took a share of their light and mixed it into the darkness, which created a disorderly flurry, from which arose a new element—*death*, resulting in darkness continuously consuming itself. It was the original human element, sent by the spirits of light to mingle with the darkness in order to overcome death. Human beings had to triumph over death from within, using their own forces. It is this *mingling* between the polarities which leads to transformation.[13] In this way, death vanquishes darkness through human effort (also see "Who is Parzival?" in Book Four).

Thus, the powers of Light and Darkness are both essential to creation, the one as important as the other. Darkness is connected to matter, as expressed in many cultures around the world, and Light with the invisible realm or the divine. As stated earlier, it is always a matter of context. Often the polarities, no matter how divergent and seemingly contradictory, nevertheless can be reconciled. In Wolfram's epic of Parzival, we will often come across apparent inconsistencies that can be resolved in the end.

As a Waldorf teacher, one constantly works with polarities, starting from the straight and curved line on the first day of school in grade one, to the center and periphery in geometry, or contraction and expansion in eurythmy. Another polarity is the spiral. We find the use of spirals in almost all cultures, in cave paintings, carved into dolmen, and as symbols in the Middle Ages. Inward spirals are calming and take the soul inward, whereas the outgoing spiral seeks the light. Interior and exterior—dark and light, death and rebirth.

I ask the students where and how the light and dark imagery is portrayed in modern culture, and they are quick to respond. Many scenes and characters from movies get mentioned, such as the 'Black Riders' from Tolkien's *Lord of the Rings,* or Darth Vader from the *Star Wars* series—one

---

13 Rudolf Steiner, *The Temple Legend: Freemasonry and Occult Movements: From the Contents of the Esoteric School*, November 11, 1904 (Rudolf Steiner Press, Forest Row, 1997), CW 93.

of the most iconic and infamous villains of the silver screen, who represents the dehumanizing element. He is dressed all in black, as are the Sith, who represent the "dark side," fueled by anger, greed, and hate. Of course, a slew of scary movies gets mentioned, such as *The Haunted, The Texas Chainsaw Massacre,* and *The Blair Witch Project,* to name only a few, where darkness and a range of opaque colors are ubiquitous. Night or forest scenes (as with the last two movies) are immediately more fear inducing.

Alternatively, Mani, (similarly to Muhammad), sought solitude in the darkness of a cave to seek wisdom. Water, the moon, femininity, rest, matter (Mutter—mother) earth, are all connected with growth and rejuvenation, and are all part of yin—the dark/black creative force. Handing out a list of yin-yang attributes helps the students to broaden their concepts and bring more objectivity to something that can easily be misunderstood and misrepresented through its paradoxical nature. Or as Oscar Wilde famously said in *The Picture of Dorian Gray* (Chapter 3): *"Well, the way of paradoxes is the way of truth."* In short, Wolfram wants us to look at the whole person, warts and all, which can be overcome—from within and from without.

Gahmuret

"Every moment of light and dark is a miracle"[14]— Walt Whitman

What kind of man is Gahmuret? We see *how* Gahmuret's heritage and inheritance directly influences and affects his life in the way he deals with the predestined outer circumstances. His motivations determine his life and, in a seminal manner, the lives of both his sons. I am reminded of the words "what motivates me shall be my destiny,"[15] from a song I heard as a teenager, which left me wondering: Do motivations have a source? If so, where are they located? Where do they come from? What makes my motivations unique? Why do I do the things I do, want the things I want, love or hate this or that? I'd never thought about it consciously before,

14 From Whitman's poem "Miracles."

15 "It's Your World" by Jam Factory from their album *Sittin' In The Trap.*

and for a while I repeatedly quoted those lyrics. Pondering the source of motivations confirmed the reality of karma for me. I was seventeen at the time, completing 11th grade.

Gahmuret comes from a reputable well-to-do noble family of knights. His father, Gandin, dies in battle, and his older brother, Galoes, inherits the kingdom of Anjou *(Anschouwe)* and all the riches, as stipulated by tradition.[16] This inheritance rule, based on Roman law, was not unique to Germany, but a well-established practice amongst several countries around the world. Though Galoes offers to share the kingdom with Gahmuret equally, Gahmuret refuses, preferring to find his fortune on his own: "But my heart is set on the heights! I do not know why it quickens so—*here*—as though it would burst. Oh where is my ambition taking me? I shall attempt it if I can" (p. 19). It explains the inexplicable aspect of Gahmuret's motivation, coming from deep within, as it will for Parzival, his son, and for all of us who experience such deep *yearning*. It's an unquestioned force as strong as a child's instinct to stand up, yet it manifests in Gahmuret as something *new* that breaks the traditional mold. It was a strong yearning, felt by many people from the ninth century onward—a need and desire for freedom.

Not content with what life offers him, he seeks to go beyond the familial limits, even though venturing into the unknown is a risk. Gahmuret's quest to make it on his own characterizes him as a self-reliant and adventurous free spirit. He does not want or need any charity, no matter how well-intentioned. By refusing his brother's kind offer, we ascertain that he is an upstanding knight, free of greed and self-centered ambition. "Gahmuret cultivated self-control and moderation in all things. He was not given to boasting, endured great honor calmly and was free of loose desires" (p. 20). He does, however, accept his brother's generous parting gifts. By responding to the full force of his yearning, he answers a question that has not fully matured within him. Many people experience such yearning, though

16 It is noteworthy that the original spelling, *Anschouwe*, relates to the German word, "Anschauung," which can mean "opinion" or "worldview" (Weltanschauung), suggesting an inner realm.

most don't pursue the call because of social norms or conventions, thereby potentially forfeiting an important part of their destiny and those who follow after. But can one discern between mere fancies and an authentic longing? In some classes this has become a topic of fruitful discussion. By following his call, Gahmuret anticipates and prepares Parzival's quest.

What many of the students appreciate in Gahmuret is that he was set on *serving* the most powerful ruler of the world, which at that time happened to be the Baruch of Baghdad. Europe, at the time, was *not* the dominant culture, while Persia was a powerful, vast, and culturally sophisticated empire. I remind the students that the story takes place in the ninth century, well before the Crusades, though they transpired during Wolfram's time. Middle Europe, compared to the Middle East, was still relatively primitive. In this respect, the term Dark Ages is an apt description. Gahmuret's willingness to fight *for* the Baruch of Baghdad, highlights his religious tolerance, considering that he, as a Christian, is prepared to fight for a Muslim. It should be noted that he does not set out to *rule* over other people or to become a dominating leader. On the contrary, he wants to *serve*, which shows great humility and generosity of soul (a true "Knecht"). His inexplicable urge to serve the "highest" finds its embodiment in the temporal world, though perhaps it was an outer expression of something deep within him that longed to serve the highest spiritual power—God. If so, it remained unrecognized and unconscious, and as a knight and a warrior, trained in the ways of the world, he chose what he understood—serving someone who rules over more than two thirds of the world. This foreshadows the immense domain over which his son Feirefiz will one day rule, albeit in a transformed manner, of which we will hear more in the last chapter of

this epic. It is worth pointing out that "Baruch" refers to the "blessed one," which we also recognize in the name of former President *Barack* Obama (an aside appreciated by the students).

The relationship between Gahmuret and the Baruch is remarkable, because it is an example of how diverse nations and their vastly different cultural traditions and backgrounds can nevertheless work together with understanding and respect. Lively discussions have ensued in the classroom regarding the ongoing strife between the Middle East and the West, which continues to this day. Throughout the years I have taught *Parzival*, there has always been a crisis in that part of the country: three Gulf Wars, Isis, Al-Qaida, and numerous civil wars, insurgencies, all the bloody conflicts in the area, in which the West was inevitably embroiled. It's as relevant as ever and seems never-ending. All the more noteworthy that the opening chapter of this medieval masterpiece offers a moving imagination of peace and unity between East and West, based on mutual admiration and understanding as exemplified by Gahmuret and the Baruch of Baghdad (Baghdad meaning "gift of god," from "Bagh" meaning "God," and "dad" means "given").[17] Their friendship represents an ideal in how distinct and diverse cultures can fructify one another and work together reciprocally. Historically speaking, we see an attempt by Charlemagne to achieve some kind of mutual respect and cultural exchange with the Harun al-Rashid in Baghdad, during the eighth / ninth century. It is time that the West renews its efforts to form bridges with the Middle East, to respect and recognize the contributions the East has made to culture. Mutual honoring is called for—which also holds true for the West's relation to other cultures it has dominated and exploited in the past.

While in the service of the Baruch, Gahmuret changes his father's coat-of-arms from a black panther to a white anchor, signifying a break from the past, his family and bloodline, indicating his emerging independence. White anchors are sewn on the horse's green caparison and more on his shield. More are sewn on his harness and on all of his green silk and velvet

17 In Russian "Bog" means "God," and in Sanscrit it is "Bagha," as in *Baghavad-Gita*.

vestments and garments. The chosen color for Gahmuret is green, which implies the growth forces of plants, the ubiquitous color of nature as well as thinking. Green is both invigorating and calming. It connotes a picture of balance, which grounds one in the world. It is the color of health, youth, and hope. Green is the sacred color of Islam. Gahmuret can be called the Green Knight, full of promise. And at the outset the different hues of green are adorned with white anchors, promising to anchor these positive attributes. The shank of an anchor is the middle between opposing hooks or flukes, a metaphor for balance.

The students are quick to note that an anchor could imply that Gahmuret is searching for a place to be grounded and inwardly moored, for meaning and purpose in life. His roaming soul desires and longs to be anchored. Though Gahmuret has set forth to find fame, fortune, and adventure, he is nevertheless seeking a destination, a place to anchor and quicten his burning yearning, which is really a subconscious aspiration to be anchored in the spirit. Possibly the Caliph would like him to drop anchor in Baghdad permanently, since he is not only one of his best fighters, but because he has become fond of him. One student suggested that Gahmuret actually wants to anchor in many places before finding his final destination—the last place to let go the anchor—in order to "learn the minds of many distant men,"[18] quoting from the opening lines of Homer's *Odyssey,* which we studied in 10th grade. The black panther is suggestive of power, strength, stealth, but also of opaque, unconscious forces which stand in contrast to the guiding light of clear thinking. It hints at a possible inner change: leaving behind the instinctive and uncontrolled urge to fight, the medieval "bloodlust," in exchange for the security of the anchor—cut from dazzling white ermine. The white anchor and the black panther again draw attention to the dance of opposites. Both crests say something about Gahmuret and his family lineage. The anchor indicates what Gahmuret needs, and the panther what he needs to leave behind or to transform. However, though Gahmuret has selected the anchor, he cannot find inner rest or a place to call home, and it becomes

18 Homer, *The Odyssey,* translated by Robert Fitzgerald (Anchor Books, 1963), p. 1.

a burden. "His Anchors had essayed neither main nor headland, they had not bitten anywhere. A noble exile, never finding billet or rest, he had to bear this burdensome device, the Anchor signs, from land to land" (p 21).

After serving the Baruch successfully, Gahmuret continues his adventures, laden with rich gifts, which surpass anything his brother could have offered him. He rides and sails to many lands, winning fame wherever he goes, fighting battles in Persia, Aleppo, Damascus, northern Africa all the way to Morocco, and throughout Arabia. His far-reaching travels foreshadow the even more extensive travels of both of his sons, which are carefully and ceremoniously listed toward the end of the epic, linking the beginning to the end. Outwardly speaking, he has achieved his goal: he has served the "highest" on the known earth and won fame and fortune wherever he went—respected by all.

Yearning

We all yearn for something.
Some more strongly than others.
Something we wish we could achieve.
Reaching out for something we do not have,
But something that is still reachable.
We would do anything to get it,
Even if we do not know exactly what it is.
It is the act of growing.
Once we have persisted through hardship,
And battled through pain,
We realize that our expectations of our goals
Were much greater than reality,
But the journey was much more fulfilling than expected.
~ Student

Belacane

"And all that's best of dark and bright
Meet in her aspect and in her eyes"[19] ~ Lord Byron

Once more Gahmuret lifts anchor and sets out into the unknown. He is driven off course by a heavy storm, which almost costs him his life, landing in an unknown part of Africa where the people are as "dark as ravens." The storm suggests a decisive change, guided by destiny. He notices that the mighty castle of Patelamunt, the capital of Zazamanc, is under siege, and he offers his services, initially for hire, until he meets the black Queen of Patelamunt. Though she welcomes his offer, she wonders whether the difference in skin color would be a "sore point with him," while also deliberating his lineage: "Is he near enough to me in birth for my kiss not to be thrown away?" (p. 24). However, mutual love unfolds between them from the moment they see each other. "He looked so very winsome that, irresistibly, he unlocked her heart which until that time her femininity had kept locked fast" (p. 25). And to Gahmuret it seems "that although she was an infidel, a more affectionate spirit of womanliness had never stolen over a woman's heart. Her modest ways were a pure baptism. . . . With this there was born between them a steadfast longing—she gazed at him, and he at her" (p. 27). Infused with love, he vows to fight in her service. From then on, they feel that their lives belong to each other.

Patelamunt is besieged because Belacane had been unwilling to give herself to Isenhart (hard iron), King of Azagouc, who loved and desired

19 Lord Byron, from the poem, "She Walks in Beauty."

her.[20] She wanted him to first prove himself worthy of her. In the attempt to prove himself, he battled without his armor and Adamant helmet, which cost him his life. As a result, his people blamed Belacane for his death, calling on their allies, a white army from Scotland, to aid them. In the two armies, one white, the other black, we again have the black and white imagery with which the chapter begins. What is important to note is that the dual armies are not fighting *against* each other, but are on the same side, besieging Belacane together.

I ask the students what they make of this and the fact that Patelamunt has sixteen gates, eight guarded by the black army of King Isenhart, and the other eight by a white Christian army. Often, the immediate response is that it makes for a welcome change, because historically speaking it is always white against black, and so-called heathens against Christians. In that regard it is surprising. Having also mentioned the importance of number symbolism, they might point out the connection between the sixteen gates and the sixteen chapters or books of *Parzival*. The astute students will also point out that Gahmuret was given sixteen squires to accompany him on his journey from Anjou. When I first began teaching *Parzival,* I refrained from broaching the "esoteric" implications of the symbolism, but because of the increasingly probing questions of the students, intent on knowing the deeper meanings of the imagery, I have ventured to say more, careful to remain as objective as possible, explaining that there are always various ways to interpret texts. However, I have been surprised to discover how acquainted many of them are regarding metaphysical symbolisms. I now offer some of these insights as examples of how deeply one can probe into this hermetic and truly miraculous literary masterpiece.

Each gate, it could be said, represents a chapter of the book, and

20 Various scholars place Patelamunt and Azagouc in present-day Morocco. Azagouc could refer to the Arabic *Az-zuqaq* (The Straits of Gibraltar). Patelamunt could be the port city of Ceuta. Charles E. Passage further suggests that the kingdom of Azagouc, further west = Tangier (classical Tingis). See Wolfram von Eschenbach, *Titurel: Translation and Studies by Charles E. Passage* (Frederick Ungar Publishing Co., New York, 1984), p. 163.

Patelamunt is a seedling-summary of the developing contents, prefiguring the unfolding story. The circular form of the city of Patelamunt links the beginning to the end. Johannes Stein in his book *The Ninth Century,* and others after him, compares Patelamunt to the sixteen-petaled lotus flower, the throat chakra, each petal signifying a specific quality, leading humanity to higher knowledge.[21] It is contained in the name Patelamunt—mount of petals. Almost every class has a few students who will know about the chakras (from the Sanskrit "cakra," which means "spinning wheel" or "mystical circle") and their placement in the body and even an inkling of what they might represent. In *How to Know Higher Worlds,* Rudolf Steiner mentions that this organ is particularly important to our modern age, and its development can throw light on the hidden aspects of destiny and karma. Eight petals or activities have been given to humanity as a gift from ancient times while the other eight need to be developed consciously. They are reflected in Buddha's "Eightfold-path." With time the instinctive knowledge of the first eight petals was lost as humanity sunk deeper into the darkness of matter. This ancient wisdom is represented by Isenhart's army, and the loss of those qualities are represented through Isenhart's death—the old wisdom of the past which is no longer available. Through the Eightfold-path, humanity is able to complete the development of the other eight petals, but out of one's own inner activity and in the clarity of consciousness. Under the command of Vridebrant, King of Scots, the forces of Buddha's path are represented, which will result in new insights leading into the future. Once they are developed and brought into movement, it will set into motion the other eight, so that all sixteen "wheels" will be activated—the ancient wisdom and new self-attained wisdom forming a whole within the human being: united, the sixteen spokes of the chakra will rotate together, and in their movement give voice to the harmony of the spheres, the wisdom of the universe, the Logos resurrected—the word, emanating from the creative transformed larynx. King Vridebrant, it will be noted, is not pres-

21 Walter Johannes Stein, *The Ninth Century: World History in the Light of the Holy Grail* (Temple Lodge Press, London, 1991), p. 92.

ent. He has left the white army in the hands of his four vassals, suggesting that those qualities that will lead to ultimate *peace* on earth are still far off (Vridebrant or Friedebrant indicates Friede—peace). Hidden within his name is the fragrance of *Saelde*, the inner peace of the soul.

The practice of the Eightfold-path is known to most 11th graders. It fits right in with the burgeoning idealism, which they seek. It is also an inroad to those students whose idealism has been injured—collateral damage of our combative age. They easily perceive people who practice *right thinking*, (ideas and educated opinions, viewpoints); *right judgement* (or decision); *right speech* (where the spoken words are well chosen, have weight, and develop logically); *right deed* (or action which causes no harm to others and is effective for the good of all); *right ordering* (of one's life according to nature and the environment, as well as the spirit or the higher ideals); *right striving* (or human endeavor, knowing what is and isn't possible); *right memory* (learning from life, the mistakes one has made, mindfulness); *right examination* (or contemplative self-knowledge, taking stock in order to go forward, while discerning between the essential and the non-essential).[22]

Names, as mentioned, play an important role in *Parzival*. Some more than others. When I ask the students what the name Belacane could imply, they immediately propose "beautiful" or "pretty," derived from the Italian "bella" or "Bellissima," the French "belle," but also "good" or "wonderful" from the Spanish "bellísimo". We can all attest to those attributes. Heinz Mosmann adds that "kane" implies "kone," which means "wife" or "bride" in Middle High German. In this context, Belacane means "beautiful wife."[23] However, I continue prodding, asking what bird the name might infer, as bird imagery is prevalent throughout *Parzival*. Usually, someone guesses the Pelican, based on the sound of the word. Johannes Stein writes in his book *The Ninth Century* that the pelican was known to sacrifice itself for its young, by piercing its breast to feed its young in times of need. According

---

22 Rudolf Steiner, *How to Know Higher Worlds: A Modern Path of Initiation* (Anthroposophic Press, 2008), Chapter Six.

23 Heinz Mosmann, *Der Parzival Wolframs von Eschenbach: Erkenntnis und imaginative Gestaltung des Gralsmysteriums* (Verlag Freier Geistesleben, 2020), p. 44.

to Basil Valentine (fifteenth-century alchemist), a person who has reached the stage of the "Pelican" has attained the most sublime and highest order, above the Raven (messenger between the spiritual and earthly worlds), Peacock (powers of imagination), and Swan (Inspiration). By choosing the name Belacane, Wolfram signifies that Queen Belacane has reached the level of intuition. The Pelican, due to its sacrificial quality, was a symbol for Christ. In this fourth degree, "the fire of Knowledge gives the strength to ray out the Spiritual Light into the darkness, the self-sacrificing Pelican."[24] This black Queen who is not a Christian, intuitively radiates spiritual light into the darkness, embodying the highest Christian ideals—qualities that transcend outer religious labels. Additionally, Belacane, due to the name's similarity in sound to Bilkis, has also been associated with the Queen of Sheba, the Arabian name for her, or Balkis as she is referred to in the Quran. Furthermore, the Yemenites call her Balkama, which is closest in sound to Belacane. Secundille, the wife of Feirefiz, who we meet later in the epic, is also associated with the Queen of Sheba, this mysterious queen, who has been called "the Soul of the Orient, or "Queen of the South" by the Ethiopians.

It is significant that Wolfram would choose a Christian symbol for a so-called "heathen." It shows that the development or the inner nobility of the person goes far beyond any labeling. Belacane is filled not only with ancient wisdom, but also has the attributes that point to the future. She is a priestess of sorts, a Black Madonna. During the Middle Ages, images of Black Madonnas began to appear all over Europe. They are always found in places where there once existed old mystery centers, which Patelamunt is. Belacane, like the other Black Madonnas, represents inner transformation. Gahmuret, through their union, has the opportunity to transform, though, as we shall see, he fails to recognize what she could mean for him.

Belacane embodies the intuitiveness associated with the fourth and highest level of initiation. In our age and going into the future, it is imperative that we get beyond outer classifications and tagging, which

24 *The Ninth Century*, p. 320.

can so easily lead to wrong judgements, but that we should rather focus on recognizing the inner qualities of a person, no matter who they are and where they are from. Belacane, it is insinuated, does not need a formal Christian Baptism. She has the purity, the virtues, the modesty, the love and compassion to the highest degree, symbolized by the single-ruby crown she wears in her headdress, also signifying her beauty of soul, the steadfastness and selflessness of thought.

It is "who" you are that counts, irrespective of race, religion, gender and so forth. Furthermore, it is time we change our attitude to the term "heathen." It has decidedly negative connotations. It is used negatively, a reference to people who are not Christians, Jews, or Muslims respectively. Like the term "pagan," it suggests rural people, people of the earth or the heath, which can also be seen as healthy and wholesome. Wolfram uses the term "heathen" without judgement, merely distinguishing between the various religions—not implying that the one is better than the other. That is made amply clear with Belacane, but also with the Baruch, Feirefiz, Secundille, and Ekuba. The other day (as of this writing) a Native American elder from the Mohawk Nation gave a welcoming address at our Waldorf School. During the ceremonial opening, Sakokweniónkwas, or Tom Porter (English name), referred to himself as a pagan, after which he spoke words of universal import that transcended any formal religion—a truly profound experience. In *Parzival*, the "heathens," "Saracens," "Moors," or "infidels" are not the enemies of the Christians. Rather, the evil element is represented by Clinschor, the ruler of Terre marveile, who holds people from all cultures hostage.

Gahmuret conquers both the black and white armies, marries Belacane, and restores peace. Up to this point, Gahmuret's character comes across favorably and his worthy attributes are undeniable. He is generous, courageous, tolerant, chivalrous, and respected amongst the Muslims and the Christians alike. Without doubt, it's remarkable for a person of the Middle Ages to transcend religious and racial prejudices by marrying an African Queen. Belacane, the black Queen, is filled with the light of wisdom, purity, and love, while Gahmuret, the white Prince of Anjou, has an inner darkness, which comes to the fore at the end of Book One. Like the magpie, he is inwardly checkered. He has a fatal flaw: *restlessness*.

Though he found Belacane, he has not found himself or a place to anchor permanently. His restlessness even overshadows his unwavering love for Belacane who is "dearer to him than life" (p. 39). The prowling spotted panther stirs in him once again. He cannot control the instinctive urges to seek adventure, to fight and participate in tournaments. Furthermore, Belacane is pregnant with his son. Even that does not deter him. He steals away "like a thief" in the dead of night, leaving only a letter behind, outlining his noble lineage for her to pass on to their son. Gahmuret wants his son to know that he is a descendent of the "British race" and related to Utepandragun and King Arthur—all the way back to his great-great-great grandfather, Mazadan ("Mac Adam," meaning "son of Adam"),[25] and Terdelaschoye, who was a *fairy*, which hints at an *otherworldly* heritage (fairy women with magical powers in Celtic lore were known as *Sidhe*, pronounced *shee*). Rudolf Meyer relates her to Morgana Le Fay, whose country was called "Land of Joy" which is the meaning of "Terdelaschoye."

> From her, two sons were born to Mazadan. They became the progenitors of the lineage of Anjou and Arthur. Fairy blood, an ancient inheritance of clairvoyant abilities, flows in the veins of this dual family tree. Both the Grail and the Arthurian stream are characterized as carriers of high spiritual powers, through which humanity should be given impulses for supernatural life.[26]

Though Terdelaschoye points to dormant clairvoyant abilities in both Parzival and Feirefiz (his half brother)—and later Gawain—it also reveals the gradual loss of this natural inborn spiritual vision in the human being, even in Titurel's lofty lineage. Looking back, it is said that Gilgamesh was

25 Mazadan also has a sound relationship to Mazda, as in Ahura Mazda(o), which means "wise." And "Arthur," shares sound similarities with "Ahura," specifically the "hu" which refers to the sun—Sun God, the divine.

26 Rudolf Meyer, *Zum Raum wird hier die Zeit: Die Gralsgeschichte (*Urachhaus, 1980), p. 57 (translated by the author).

two-thirds god and one-third human; the Pharaohs were half god and half human; the Greek heroes were one-third god and two-thirds human. Finally, Parzival and his family line were left with remnants of fairy blood. Clearly, a renewal of spiritual vision is called for. Furthermore, this fairy element has qualities that can stir up passions in the knights, which can easily lead them astray and into danger, not unlike the sway of impish will-o'-the-wisps.

We even hear the fairy or fay aspect in Feirefiz's name, which, when conjoined with "fiz" or "fils," ("son"), suggests "son of a fay." Feirefiz has also been interpreted to mean "vair fils" meaning "pied son," or "colorful son." Gahmuret ends the letter with the words: "You can still win me, if you will be baptized" (p. 39). It contradicts how he thought of her only a few months earlier when it seemed to him that her "modest ways were pure baptism, as was the rain that fell on her—" (p. 27).

The manner in which he leaves is upsetting to students. A girl once laughed out loud in pure derision after we'd read the letter, proclaiming, "That's like the classic email breakup." "Worse," cried another, "it's a text message breakup. What a dis." Gahmuret had entirely lost their respect, agreeing that it was a cowardly and irresponsible act—him slinking away at night, leaving a letter, but taking a boat full of gold, all while she's pregnant. "Some things don't change," another added.

Belacane would have done anything for Gahmuret, including getting baptized. It causes her to wonder about other possible dalliances. "To whom else has the courtly warrior left the fruits of his love" (p. 40). Her trust and faith in him have been deeply shaken. Belacane never recovers from the pit of grief caused by Gahmuret's desertion, dying soon after the birth of their son, Feirefiz, who was dappled both black and white: "His hair and all his skin were particolored like a magpie" (p. 40). Hearing this, a multiracial girl who always sat in front of the class exclaimed, "I guess the people of the Middle Ages had no clue how it really works," and she laughed. "But I get it, it's supposed to be symbolic."

Belacane dies of a broken heart. It is the second woman who dies because of Gahmuret's restlessness, the first being his mother, who died shortly after he left Anjou to serve the Baruch of Baghdad. Meanwhile, Gahmuret is tossed around on the windy sea for a year, having forfeited his anchor for lack of loyalty and steadfastness. He had arrived in Zazamanc midst a storm, and he departed in stormy and wind-tossed conditions. He could have stilled his spiritual yearning with Belacane. She had steadfastness and purity of soul, wisdom, and great love in her heart for him. She had the qualities he needed, but he could not recognize what he had in her, just like he could not understand the true meaning of his yearning for the highest. A Black Madonna does not judge the other for their shortcomings, but rather, she looks to see what and who they will *become*. However, Gahmuret forfeited his chance to learn from her, to question the true meaning of their encounter and what it could promise him. He did not ask after or pursue the potential of their relationship. Gahmuret didn't open himself up to her in a receptive manner, which would have filled his inner darkness with knowledge-imbued Spiritual Light. He was not ready for her and what she had to give. Mari Evans' powerful poem "I Am a Black Woman" ends with the lines, *Look / on me and be / renewed*. Gahmuret did not take time enough to truly "look" and let himself be renewed and transformed by Belacane. He could not slough off the old forces within him. Feirefiz, the son of the Black Madonna, together with Parzival, will be able to redeem this failure in the future. Failure always has the potential to birth something greater. It's not a justification, but a life lesson.

A few years back, after meeting a friend for coffee in Lenox, Massachusetts, I went to the local bookshop as I am wont to do. Serendipitously, there was a reading and book signing by the author Pir Zia Inayat-Khan, who was reading from his new book *Saracen Chivalry*, which is a treatise by Belacane to her son Feirefiz. In the text Belacane counsels young Feirefiz in the mystical ways of chivalry. The author states that it belonged to Feirefiz's most precious possessions, which he treasured throughout his life. It offers an insight into medieval chivalry from the view of an African woman that highlights Islamic wisdom in a beautifully written and accessible manner.

The mystical Sufi teaching is expressed directly through Belacane, filled with wisdom from a non-European perspective. Through the wisdom filled and understandable content, the Eastern and Western streams can find common ground. In a way it accomplishes for our time, at least in part, what Gahmuret set out to do.[27]

While reviewing the *Parzival* block a few years ago, Kailani,[28] an African American, said how much she'd loved the section with Gahmuret and Belacane the most: "I was really moved by their relationship." This was immediately followed up by Drake, also African American, who said, "It's good to hear about people from Africa, and a black Queen who has power. I appreciated that the black woman was not only described as attractive, but also as noble, kind, and wise. Hardly any books that are studied at school have that. All the books we studied in public school only had white people." I was particularly glad of his comment because he tended to be withdrawn in class.

Queen Belacane is the first major female character to play an essential role in the epic. Though we do not meet her again, she lives on through her son and her influence is felt throughout.

Discussion Topics and Questions

- How did your relationship to your family or the adults around you change when you became a teenager?
- How many nationalities are represented in the class or in your family?
- How have your parents' decisions influenced your lives?
- How many names for "God" can we come up with in the class?
- Can you distinguish between authentic yearning for something

27 Pir Zia Inayat-Khan, *Saracen Chivalry: Counsels on Valor, Generosity and the Mystical Quest (*New Lebanon, NY, Suluk Press Omega Publications INC., 2012).

28 Names have been changed.

more profound and mere fancies?

- Do you have a family crest? What would your own crest or emblem look like?
- Discuss the symbolism of a besieged castle.
- Was it right for Belacane to have Isenhart first prove himself to her? What justifies her? Did she really love him? Was she ready for his love? Did she feel pressured?

Illustrations:

1. *Parzival* book cover (Ingrid Pilgrim)
2. Black/white polarity
3. Black/white polarity and poems (Goni Ronen)
4. Armored Knight
5. Four Degrees of Inner Development (Jae-Yeon Yoo)

BOOK TWO

Herzeloyde

"We all stand on the shoulders of our ancestors." — Chinese Saying

In Book Two we are introduced to Parzival's mother, Herzeloyde ("heart suffering"). Who is she? What is her influence on Parzival? How can we understand her? What is her heritage?

Queen Herzeloyde is anything but weak and submissive. She is a person who takes life into her own hands. Her choices are based on the realities of life and outer circumstances. Herzeloyde lost her first husband in battle, leaving her a widow on her wedding day before her marriage to King Castis was even consummated. She is now the Queen of two realms, Norgals and Waleis, and needs a worthy husband to help protect her lands. She organizes a tournament where she will choose the most commendable knight. She has no intention of succumbing to an arranged marriage or letting herself be vanquished, abducted, or wooed, which was often the case in medieval times.

Gahmuret, who ended up in Spain after deserting Belacane, hears about the tournament in Kanvoleis[1] from his cousin, and decides to participate, *not* to gain a wife but for the sheer thrill and lust for battle. Eschenbach describes his arrival in grand terms. Herzeloyde, observing his entrance, does not, however, "rate it so highly" (p. 42), though she is curious about this King of Zazamanc who wears a mantle of green samite and whose attendants are both "infidels" and French. Though she is not taken by the splendid outer accoutrements, something does stir in her, a premonition of sorts. Her interest in him has awakened and she has an intimation of their mutual destiny. Gahmuret erects his pavilion in the *inner* circle, as directed by the Queen, his pendants displaying three ermine anchors each, which suggest the three women vying for his anchorage.

Queen Herzeloyde is clearly disappointed when he does not initially appear in the preliminary jousts: "Ah, where is the man of whom I have heard such marvels" (p. 46)? Judicious Gahmuret is only taking a moment to observe the others, instead of simply rushing headlong into the "hurly-burly." When it comes to battle, he keeps his cool—his head.

The games set the stage for the tone and tale of the epic. The participants are from a diversity of clans and we are introduced to some of the consequential players of *Parzival,* such as King Lot of Norway, his son Gawain (as yet too young to joust), his cousin Kaylet, Gurnemanz, and many Britons under Utepandragun, all within the *inner* circle (representing King Arthur, who went in search of his mother who fled with a magician, Clinschor). And each of the main characters has certain planetary characteristics, which become evident during the course of the story. It gives a glimpse into the multitude of players that appear in *Parzival* (around 250), which points towards the great diversity of people and circumstances found on Earth. Outside the village in the *outer* circle, more knights are gathered who will play noteworthy roles later on, such as the King of Ascalun, Cidegast of

1 Present day Colmar according to some scholars.

Logroys, and the brutal Lähelin. There is little love lost between the outer and inner circle, which adds ferocity and excitement to the games—an opportunity to indulge their bloodlust. It is another example of the polarities— such as black and white, light and dark, spiritual and physical, male and female, love and hate, in short, the ongoing yin and yang of life—which are continuously seeking to be reconciled.

Gahmuret does indeed participate in the Vesper Games, which precede the actual tournament. In these, Gahmuret proves himself to be the most outstanding warrior by far, and Herzeloyde has made up her mind: "Yet when all is said and done, I believe that Gahmuret's deeds have won most praise" (p 51). Gahmuret leads the inner circle to sure victory. Herzeloyde sees no need to have the actual tournament. None can surpass Gahmuret.

Gahmuret still shines brightly at the outset of Book Two. His accumulated riches include the gifts from the Baruch of Baghdad, the spoils of his extensive journeys, and the wealth from the combined Kingdoms of Zazamanc and Azagouc (Isenhart's former kingdoms), acquired through his union with Belacane. He also inherited Isenhart's splendid pavilion and armor, especially the glorious Adamant helmet that has magical properties, able to withstand the most vicious spear thrust. The helmet, which is adorned with an anchor, will ultimately prove to be his downfall. However, up to this point, the outer trappings are a true reflection and expression of his positive attributes, which Herzeloyde and the others recognize: "There were many who, finding themselves on his line of attack, cried, 'Look out, here comes the Anchor!'" (p. 51). It is the very reason why Herzeloyde chooses him without even waiting for the actual tournament to take place.

The anchor on the Adamant helmet and elsewhere is mentioned numerous times to underscore its symbolic importance. So far, the anchor in Gahmuret's life has not found its permanent resting place, but rather seems to underscore his ongoing restlessness, like a boat meant to visit many harbors instead of mooring in only one. Herzeloyde, however, finds *her* anchor in Gahmuret.

The moment she *recognizes* him as her lover, partner, and protector, things start to unravel for Gahmuret and get "complicated." First, he gets a message from Queen Ampflise of France, whose husband had died in battle, confessing her longing, love, and passion for him, and offering him the crown. Then he hears of his brother Galoes' death. With that, Gahmuret inherits the kingdom of Anjou. Thirdly, he is told that his mother had died—the loss of her husband and son had been too much for her. On hearing this sad news, he retreats from the Vesper Games—but the cards have fallen. Herzeloyde is determined to make him her husband. She pursues her decision and when she is ceremoniously received in his Pavilion, she looks him "up and down," which promptly confirms that she likes him—clearly a more rational approach than the meeting between Belacane and Gahmuret.

This is not a picture of a woman needing to be saved. Quite the opposite. It highlights a woman who knows exactly what she wants, à la Sarah Vaughan's song, "Whatever Lola wants, Lola gets," and, of course, Herzeloyde wants Gahmuret. Though Gahmuret is the host in his Pavilion, she states with great self-confidence, "Yet I am Mistress of this land. If it is your pleasure that I welcome you with a kiss, I assent to it" (p. 52). It is clear to him "what she wants," and he replies diplomatically that all the other lords be kissed as well. As Gahmuret is about to sit down,"she caught at him and pulled him down beside her on the other side" (p. 52). Moments later, after Gahmuret is lavished with praise from his maternal cousin Kaylet, it is determined and accepted by the men of all countries, including the British, Irish, and French, that there will be no formal tournament and that the victory clearly belongs to Gahmuret. Herzeloyde confidently states, "You must give me satisfaction in the claims I have on you" (p. 53). This puts Gahmuret in an awkward position. Both the Queen of France and the Queen of Waleis and Norgals are vying for him, yet Gahmuret pines for his wife in Africa and his conscience plagues him: "I am full of longing for the Queen," he tells the others, who chide him for looking sorrowful when he should be happy at having won Herzeloyde. "I left a lady at Patelamunt the memory of whom—pure sweet woman! —*wounds me to the heart*"[2] (my italics).

2 It foreshadows the love trials of Parzival and Feirefiz.

Gahmuret adds, "Now many an ignorant fellow may think that it was her black skin I ran away from, but in my eyes she was as bright as the sun! The thought of her womanly excellence afflicts me, for if noblesse were a shield, she would be its center-piece" (p 56). There is no mistaking his true and authentic love for Belacane. She is not merely an "exotic" flower he picked for himself, as some scholars assert. It also highlights the importance of the inner light in all people, in contrast to the outer skin that varies from person to person, even within a race, culture, or family. However, his noble words are blemished and diminished when he blames Belacane for his abandoning her, claiming she stopped him from fighting jousts. Similarly, to the baptism claim, she would most certainly have allowed him to fight had he only asked and talked to her, communicated his true reasons for wanting to leave. He is projecting his own guilt and failings onto her. Gahmuret's physical need and drive to go out and joust overshadowed his loyalty to her. He lacked *steadfastness*. And now the "dark" side of his character is getting exposed. However, in his defense, he does continue to put up a bit of a fight, replying to Herzeloyde's repeated spousal claim, "I have a wife, Ma'am . . . whom I love more dearly than life itself" (p. 57). Yet, Herzeloyde is not dissuaded, insisting that he give Belacane up. Still, he argues that the actual tournament never took place, so he is under no obligation.

He is put into a difficult position of choosing between three queens: Belacane, Ampflise, and Herzeloyde. His name, Gahmuret ("Gach-amuret"), which suggests "quick to love," rings true.[3] Unable to get out of the situation, Herzeloyde calls on an arbiter to judge the situation. According to the judgment, Gahmuret is ordered to uphold Herzeloyde's claim. On hearing the decision, she simply states, "Sire, . . . you are now mine" (p. 58). Gahmuret finally gives in, albeit on the condition that he be allowed to leave for a joust once a month, unhindered. This she grants to him.

Herzeloyde's perseverance and determination to marry Gahmuret highlights her strength and clear-sighted aim. She is not a woman to be

3 The "Gach" in Middle High German means "impetuous," "rash," and "eager", which implies his inner need to hurry from one place to another, to fight, and to rush into relationships. And "Amur" = Love.

deterred. And that, too, will be part of Parzival's heritage. Furthermore, her persistence and feistiness are admired by the students. Herzeloyde pays a steep price for her rational and resolute insistence. Most students are disappointed that Gahmuret was unable to stand up for Belacane, letting his convictions be subjugated by a mere outer court. For all his positive attributes and prowess as a knight on the battlefield, it exemplifies a serious character flaw.

For a while the two are happy with one another and deeply in love, even though it began more like a self-arranged marriage on the part of Herzeloyde, and had little to do with love but more with law, and was not born out of Gahmuret's free choice. True to the agreed upon condition, he participates in a tournament once a month until the Baruch of Baghdad once again requests his assistance, to which he honorably complies. Though he does not abandon Herzeloyde, he does leave her to go into battle. Every day she hopes for his return, and after six long months, she has a nightmare, which can be seen as a vision from the future, not only in her personal life, but in the greater cultural life. "For now, she marveled at how she was mothering a serpent which rent her womb and how a dragon sucked at her breasts and flew swiftly away and vanished from her sight! It had torn her heart from her body" (p. 62). The true meaning of Herzeloyde's name—heart suffering—is now revealing itself in full force. We might ask: To what extent do we feed the dragon of our time, and in what ways do we embody the dragon? There will be consequences either way, so it behooves us to transform that which we feed.

Straight thereafter she is informed that Gahmuret died in battle. A treacherous knight had smashed a flask of blood from a billy goat over Gahmuret's Adamant helmet, which rendered it spongy and soft. Ipomidon of Babylon, the enemy of the Baruch of Baghadad, who sought revenge, thrust his spear through the softened Adamant, killing him shamefully. The news pushes Herzeloyde to the brink of sorrow and she comes close to ending her life. Only the fact that she is carrying Gahmuret's child stops her. To kill herself would be like killing Gahmuret all over again.

The powerful and grim nightmare coincides with the news of Gahmuret's death, foreshadowing Parzival's birth, the nature of his character, his ultimate departure, and the struggles and sufferings that await him. "Her losses grow apace. Sorrows to come are on the way to her" (p. 62). It is a turning point. Her life will never be the same. Her loss is irretrievable—her former existence expunged. Her only option is to move forward toward an uncertain future, accompanied by the certainty of intense suffering, *Leiden*. The tenor of her suffering is a microcosm of the age to come. The pain confirms humanity's irretrievable loss of spirit as it enters more deeply into the physical world, no longer carried and shaped by the Apollonian formative forces—the wisdom of the ancients, the heathens. It is a vision of the birth of the *consciousness soul*, the painful labor pains where humanity,

as a whole, suckles the serpent, the dragon. The vision heralds the future, a time when all people will have to suffer and endure the painful stages of self-development within the confines of an increasingly materialistic and self-centered age, having to navigate through the different junctures to some form of fulfilment—a quest to overcome and find oneself in freedom for freedom. The vision of Herzeloyde applies to us all. We cannot escape it—its horrors will show itself to us as wakeup calls. Life as we know it cannot continue; we have to start shaping it from out of our own innate forces. And the upcoming story of Parzival offers all striving human beings a masterplan to the authentic self.

Book Two deals more with social issues and questions, and in that regard, it has similarities with the Gawain section of *Parzival*—people arguing, manipulating, and using laws for their own end, discussing rules and regulations. The end of Book Two does, however, reestablish Gahmuret's character. His positive attributes and achievements shine through once more, highlighted by the epitaph that the Caliph engraved on Gahmuret's Adamant helmet that was fixed securely onto the cross above his grave. "Baptized, he followed the Christian rite. It is no lie but truth to say that his death distressed the Saracens" (p. 67). Gahmuret strove to unite the East[4] and the West, to balance the polarities, and to bring all that is divisive into harmony. He exhibited exceptional tolerance and generosity towards all people. He was all-inclusive and free of prejudice. All were treated equally, according to their station.

Humanity is still trying to live up to those ideals, especially in the roiling mess of the Middle East. Gahmuret had the potential and most of the attributes to make it happen, but lacked two essential elements: steadfastness (through his inability to curb his restlessness), and the power of clear thinking. The latter is made evident in the way he died. The magical Adamant helmet which he received symbolizes the powers of crystalline thought. However, he had inherited the helmet from Isenhart, a heathen, and its power was not his own. Furthermore, it represented the old star wisdom which he lacked, lost, and could have regained. He had not developed the power to think in a living, flexible, and clear manner. Therefore, through the dark forces of magic, the billy goat's blood, which in various cultures signifies the lower sensual instinctive forces, he was vanquished. He did

4 The East included Africa during the Middle Ages. Today the boundaries between East and West are blurred and represent more of a religious and cultural divide rather than geographic. The time has come to overhaul these dichotomous terms.

not have his hot urge to battle under control. The instinctive "bloodlust" was stronger than his rationality and clarity of thought, expressed when Gahmuret reverted back to using his father's blazon of the spotted black panther. For him, the anchor had become a symbol of his detachment, his roaming from place to place. He never really took to the anchor, and never sought the depths to which the anchor has to drop in order to bite the solid ground. He could never go inward and anchor himself in the deeps of the spirit, though he got to know the world and lived out his drive to fight. This leitmotif runs throughout the epic, foreshadowing the task and mission of Parzival: to find inner steadfastness and control over his feelings and actions by developing the forces of thinking, warmed by compassion. Control over mind, body, and soul—imbued with love—is an imperative of our age, which encapsulates Parzival's journey.

Who Is Herzeloyde?

"Because philosophy arises from awe, philosophers are bound in their way to be lovers of myths and poetic fables. Poets and philosophers are alike in being vast with wonder." ~ Thomas Aquinas

There are historical realities to be found behind many of the personalities and imaginations in *Parzival.* Except for giving some brief background information regarding the ninth and the twelfth/thirteenth centuries to the students, I do not elucidate too much on historical perspectives. However, for the teacher, the more esoteric background material helps to give breadth and depth to the deeper layers of the epic. Rudolf Steiner has given numerous indications in this direction, though some remain enigmatic. I use the evidence to enter meditatively into the respective characters.

In volume four of Steiner's karma lectures, which he gave in 1924, he talks about the successive lives of Herzeloyde. We are not told of a specific historical personality behind Herzeloyde during the ninth century, though Steiner, in reference to legendary figures of the Middle Ages, and specifically to Herzeloyde says, rather inscrutably, that she "is not really historic, but more historical than history."[5] In living out her legendary existence in the epic, she complements her previous incarnation as Julian the Apostate.

Julian was born in Constantinople, nephew of Constantine I, in 331 CE. He led and endured a tumultuous life, which started with his mother's death, followed a few years later by the murder of his father and the massacre of most of his relatives by his cousin Constantius II, who took over after the death of Rome's first Christian Emperor. Julian received his education through the eunuch Mardonius, who introduced him to the beauty of the Hellenistic culture, where he fell in love with the works of Homer, Hesiod, and the philosophers. However, he was a lonely child and often sat by the Bosporus, gazing up at the stars, intuiting their wisdom. In his eleventh year, he was sent to the grim fortress of Macellum in Cappadocia, severed from his beloved tutor and raised as a Christian. The loneliness he'd known as a child only intensified. At sixteen, after his release, he visited many Greek city-states before settling in Athens. Being barred from public life allowed him to pursue his studies, which led to his rejection of Christianity in his twentieth year, in favor of Neoplatonic Hellenism; hence the name Julian the Apostate. He had a natural penchant for the ancient wisdom and was initiated into various Mysteries, of which the Mystery of Mithras was most important.

Julian was summoned to Milan, where he expected to be executed. Instead, raised to the position of a Caesar, he was sent to Gaul, where he led successful raids against the German tribes. His soldiers admired and respected him, which enabled Julian to become Roman Emperor in 361 CE. He immediately set about reorganizing the Empire to run more efficiently, but also restoring pagan rites and sacrifices, though he kept some of the Christian elements that he respected. He did experience a conflict between the old wisdom and the new elements found in Christianity. In 363 CE, during an ambitious campaign in Persia, Julian was treacherously murdered, presumably by one of his own people for either revealing secrets of the Mysteries or for his rejection of Christianity.

5 Rudolf Steiner, *Esoterische Betrachtungen: Karmische Zusammenhänge*, GA 238, p. 87 (translation by author).

In the karma lectures, Rudolf Steiner indicates that Julian the Apostate would have been well suited to incorporate Christianity into Europe, better than all the other Emperors because he had deep spiritual insights. He had a profound understanding of both Christianity and ancient wisdom. The tragedy is that he was not able to unite the old sun wisdom of Mithras with its incarnation into Christianity. The world was not yet ready for a reconciliation between the Eastern and Western Sun Mysteries.

Knowing, through Steiner, that Herzeloyde is the reincarnated Julian helps to put things into context, enabling one to see the larger context and her role in the unfolding development of the Grail story. For instance, it is interesting to note that Julian's mother had a dream-vision of giving birth to Achilles shortly before Julian's birth,[6] which not only throws light on Julian's life but reminds one of Herzeloyde's nightmare before giving birth to Parzival, which reveals essential aspects of Parzival and his unfolding destiny.

It is further interesting to note some similarities to Gahmuret's life, almost like a mirroring. Julian and Gahmuret both traveled extensively in the West and the East. They both shared a deep connection to the East and the ancient wisdom. And they both met an untimely death on the battlefield through treachery. As mentioned, Steiner says that more than most early Christian leaders, Julian could have brought Christianity to Europe in a more balanced manner. Both leaders failed in the unification of East and West. Herzeloyde, in her love for Gahmuret, is reliving aspects of her previous incarnation.

Herzeloyde, as we shall see in the following chapter, retreats and isolates herself. The outer movement of Julian/Gahmuret is turned inward. She needed it to reconcile the conflicts and oppositional states that Julian experienced in his own life. In Soltane she becomes an anchoress of sorts, thereby serving as an anchor for the departed Gahmuret. Steiner describes her life as a peaceful and warm cloud that floats over the life of Julian the Apostate, intensifying the inner life of the soul. "And so the soul became

6 Nina Göbel, *Julian: Herzeloyde: Tycho Brahe* (Goetheanum, Freie Hochschule für Geisteswissenschaft), 1987.

enriched, richer in the manifold inner impulses."[7] The law of contraction and expansion holds true over a succession of lifetimes, just as one can observe it within one lifetime. After the more outward incarnation of Julian, also present in Gahmuret's life, she turns inward—a time of gestation. She sacrifices her own life for Parzival, giving him the foundation he needs for his unfolding. She is and remains a widow, another theme that runs throughout the epic. As modern people, we all become "widows" in a manner of speaking—feeling the loss of the other, leaving us inwardly isolated, incomplete. The contraction becomes extreme through the loss of Gahmuret, followed by Parzival's departure. Yet, it is what she needed in order to internalize what had transpired in the previous incarnation, and what is living itself out in the incarnation as Herzeloyde. Though she fails to unite the outer and inner world in her incarnation as Herzeloyde, she is developing the forces of love, selfless love, Grail love. Gahmuret failed to unite East and West, North and South, and Herzeloyde failed to unite inner and outer, the spiritual and the physical. Parzival's journey will represent the prototype of how to reconcile these polarities—those that keep humanity so separated and fractious. One can also view his journey as the path to the *source*.

In Herzeloyde's subsequent incarnation as Tycho Brahe, the Danish astronomer, known for his accurate and scientific observations, one can see an attempt at uniting the polarity between the geocentric cosmology of the Ptolemaic system and the Copernican system that positions the sun at the center of the universe. There is an entire worldview attached to either outlook. However, it goes beyond the scope of this book to go into further detail about his endeavors. In Tycho Brahe, the contracted soul once again expanded out into the universe, but consciously, out of a spiritually inspired intellect.

Gahmuret vacillates between the polarities: East and West, light and dark, Christianity and Islam, masculine and feminine, outer and inner,

7 Steiner, *Karmische Betrachtungen*, Band IV, p. 88.

contraction and expansion, war and peace, success and failure, and fire and water. Gahmuret cannot find the middle way, which will be Parzival's task. In Belacane and Herzeloyde, we have the black and white motif. It's easy to observe the differences between his two wives, yet there is more that unites than separates them. They are both forsaken by Gahmuret. Herzeloyde's name—heart suffering—also holds true for Belacane, for the black Queen dies from the acute pain of his desertion. Likewise, Belacane's name holds true for Herzeloyde, for they are both beautiful ("bel"), and Herzeloyde, by sacrificing her life for Parzival, has a Pelican's devotion to her young. Merged together, they are as one: ancient wisdom of the stars and nascent wisdom reaching for the stars—the outer reaching down, the inner reaching up, making a whole when merged together. Gahmuret was simply not ready to unite these divisions. The opposites thus remained separate, but future bearing seeds were sown, ensuring that the polarities would blossom forth in the splendor of variegated wholeness, through the efforts of Feirefiz and Parzival and the eternal feminine, which—as Goethe says—draws us upward and on.[8]

Discussion Topics, Questions

- What is your birth-biography? How has it shaped your life? (Can be discussed in groups. Needs to be approached delicately.)
- Can dreams inform the future?
- Place yourself into the position of Herzeloyde or Gahmuret: What would you have done in their place, given the context?
- Have you ever had premonitions of something about to happen—little warning signs? When did you heed them, when not?
- Do you recognize patterns in your life?
- How much of yourself do you reveal to others?
- What social norms do you suffer under? To what extent are they restrictive? What are the positive aspects of social conventions?

8 Goethe, end of *Faust,* Part Two.

Do you have your own social norms? Do they make you feel safe or thwart your potential?

- How often is an adolescent a dragon to their parents?
- Compare and contrast Belacane and Herzeloyde.

Illustrations:

1. Suffering heart (Violet Middlebrook)
2. A Dream of Dragons (Gabriel Lopez)

To us it is given
At no stage ever to rest;
The active human being
Must live and strive
From life to life
As plants grow
From springtime to springtime;
Through error and truth,
From fetters into freedom,
Through illness and death,
Upward to beauty, health and life.[1]
~ Rudolf Steiner

BOOK THREE

OUT OF THE sixteen books, I spend the most time on Book Three. In Chrétien de Troyes' version, it is the opening chapter. Here we meet Parzival for the first time. Many of the seminal themes are found in this chapter, forming and establishing the foundation for later developments, both in plot and content. It speaks directly to the inner life of the students, which lives itself out in many different ways.

NATURE BOY

"The greatest thing you'll ever learn
Is just to love and be loved in return."
~ Eden Ahbez[2]

BY RIGHTS PARZIVAL should be surrounded by knights, ladies, and courtly society, educated according to chivalric traditions. After all, he is heir to three kingdoms: Waleis, Norgals, and Anjou (*"Anschouwe"*). Yet, he

---

1 Translation by Arvia Ege, modified by the author.

2 From the song "Nature Boy," composed by Eden Ahbez and made famous by Nat King Cole.

knows nothing of them, having grown up in the wilderness far removed from any form of civilization. The father principle is missing entirely in his life, and when he does meet it, the lessons come hard and fast, which creates inner conflicts, thereby also giving him the momentum to grow beyond his age and with great impact. That familial severance prompts a search for completeness. Many heroes have lost their fathers or are orphans. Telemachus grows up without Odysseus and is prompted by Athena to go in search of him. Forrest Gump's father has gone on "vacation," and Moses is abandoned in a basket. Furthermore, fairy tales with absent fathers are numerous, which is also true for popular superheroes, such as Batman, Spiderman, and Luke Skywalker. When the father is absent, the hero is forced to find himself through his own actions, for which he must take full responsibility.

Parzival is living with his mother and a handful of servants in Soltane. The name itself suggests *sol*-itude, i-*sol*-ation, and de-*sol*-ation. It is by design. Herzeloyde, out of her great suffering and loss, does not want Parzival to succumb to the same fate that befell Gahmuret, Castis (her first husband), Galoes, Gandin, and most knights of the time. In Chrétien's version, Perceval has two older brothers who also get killed, one of whom has his eyes pecked out by a raven/crow, as described in one of the earliest of English extant ballads called *The Twa Corbies*, which I usually sing with the classes each year.[3] Herzeloyde does not want to lose Parzival as well. Therefore, she leaves all her lands, fame, and fortune behind and makes her home in the thickets of the forest. She forbids any of the servants to mention a word of the ways of the world outside their self-imposed sequestered sanctuary. She keeps his heritage from him by scrupulous design, so that he will never be tempted by what he doesn't know. It is an idyllic Edenic hideaway in which the young boy can play and roam freely through the wilds of the woods with no restrictions. He grows up as a Nature Boy, surrounded by wildlife wonders and embedded in the rhythms of the seasons, which inculcate a moral goodness in the receptive soul of the child. The word "nature" has

3 As learned from my Irish friend Norman Skillen, who also taught *Parzival* for many years.

its source in “natus,” meaning “born,” or “nasci,” in which we hear the word “nascent,” referring to the beginning of things. The name Soltane, though it refers to a solitary existence, also has another meaning hidden within the word, as the students point out correctly almost every year when I ask them what the name Soltane could mean. “Sol” in Spanish means sun, as does “soleil” in French. In fact, the relation to the sun is usually mentioned first. Parzival has a sunny and bright childhood, enveloped by the love of a doting mother. Though isolated in the wilderness of nature, he can enjoy the warmth and brightness of the sun.

As part of our discussions, I ask the students about the pros and cons of growing up like Parzival. They tend to be critical, especially of Herzeloyde’s overprotectiveness, her “smothering,” claiming she acted out of fear, and that it was obvious it couldn’t last. Almost reluctantly, they admit that she loves him and only wants to protect him from the dangers of the world, especially certain death in battle. Often, these discussions around Parzival in Soltane can get quite heated. One student who grew up in the projects and had attended a public high school with over a thousand students was adamant: “You have to watch your back early on. That’s the reality. You can’t be spared and protected from the stuff that happens. You gotta learn to fight, learn the ways of the street.” It was his first year at our Waldorf school, and ironically his mother had removed him from the city especially because of the deleterious effects of his previous surroundings. She did exactly what Herzeloyde did—protecting him and his siblings. When children are nurtured and protected from the harsh world, they gain the strength needed to get them through the hard times that will inevitably meet them later in life, in one form or another.

The benefits of growing up in nature are numerous: clean air, quietude, ample space, the beauty of the natural surroundings, the life of plants, birds, and animals, a time to learn through play, experiencing the elements. In a recent class, someone mentioned the growing popularity of “forest schools and kindergartens” that have sprung up all over the world. Not for nothing do we have the saying: Nature is our greatest teacher. It is the source of both earthly and divine wisdom, embodying the lawfulness of all lifeforms.

Or, as William Wordsworth says: "*Come forth into the light of things / Let Nature be your teacher.*"[4]

We discuss the artificial norms of society, back then as today. Growing up removed from societal customs and traditions allows for greater freedom and independence, where one can learn through trial and error, unencumbered by rules and regulations. Parzival does not have to follow the manifold courtly dos and don'ts. He is kept ignorant of the contemporary life around him. He does not learn the traditions and customs of his time, the consequences of which Parzival will have to bear. He remains blissfully ignorant of the royal routine, but he exults in life. The conventions of "polite society" can easily lead to prejudice and stifle healthy questioning that comes naturally to children. These customs can become a costume that people don, behind which they hide, serving as a form of disguise. Undoubtedly, Parzival will be regarded as a fool when he enters the greater world. It will all be new for him, and that will make him more conscious of what is expected and required, and it will have more of an impact on him. Having been kept ignorant, Parzival will see the outside world with fresh eyes. He won't just take it for granted. Though his lack of a normal education is initially going to work against him, it will ultimately thrust him into the future as an agent of change with immense impact.

I ask the students if Parzival's sequestered situation reminds them of other great personalities that have initiated great changes in the world. Intermittently someone mentions the Buddha, which is maybe the most apropos example of this phenomenon. Like Parzival, Siddhartha Gautama

4 From Wordsworth's poem "The Tables Turned."

was sequestered from the world, though in his case, it was in reverse. He was isolated in his royal surroundings, lavished with luxuries, and (like Parzival) kept away from death, ugliness, and illness. When he could stand his imprisonment no longer, he broke out and was shocked into reality by what he saw—the sufferings of the world (unlike Parzival initially). After a time of wandering and searching, Siddhartha found enlightenment under the Bodhi tree. From then on, he was known as the "Awakened One," or the Buddha. Had he not initially been removed from the realities of daily life, he might never have been as influential. He brought something new into the world: *compassion* and intentional self-transformation. It is interesting to note that the appearance of the Grail stories in writing coincided with Francis of Assisi (1181–1226), who is, in many ways, the Christian Buddha of the Middle Ages. Like the Buddha, Parzival's task is to bring a new impulse to humanity.

A student once asked if the people in the Dark Ages would even have heard of the Buddha. Knowledge of the Buddha had been lost and forgotten, like so much else from the ancient world. However, a certain legend could be found all over Europe and the Middle East, which belonged to the most popular stories of the time: the story of Barlaam and Josaphat, appearing in a wide variety of versions. It was prophesied to a king in India that his son would achieve great things. Therefore, the father protected and took great care of him, ensuring that he would receive only the best and most precious that life can offer. He kept him from knowing about the sorrows and sufferings of the world. However, one day, young Josaphat did venture out of the palace to witness sickness, leprosy, old age, and death. Greatly distressed, he returned to the palace, where he spoke to Baarlam, a wise man and Christian. They talked about the experience and over time Josaphat became a Christian. The close resemblance to the story of the Buddha is unmistakable. There is evidence that the Manichaeans helped to spread the story and there are many spellings of the name Josaphat, depending on the language, such as Jodasaph, Yudasaf, and Budasaf (Arabic), but its etymology is clear: it is the Sanskrit word for Bodhisattva. According to Steiner, it shows that the great being, the Bodhisattva who lived in the

Gautama Buddha and who paved the way for the Christ, absorbed and became a Christian. Gautama Buddha did not remain the same as he was in 600 BC, but evolved, developed, and transformed, as is only natural with all beings.[5] One has to remember that Steiner is talking about the cosmic Christ, seen from an esoteric point of view.

Parzival, however, approaches his *gradual* awakening through his own failings and imperfections. He has to learn and relearn what it means to be truly human. Buddha was prepped to be a leader and king, but woke up to the plight of the world. Parzival was kept from being a king of his lands, and had to *start from scratch*, confronting his own plight and flaws. The world becomes the arena of self-confrontations and development, and it takes many adventures ("*aventure*") and many people to help Parzival find his destiny—his eternal individuality.

Other examples come to mind, such as Muhammad, who came from a prominent family. His father died before his birth, and he was sent off to live with the Bedouins in the desert. At an early age, his mother died and he became an orphan, forced to lead an unprosperous life under his guardians. Muhammad's inner and outer isolation—self-imposed in later life—led to his revelations. Another student brought up John the Baptist who retreated into the wilderness at an early age, leading an austere and simple life until he began preaching and baptizing. Or then there's Nelson Mandela, son of a chief, who spent the happiest years of his childhood in the small village of Quno in the Transkei, listening to stories and herding cattle. There were no roads and he learned by observation, immersed in nature. There are numerous parallels: born into noble stock of leaders and warriors, steeped in nature, death of the father at an early age, and growing up far removed from the modern ways of life. Describing his childhood, Madiba writes:

> From an early age I spent most of my free time in the veld, playing and fighting with the other boys of the village. We were mostly

5 Rudolf Steiner, *Der Orient im Lichte des Okzidents* (Rudolf Steiner Verlag, Taschenbücher aus dem Gesamtwerk, 1977, GA 113), pp. 193-194. In English: *The East in the Light of the West.*

> left to our own devices [like Parzival]. We played with toys we made ourselves, moulding animals and birds out of clay and building ox-drawn sledges out of tree branches. At the end of the day . . . my mother would enchant us with Xhosa legends and fables that had come down from numberless generations. These tales stimulated my childish imagination, and usually contained some moral lesson."[6]

At the outset, Parzival is a foolish boy-man, a dullard, and an impulsive, unrefined person. He is not unlike the mythical Adam, before experiences wake him up to himself and the world around him; or Enkidu from the Mesopotamian *Epic of Gilgamesh*, the wild man who grew up with the animals, ignorant of civilization and society. Parzival, endowed with the dormant qualities of his lineage had to be removed from society in order for him to reenter and bring about the needed change, which otherwise would not have been possible. To reiterate: often, it takes someone from the outside, with fresh eyes, to bring about change, be it in an institution, business, corporation, school, or government. We don't have to look too far to recognize that those who bring huge changes (both positive and negative), aren't necessarily the ones to be formally trained or educated in the specific fields. Steve Jobs and Bill Gates, for instance, are the prototypical "college-dropout billionaires," arriving at their innovations through unconventional ways, having pursued their visions in their own unique ways (true for many American "self-made men"). In the arts, Vincent van Gogh is a prime example, and in music it's Erik Satie. The same is true for many women (most of them unrecognized in their time and even now), such as Hedy Lamarr, the successful actress and inventor, who contributed substantially to the inventions of GPS, Bluetooth, and even Wi-Fi technology. And then there is Rudolf Steiner whose initiatives gave innovative and renewed impulses in the realm of architecture, art, movement, sculpture, music, education, agriculture, and medicine, though he had not undergone any

6 Nelson Rolihlahla Mandela, *Mandela: An Illustrated Autobiography*, Little, Brown and Company, 1994, p. 8.

formal training or education in any of those disciplines. He too grew up in a relatively sequestered and simple manner, at one remove from conventional society. Major cultural, artistic, and scientific shifts often come through the side door. As the famous saying goes: "The revolution will not be televised."

Parzival's unconventional education develops through significant encounters, each one taking him a step forward, teaching him something he needs in order to fulfill his destiny, guiding him toward his end goal. Parzival, through his encounters, lays out the blueprint, the archetypal path that we all—as humans—have to undertake, in one way or another, in order to bring humanity forward in a healthy, helpful, and vital manner, though different for every person. Encounters have the potential to be transformative.

Encounter with the Birds

"Look sharply
After your thoughts.
They come unlooked for,
Like a new bird
Seen on your trees."
~ Ralph Waldo Emerson

Encounters play a pivotal role in Parzival and each one sheds light on all subsequent encounters, regardless how they manifest—big or small, outer or inner. Though he was born to Herzeloyde, who influenced his infancy and early childhood in a most fundamental manner, I do not, strictly speaking, consider her to be his first encounter. She was his home and together they were as one, just like he and the surrounding nature were experienced as an inseparable whole. Parzival was embedded in her all-embracing love. The first encounter that jolted him from his timeless Garden of Eden was with the birds.

Gahmuret, we remember, wanted to serve the highest ruler. In his case, it meant the most powerful on earth. Parzival is also drawn to the "highest,"

but in this case, the birds up above. Wolfram writes that Parzival was "cheated of a royal style of life in all things . . . except that he would cut bow and arrows with his own hands and shoot at the flocks of birds there" (p. 71). We see Gahmuret's nature welling up from the depths of Parzival's soul in his desire to forge weapons and hunt. Parzival "had no care in the world save the singing of the birds overhead. Its sweetness pierced him to the heart" (p. 71), sensitively stimulating his feeling life. It is the first time that he is deeply moved inwardly by something in his surroundings. However, it also leads to conflict. When he shoots them, he weeps bitterly and runs to his mother, not understanding why they ceased to sing. It's also the first time that we hear of him crying. As we talked about this scene in class a few years back, one of the girls was puzzled about that phenomenon, asking, "Really, he didn't know that they were dead?" I nodded, restating that Parzival simply did not understand how life could leave the birds. All that he wanted was to have them close by. After a moment's silence she said, "Ah, that is so sad, it brings tears to my yes. I'm sorry, but it really does."

Crying, however, like laughing, is a cathartic experience, a transformation of sorts (I remind them of the 9th grade Tragedy & Comedy block and our discussions around laughing and crying). He has no understanding of death, nor can he recognize the correspondence between outer circumstances and inner soul conditions. It is this inexplicable desire for the *heights*—the birds above him—and the beautiful singing, which he wants to reach and bring down to earth. The birds represent the heavens, something worthy to be attained. It's a subconscious longing to bring heaven down to earth.[7] He was unable to explain his vexation to Herzeloyde, just like Gahmuret could not explain the ache he felt before setting out on his adventure. It is a yearning that goes beyond the physical: the yearning for something more, higher, spiritual—the lost paradise, no matter how beautiful the earthly world might be. Herzeloyde, on observing Parzival "gaping" up a tree, misunderstands his affliction, and sees it as a threat to the "perfect" life in Soltane. She intimates correctly that this longing might lead him away from her, and into danger. In her attempt to thwart the impulse, she orders the birds killed, which only helps to precipitate the moment when he will leave her. It reminds one of the inescapable forces of fate that run through Greek mythology.

On seeing their demise, Parzival confronts his mother, wanting the wanton killing stopped, which gives her pause to think: "Oh, why do I forget and thwart the will of Him Who is God on *high?*" (p. 71)? The birds are brought into connection with God. Like God, they live in the heights. They sing the praise of life. They are reminders of spirit, recognized throughout the ages in diverse cultures in myriad ways. Parzival's encounter with the birds leads to a brief but decisive discussion about God and the devil, good and evil (see next section): God, as the creative life force, and the devil as the personification of temptation and distraction.

Birds are associated with thinking and wisdom in many cultures, as exemplified in the symbolism of feathers with the indigenous people of America. Their striking feathery headdresses represent leadership, wisdom, and sovereignty. Feathers are a postal service to the heavens, delivering and receiving messages. We also have idiomatic phrases, such as, "feather in your cap," to denote success, achievement or triumph in one form or another. In

7 We are reminded of the words from the Lord's Prayer: "Thy will be done / On earth as it is in Heaven."

Christian symbolism, feathers represent closeness to the spirit and God. In the Bible, Noah sees the dove after the Flood, filling him with hope for the future. It is said that for the Native Americans the eagle was the favorite of the "Great Spirit." In almost every country around the world, the eagle is associated with strength, freedom, sovereignty, and truth. In ancient Egypt, the sacred Ibis is connected to the God Thoth, whose head depicts an Ibis, and who signifies wisdom, knowledge, truth, and all learning. The feather, with its airy and light quality, denotes an array of virtues. The film *Forest Gump*, most famously starts with a feather floating down from the sky—the heavens—and ends with the feather floating away.[8] In many parts of Africa, the bird has been acknowledged as the creature of freedom; and the gods could choose to raise the human soul to the sublime state of a bird, after traversing through many earthly incarnations. According to Credo Mutwa, only the realm of the stars is higher.[9]

Parzival unconsciously yearns for the spirit, something higher, beyond the physical realm. It alludes to his thinking capacities, which he will have to develop in order to achieve his goals. "[A] feather holds something tremendous: it holds the secret of how thoughts are formed."[10] The eagle is the most potent symbol of higher insights, though all birds incorporate those ideals. Bird imagery fills the pages of Parzival. They will accompany Parzival throughout the epic in profound ways, each one denoting a different quality. They offer clues to Parzival's soul-spiritual development at every step of the way—his beginning into thought control. At this stage, however, the individual birds are not named; no qualitative and symbolic differences are suggested.

---

8 Halfway through a *Parzival* block, some students voiced that they'd watched *Forest Gump* and noticed many similarities to *Parzival*. They asked whether we could watch the movie during class. I am not one to watch movies during class time, but I consented on the condition that they organize everything themselves. I didn't think they would, but they did. After watching the movie, we discussed all the similarities, and I was impressed with what they discovered and noticed. It helped them to connect to the thematic content of *Parzival* with enhanced enthusiasm.

9 *Indaba, My Children*, p. 610

10 Rudolf Steiner, *Man as Symphony of the Creative Word* (Rudolf Steiner Press, 1991). p. 16.

"Oh Mother, What Is God?"

"Ignorance is the curse of God; knowledge is the wing wherewith we fly to heaven."
~ William Shakespeare, — *Henry VI, Part 2*; Act IV, scene vii

The Brief talk with his mother about God and the Devil opens the lid to Herzeloyde's worst fear—that Parzival might leave her to pursue a knightly life, which caused Gahmuret's death. All humans are confronted with the question around good and evil, the beings or forces through which we experience all that is good or bad: otherwise known as God and the devil (with equivalent terminology subject to respective cultures). Depending on the students and who is in the class, this topic becomes a point of thoughtful discussion. The question *who or what is God?* comes up again and again. It is a question that infuses a great body of literary works, each one from a slightly different angle. Looking back to the 9th grade curriculum, one can remind the students of Oedipus' relation to the gods, or the famous line of Lorraine Hansberry's *A Raisin in the Sun*: "I don't believe in God . . . There simply is no blasted God! There is only Man, and it's he who makes miracles."[11] I also might refer to the famous "Gretchen question" from Goethe's *Faust*, which we discuss in the senior class, where Gretchen asks Faust about his relationship to God. Students relate to this question very differently, depending on their age.

Herzeloyde keeps it simple, depicting God as "brighter than the sun," while the "Lord of Hell" is labeled as black. She teaches him to discern between light and darkness. This section reminds me of the time I traveled through Bali and asked the guide at Pura Besakih, a vast complex of temples, what the black and white checkered sarongs signify that are wrapped around many statues and even trees, or worn by the *legong* dancers during their *kris* or sword dance. He explained that the white means the good and the black means evil, both of which we carry within us. Up to that point, Parzival's world has been good—utterly good. His world was united and wholly

11 Lorraine Hansberry, *A Raisin in the Sun*, act 1 scene i (Penguin, 1988), p. 51.

undivided. The ideal for a child in the first seven years is to be surrounded by goodness, which gives the child confidence and strength to live, act, and work positively later in life. Finding out that the world is divided into good and bad, light and dark, opens the inner life to the possibility of doubt in seed form. Herzeloyde does not intend it to be taken literally, which, of course, Parzival does when he sees the knights shortly after. In the physical world "all that glitters is not gold," as the well-known proverb says. One has to be discerning. Yet, for the inner life, the imagery holds true. "His mother told him about light and darkness and how different they are" (p. 72). She is teaching him a fundamental Manichean, Zarathustrian, or Taoistic lesson, based on the duality of light and darkness. Herzeloyde does not explain anything, leaving it pictorial, her answers meant as an orientation gift.

Like Parzival, we have to begin to *love* that which is hidden from us, which keeps us in the "dark" of unknowing. We have to arrive at the right relationship to our own inferiorities, vulnerabilities, suspicions, prejudices, and fears—only then can the inner darkness be embraced, accepted, and transformed into a womb that gives birth to light. Our age demands for us to wake up from the darkness of the unconscious realms, as C. G. Jung stipulated. Remaining oblivious and ignorant of the needs of the world is no longer a viable option and has no place in the development of humanity. And should humanity refuse to wake up to the needs of the world and its people, then the darkness of unconsciousness will have negative consequences; it will not have the creative, womblike forces, but the opposite: the cold forces of hardening intellectualism and death. Wisdom must be brought into the day consciousness. Ignorance cannot continue to be bliss—not if we want to be responsibly free. In the past, wisdom was in the hands of the gods, the initiates, the sages, the priests, the pharaohs, the heroes, the leaders. People were initiated into secret knowledge. Those times are irrevocably over for all but a few outliers. We cannot rely on them and their in-*sights* any longer. Living in modernity necessitates that we all take responsibility—for ourselves and the world. Instincts alone will not bring us forward. Nor the reliance on atavism. On the contrary, we are called to work on developing our faculties of imagination, inspiration, and intuition. Bringing things to consciousness is opening up to the light. Ignoring the needs of the time is succumbing to the shadow, is keeping us in the dark. The story of Parzival is the story of gaining the inner light, of the emerging consciousness leading to the recognition of the needs of the world for the health of all. It is the path to the Holy Grail of higher knowledge that encompasses goodness, beauty, and truth—to completeness. The term "Holy" means "to make whole." The Grail can transform and make us "whole." Until then we feel "un-holy" or "un-whole," i.e., incomplete.

As mentioned earlier, the black-white, light-dark imagery is found in all the major world religions, and it marks the core of Persian Zoroastrianism, which belongs to the oldest continuously practiced religions in the world. This duality of good and evil, which includes the concept of hell, is described in the Avesta ("religious text"). Ahura Mazdao, "The Wise Ruler," is a lofty being of brilliant light, in contrast to Ahriman, who is connected to hell and darkness. Ahriman became the most powerful adversary to Ahura Mazdao. Black and white imagery is used throughout the Avesta, and the imagery is continued in the Manichean teachings of Mani, who melded Zoroastrianism with Christianity, and which is concealed in *Parzival*, well disguised, especially because of the Catholic Church, who considered any alternative view of Christianity to be heretical, resulting in the systematic persecution of the Cathars, Manicheans, Albigenses, amongst others. However, it has been forgotten how influential the Manicheans were, all the way to India and beyond to China, where some of the ancient Manichean texts were discovered. I mention this because it goes beyond any so-called white European thinking. Modernity is the result of influences from northern Africa, Persia, India, and the far East. In our global age, we have to see things in a new light, honoring what has been accomplished and practiced in the past, but transformed into what has relevance today. One of the greatest essentials is for humans to arrive at a right and true relationship with one another, no matter what the differences might be. Unfortunately, there is a lot that obscures clarity of thought. Herzeloyde's depiction of God is based in a Zarathustrian, Manichean, and Eastern worldview rather than in Western Catholicism.

Herzeloyde means well when she advises Parzival to turn away from the devil and "treacherous despair" because she does not want any harm to come to him. But Parzival needs to confront the *D-evil* in order to transform that force—to love him into *goodness,* just like the modern human being needs to confront the wasteland and transform and work it into something Good, so that it can once again nourish humanity. For the devil—an active personification of our unconscious drives, urges, and desires—functions in the darkness, which shows itself in the inability to control and understand parts of who we are. When Faust asked the devil who he is, Mephisto answered: "*Part of that force which would / Do evil evermore, and yet creates the good.*"[12] The devil, just like the darkness, has its place.

Herzeloyde does not want to lose Parzival or have him die in battle. She has experienced enough of that. Pictorially, she gives him the gift of duality and how life oscillates between the opposing forces. He will have to discover for himself the different shades within the polarities, how they intermingle and fructify one another; how they form a bond, how the one lives in the other—always in motion, the one growing into the other, the tides and gifts of color, always uniting, always finding each other's sweet spots, like two melodies singing around one another, within the atmosphere of change and development—invoking the best: yin-yang's black and white uniting in an ultimate love relationship.

Knights in the Forest

"That which we do not bring to consciousness appears in our lives as fate."
~ C. G. Jung

Some time passes and Parzival continues to hone his hunting skills. On one of these hunting excursions, he hears the sound of hoofs and he *hopes* it might be the devil. Instead of running away, he is ready to fight him, which shows his immense self-confidence and courage. Like Gahmuret, he is

12 Goethe, *Goethe's Faust*, translated by Walter Kaufmann (Anchor Book 1961), p. 159.

fearless. It turns out to be three knights. He thinks that they must be gods, the way their resplendent armor shines in the sun. He immediately falls to his knees on the path and cries, "Help God! . . . Thou hast the power to help!" (p. 72)! Unwittingly, of course, they do help in that they precipitate his leaving Soltane.

The students often smile, commenting on his simple stupidity ("*tumben*") to think that the knights are gods. Parzival has never seen people fully armed from "heel to crown" before. Seeing them tower above him on their mighty steeds is a formidable sight for him, the shock of which triggers the latent knight within him. However, it is not such an uncommon human trait to mistake mortals for gods, which, if the opportunity allows, is worth discussing. There is plenty of evidence for this, as Anna Della Subin poignantly points out in her topical book, *Accidental Gods*,[13] supplying detailed and ample examples, such as Christopher Columbus, Cortez, Pizzaro, Hailie Selassie, Krishnamurti, and many more. Some abused their power to harrowing effects. Of course, going back in history, many leaders, heroes, Pharaohs, Prophets, Emperors were considered divine, and *not* by accident, having gone through stringent initiations. Some initiates had undisputable godlike power, making them worthy of veneration, like Buddha and Zarathustra. Nonetheless, humans are quick to deify others, such as tyrants and charismatic politicians. We only need to think of the quasi-divine status of Stalin, or the leaders of North Korea's totalitarian regime, or the lamentable deification of Trump by some of his

13 Anna Della Subin, *Accidental Gods* (Metropolitan Books, 2021).

misguided supporters. Furthermore, adolescents commonly idolize their sports and pop heroes like gods, pasting their bedroom walls with posters of them. We live in a society obsessed with glamour. Then there was the Islington graffiti stating that "Clapton is God," which morphed the lead guitarist into a global myth. Or Robert Plant beatified as the "Rock God." This devotion in teens is normal and can transform into something that propels them to pursue their true goals and ideals later on. Parzival, like most young people, is caught up in his senses. For him it was the dazzling armor and the sleek steeds. Today it might be a sports car, the latest device, bling, or trendy designer clothes. The outer world through the senses has a magical allure.

In Parzival's case, it underscores his simpleness, fueled by his mother's words of the brilliance of God, taken literally. "This stupid Waleis is slowing us down" (p. 72),[14] spoken by one of the impatient knights, accentuates his foolishness. They don't *see* who is in front of them. It's an example of prejudice based on appearance and different behavior, which can have far-reaching consequences. However, their overlord, Prince Karhnahkarnanz, rides up on his splendid Castilian. He is even more magnificently attired, adorned with tiny golden bells attached to the stirrups, legs, and arms that ring and jingle musically with every move. One can compare Parzival to a boy who has only seen self-made go-carts, suddenly coming across a Lamborghini or Ferrari. For Parzival it's an otherworldly apparition, literally enhanced by all the bells and whistles, which convinces Parzival even more of the fourth knight's godliness. Parzival calls on God and falls to his knees to pray when Prince Karhnahkarnanz starts to question him. And like many of the humbler "accidental gods" mentioned by Anna Della Subin, Prince Karhnahkarnanz says, "I am no God" (p. 72), explaining that they are *knights*. Thereby, he unknowingly unlocks the door to Parzival's destiny, which will indeed ultimately lead him to a true understanding of the inner power of the creative light. For Parzival, the knights and

14 Waleis is often associated with Wales, from where we have the story of Peredur, which has similarities to the story of Parzival. However, Waleis in Eschenbach's version is not situated in Wales, but in middle Europe.

knighthood become the next best thing to God. He is utterly taken by the outer trappings and wants to be like them, which prods and awakes the questor in him. The yearning that he felt in his encounter with the birds and their celestial singing is finding a potential outlet, albeit outer.

Karhnahkarnanz's arrival is a *kairos* or an opportune moment. Up to now, childlike Parzival has led a life steeped in the eternal present. He is arriving at the threshold of time, hastened by his meeting with the knights. The Greek word "Kairos" means "opportunity" or "encounter," and each encounter becomes an opportunity—an occasion to grow. But so much depends on what we do with the opportunities we are given. They are auspicious moments, inviting a decision, an action. However, inactivity and failure to act appropriately is rooted in every opportunity. Kairos time often leads over into chronological time. Living life according to Kairos time allows us to recognize the opportunities presenting themselves in a conscious manner. Parzival receives a succession of momentous opportunities but lacks insight to interpret and live them fully. He is still dull of mind. His repeated failures will thrust and sentence him to serve chronological time, steeped in trials, errors, hardships, and mounting suffering. Kairos time and chronological time (Chronos) are interlinked, the one attending the other on the journey toward self-development. Time is an ordering principle, and earthly life is in need of ordering, of unfolding, of blossoming and bearing fruit. Parzival, from this threshold moment of meeting the knights, will set out to put his own life in order—the opportunities and encounters in concordance with what wells up from within.

It is the fourth knight who recognizes Parzival's high and noble birth—in stark contrast to the three other knights who took him for a foolish Waleis. Prince Karhnahkarnanz has heart, as his name suggests: "Kahrnahk" or "Karnak" in Sanskrit means "heart" or a "chamber of the heart." "Karna" also implies "wealth." "Karn" appears twice in his name and means "ear" in Sanskrit, suggesting "to listen." Thus, Karhnahkarnanz, in our poetical and playful approach, could be interpreted as a "listening heart of wealth." He sees that Parzival is worthy of becoming a knight, whereas the other three knights "were angry that their prince stood talking with this fool of a boy"

(p. 74). However, the prince not only lavishes continued praise on Parzival, but blesses him, "May God protect you" (p. 74). If only Columbus, Captain Cook, Pizzaro, Cortez, and many of the other "gods" could have had the same princely qualities of Karhnahkarnanz, centuries of suffering might have been avoided, at least lessened and partially allayed. In this pictorial depiction, the three knights only see Parzival as a simple supplicant and a fool who they want to exploit and use for their own purposes, in contrast to the single but heartfelt voice of the fourth knight. Karhnahkarnanz is the first true and noble knight Parzival encounters.

Throughout this episode, Parzival does not answer any of their questions but persists on asking questions himself. There are different qualities to the asking of questions, but they all relate to wanting to know the "source" of things, be they outer or inner, conscious or unconscious. For now, his questions remain childlike, similar to an infant asking a torrent of nonstop questions about the world.

The reason why these knights are in the wilderness of Soltane is because Imane de Beafontane, a young woman, was abducted by Meljahkanz and another man. Parzival is too enraptured to answer or heed any of their questions. What's noteworthy is that it is the first time that Parzival hears about a crime. He has no conception of it and cannot *hear* it, remaining dull to the plight of other people. He has no soul connection to that hapless young woman, no empathy, let alone compassion. The name Imane in French and means "faith" or "belief," and Beafontane means—as the name suggests—"beautiful fountain." It also has African connections. Orland Bishop in his book *The Seventh Shrine*, writes about "Imani" in a most beautiful and insightful manner, which relates thematically to the seminal abduction of Imane in *Parzival.* "Imani is faith, the inner preparation to decide for a particular future out of one's own experience of freedom," followed by, "The power of Imani is to ask the question—how do we prepare ourselves to be a giver in this world?"[15] Parzival, at this early stage is far from asking the necessary questions; he still needs to suffer through

15 Bishop, *The Seventh Shrine*, pp. 155-156.

much inner preparation before he will be able to decide freely about his own future. Yet, the Imane incident heralds Parzival's path to himself so that he may become a giver, rather than a taker. In a way, the Imane episode is seminal—the seed of Parzival's entire development, mirrored in Orland's words that seem to be written specifically for Parzival:

> The process of *Imani* initiates the human being into the self-consciousness that knows itself as the speaker, the inner creative utterance of what becomes thought, speech, and action. It is a movement from the seed of life, in the inner sanctuary, into the fruit of life. *Imani* is the . . . fulfilment of consciousness from its inner predisposition *to create a deed out of nothing* (author's italics).[16]

Since the "#MeToo" movement against sex crimes, abuse, and harassment, I have given this part of the scene more emphasis during class. The students should not for a second think it was only a medieval issue that happened a long time ago, and they don't, of course. There are countless examples: "Lolita" stories of older men abducting young girls, not to mention the rape pandemic across the world, especially in war zones (think Congo, Taliban, Iraq, Ukraine); or in antiquity, the Rape of the Sabine women, where the early Romans carried them off. The custom of carrying the bride across the threshold on the wedding day goes back to the abduction of the Sabine women, though other interpretations arose later. Then there are the thousands of Yazidi women who were abducted by Isis fighters and repeatedly raped, beaten, and sold as sex slaves.[17] It is a theme that we meet a number of times in the epic. The students are highly disturbed by the modern predominance of sex slavery and abuse. And, of course, there is Princess Leia from Star Wars who gets abducted by Darth Vader, the "dark father," representative of evil, as mentioned by one of the students during a discussion. Meljahkanz is also associated with darkness: "melas" or "melan"

16 Ibid., p. 157.

17 See Nadia Murad's book *Last Girl: My Story of Captivity and My Fight against the Islamic State*. (Tim Duggan Books, 2017).

means black, which is an allusion to his inner darkness toward the feelings of others—his light obscured by the inability to see the consequences of his actions. In Homer's *Odyssey*, the disloyal goatherd is called Melanthius and his sharp-tongued sister Melantho, both alluding to their soul darkness.

Imane's last name, Beafontane, means "beautiful fountain," and relates to the healing and life-giving substance water, essential for all of humanity and life, and the essence of baptisms. It suggests that the ailing spirit needs healing and watering. The water motif is prominent in all great literature, sacred texts, and holy books. If the students have had the "Bible as Literature" class (10th grade), I remind them of the water symbolisms found in the Bible. Furthermore, the sites of the ineffable Black Madonna all over Europe and North Africa are always situated by a well, spring, lake or body of water. Imane Beafontane, a minor character, nevertheless has a seminal place in *Parzival* in that she is mentioned right in the beginning, before Parzival even sets out on his developmental adventures.

During his upcoming journey, he will need "Imane," that is to say, "faith" in himself, in order to overcome the adversaries of the world, the pain and suffering of others. When the knights gallop off in hot pursuit, leaving the fool gobsmacked in the dust, he is oblivious of what has just been set into motion.

Advice, Grief, Departure

"We learn to walk by falling and come to truth only through error."
~ Johann Gottfried Herder

Herzeloyde is asleep while this life-changing encounter occurs. Like Odysseus, who fell asleep at crucial moments, one cannot help but think it was meant to be. With Odysseus, as with Herzeloyde, the misfortunes are ill or well-timed, depending on how it is viewed. It's a question of wakefulness, as much as a question of necessity. When are we asleep to a situation and when should we be awake? What are the consequences?

It is reminiscent of Herzeloyde's troubled sleep immediately before

Parzival's birth, during which she had suffered the vision of a dragon suckling her breasts, tearing her *heart* from her body before flying away. "Never since has such anguish befallen a woman in her sleep" (p. 62). On waking, the feeling of intense loss had coincided with the searing news of Gahmuret's death that had caused her to faint. The piercing premonition and apparition of loss, coupled with the death of Gahmuret is another apt metaphor for the loss of the spirit, coupled with the inconsolable grief that the human soul will subsequently have to endure during the consciousness soul age. Some things are inescapable, no matter how hard we try to prevent them. Our modern age, fraught with ongoing disasters, can only lead to one positive outcome—a call for us to *wake* up, become more *aware* and *do* something. Blaming the "evil doers," though satisfying, will not solve the problems. Wishful thinking for bygone days is also of no consequence. Only conscious recognition of what is and what needs to be done will offer a way forward. But the road is paved with adversaries and impediments, and the resolutions will vary from moment to moment, from issue to issue, from person to person.

When Parzival goes to tell her of his encounter with the knights, she falls to his feet in a swoon. Recovering, she wonders desperately how she can dissuade him from his purpose, though she knows his mind is made up and set on departure. Indeed, she's partly responsible for having answered his questions. Herzeloyde can barely keep him from leaving on the spot, persuading him to at least stay the night, so she can ready some clothes for him and give him some advice, which is shockingly brief: avoid crossing murky fords, greet all people, be willing to learn from a wise and grey-haired man who offers to teach you, and "win a lady's ring and greeting" (p. 75). Herzeloyde does not clarify what winning a lady's ring and affection truly entails. Like the other three pieces of advice, he takes it literally. It's her hope to have him return to her, should his heart get broken. The word advice has "vice" tucked into it (not etymologically but poetically speaking), just like in German, "Ratschlag" has "Schlag" (schlagen), to "beat" or "hit" hidden in the word. Advice can easily be taken the wrong way, ending up causing pain. Especially as parents or teachers, we have to be careful how we give advice. What we say has an effect.

While reading *Saracen Chivalry*, by Zia Inayat Khan, I couldn't help thinking about the contrast between Herzeloyde's abbreviated advice compared to Belacane's comprehensive book of counsels written for Feirefiz. Her treatise is comprised of meaningful and expansive guiding principles in how to lead one's life. Parzival's path is to forge his own way ahead, learning from the book of life, where he is destined to fail, to make mistakes, and act callously. However, his repeated stumblings will serve as the ultimate and necessary preparation for the modern age to come that is solely based on rational scientific thinking, where spirituality no longer has an overarching influence and power. In the prevailing intellectual age, there is little one can rely on. Even within one's own family nucleus, there might be a slew of diverging viewpoints. That was not the case in the past, especially not under a theocratic society. Now we have to find our own way, which is exactly what Parzival does—the trailblazer of the modern human being. It's the path toward freedom, which is never easy. Unfortunately, many places on earth are still forced to live according to restrictive rules and regulations—theocratic carryovers from the past—that impede the emerging need for individual and communal freedom.

Herzeloyde does, however, allude to Parzival's background for the first time, by mentioning Lähelin, who seized their realms, Norgals and Waleis, killing the princes in charge. Parzival vows to punish Lähelin.

The next morning, dressed in fool's clothing, chosen and made by Herzeloyde in the hope that he might return to her loving arms, he happily sets off, riding on an old nag, eyes firmly set on the future. He had heard and responded to the call and his first quest is underway: *to become an Arthurian Knight*. Dull of mind but filled with purpose, he rides off, not even bothering to turn around to bid his mother farewell, oblivious to her fate. He's leaving home in order to find his true home. At that moment his doting and loving mother sinks to the ground, lifeless. Death by grief. The full import of her name—Herzeloyde—has found its tragic conclusion. Parzival, the dragon, has torn her heart from her body, as the vision prophesied so many years ago. There are only so many losses one can bear, and this was one too many for this suffering soul. Her grief is as deep and true as her love for her son and Gahmuret before him. She has no more reason to live and she knows he will not return. She's done what she could for him. In a way, her death gives her the possibility of accompanying him in spirit. In death she can be closer and more helpful to him than in life.

Though the students might generally not have too much sympathy for Herzeloyde, having kept him from greater society, they feel her loss. Herzeloyde's grief was, however, not solely for herself but for the suffering she knew Parzival would have to go through. Grief is a potent force. Yesterday, as of this writing, a grieving husband collapsed and died of a heart attack two days after his wife was shot in the Ulvade school shooting that claimed the lives of nineteen children. "He died of grief," the reporter said on the news.

We all suffer grief in one form or another throughout our lives, some more than others. Though we need to wake up and learn from our own grief, what is more important is to recognize, read, and enter into the grief of others in the most compassionate way possible. In the Americas, we have a duty to acknowledge that the "Middle Passage created one of the larger outpourings of grief within the frameworks of human history. . . . This event of the Middle Passage was seen in the spiritual world as a call to the ancestors to come directly into the experience of loss."[18] What Orland Bishop writes here is true within the larger scheme of things as much as in the personal. Grief runs throughout *Parzival* as an ongoing theme of *Paradise Lost* and *Paradise Regained*, though distinctly different from John Milton. It is the human story. As humans we have to endure Grief, and realize, as Orland writes, that it is part of our development, our *initiation* to find our emerging selves—if we are brave enough to *see* and *be* the light, as Amanda Gorman reminded the world in her poem "The Hill." John the Evangelist had the same message about 2,000 years earlier when he pronounced, "While you have the light, believe in the light, that you may become light" (12:36).[19]

Orland continues in the same section, which can apply to Herzeloyde and all of us: "Grief is an opening to the other world. . . . Grief is a submersion in

18 Bishop, p. 21.

19 Based on the New King James version, slightly modified.

the latent powers of the soul, in order to awake to higher levels of striving to substantiate our true purpose. . . . Grief awakens us to our purpose and our path." And lastly, "Grief evokes from the earth a creative force that can be called a shrine." Though Herzeloyde dies, it inaugurates Parzival's path of initiation. Her death through grief facilitates the entire arc of his development and transformation from a fool to the Grail King, the prototype of the modern human being's initiation into the higher self.

Parzival unwittingly has made himself culpable. By leaving, he severs the physical bond to home and to his mother. All dependence on familial blood ties must initially be broken along the long road to the Self, to the Grail—of which, as yet, he knows nothing. Independence demands separation after which a new and freer relationship can be sought. His impatient departure causes her death. He has no regard for his mother's feelings—does not pick up on them—and is totally oblivious to what she might have gone through. His mind is solely on his personal quest. Previously, he'd shown no empathy for the abducted Imane, nor for his mother when she swooned after he told her about the knights. He'd remained dully indifferent.

Often, during the 11th grade year, while talking to parents—mostly mothers in this case—they lament the fact that they are losing touch with their children, and that they—mostly sons—have stopped talking to them about their private lives. I encourage them not to take it too personally as it belongs to the journey of self-discovery, and shutting out the parent is part of it. These mothers are experiencing a Herzeloyde moment.

In the ancient mystery centers, the disciples were taught about the stage of *homelessness* through which they would have to pass in order to attain higher states of consciousness and inner freedom. In a sense, Parzival was already born into homelessness, in that he was utterly removed from chivalric society and the attendant social norms. Mother nature was his home, coupled with the unwavering love of his mother. No teacher or initiate had to send him out to learn the lessons of homelessness. It came from deep within himself, as it does for any modern seeker of the spirit in

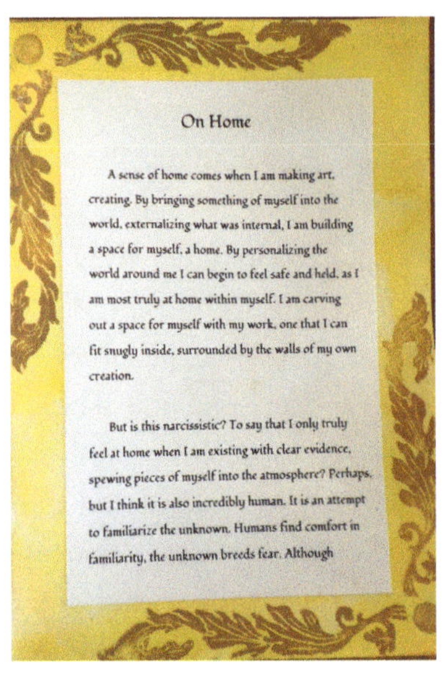

On Home

A sense of home comes when I am making art, creating. By bringing something of myself into the world, externalizing what was internal, I am building a space for myself, a home. By personalizing the world around me I can begin to feel safe and held, as I am most truly at home within myself. I am carving out a space for myself with my work, one that I can fit snugly inside, surrounded by the walls of my own creation.

But is this narcissistic? To say that I only truly feel at home when I am existing with clear evidence, spewing pieces of myself into the atmosphere? Perhaps, but I think it is also incredibly human. It is an attempt to familiarize the unknown. Humans find comfort in familiarity, the unknown breeds fear. Although

the present age of the consciousness soul. He was—albeit subconsciously—his own teacher, sending himself off into the different and accumulating stages of homelessness, weening himself not only from Soltane but a long series of cultural epochs that were, up to now, still imbued with the vibrant and guiding life of the spirit. However, when he rode forth on his nag, dressed as a fool, he trotted away from his sunny, simple, and paradisal Soltane home into the tough terrain of heartbreakingly harsh homelessness. As Joseph Campbell would say, "The Hero's journey has begun."

In the eyes of the world, Parzival is a fool. Many of us feel like fools and make sure that we do not get perceived as such, working hard to appear professional, even if we secretly admit that we are suffering from "imposter syndrome." Our age thrives on specialization, which is one way to overcome the feeling of inadequacy. Yet, no matter how specialized we are, in the light of the spirit, we remain fools. It cannot be otherwise. Humanity has descended into matter to such an extent that the living spiritual world is securely cut off from most people. For some the abyss is overcome through faith, yet the chasm remains. The yearning for something more is growing stronger, and if not that, then the recognition of the spirit's necessity, given the circumstances of the earth's ever-mounting problems.

In most cultures over the centuries, the *fool* has had an important role to play, and still does in various forms. The greater truths let themselves be conveyed through tragedy and comedy. Others help us to see the truth, often through laughter. It takes awareness and wit to laugh at ourselves. It's essential on the path of self-development. The Celts had the Great Fool in the form of *Amadan Mor,* or just *amadán,* which is used both with endearment or as an insult. In the East, the Great Fool comes in the form of *Li Tiehkuai*, and for the Native Americans *heyoka*. And then we have the court jester (who we also briefly meet in Book Five), used so effectively by Shakespeare. Comedians like Charlie Chaplin or Buster Keaton played the "fool" so endearingly while spreading little gems of wisdom. We can relate to them because we see ourselves in them.[20]

Jeschute

"We shall awaken from our dullness and rise vigorously toward justice. If we fall in love with creation deeper and deeper, we will respond to its endangerment with passion." ~ Hildegard von Bingen

Ready or not, here I come! That phrase from playing hide and seek comes to mind in relation to Parzival's rapid departure. It refers as much to the people Parzival will meet as to himself. Parzival is utterly ill-equipped for refined and civilized society. Parzival happily bumbles along, seeking to fulfill his quest, blissfully unaware how unprepared he is for life out in the world after years of insouciant solitude in Soltane.

Parzival rides off, unencumbered and excited like a boy off to the circus. He comes across a murky ford, which he could easily have crossed, but remembering his mother's words, refrains. He has not yet learned to be discerning in what he observes. The stream only appears dark because of the abundant growth of flowers and grass. Hence, he rides along the stream and even spends the night in the woods—his first alone—before crossing

20 *Healing the Fisher King*, pp. 42-45.

at a place where the ford is clear. Crossing the river is a firm demarcation between his familiar life in Soltane and the unknown ahead. Like Julius Caesar crossing the Rubicon, there is no turning back. It's the threshold to a new life, where he will be forced to learn from his own experiences and ultimately take responsibility.

Life does not wait long to test Parzival. In a meadow on the embankment on the other side of the stream, Parzival encounters a maiden lying in a pavilion, asleep. In Chrétien's version she is not named and it is assumed that Wolfram called her Jeschute, based on the French word "gisoit," which means "lay," referring to her "lying" exposed in the tent, thus vulnerable to an unwelcome intrusion or sexual assault. Eschenbach describes her in a most sensuous manner. "Thus lay the loveliest challenge to adventure imaginable" (p. 76)! Though she is described in a sexually alluring manner, Parzival is drawn to her *not* by any erotic arousal but solely by the ring on her finger, which reminds him of his mother's words: "Waste no time, but kiss and embrace her." Again, he takes his mother's advice literally and wrests the ring from her in a rough and dishonorable manner, with no concern of her feelings or respect for her space. He ignores her shocked bewilderment, no matter how much she wails, forcing a kiss off her and crushing her breast to his. And for good measure, he also tears a brooch from her shift. By all accounts it is an inexcusable act of overt sexual harassment and abuse.

She is still in fear that he might rape her, and when he complains of hunger, she asks him *not* to "eat" her, but he is merely craving food and not her flesh, proceeding to gobble down the available bread and partridge, helped along by "heavy draughts" of wine. Incidentally, symbolically the partridge is associated with new love. Parzival is clearly making a literal mess of his first endeavor to win a lady. His craving for food satisfies his bodily drive, and luckily for her, his sexual urges have not yet stirred in him, but he has clearly committed a serious transgression without the slightest concern for her or its ramifications.

In a modern context, the disconcerting fact is that many adolescents—and predominantly boys—invade the space of girls, trying to "win" their bodies, and thrusting sexual expectations on them, gained from questionable sources, such as social media, movies, and porn sites. A great deal of damage is done in this sphere, confirmed by the students in class during the discussions. It is crucial that parents, teachers, and guardians have open and thoughtful discussions with the respective adolescents on the topic of relationships and sexuality—beyond what is offered in the sex education programs. If the sacred importance of human interaction is not addressed, especially in the realm of healthy intimacy, then it continues into adulthood resulting in dire consequences that can lead to all sorts of complications.

Parzival rides off, delighted by his illicit plunders but dully indifferent to the plight of Jeschute who is left to deal with the consequences of Parzival's actions. As soon as her husband Orilus returns, he accuses her of cheating on him, punishing her by forcing Jeschute to continue wearing the scant shift in which Parzival had found her, and insisting she ride behind him on her palfrey, which he will keep underfed. Furthermore, he destroys her costly saddle, while forcing her to use rough ropes for a bridle—all to spite her, making her ride as uncomfortably as possible. This "punishment ride" will last for an entire year, all because of Parzival's dumb and thoughtless deed. Forcing the horse to go hungry is a symbolic imagination for Jeschute's spiritually starved state of soul, caused by a fool and a jealous husband. Orilus' despicable actions are meant to degrade her dignity, and they are an affront to her intelligence. She is shamed and made to look foolish. Orilus, whose name is associated with "pride" by many authors, is the epitome of jealousy, which blinds his trust and belief in the other, making him unable to judge a situation clearly and in a levelheaded manner. When I ask the students what "Je" means (pronounced in French), they will answer, "I" (and "Yo" in Spanish). When I ask for the possible meaning of "schute," those who know French will say, "fall" (*chute*). "Je chute" meaning "I fall," describes her changed circumstance perfectly—sadly through no fault of her own.

They ride off, with Orilus eager to avenge himself on Parzival: "I would try my fortune against him though he breathed fire like a dragon" (p. 80), an allusion to Herzeloyde's terrible vision, and Parzival's dormant, untamed strength, waiting to be unleashed. Ironically, Orilus' emblem is the dragon and these two dragons will meet up at a future time when fortune will offer the opportunity to right the wrong. Orilus and his siblings play a significant role in Parzival's self-development, and as the epic evolves, we begin to see the interconnectedness of the main characters. It is in moments like these that I remind the students to become aware of their own encounters and how they might point toward the larger "karmic" scope of their lives.

The students tend to get angrier at Orilus' treatment of Jeschute than at Parzival. Many see it as medieval barbarity dominated by men. In response I ask: "Are we free of it today? Is it so different? To what degree have we progressed?" Over the last couple of years, global statistics of domestic violence (predominantly against women), have risen during the pandemic at an alarming rate, and it was already upsettingly bad beforehand. Hundreds of articles and news reports warning and reporting on the shocking surge are disturbing reminders of the problem. Depending on the class, this topic leads to eye-opening discussions.

Sigune

"Why not live as light in the world?" ~ Leif Garbisch

Parzival, oblivious of the dangers of his pursuer, hurries along, fixated on reaching King Arthur and becoming a knight. His foolishness is underscored by greeting everyone he meets, because "that's what my mother told me." This, too, is reminiscent of the beginning of the film *Forrest Gump*, where Forrest is talking to the woman on the bench, always quoting his mother. A student once pointed out the similarities to Parzival in the film *The Waterboy*, starring Adam Sandler, in which Bobby, the protagonist, is a somewhat differently abled person living with his overprotective mother. Parzival is not yet able to greet anybody purely out of his own volition, but because his mother said so. For him, whatever his mother advised is tantamount to doing the right thing. His inner life is dormant and dull, and it's as if he has on soul blinders, but his happy-go-lucky nature stands him in good stead. He is not weighed down by anything and he has a natural abundance of self-confidence in an endearing, childlike way (which is not the case in Chrétien's version). He is locked into his own ignorance but has no bad intentions, none whatsoever. His quest rises up from ancestral depths, guided along by an arcane sense of will that leads him into situations of self-confrontations, which our dealings with other people essentially are. As fast as he is hastening to satisfy his quest, so the quest is hurrying toward him—for his own good, though it will first result in severe suffering. It is emblematic of youth to be blessed with the ignorance of the future, otherwise the idealistic quester might not muster the forces to continue with life.

Nonetheless, it's only been a night and a day and already the Pure Fool has inadvertently caused his mother's death and an abominably distressful situation for the faultless Jeschute. Inner awakening is called for. It is answered by a timely nascent destiny directive that comes in the form of another encounter—brief but significant.

Parzival rides *down* the slope on his nag, when he hears a woman's voice lamenting. In a way, the plaintive sounds serve as an echo for the undue suffering he has just caused Jeschute. It's also an apt metaphor for his first tentative *descent* into the earthly realm and his inner life. Waking up to oneself always feels like a downward climb, and for many 11th graders it can feel like plummeting into the depths of confusion.

Next to a cliff he sees the maiden Sigune holding a newly slain knight, Schionatulander, lying in her lap. Parzival is confronted with a picture of inconsolable grief, caused by death—the antithesis of the Jeschute encounter, which brimmed over with intoxicating sensuality and life forces. Up to this moment, he's been spared the direct confrontation of such misery (had he turned around on leaving his mother he would have witnessed a grief just as intense, followed by death). This image of profound sorrow makes an incision into his heart, just wide enough to let Sigune's words of grief enter, like the first shimmer of soul consciousness. It is a most poignant and poetic imagination of the conception of the consciousness soul age, with Parzival as the first representative of this evolutionary era, representing the path of gaining worldly and mystical insights out of one's own inner forces. She is newly widowed—the most recent in a long line of widows, going back generations, both in his own family and in humanity, such as Isis pining for her Osiris after he was murdered by Seth.

During the *Parzival* block, I hang a framed poster of Michelangelo's Pietà on the wall, referring to it whenever we come to the meeting with Sigune. They, of course, know it from their History through Art block

in 9th grade. It is the image that depicts the virginal Mary holding the crucified Christ in her lap, imbued with the love of both a mother and a lover. The singular sculpture shows her grief in the ruffled folds of the garments that surround her, in contrast to the purity of her most celestial face. This sublime sculptural masterpiece, which Michelangelo sculpted when he was a mere twenty four years old, captures the mood of the grieving Sigune over the slain Schionatulander perfectly, a quintessential image of the grieving widowed human soul—that widowed soul living in all of us (Old English "widewe," from the Indo-European word, "be empty").

For many years we took the seniors to Italy on an arts trip, which simultaneously served as a retrospective to much of what they had covered during their years in Waldorf. It was my good fortune to be part of that trip over an eight-year period (inaugurated by my wife, Martina), and year after year, we would stand in front of the Pietà in St. Peter's Cathedral, some choosing to capture the masterpiece in their sketchbooks. I was always glad when someone recalled Sigune holding her newly deceased lover in her arms.

But for Parzival, it will take time for the image of sorrow to settle in. Initially, he still follows his mother's advice, greets Sigune and pummels her with questions. The full impact of the weeping lady with the dead knight on her lap eludes him—it barely registers. It's beyond his comprehension, as exemplified with the unabashed self-evident statement: "It looks to me as if he's dead, ma'am" (p. 80). He is well meaning, of course, and it's just part of his chatter. He does, however, immediately offer to avenge the death of the slain knight, an embryonic expression of pity wrapped within an ancestral impulse.

Though consumed by grief, Sigune hears and recognizes his noble birth and good stock at once, just as Prince Karhnahkarnanz had. She asks him his name, but he has no clue; just like "the majority of [humankind] he is ignorant of his eternal reality."[21] He answers with what his mother and the servants called him—*bon fiz, cher fiz, and bea fiz* (good boy, dear boy, beautiful boy).[22] With those words, Sigune immediately realizes who he is and gifts him with his own true name: "Upon my word, you are Parzival!" (p. 81) It is the first time that his name is mentioned. It seals the moment of his emerging self-awakening, giving him an experience of his unique eternal I through his name. She also tells him that it means "pierce through the middle,"[23] ("*deiswâr, du heizest Parzival, der nam ist rehte enmitten durch*"[24]) which lends meaning to his deeper self, his destiny dictum, his unfolding individuality, by conferring a quality, a character trait. Stein writes: "Thus Parzival learns his true name. It is the name of the spiritual force of *light* that penetrates the *darkness*."[25] It can also be seen as a pathway of knowledge that leads him from dullness ("*tumpheit*"), through doubt ("*zwifel*") to blessedness ("*Saelde*")—through the darkness of death to the brightness of life. Parzival receives his true name just after Schionatulander's death, having receded from life to follow the dog Gardevies with the starry script into the realm of the stars, the *source*. Gardevies means "guardian of the way/path." Sigune was reading the starry script on its bejeweled inscrutable collar and leash when it ran away. She had promised Schionatulander her love if he brought the dog back. Alas, he was killed before he could return

---

21 Stein, p. 123.

22 In Chrétien's version it is: "Dear son, dear brother, dear master."

23 Or "pierce through the *valley, heart, abyss*," depending on the translation. However, "middle" is most correct according to the Middle High German.

24 Lachmann, III, 140, 16/17, p. 75.

25 Stein, p. 124.

with the dog. From now on Sigune becomes the guardian of Parzival's path—his path towards star knowledge, towards the attainment of the Grail. At this stage, however, Parzival is at the outset of his earthly life, while Schionatulander has reached his end. The two are forever bound to one another. Parzival has received the source-seed of strength to make his way through life, no matter how tough, freckled with failure, missteps, doubt, impediments, and accrued guilt. Yet, the connection with the source must remain intact throughout, even when threadbare and threatened. I ask the students if they have a sense of life's source, what that could mean or look like, and how one could maintain it in our day-to-day lives. It's a theme that goes throughout Parzival, so we can revisit it often.

What is significant is that Sigune not only recognizes him, but sees him for who he truly is, his hidden qualities. While living in Empangeni, a little town in KwaZulu-Natal, I always loved the Zulu greeting, "Sawubona," which means "we see you." It is often answered with "Yebo, sawubona," which translates as "yes, we see you too." Sigune truly does "see" Parzival. What if all our salutations could contain that seminal thought?

Sigune then proceeds to fill out the picture of his life: "I will tell you plainly who you are" (p. 81), telling him that they are cousins and that his father was an Angevin and his mother a Waleis born in Kanvoleis (sister of Shoysiane, mother of Sigune), and that Parzival is also King of Norgals. She enlightens him to the backstory to his life, thus bringing his circumstances into context. She tells him of the two brothers who have wronged Parzival: Lähelin, who robbed him of his two kingdoms, already mentioned by his mother, and his brother Orilus, who just that morning killed her lover Shionatulander, while defending Parzival's land.[26] It was Orilus who years earlier had killed Galoes, Parzival's paternal uncle. Clearly, it is high time that Parzival becomes privy to his past in order to set things right. But it is a lot to digest all at once, let alone to fathom the scope of what he has been told. The interconnectedness between the people he meets is

26 The backstory of Schionatulander and Sigune is found in Wolfram's fragment *Titurel*, and more extensively in *The Younger Titurel* by Albrecht von Scharfenberg.

beginning to become clear. He does, however, begin to recognize her grief and the disgraceful manner of Schionatulander's demise, wanting to "settle the account" immediately. Feeling empathetic and in line with his noble heritage, he is moved to avenge the shameful deed. Sigune, however, sends him in the wrong direction, fearing that he would not fare well in a fight against Orilus, an experienced and ruthless knight. It would put an end to Parzival's quest and leave his destiny unfulfilled. Nevertheless, she points him in the "true" direction, "right" for his destiny and his future.

The name Sigune is said to be an invention of Eschenbach, but because he is playfully particular about the names of his characters, we try to figure out in class how and why Eschenbach might have chosen "Sigune." Students love to come up with ideas themselves, and I have learned to listen to them. Sometimes their off-the-cuff thoughts might be worth as much as those of scholars. I have become much more daring in interpretations through the fresh imaginations of the students.

A safe place to start is with the sound of the word, foremostly looking at the German and the French. It does not take much to come up with "Sieg," which means "victory," in German, and "une," which could refer to "one," (Uno or Eine), but also to "ohne," the German word for "without," which expresses loss. So, it could mean "One Victory" or "Without Victory" or "Victory despite of Loss." And victory suggests a battle. Of course, this kind of speculation is poetic rather than scholarly. Some years later, our in-class discussions were verified when I read the fragments of Wolfram's *Titurel*, where he calls her "Sigune the victorious."[27] Charles E. Passage, who translated *Titurel* into English, also suggests that Sigune could be an imperfect anagram of "Cousin."[28] Furthermore, "Gun" or "Gund" also refers to battle, specifically: "in battle to preserve the mystery,"[29] which fits the enigmatic character of Sigune. "Le signe" also refers to a "sign," "indication" or "gesture." Sigune can "read" the "signs" of Parzival and "indicate" or "gesture" which way he should go next. The French word

27 Wolfram von Eschenbach, *Titurel* (Frederick Ungar Publishing Co. New York), p. 23.

28 *Titurel*, p. 198.

29 Theo Herrle , ed., *Reclams Namenbuch*, (Stuttgart Philipp Reclam Jun, 1981).

"signer" implies that she "endorses" him. Sigune, too, can be associated with a bird, similarly to Belacane, namely the "swan," which in French is "cygne." Basilius Valentinus places the swan on the third degree of inner development—"where Inspiration as the Divine Word, the harmony of the spheres, sounds forth."[30] And each time they meet Sigune the "cygne" is an inspiration to Parzival, first perceived in a dull and instinctive fashion, but increasingly more conscious, until, after their fourth meeting, she will inspire from beyond. Lastly, her name is also closely related in sound to the German word "Segen," which means "blessing," and she is truly a blessing in Parzival's life.[31] Though Wolfram supposedly made up the name, it is possible that he borrowed it from Norse mythology, as his all-encompassing knowledge was exceptional. The oldest known goddess from *The Edda*, best recognized for her loyalty and compassion, even under the most trying situations, was Sigyn, whose name means "Friend to Victory." She took pity on her husband Loki, who was undergoing severe punishment by the Aesir for killing their beloved Baldur. Enduring great discomfort, she held a cup to catch the drops of fiery venom that dropped from the serpent's fangs positioned directly above Loki's head. Sigyn, or Siguna, as she is sometimes translated as, is the epitome of a loyal wife, as is the Siguna of *Parzival*. Nowadays, Sigyn is best known in popular culture as a Marvel character and has a prominent part in the world of the Avengers.

Both Sigune and Schionatulander keep him connected to the spiritual world, both in their own way. To determine the meaning of Schionatulander's name, however, is more difficult. Karl Bartsch suggests that Wolfram derived the name from *Li Joenet de la Lande*, meaning "The Youth from the Moor," or *li joenet u l' alant*, "the young man with the (hunting) dog."[32]

Although there is a heart-wrenching sense of loss around Sigune, it only serves to highlight the tremendous achievement that we see in her, confirmed by the subsequent times she appears in Parzival's life. Her loss helps Parzival achieve his quest—for *him* to become "victorious" in

30 Stein, p. 320.

31 Mosmann, p. 493.

32 *Titurel*, p. 194.

"battle." Up to now, Parzival's quest is more like an ineffable urge that rumbles through the dark terrain of his subconscious. It's an impulse-quest, which he is pursuing in a swift but almost lackadaisical manner. However, the encounter with Sigune gives the rather random quest direction and heralds the dawn of self-consciousness.

He leaves the suffering Sigune, recklessly impatient to fight. Although he's only dimly aware of what he's gained, he's a changed person through Sigune's seedling gift of self-knowledge: he now knows his true name, that he is a king, that others suffered and lost their lives fighting to defend his lands, that his family extends beyond the confines of Soltane, and that he has a duty to reclaim what is his due. Parzival is no longer utterly ignorant of his past and the future has a lot in store for him, for the sake of the world. He witnessed the finality of a human death and the fidelity that transcends those bounds, encapsulated in the powerful pietà image that will accompany him as an enduring source of strength throughout his travails. However, he cannot yet decipher his own guilt, even though Sigune's image of holding her dead lover mirrors his culpability. Sigune knows full well that sending Parzival in the "wrong" direction will ultimately lead him in the "right" direction. Sigune, the one who has to live without her lover, has given Parzival the first directive to be victorious over his upcoming tribulations, and renewed hope.

Fisherman

"Here is home, where I am in the present moment." ~ Student

He rides off along the broad road toward the people of Britain, again greeting everybody he sees like his mother had advised, which keeps his eyes directed outward on others and on the world around him. It keeps him from becoming too self-absorbed in his one-track desire to become a knight. The morning verse for Waldorf students from grade five upwards begins with, "I look into the world," which serves as a prerequisite for looking into the soul, addressed in the second part of the verse. In his childhood years in Soltane, the verse for the first four grades fit perfectly, beginning with, "The sun with loving light, makes bright for me each day."[33] So far, he's been bathed by the beauty of a sunlit world, able to look at the world and get to know the stones, plants, and animals, which have given him an intimate connection to nature, though few and extremely limited opportunities to interact with people. And at night the firmament twinkles its gentle silvery specks of light on him. Since crossing the shallow ford, his lot is to encounter an ever-growing diversity of people. He has no prejudice and greets them all the same—an ensouled humanity, each one giving the spirit a home.

It is evening, he is weary, famished, and needs a place to sleep. At a large house he asks for food and accommodation. The churlish fisherman sees only a poor fool and does not recognize his noble ancestry, dismisses him with the words, "I'd not give you half a loaf in thirty years" (p. 82). The number thirty appears often throughout the epic, denoting, in part, a large amount. However, when Parzival offers him Jeschute's costly brooch in exchange, his whole demeaner changes and he becomes a sleazy sycophant, inviting him to enter, promising to treat him with respect. He is not only exploiting Parzival's "tumpheit," but his trusting unworldly innocence or trusting naiveté, which, on a larger scale, has happened to entire peoples, as we know all too well.

The Fisherman, representing the unsavory ways of the world, is a minor character, yet cannot be dismissed. He serves as a contrast to that other Fisherman, the one Parzival will meet later on, referred to as the Angler, the wounded Grail King. The former shows him the way to Arthur's Court in Nantes, and the latter guides him toward the Grail Castle. The meeting further underscores Parzival's foolishness for blindly trusting this deceptive churl. The Fisherman only flatters him once he has the gold. In *Parzival*, things often come in twos, the first denoting what needs to be overcome and left behind, while the second points to what needs to be attained.

In all likelihood we've all been hoodwinked or taken advantage of in one

33 From the Morning Verses given to the teachers in 1919 by Rudolf Steiner.

way or another, especially in our youth—paid too much for something worthless or coerced into signing a document under duress. It easily happens while traveling in countries with different customs. Moreover, our über-capitalistic for-profit system supports and fosters this kind of exploitative conduct. The boorish Fisherman is a ubiquitous character in our daily lives. Parzival is a right sucker in comparison to wily Odysseus, whose sharp and crafty mind averted him from succumbing to multiple traps along the way. Our guileless dullard will have to learn the ways of the world the hard way, just like most of us. Yet, even villains can help us along the path to ourselves in a roundabout way.

The next day he rides on alone toward Arthur and his Round Table. Eschenbach takes the opportunity to once again emphasize his foolish appearance, his decrepit stumbling pony and the homespun attire of both the nag and the simple lad.

At this point, I might ask the students to put themselves into Parzival's position, to imagine what it might have been like coming from a safe and secluded place, only to be thrust into new surroundings where everybody is different and where you might get mocked, jeered, or discriminated against. There are so many reasons why one might feel inferior or out of place, which the students quickly name. However, the unassuming Parzival is saved, so far, by his ignorance and happy-go-lucky demeanor. He simply has no understanding of these social differences. Nor does he care. In his case, ignorance is bliss. Pain, loss, and shame will catch up to him soon enough.

The Red Knight

"Careful what you wish for." ~ Old Adage

Near to Arthur's Palace, Parzival meets Ither of Gaheviez, a knight of high repute, widely known as "The Red Knight." Both the knight and his charger are red all over, from the armor to his hair to the sword, shield, spear, et al; so red that it hurts the eye. And in his hand, he holds a red goblet. Eschenbach puts great emphasis on the color, which leaves an

indelible impression. In fact, the color red is mentioned fourteen times, which once again alludes to the importance of fourteen, which symbolizes the beginning of things, spiritual growth, and also love. Of course, there are always negative attributes attached to anything, and in this case, it refers to irresponsibility. It's a good place to pause and have a discussion on the color *red*, its qualities and symbolic significance. The students are quick to associate red with passion, anger, arrogance, aggression, love, courage, royalty, blood, heat, fire, activity, danger, and the choleric temperament (referring to our study of the four temperaments during the Tragedy and Comedy block in 9th grade). Red is a commanding color. In our further discussions, we can add qualities that indicate inner warmth, liveliness, dominance, the living luster of life, and early growth (first red and then green in plants), which is particularly pertinent to Parzival as he is still at the outset and beginning stages of his gradual growth. Furthermore, red is generally recognized as the most colorful of colors (in its use and effectiveness); it shines out strongly and invigorates. It is also the color that is mentioned most often in *Parzival*, beyond black and white, as red is recognized as the color of transformation. Interestingly enough, red is the closest to darkness, situated, as it is, next to the black along the prism's spectrum, which means that red starts to appear when darkness pushes into light. As the darkness lessens in its shifts into the light, the red transitions into orange, yellow, and eventually into pure light, which suggests Parzival's slow transformation, alluded to in the first paragraph of the epic.

A phenomenological approach to color helps to keep it objective. Red, like any other color, is permeated with strong contrasts in regard to its qualities, morally and otherwise. Red is predominantly recognized as the color of love, for it is, like no other, the color of transformation. Red is the color of Mars, and Ither embodies the qualities of that fiery planet. He is rash and rebellious, as is Parzival, who will be named the Red Knight. Those reckless qualities, however, will have to be transformed, especially his foolish and impetuous speech—from wild and thoughtless remarks to words of wisdom.

The Red Knight, after remarking on Parzival's beauty—blessing the mother who bore him—gives him a *task*, his *first:* to deliver a message of apology to Queen Guinevere[34] for spilling red wine on her lap in angry haste when Arthur judged against him regarding a land claim. The message includes a challenge for any of Arthur's knights to retrieve the cup that he took, so that they might uphold their honor. The spilling of wine can be likened to the spilling of blood—of death (in contrast to the life-giving Grail vessel). Guinevere (Gwenhwyer/Gwenhwyfar from Welsh and Celtic roots) means "white fairy, white shadow, or white phantom," which emphasizes the image of white and red. These two colors are often found in fairytales and they tend to foreshadow misfortune. The cup is also associated with kingship. In this case, the Red Knight snatched it away as an affront to Arthur and his rulership. Now, the holder of the cup is asking the future Grail King to deliver a message. Thickly wrapped in this encounter is the conception of Parzival's true quest. It will be Ither's *last* task he gives. In a manner of speaking, the Red Knight is tasking himself out of commission, or into another iteration of himself—the phoenix arising from its ashes.

At this stage, none of Arthur's knights who are present at the court have the will, gumption, or inner motivation to challenge the Red Knight, which also implies that they are not ready. Little does Ither, the Red Knight, realize that he has summoned his own death. Little does Parzival realize that he has accepted the task that will birth his new life.

---

34 I have chosen the more common spelling of Guinevere over Hatto's Ginover.

King Arthur's Court

"Good judgment comes from experience, and often experience comes from bad judgment." ~ Rita Mae Brown

Parzival, who only wants the splendid armor, happily obliges and enters Nantes, where his foolish appearance immediately creates an amusing spectacle, with children following him through town until he enters Arthur's court, where he sees so many magnificent knights that he is unable to distinguish the true Arthur. "I see a lot of Arthurs here—which is to make me a knight?" (p. 84). It shows his childlike innocence, and hints at Arthur's diminishing power. The theme of recognition plays an ongoing role. Apart from the first three knights and the greedy Fisherman, his noble lineage is once again recognized. Parzival, however, only sees the outer trappings of the knights, not the qualities that make up the person. Learning to distinguish and correctly gauge and bring into harmony the outer and the inner—that too needs to be consciously attained.

Like many young people, Parzival wants immediate gratification for his uppermost desire: "Now don't put me off any longer but do what it takes to make a knight of me" (p. 85). Only a person not schooled in the codes of chivalry would speak in such a brash and brazen manner to a king. His bold behavior makes an impression and he rattles at the norms. Parzival certainly succeeds in that, like the simpleton in fairytales. It also underlines the impatience of youth. To Parzival, it feels like he's gone "unknighted" for a year, though it's only been three nights since he saw his first knights. His foolish complaint reminds me of Robert Frost's oft repeated quote: "Grievances are a form of impatience. Griefs are a form of patience." In youth, however, impatience has its place; it's the momentum behind the desire for change. But if left unchecked, it can lead to the death of things and create a great deal of suffering, exemplified in Faust's mighty *curse speech* (as I call it), which he ends with the shattering words: "A curse on hope! Faith too be cursed! / And cursed above all else be patience!"[35] One only has to

35 Goethe, *Faust*, p 179.

look at the consequences of aggressive colonialism, where impatient greed spread misery for millions; or, for that matter, the for-profit healthcare system here in America that has little true concern for the people. And so it goes. Luckily, one might say, Parzival will have his share of grief soon enough, which will, over time, temper his impatience.

Lady Cunneware

"True humor springs more from the heart than from the head; it is not contempt; it's essence is love." ~ Thomas Carlyle

The reluctant King Arthur is easily persuaded by Sir Keie to let greenhorn Parzival fight against Gaheviez, though it might kill him. As Parzival impatiently leaves Arthur's hall, he observes a scene on the low balcony above him that grieves him deeply. Lady Cunneware, sitting together with Queen Guinevere and other knights and ladies, bursts out laughing as Parzival rides by. Up until this moment, she has never laughed before, and unbeknownst to the young fool, it has been prophesied that she would not laugh until the arrival of someone who would win supreme honor to Arthur's court. Sir Keie, angry that she would dare to laugh at this idiot who is as unknightly as it gets, beats her severely with a staff, cutting through clothes and skin, drawing blood. This causes the mute Antanor—considered a fool—to speak. Likewise, he had renounced any form of speech for the same reason as Lady Cunneware. His words now emphasize the portentous moment very publicly: "God knows, Sir Seneschal [Keie], it was because of the boy that Cunneware of Lalant was beaten. He will fritter your jollity away for that one day, however lonely and friendless he may be" (p. 87). The prophetic words also earn Antanor a bitter beating. Parzival, witnessing their barbaric thrashing on his behalf, is deeply angered. His hand clutches his javelin, but because of the throng of people, he refrains from hurling it toward Sir Keie. It is the *first* time that he consciously perceives the suffering of others because of him. Parzival is impulsively outraged at the brutality and gross injustice of the beating, which arouses a fiery empathy for the hapless victims. The impact of this moment is made clear in Parzival's words to Iwanet just before he leaves King Arthur's Court: "Her pitiful words have moved me deeply, not merely brushing against my heart—no! the lady's undeserved sufferings are lodged at its core" (p. 90)!

It is yet one more example of the egregious treatment of women. We saw it with the abduction of Imane, with Jeschute, and now with Cunneware. It should enrage us like it enraged Parzival, to ensure that we speak up or act decisively should we witness such ill treatment.

Why laughter? What is so special about Cunneware's laughter for which she is so unjustly repaid? It serves as an impetus to Parzival's development, spurring him on toward inner maturity. Laughter is like light in the darkness, a release from tension, a resolution, or a restoring of balance. Laughter holds a special place in fairytales like "The Golden Goose" or "The Princess Who Never Smiled." In each case the respective Princesses laugh or smile when they behold the simpleton or lowly peasant boy, because they recognize something special in them. Laughter reinstates hope and happiness, dispelling the pain of a weighed down soul.

Lady Cunneware's laughter is like a new dawn—of fresh things to come. It is a promise of hope, rejuvenation, of change, healing, and the fulfilment of a need. Her laughter marks a turning point and is a recognition of the genius hidden within Parzival. He cannot yet recognize his own potential and it has to come from the outside. The laughter is underscored by the beating Cunneware and Antanor receive, which imprints itself on Parzival's psyche. Honest laughter coming spontaneously from the heart, fills the air with wonder and is infused with the glint of the miraculous. Like crying, its polar opposite, it's a fundamental human emotion that can strengthen the individuality and refine the inner life. Sorrow tends to isolate, but laughter is communal; it vivifies, restores, and builds relationships. Memorable examples of laughter include Homeric laughter, Zarathustra laughing at birth, or of the biblical Sarah who laughed out loud on hearing she's with child despite her old age, prompting her to name her son Isaac, which means laughter.[36]

In regard to Parzival, it indicates that he has the strength within him to bring about great change, which will amend the course of the future. In *Peredur*, a Celtic precursor to Eschenbach's *Parzival*, and in Chrétien de Troye's *Perceval*, we have similar versions of the maiden who refrains from laughing until the simpleton arrives (only Eschenbach provides her with a name). We must remember that Eschenbach is consciously throwing light on the hidden dimensions of the spiritual realities with the skill of a master artist. Be it as it may, Lady Cunneware, by sacrificing her laughter, has gained inner strength of perception that allows her to see *through* the fool's clothing and behavior, not only to his potential but to the fulfilment of his future development. And through her laughter she conveys the truth of Parzival to the community, as her name implies: In "Cunne" we have the word "kunnen," to "know" and "understand," or "Kunde," which means "news," "message," or "tidings," as in "good tidings," ("gute Kundschaft").[37] "Ware," the last part of her name, is easier for students to deduce, since "wahrheit" means "truth." Cunneware's laughter is thus a "message of truth" that heralds hope and honor for Arthur's Court, which is clearly in need of renewal and rejuvenation. This is partly indicated by the Red Knight's land claim, and underscored by Arthur letting the idiot Parzival fight against the honorable knight who has the highest standing. Others before Cunneware had recognized his noble stock in his handsome visage, but through her prophetic laughter, she sealed the authenticity of the prophecy.

King Arthur's court must have had high expectations regarding the knight who would be deemed worthy of receiving Cunneware's laughter.

36 Dagmar Fink, *Das Wunder des Lachens* (Verlag Freies Geistes Leben, 2001).

37 Mosmann, p. 89.

All the more disappointing for someone like Sir Keie to observe such an uncouth boy-man showered with her golden laughter. Sir Keie's name is an allusion to the Cynics, the Greek philosophical school of thought that had declined and become decadent, especially in the modern intellectual context.[38] The intellect alone cannot grasp the prescient insights of someone like Cunneware. Indeed, things are often not what they seem or what we expect them to be. Furthermore, it teaches us that we should not judge a person too quickly, which holds true especially for teachers. Over the years I have observed numerous students graduate who had struggled in one way or another, only to shine a few years later, having come into their own. Many of them went on to achieve remarkable accomplishments, changing the world for the better in astonishing ways. Nor is the status quo necessarily always to be followed. Change often comes from where we least expect it, not only in myths and fairy tales, but in real life.

For Parzival, as for each and every one of us, it is of the greatest importance to be recognized for who we are. It fosters inclusion. Especially when we are young, we do not necessarily know what our futures might look like and how we might attain our goals. During the block on Homer's *Odyssey*, I always endeavored to focus on "how" Odysseus overcame his challenges. In *Parzival*, apart from looking at the "how," I focus more on the "why." At the outset of the quest, this tapping forward in the darkness or the unknown is normal, especially in our age, where it is mostly *not* prescribed in what direction we must go. We divine our way forward. Parzival has no idea that he will be the consummate Grail knight, but Lady Cunneware intuits his path. She is like an angel for him, with whom the knowledge of his higher Self is held in safe hands.[39] It is almost as if the threads of a karmic bond have found each other, which lead through and out of the labyrinth of their respective destinies. That there is an intimate and overriding connection between them is made clear as the story progresses.

Lady Cunneware's laughter sets many things in motion, not only for

38 See Heinrich Teutschmann, *Der Gral Weisheit und Liebe* (Philosophisch-Antroposophischer Verlag am Goetheanum, 1984), p. 162.

39 Fink, *Das Wunder des Lachens*, p. 37.

Parzival but for all the knights, be they from Arthur's Court, the Grail Castle, or from Gawain's Castle of Wonders. Furthermore, her laughter is a warning to traditional codes of honor and chivalry that will soon have run their course, that will lose their meaning, and will fall into corruption and erode away. A student once asked, "What's an example of something that is accepted today as being okay but will be seen as bad in the future?" We'd been discussing the changing attitudes in regard to women, gender, and race, and how one simply cannot talk about those themes in the same way anymore, that we now consciously choose different vocabulary and are more aware of the hurt caused through prejudice. It was an excellent question and it gave rise to a stimulating conversation, though the answers remained inconclusive. Some examples they came up with included social media abuse, junk food, for-profit thinking, educational systems, environmental exploitation all still accepted at this stage by the society at large, though criticized by a growing minority.

Lady Cunneware, who blessed him with revivifying laughter, is—ironically enough—the sister of Orilus and Lähelin, the very knights who had wrested two of Parzival's kingdoms from him. She is a counterforce to their lust for power, self-seeking control, uncultivated drives, and greed. She, like Sigune, keeps Parzival connected to the *source*, to the spiritual font that he will need for his own inner development.

The Fight

"Experience is the name everyone gives to his mistakes."~ Oscar Wilde, from *Lady Windemere's Fan.*

As soon as Parzival approaches the Red Knight, he forgets what has just happened and only has eyes for the armor and fine horse, requesting it as his right in a rude and rash fashion, behaving like a mean mugger rather than anything remotely like a knight. He lives in the moment, reacting and responding to what's in front of him. Furthermore, he assumes, wrongly, that the noble warrior is Lähelin, who robbed Herzeloyde of two of her kingdoms, as if that claim would justify Parzival's violent conduct (years later, the hermit Trevrizent wonders whether Parzival might be Lähelin). The Red Knight, of course, will have none of that and thrusts him away with such force that nag and fool tumble to the ground, followed by a swift blow to the head with the shaft of his lance, drawing blood. It was meant as a warning to Parzival, but it only serves to enrage him. Impulsively, he throws his self-made javelin, piercing the unfortunate warrior through the eye, in the gap between helmet and vizor, causing instant death. Nor does Parzival show any remorse, though the ladies and knights who bear witness to the sham of a joust suffer tears of grief. The Red Knight bore a similarly ignominious death to Gahmuret who succumbed at the hands of Ipomidon. Both were killed by a stroke to the head, the seat of thought, suggesting that the thinking capacity was not sufficiently developed. In order to overcome his father's heritage, Parzival must develop and gain control over his thought life. But it will take more than a blow to the head to wake up and stir Parzival's thinking faculties. It is noteworthy that the name Ipomidon comes from the "classical Greek Hippomedon, 'horse ruler,' from the story of the 'Seven against Thebes,' known to medievals ... by Statius."[40] Horses symbolize intelligence, and Gahmuret's thinking intelligence was snuffed by a lance thrust through his helmet, which left a splinter of the shaft in his head.

We see that anger is the immediate impetus behind the killing of Ither, the red knight. Anger has its place. It wakes people up, yet can easily blind them to the consequences of their crude and hasty actions. We recall the

40 Eschenbach, *Titurel*, p. 179.

epic anger depicted in the opening line of Homer's *Iliad*: "Anger [mênis], be now your song, immortal one."[41] Anger drives Achilles back into the battle in the tenth year of the siege on Troy. Likewise, in a moment of undiluted wrath, Parzival threw his homemade javelin (javelot), killing Ither, which is a dishonorable start to his journey as a knight. It's the wrath that leads young people out into the streets to protest the injustices of the world. It's the anger I felt when I hit the streets of Johannesburg in South Africa, protesting against the reprehensible apartheid system during the July Riots of '76. Parzival's anger, however, is not based on any righteous cause. It played itself out on a juvenile delinquent level. Over time his *mênis* will transform into *Metis*—measured action (Goddess of wisdom and providence)—but that will take time, painful experiences, and ongoing suffering. Parzival saw red—literally and figuratively—and reacted instinctually. Like Cunneware's laughing, it sets things in motion, however from the opposite end. As yet, he is far from the years of discretion when he will dearly regret this degrading deed.

He does not understand the consequence of his action and its long-term ramifications. He has killed a kinsman, for Ither of Gaheviez was married to Lamire, Gahmuret's sister.[42] Furthermore, he is also related to Ither by blood, their lineage going back to Mazadan and Terdelaschoye. However, he will only find this out much later from the hermit Trevrizent. It is another severing of blood ties, both on his father's and mother's side. Herzeloyde's lineage through Titurel is also in need of rejuvenation, as it is in the process of dying out and the Grail stream is waiting for the person who will bring new life and lead it in a new direction.[43] The fledgling knight has much to accomplish before he can bring honor to Arthur's court and be the true embodiment of a perfect knight. Cunneware's prophetic laughter blessed the fulfilment of his future self. We all have that higher self within us.

Parzival has no idea what to do with the armor, how to loosen it from the

41 Homer, *The Iliad*, translated by Robert Fitzgerald (Anchor Books, 1975).

42 It is inconclusive whether they were married or whether Lamire was his mistress.

43 Rudolf Meyer, p. 57.

knight, let alone put it on. The helpful Iwanet guides him through the process, giving helpful basic advice in how to use a lance and a sword and how to maneuver behind his shield. Furthermore, he suggests that he leave his quiver of javelins behind because it goes against chivalry. However, Iwanet is not able to persuade Parzival to forego his fool's attire which his mother had made for him. Though he now looks like a handsome and noble knight, he is still a fool underneath it all. He is an imposter knight, though he does not suffer from "imposter syndrome" as many of us might. And through all of this, Parzival can hardly contain his impatience, eager and raring to ride off, just like when he left his mother.

This episode with young Iwanet highlights the fact that even a page has more sense and earthly knowledge than him. Parzival's simple mind thinks he has *won* the horse, armor, and knighthood, just like he thought he had rightfully followed his mother's advice and *won* the Jeschute's ring. Instead, his act of impulsive force caused undue grief, suffering, death, and *loss* in the process—*loss* for himself, the greater community and them. In this, his first battle, he has broken all the rules of chivalry. Yet, it is not entirely his fault. King Arthur and Sir Keie, the leadership, hold some responsibility, for they enabled him, though it was abundantly clear that Parzival is a country bumpkin, blissfully ignorant of the chivalric codes. He simply craved knighthood like a child yammering after a toy. We only need to look at some of our own leaders, political and otherwise, to see how innocent lives are lost or impaired because of their poor decisions. Sigune showed more sense when she directed Parzival away from Orilus.

Although Parzival does not recognize his own reprehensible action, he does internalize the unjust handling of Cunneware, telling Iwanet to report the following to King Arthur:

> Tell him of the deep disgrace I suffered: a knight offended me by striking a young lady who honored me with her laughter. Her pitiful words have moved me deeply, not merely brushing against my heart—no! the lady's undeserved sufferings are lodged at its core. (p. 90)

He departs, leaving the women in grief and bereft of laughter, though he himself feels no compunction for his deed. Conversely, he has no intention of returning to Arthur's Court before he can right the wrong that was meted out to Lady Cunneware because of him.

Gurnemanz

"We must always change, renew, rejuvenate ourselves, otherwise we harden." ~ Johann Wolfgang von Goethe

It's important not to lose sight of the absolute purity of Parzival's foolishness. Pondering his "pure" foolishness helps us to put things into context. We associate "pure" with a substance that is uncontaminated, flawless, perfect, authentic, genuine, clean, untainted, natural, uninfected. It also has the connotation of someone being virtuous, ethical, honest, upstanding, irreproachable, and *guiltless*. Yet, since leaving the paradisal Soltane, he has made himself culpable and responsible for the death of three people in a very short time: his mother, Schionatulander, and Ither of Gaheviez. But, as far as his intentions are concerned, he is utterly free of any contamination. Through his circumstances, he does not know any better, and it is because he is following the advice of others to a T—trusting blindly in their authority—that he utterly lacks the ability to read situations. He has no way of knowing or understanding the context in which the advice was given. In that way Parzival is an infant, in the original sense of not being able to speak—*en-fant*. Everything is taken literally, and the connections he makes are based on his literal view regarding all aspects of outer life. He has not yet learned how to read life, the signs of the outer world, and so he comes across as a dimwit, lacking worldly wisdom and all vestiges of *common* sense. However, in regard to his potential, he is anything but that. In fact, his foolishness underscores his genius. There is honesty in his perception of the world, no falsity whatsoever. It's almost as if his foolishness has been nurtured in a chrysalis of purity, so that he will be able to *absorb* the lessons of life in an exponentially enhanced manner. His foolishness highlights his potential—in fact, it necessitates his ability to make his achievements possible. All that, of course, does not excuse any of his misdeeds for which he will have to bear the consequences. The laws of karma are irrevocable.

We have a pertinent example of his childlike purity when he approaches the Castle of Gurnemanz with its multi-clustered towers. Awestruck, he thinks that Arthur must have sown them, rationalizing that his mother's men cannot farm like this, yielding such impressive results: "Of the crops she has in the forest none grow as high as this, yet there is no lack of rain" (p. 91). There is something endearing and ingenious about this image, equating the castle and its many spires, towers, and ramparts, with a crop. Parzival has been kept sequestered from this kind of "growth." He does not have the capacity to fathom what his eyes behold. Incidentally, I recall entering a toy store recently where a little boy marveled at the beauty of some polished stones. I overheard him telling his mother that he wanted to plant the stones in the ground, water them, and harvest many more colorful stones once the stone-trees were fully grown. It reminded me of Parzival's childlike worldview.

This description of the many-towered castle comes right after Eschenbach's portrayal of Parzival's new horse. His rickety nag has been left behind without another word (presumably a gift to Iwanet for helping him, as related in the Chrétien version), and it is the tremendous agility and speed of this new charger that impresses. It is impervious to heat, cold, or heavy going. Most striking is the distance and pace with which he travels "Fully armed the naïve young man rode it in that one day as far as an old campaigner, minus his gear, would never have attempted had he been asked to ride it in two!" (p 91). Not once does he rein him in. On the contrary, he rides the wave of his horse's momentum without imposing his own will. And what a thrill it must be, after riding on the old nag of a horse, and how freeing. Horse and rider are meant for each other and become one. Horses represent deep-seated and—at this stage—unconscious intelligence, filled with wisdom, not unlike that of bird migrations, which leads him on. Parzival is unconsciously intelligent but intellectually and socially stupid. He is driven by instinctive unbridled will. Thinking has not yet entered the will. He is a bit like a centaur, half man, half horse—with more horse than man. Yet, he has a dormant sense of Pegasus within him—the ideas flying toward the spirit. However, the speed of the horse mirrors the rapacious speed of his development and ability to learn, spurred by his impatience, still unencumbered by any feelings of guilt or remorse. The strength and pace of the horse are second nature to him. At this stage, destiny is leading him. In the future, he will have to lead destiny, which is true for all of us.

It's almost as if Gurnemanz is expecting Parzival when the path and horse lead him to the grey-haired knight sitting under a linden tree—associated with truth, prosperity, and love. Parzival greets him and says at once, "My mother asked me to seek advice of a man whose locks were grey" (p. 92). Gurnemanz de Graharz immediately hears from the manner of his simple speech that this knight is in serious need of advice, though he appears magnificent on his red charger. Gurnemanz agrees to teach him on one condition: that he *must* adhere to his advice. He agrees and Parzival is invited into the castle. Initially, he stubbornly refuses to get off his horse and only after much cajoling does he oblige. And when he is finally convinced to remove his armor, everybody is aghast that he is still wearing the fool's attire underneath. Clearly, this young knight is in need of worldly knowledge and knightly conduct.

The next morning, after a night's rest, maidens enter to bathe him, which he enjoys, though he becomes embarrassed toward the end, insisting they leave. Wolfram, insinuates that Parzival was sensually aroused, adding: "I fancy they would have liked to see if he has sustained any harm down below" (p. 94). ("*ich waen si gerne heten gesehn, ob im dort unde iht waere geschehn.*"[44]) This indicates his emerging sexual maturity.

After Parzival is given new clothes and nourishing victuals, Gurnemanz asks from where he has come. He is dismayed to hear about Ither's death, declaring that from now on he should be called the "Red Knight." What's implicated is that Parzival, as the new Red Knight, needs to recast the negative attributes of the color red to the positive: controlling his impulsive

44 Lachmann, III, 167, 27-28, p. 28.

and impatient nature, containing his bloodlust and compulsion to fight, and overcoming his lower urges, desires, and passions by strengthening his individuality, for blood is the carrier of the I. The Red Knight, true to the color, becomes the symbol of change, of which he will only become fully conscious after he has been to the Grail Castle, and once he starts his search for the Grail. The old ties that bind one to family, clan, tribe, nationality or culture first need to be overcome, before they can be chosen freely out of the conscious strength of the individuality, where the new community gradually begins to include all of humanity, irrespective of the bloodline.

Gurnemanz not only becomes a father figure to Parzival but his first official teacher, gently and firmly advising him of chivalrous conduct. Parzival needs to be instructed in even the most basic of actions like the etiquettes around eating, bathing, and dressing. Once the outer aspects and his wild spirit have been taken care of, Gurnemanz tactfully advises him in the use of words: "You speak like a child. . . . Why do you not stop talking of your mother and turn your mind to other things" (p. 95). First, with the clothing, and now with the refinement of speech, Gurnemanz weens him from constantly referring to his mother. Effectively, he cuts Parzival's apron strings, educating him in the courtly ways and customs. Gurnemanz recognizes Parzival's potential and his ability to lead. Under his guidance, Parzival is quick to remedy his unformed ways, learning and remembering the eleven codes of chivalry, which include: 1) don't lose your sense of shame; 2) protect and show compassion to the needy; 3) bear wealth or poverty in an appropriate manner; 4) uphold fine manners becomingly; 5) do not ask too many questions; 6) connect thoughtfully to the world with your senses so that you may be guided to wisdom; 7) show mercy to a conquered knight and let him live; 8) cleanse yourself once you remove your armor; 9) be of good cheer which will help you to gain honor and praise; 10) respect and honor women and never lie to them; 11) husband and wife are equal, like the sun spreading its light. (p. 96) The fifth code, "do not aske too many questions" ("*irn sult niht vil gefrâgen*"[45]), will be the cause of

---

45 Lachmann, III, 171, 17, p. 89.

great pain, because—again—he will take the advice too literally. However, they are not meant to be followed like a dogma, but have to be made one's own. The unmentioned and unwritten twelfth code cannot be imposed from the outside but must arise from within, specific to each occasion. This all-encompassing code cannot be taught, only learned through hard-won experience over time, when time becomes space.

After hearing and absorbing the codes of honor, Gurnemanz teaches him the knightly arts of horsemanship and the use of weaponry. Already within the first day, Parzival outstrips all the other knights, his royal heritage shining through and impelling him on. Over the next few days, he works on honing his astonishing skills. To this, Johannes Stein, referencing Steiner, states: "Inherited faculties are the forgotten experiences of earlier generations."[46] (See "Who is Parzival?") In his earlier years, these gifts hold him in good stead, but on his journey to develop his individual faculties, there will be much to prevail over. Parzival is only "slow to learn" when it comes to inner development.

Gurnemanz, who has lost three sons, sees Parzival as his fourth, and hopes that he will wed his daughter Liaze, though he leaves them free to find each other. However, after fourteen days, Parzival, who has surpassed the other knights in all the disciplines, longs to set forth and prove himself in knightly combat "before he would warm to what are called a woman's arms" (p. 98), which clearly reminds one of Gahmuret and how the urge to fight pulled him away from Belacane and Herzeloyde. Yet, there is a difference. He has not touched or given himself over to Liaze. He is leaving because he still needs to find himself and his task in life. He has learned the codes of chivalry and knightly ways, but he lacks experience. He has to find his own way in life. Most of us can recognize that impulse in ourselves. Like Gahmuret, when he first set out to serve the highest, Parzival is keen to set out to find his calling. He has learned all he could from Gurnemanz. The fourteen years it takes to become a knight—from page to squire to knighthood—he achieved in fourteen days. Though he was kept insulated

46 Walter Johannes Stein, *The Death of Merlin: Arthurian Myth and Alchemy* (Floris Books, 1989), p. 65.

in the isolation of Soltane, he has made up for lost time. Parzival arrived as a fool and leaves as a knight. There is a powerful pedagogical lesson in the above scene. Not everything needs to be learned as early as possible. In fact, we do damage if we thrust intellectual education on children too early. Waldorf education, amongst others, has proven this point for a hundred plus years. May it not lose that fundamental insight.

Gurnemanz appears in several medieval tales under different spellings, which suggests that he was once a prominent figure, though he is now mostly remembered as Parzival's counselor and teacher.

Discussion Topics, Questions

- Parzival was moved by the birds. Do you recall what first moved you inwardly, based on an outer sensation or experience (could be embodied as a poem)?
- How do you relate to the singing of birds?
- What encounters have been transformative in your life?
- Discuss the theme of people treated, worshipped, or taken for gods.
- Examine gender inequality and what can be done about the phenomenon of sex trafficking.
- If you have lost someone close, do you feel their presence?
- What is conscience? Do you have a sense for it?
- Have you ever experienced a "crossing the Rubicon" moment?
- Have you ever woken up to your own guilt at a much later stage?
- Do you have a sense of your own true source? How can the connection to the source be maintained?
- Can we recognize when others act without fully comprehending the consequences? Give examples.
- What are modern-day examples of the exploitive Fisherman?
- Are you able to recognize a person for who they are? Have you been mistaken? Give examples of seeing through outer appearances.
- Debate youthful impatience versus inexcusable impatience.

- Does destiny lead you or do you forge your own destiny?
- What rules and regulations or codes of behavior are deeply ingrained in us?
- What is the ideal form of education? Are the so-called experts worthy of our respect? If not, why?
- Which of the codes of chivalry are or might still be appropriate today, in one form or another?
- There is always an impulse and vision behind a quest. What are these motivating forces? Are they inner or outer?
- Are we aware of the value of things, objects? Do we value what we have? Have you ever discarded something that you later regretted, especially when you discovered its value?
- Discuss jealousy, based on Orilus' reaction to Jeshute.
- Examine your own motivations. Name them, question them, accept or discard them.

Illustrations:

1. Rudolf Steiner verse
2. Coat of arms
3. Ma'at, goddess of truth, balance, justice, and order, depicted with wings (Valley of the Kings, Luxor, Egypt).
4. Personalized Coat of Arms
5. In-class writing on "Home" (Violet Middlebrook)
6. The murky ford (Alexander Madey)
7. Framed photo of Michelangelo's Pietà
8. Coat of Arms (Rosabel Mongan)
9. Ballad
10. The Red Knight (Rosabel Mongan)

BOOK FOUR

Belrepeire

"Everything that is in the heavens, on earth, and under the earth is penetrated with connectedness, penetrated with relatedness."
— Hildegard von Bingen

We see a very different young man depart from Graharz to the one who'd arrived two weeks prior. He was no longer a carefree simpleton who'd fancied himself a knight, but a well-bred chevalier "whose eyes were at the mercy of his heart" (p. 100). He is overcome with sadness due to his infatuation with sweet Liaze. His thoughts are focused on her, which shows that his inner life is continuing to stir and awaken. Whereas he'd left lovely Jeschute without another thought, his mind is now caught up in feelings for Liaze, who showed him every honor and friendship, yet stopped short of offering him her love, though she would have been dutifully willing had he proposed. For the first time, he experienced the harsh pangs of love, over which he has little control, exemplified and underscored by his inability to curb his horse (in contrast to the thrilling and carefree ride a fortnight earlier after "winning" Ither's horse). Nevertheless, Parzival does not go astray, for the horse shoots swiftly ahead between mountains and through forests and fields to where he needs to go. The horse, to reiterate, symbolizes Parzival's higher intelligence within the depths of his subconscious that knows exactly what to do and where to go.

Often in life we can have the feeling that we are led toward something significant that we could not possibly have planned or foreseen ourselves. This holds especially true for young people making their way in the world. Often, we can have the sense that the wisdom within our will is leading us to where we are meant to go—an invisible guide. Reading Julianna Margulies' memoir *Sunshine Girl* recently, I came across the line that her grandfather told her: "You never know what's going to happen. If you make a left instead of a right, you might bump into the man you're going to marry."[1] This can lead to good discussions, depending on the students and the class, and I ask them whether they have ever had a similar experience, a significant encounter, or conversely, avoided a calamity. The world is full of examples, such as the 9/11 survivor stories, where, through some twist of fate, people's lives were saved: taking a random cigarette break, a different subway route, or simply oversleeping. There are many occasions during literature classes where one can talk about fate, destiny or luck, and it's interesting to note the differences in what students say, depending on the grade level.

In the case of Parzival, one has the clear sense that he is led by his own subconscious wisdom. However, the more one develops, the more one needs to take life into one's own hands. It's a bit like the gift of falling in love, which is followed by having to work on the relationship.

Parzival has no clear plan or intention. He is still like Gahmuret, "looking for adventure," open to what the path he's on will bring. By the end of the day, he reaches the port city of Belrepeire in the kingdom of Brobarz (Bro-barz, country or region of bards; also interpreted as "wilderness").[2] The nature around is wild, with cliffs, gorges, and torrents of water spilling out into the

---

1 Julianna Margulies, *Sunshine Girl: An Unexpected Life* (Ballantine Books, 2021), p. 149.

2 *Titurel*, p. 168.

ocean. He will need to cross a rickety bridge that swings precariously over the gushing water in order to reach Belrepeire, a city well defended, with sixty knights shouting for him to retreat. They assume he is Clamide, their enemy.

Parzival is not deterred, and when his horse refuses to cross—afraid and startled by the loud cries of the knights and the swaying bridge—Parzival dismounts and leads the frightened horse across, knowing that they could both plummet into the torrents. Parzival is no longer the reckless fool. Leading the horse across shows that he is beginning to use and control his intelligence.

He comes to a battlefield and rides toward the palace. Knocking on the large gate, a lady opens and lets him know that they have suffered enough and he should go. However, he offers his help, and with the Queen's permission he is allowed to enter Belrepire—a "fair" or "beautiful" place to "repair" or retreat to, as the name suggests.[3]

Condwiramurs

A vision appeared in his velvety sleep
One of gentle water lapping
And of musky silken white, swimming
In a sea of overshadowing grief.
~ Jae-Yeon Yoo (Student)

The situation in Belrepeire is dire. The inhabitants are besieged by Clamide and his men. Many knights have died during battle and all are suffering from starvation due to the impinging famine. Initially, he does not recognize the severity of their plight, indicating that he is still not yet awake enough to the needs of others. On the lawn by a linden tree, they remove his armor, wash off the iron rust, and give him a mantle to wear. On the stairs leading up to the grand palace, he is introduced to Queen Condwiramurs, and after the customary welcome kiss, she takes his hand and leads him to

3 *Titurel*, p. 190.

their seats. Eschenbach proceeds to highlight her unsurpassed beauty that excels all other women. The beautiful pair is admired by all around.

For many years, the *Parzival* block coincided with Valentine's Day, which celebrates love and romance. Many students take it seriously even though they might make light of it. It's a good opportunity to offer a variety of imaginations on the theme of love and relationships. And *Parzival*, in essence, is all about love, and one could say it is an *Initiation through Love*. Love is expressed in myriad forms, from the basest—the anti-love of rape and abduction—to the most sublime and ideal, as the union between Parzival and Condwiramurs. In our modern world dominated by the media, young people are bombarded with all sorts of depictions of relationships, which leave deep impressions, yet can cause severe inner turmoil and distress because they think that what they see on the screens is how one should behave in relationships. In contrast, the meeting between Parzival and Condwiramurs is one of the most mystically beautiful meetings between two souls to be found in world literature. Celtic literature expresses for the first time the awakening of romantic love, in contrast to earlier times where all "love" was closely related to blood ties. Heretofore, marriage was basically a business transaction, dependent on traditions, customs, and rituals. It was inescapable, especially in pre-Christian times, exemplified by Egyptian customs, where familial marriage, even between brother and sister was acceptable. Marriage between different races was condemned. Similar traditions are still in place to this day in many parts of the world. However, individual love began to come into its own during the Middle Ages, of which Celtic literature tells, with stories like Tristan and Iseult or Erec and Enide. Romantic love is the right to choose one's love freely, and there are very few students who will argue against that, though we've had students from other countries who volunteered information about their own parents' arranged marriages which had worked out well. Yet, they also admitted that others had not. One student came to us to escape an arranged marriage. Freedom in love relationships is the prerequisite to freedom in thinking. In Greek mythology, romantic love was deemed destructive. However, romantic love became an integral part of chivalry, and the troubadours highlighted romance, as heard in so many of their poems and songs.

Condwiramurs means "guide to love" or "conduit of love" (Old French: *Coin de voire amour*). And she guides Parzival in his struggles to find, comprehend, and live the breadths and depths of love. She takes the lead in their relationship, which is made evident from the moment she takes his hand to guide him to their seats. It is a very different Parzival from the one who forced a kiss and stole a ring and brooch from Jeschute. Initially he is reminded of Liaze, the first woman to stir his feelings, though Condwiramurs eclipses Liaze in beauty. Parzival, in stark contrast to his former self, refrains from asking any questions, adhering to Gurnemanz's advice too literally, which causes Condwiramurs to question and doubt herself, thinking that he is looking down on her. Eventually, she takes the initiative and asks him from where he has come, which alleviates the awkwardness between the two. This aspect of when to talk and when to keep silent is a good topic of discussions to have in class, though I only tend to broach the topic fully when Parzival arrives in Munsalvæsche, where his silence is the cause of great disappointment and sorrow.

When Parzival tells her that he has come from Gurnemanz, she is amazed at the distance he's traveled, riding in one day what others would have a hard time covering in two. Once again, we have the theme of speed, which indicates Parzival's tremendous power of will and rapid development. The emphasis, however, is still more on the *outer* aspects of his development, rather than on his inner maturation that takes more time to develop—this hero who grows slowly wise. However, it foreshadows his spiritual agility, reminding one of Odin riding Sleipnir, the eight-legged horse. Eschenbach constantly reinforces the various themes through repetition, though each time the quality is slightly different.

It turns out that Condwiramurs' mother was Gurnemanz's sister (unnamed), which makes him her uncle and Liaze her cousin. Interestingly enough, Gurnemanz is also the grandfather of Schionatulander. It is usually around Book Four that students begin to notice the familial connections, commenting on how everybody seems to be related, asking if there is a reason for that and how it fits into the greater puzzle of the epic. It offers the opportunity to talk about the *synchronicities* of life (as coined by C.G. Jung). I prod them to become more aware of the connections that keep on happening within the book and within their own lives. These familial ties, however, still belong to the past. They had their place, but Parzival, as we shall see, represents a new element in human evolution that transcends the ties of old.

It is at this moment that her paternal uncle Kyot, Duke of Katelangen, promises to supply them with some food from the hunting lodge that he shares with his brother. He, in turn, is the father of Sigune. That there is the promise of *food* is significant, for it suggests that the meeting of Parzival and Condwiramurs spells the end of the famine. Food, like most other outer objects, are symbolic of inner changes. Through their nascent love the starving souls are fed. A besieged castle is often a picture of soul deprivation. We saw something similar with Belacane, when her sixteen gated castle of Zazamanc was besieged. It showed her anguish at the loss of Isenhart. It is an oft repeated theme in fairy tales. Love nourishes, and when the Queen receives such nourishment, her realm also benefits. The food is brought and now we can observe how it is used.

We remember how Parzival gobbled up the food in Jeschute's pavilion, or how he tucked into the food when he first arrived at Gurnemanz's castle, annihilating the food with such vigor that it amused Gurnemanz, and one can imagine him rolling his eyes and shaking his head. When the bread arrives, Condwiramurs first shares it out to her people, and—on Parzival's suggestion—did the same with the cheeses, meat, and wine. Parzival has become more circumspect and aware of the plight of the others. However, one wonders to what extent it has to do with being in the proximity of

Condwiramurs, the guide of love, rather than coming solely from himself. The two of them barely get a slice of food. They both hold back and abstain, except for little morsels, once the others have all received some nourishment. It shows restraint, an important lesson that Odysseus also had to learn. Conscious refraining of food and other bodily urges, is an important part of spiritual development, and such renunciation or conscious suppression of direct gratification is a way to prepare oneself to be *spiritually effective*. Rudolf Steiner points out that "one will reach a certain level in the spiritual world when one fasts or does something in another way to suppress wishes and desires, in order to tame them. And the greatest spiritual results . . . will always be preceded by such a preparation, which includes the renunciation of wishes, desires, impulses of will that arise in us."[4] Condwiramurs brings out the best in him.

Mystical Midnight Meeting

They lay close, but not touching,
Attracted like a summer's day to sunshine,
Yet held apart by innocence
And the purest beam of light.
~Jae-Yon (Student)

The meeting between the two young lovers is otherworldly. If Parzival started out as a "pure" fool, he and Condwiramurs now prove themselves as "pure" lovers. Parzival is led to a magnificent bed in a chamber lit up by many costly candles. In the depths of night, in an almost dreamlike manner, Condwiramurs noiselessly makes her way to his chamber where she kneels by his bed, her tears of sorrow falling on Parzival, who wakes and asks her to join him in the comfort of the bed, promising that no limbs would embrace each other. They provide inner sustenance to one another, their soul-warmth offering an intimacy that supersedes any desire that still

4 Rudolf Steiner, *Die Evolution vom Gesichtspunkte des Wahrhaftigen*, Berlin, 14 November 1911 (translated by the author), Rudolf Steiner Verlag, 1987, GA 132, p. 43.

lies mutually dormant within them, waiting for the right moment. This meeting of kindred souls is based on something metaphysical, an intimation of what they mean to each other. Nestled in bed, she tells him her tale of woe, and he listens with an open heart, absorbing every word, which steels his resolve to help her and her realm. This meeting is a manifestation of a dream encounter. When we dream about someone who we have just met, it tends to suggest that we have a karmic connection to them. It is worth following the unfolding of such a relationship consciously.

There's a palpable change of mood whenever we cover this scene in the class. I endeavor to retell it in an objective and intimate manner, conveying the atmosphere of two lovers who meet in the middle of the night, sharing a bed, not touching, though their souls merge more powerfully than any physical embrace. Condwiramurs unburdens her soul, shares her anguish, and confesses her fears, knowing that her words will be received with empathy and respect.

Condwiramurs tells him how Clamide and Kingrun, his seneschal (the chief supervisor who takes care of administrative and other duties), have laid waste to her kingdom, killed many of her knights, and that only Belrepire is left. Clamide is trying to bend her to his will, but she won't let herself be forced into a relationship with him, preferring to throw herself from the castle's high walls into the moat than give herself to Clamide. She is an orphan, and her story is a story of an orphaned soul. Simultaneously, her situation in Belrepeire is a powerful depiction of the orphaned soul of humanity, being forced to comply and give in to so many of the cold-hearted outer circumstances of our socio-political and technocratic modern ways. It is the orphaned soul, yearning to be united with Paradise Lost—the spirit. Parzival gives his word that he will do everything in his power to help her. She departs as mysteriously and stealthily as she entered, with not a soul aware of the chaste midnight rendezvous.

Victory, Wedding, Justice

"A Thing of beauty is a joy forever." ~ John Keats

The next morning, Parzival rides out to fight his first battle as a true and trained knight. Kingrun, far in advance of his troops, clashes with Parzival and is quickly vanquished. Parzival shows mercy and sends him off to Lady Cunneware to offer his oath of surrender. Parzival also asks him to convey the following message: "I shall not return till I have wiped out the dishonour which I share with the lady who greeted me with laughter and endured such violence for it. Tell the lady I am her most humble devoted servitor" (pp. 108-9). It is the first of many knights he sends back to Cunneware, the lady who recognized his potential through her laughter. What he does not yet know is that she is the guardian of the spring, the place of renewal. In sending the knights to Cunneware, he not only conveys honor to Arthur's court, spreads his fame, but, most importantly, keeps his connection to the source, which ultimately will lead him to the Grail.

After this inaugural conquest, Queen Condwiramurs decides that "in view of his splendid victory over Kingrun he must be her lover". Like Herzeloyde before her, it is she who decides and is decisive. She won't be forced or coerced into marriage, but follows the dictates of her own heart, and Parzival is only too glad to oblige. Immediately after this public declaration, two boats are driven into the harbor by gale winds, laden entirely with food, as if ordained by God. Like before, the soul nourishment of love supplies food, enough to feed them all for a long time.

The inner development and change affect the outer. Parzival, who is now set to become the Lord of Belrepeire's citizens pays the merchants double for all the food, which shows gratitude and great generosity. Furthermore, like before, he parcels out the food in small lots to ensure that the people do not gorge themselves and not overload their stomachs. He is demonstrating the wisdom of a true leader.

To celebrate their nuptials, they share one bed together, though they choose to enjoy the tempered warmth of each other's company instead of immediately succumbing to the hot desire of physical embrace. The restraint comes naturally to them and is not forced. The soul connection overrides all else. The next morning, she ties her hair up with a ribbon to show she has become his wife. "Then this virgin bride bestowed her lands and castles on him, for he was the darling of her heart" (p. 110). For two nights they enjoy their soul intimacy, only consummating their love physically on the third night. All in all, they lay with unentwined limbs for three nights—if one counts the night when she first crept into his chamber. It reinforces the profound picture of their ideal love where the physical merger follows the soul-spiritual union—a confirmation that seals their bond. The manner of their relationship, coupled with the circumspect way they dole out the food, shows that Parzival is no longer impatiently impulsive. Patience translates itself into care, respect, and well-being for others, and the ability to listen, truly listen to others, in this case the needs of Queen Condwiramurs. The unfurling of their union is a beautiful example of the intermingling between soul and spirit within the physical realm. She ensouls and unlocks his spirit that up to now has been encased within the confines of a dulled consciousness. And in doing so stirs his eternal self, prodding his *Ur*-memory, linking him to a primal part of himself, which lives deep within the unseen parts of himself. Though Parzival has become a listener, he has not yet found his voice. What does it mean to find one's voice? How did he lose his voice, poignantly expressed in his hesitancy to ask any questions? Humanity, like Parzival, has lost its voice; in other words, the connection to the source. And the tragedy of our present age is that it does not realize what it has lost, and the extent of its loss. It still lives within the arrogance of the intellectual accomplishments. I saw a sign recently at our school's Lost and Found (after a year's worth of accumulated lost clothes): *"Find what you did not know you'd lost."* How apt. And what a painful journey for the individual seeker and for humanity as a whole. Humanity relies on the individual attainments to draw it into its destined future.

However, Clamide is still determined to force Condwiramurs into his arms, and to obtain her lands. The danger is not yet over and battles between the two armies ensue, which highlights Parzival's ability to lead an army against an unrelenting enemy. In the subsequent skirmishes, people suffer and die. Greed, power, self-importance, and selfish desires on the part of those in authority always create destruction and loss for others. Then and now. Will we ever learn from these examples through the ages? How do the various heroes comport themselves? Who is worthy of emulation? What is the right thing to do when one is confronted with situations that lack ethics and put entire communities at risk? In *Parzival* there are many examples of injustices, though each time the "attacks" highlight a different aspect of the human condition, and it helps to compare and contrast the various battles. In this case, Parzival can be compared and contrasted with Gahmuret fighting against the black and white armies in Zazamanc for Queen Belacane. In his stalwart defense of Belrepeire, Parzival shows himself to be *le fils du roi* Gahmuret. On all accounts he has become Gahmuret's equal, exhibiting generosity, courage, strength, self-control, and moderation.[5] But is he equal to the task he is meant to accomplish? Now it's a matter of fulfilling the hidden goals of his own veiled destiny, which begs the question: To what extent do we sense our own destiny and how it changes over time in regard to desires, wishes, and goals? In order to hone that faculty, we have to refine our sense of self. Teaching Parzival or any other books that deal with the big questions of life supports the discovery or uncovering of these higher goals.

When Clamide hears from his own warriors who were captured and released that there is enough food in Belrepeire to last them a year, and that the Queen now has a husband who "has all the marks of high decent"

5 See *Parzival*, translated by Hatto, p. 20.

(p. 113), he challenges Parzival to a single combat. Parzival triumphs once again, and, showing mercy as Gurnemanz had advised, also sends him off to the Britons to pay respects to Arthur and to surrender, like Kingrun, to Lady Cunneware to serve her and do her bidding. "After swearing his oath, the man who had come to grief through his own arrogance left the field" (p. 116). How many times do we suffer grief through our own arrogance? It's a good question to ask the students, rhetorical or not. The theme of arrogance is portrayed in a multitude of literary characters, such as Oedipus, Macbeth, and Doctor Faustus; or Xerxes, Napoleon, and Hitler from history. Each time it serves as a warning: "Pride goes before destruction, a haughty spirit before a fall."[6]

Eschenbach once again writes in detail about Clamide's arrival at Arthur's court, just as he did with Kingrun. It underscores the importance of justice, of righting an observed wrong. Their arrival brings it to public consciousness, heard by all, including Sir Keie, the one responsible for the beating, who says in the way of a feeble excuse: "I did what I did for the sake of courtly standards and with intent to improve your manners, for which I now suffer your [Cunneware] ill will" (p. 117). Sir Keie stands for the outdated social norms of courtly life and codes of honor. Our present age is crowded with Sir Keies. It is an example of why we need people like Parzival, who, through their upbringing, naturally think outside the box, not adhering to conventions but to what is morally right, and in this case, Sir Keie's action was a despicable moral action against women and people as such. Injustices need to be addressed, regardless of whether they are accepted by the social standards of the day or not. Speaking up is hard to do, when society at large still acts differently. It is an essential subject to discuss with students. *Parzival* offers ample opportunity to discuss the topical and ever-important theme of justice.

The bloody and ongoing conflict, which has rendered Brobarz almost uninhabitable, gives way to joy and happiness that quickly spreads over the land. Peace is restored and prosperity returns. Parzival, who has now

6 Old Testament, Book of Proverbs, 16:18

inherited great wealth from Tampenteire, his father-in-law, doles out his riches to his people, winning their hearts. And like his father before him, he enjoys riding out to participate in many tournaments, and inevitably, he also leaves Condwiramurs. However, there is an important difference: unlike Gahmuret, who deserted Belacane in the dead of night or left Herzeloyde to fight for the Baruch of Baghdad, Parzival requests permission to leave for a brief time—heard publicly by many knights and ladies—in order to see how his mother is faring. He does, however, add as an afterthought, "and also in search for adventure" (p. 119), which suggests that he has not quite overcome Gahmuret's restlessness. Welling up from deep within him is the wish to reconnect with his mother. Like Odysseus (whose mother also died after his departure from Ithaca), the only place that he can reconnect with her is in the beyond. For the Greeks, it was the realm of shades, the underworld. For Goethe's *Faust*, it is the realm of the "Mothers." For Parzival, he will have to gain access to the realm of the dead, which is the realm of the spirit, the world beyond Maya, the world of indisputable Truth. In the words of Linda Sussman: "Condwiramurs awakens Parzival's heart, and out of that awakening the first hint of self-reflection emerges in

Parzival."[7] Though it saddens Condwiramurs, she will deny him nothing and her love will be a guide wherever he goes. And so, without an entourage, he leaves her, like once he left his mother, and rides away alone. Little does he know how long and convoluted the journey will be. Herzeloyde gave him four pieces of advice before he left her. Gurnemanz gave him eleven codes of chivalry to accompany his journey. Their gifts, though helpful, contributed to his failings. Condwiramurs only has one gift for him: Love. A radiant Love that will sustain him throughout his far-reaching travels until their moment of reunification and bliss at the Grail Castle.

WHO IS PARZIVAL?

"Those who were observed dancing were thought to be crazy by those who could not hear the music"~ Friedrich Nietzsche

ANYBODY WHO PREPARES to teach *Parzival* in a Waldorf school—aware that the knowledge of esoteric streams is imparted exoterically through mythology and legends—senses the overarching significance of the individuality of Parzival, which gives rise to the question: Who was he? Thus it was with Johannes Stein, who—as was his want—went straight to Rudolf Steiner shortly before teaching the first block on *Parzival*, and asked him whether Parzival was as important as Skythianos or Zarathustra, to which Steiner replied, "Oh no . . . much higher."[8] Steiner already talked about this topic many years before in a 1906 lecture in Munich, where he refers to the three Bodhisattvas—Skythianos, Gautama Buddha, and Zarathustra—as the most lofty leaders of humanity, adding, "Now there is named a fourth individuality, behind which there resides for many, something that is even higher, more profoundly powerful than the three beings, named as Skythianos, as Buddha, and as Zarathustra. It is *Manes*

7 Linda Sussman, *Speech of the Grail: A Journey Toward Speaking that Heals and Transforms* (Lindisfarne Press, 1995), p. 56.

8 Bernard Lievegoed, *The Battle for the Soul* (Hawthorne Press, 1994), p. 81.

[Mani]."[9] To me this came as a revelation, having studied the grand and far-reaching contributions of these lofty leaders of humanity. Mani is the last of the three previous incarnations Steiner mentions in regard to the individuality who appears as Parzival in Eschenbach's epic.

The first goes back to ancient Egypt where he emerges as the Young Man of Sais.[10] This youth, chosen and called to be initiated into the old Mysteries, had an insatiable desire for knowledge, but the asking of questions was strictly forbidden. Back then, the appropriate time for the neophyte to be initiated into the various levels of knowledge was exclusively decided by the priests. The Young Man of Sais wanted to become a *son of the widow*—Isis, the widow who mourned Osiris—just like the priests. The impatient youth burned to know more about the veiled Isis. He felt impelled to look at her form, to know her essence, and the secrets she could impart. He had already learned a great deal, but was driven to know the very truth and meaning of life. Thus, he approached the silent statue and lifted her veil to satisfy his questing spirit. Beneath the veil he saw written: *I am the All, the past, present, the future. No mortal may lift my veil,*[11] which immediately cost him his life. Through his action, the Young Man of Sais broke the spiritual inertia of the time, allowing something new to seep in. It symbolized how fixed and immovable the wisdom of the Egyptians had become.

This individuality returned as the Youth of Nain, once again the *son of a widow* (Luke, chapter seven), and became a disciple of Christ after he was raised from the dead. In him, according to Steiner, lived the cumulative essence of the entire third cultural epoch—the Egyptian-Chaldean spirit.[12] "He was the first human being who received a Christian initiation, with

---

9 Rudolf Steiner, *Der Orient im Lichte des Okzidents*, 9. Vortrag, (Rudolf Steiner Verlag [Taschenbuchausgabe], 1977), GA 113 p. 191 (translated by the author). (In English: *The East in the Light of the West*)

10 Poetically immortalized in Schiller's poem: "The Veiled Statue at Sais."

11 Plutarch on Isis and Osiris.

12 Rudolf Steiner, *Zur Geschichte und aus den Inhalten der ersten Abteilung der Esoterischen Schule* 1904-1914 (Rudolf Steiner Verlag, 1984), GA 264, p. 228. (In English: *From the History & Contents of the First Section of the Esoteric School.*)

Christ Himself as the hierophant."[13] As they carried the newly deceased Nain out of the gate (accompanied by many Egyptian initiates), Steiner compares Nain's wailing and weeping mother to the goddess Isis. The awakened Youth of Nain is returned to his mother, and it is now up to him to unite with Isis. The surrounding people recognized that a great prophet had risen from the dead. From then on, the Isis force could be experienced on earth. However, Steiner makes it clear that his initiation through Christ would only take effect in the following incarnation.[14]

The Youth of Nain reincarnates as Mani in 216 CE, a Persian prophet and founder of Manichaeism, in which the results of Nain's initiation by Christ found their full manifestation. The scope of Mani's influence was largely forgotten until relatively recently, most importantly since the singular discovery of the *Mani Codex* in 1969, a papyrus collection from upper Egypt (Asyut) and sold to the University of Cologne, Germany. It is so small that it can fit into a matchbox. "On each parchment page, written in a wonderful script, are twenty-three lines. The writing is small and quite elegant."[15] Other sources also exist, some of which are contradictory, but the *Cologne Mani Codex* (CMC) offers some of the most important insights into his biography and work.[16]

According to Steiner, a learned merchant left four books to a widow when he died. She, in turn, passed them on to her freed slave just before she died when he was only twelve years old. He inherited all her wealth, including the four books by the great Skythianos. This wealthy widow had bought the boy when he was seven years old from a poverty-stricken widow. She reared him like a son, educated and freed him. Later, aged eighteen, he changed his name from Corbicus to Mani. He became a teacher with a huge following, traveling the world, spreading his teachings

13 *The Battle for the Soul*, p. 84.

14 Rudolf Steiner, *Das Lukas-Evangelium* (Rudolf Steiner Verlag, 1977), GA 114, p. 197. (In English: *According to Luke*)

15 Virginia Sease and Manfred Schmidt-Brabant, *Paths of the Christian Mysteries: From Compostela to the New World* (Temple Lodge, 2003), p. 70.

16 See also *Mani & Rudolf Steiner* by Christine Gruwez (Steiner Books, 2014).

as far afield as China, founding schools and congregations along the way. In 276 CE, he was accused by the Persian magicians of high treason and executed. However, his teachings continued to spread, until the Catholic Church systematically and ruthlessly expunged almost all traces of Mani's work. This was largely due to Augustine who became a vehement critic and enemy of Mani's teachings, having been a Manichaean himself for ten years. The time was not yet ripe for middle Europe to understand the deeper and more spiritual implications of the Manichaean stream. Lievegoed writes:

> A characteristic element is that he always places the all-encompassing images of development in the duality of light and darkness. After all, Mani was a Persian who lived in the latter days of the impulse of Zarathustra. ... Every light creates darkness. In other words, when something good is done, at the same time the shadow of the good is created. ... You can't push the shadow aside, no you will have to take it with you in your development.[17]

This is important to understand when studying *Parzival.* In a related way Virginia Sease writes:

> The teachings of Mani are often characterized by what differentiates them from Christianity, especially in regard to the concept of evil. The Manichaeans say that evil is just as eternal as good—evil and good are equally old, while Christianity, of course, states that spirits that were originally good fell away from God. A vast difference is apparent in these views.[18]

The idea of entering into darkness with love, gentleness, and compassion is quite radical, but it offers a solution for the problems we are facing today and increasingly so in the future: Loving the darkness is giving birth to the light.

Before the *Cologne Mani Codex* was discovered, numerous other texts were unearthed in the Xinjiang region in western China in the early 1900s

---

17 *The Battle for the Soul*, pp. 86-7.

18 *The Paths of Christian Mysteries*, pp. 71-72.

and along the Silk Road. These extensive discoveries were closely connected to the Uyghur people (recently in the news for the abuse against them by the Chinese). Further important Manichaean documents were discovered in North Egypt, all written in Coptic. It is not without reason that these documents have now come to light. More will follow, for we have entered a new age, where culture has to change toward the spiritual on a global scale in order to balance out the dominance of the material world.

It is interesting to note that all three incarnations emphasize widows and the *son of the widow*. This continues in the Parzival incarnation, where he is born to Herzeloyde, twice widowed (as was Isis). As Christine Gruwez writes

> the term "the son of a widow" here means that the "father principle" is not present. In other words, there is no transmission (the teaching and handing on) from teacher to pupil as regards the achievement of esoteric wisdom. A "son of a widow" is someone who begins to school himself in wisdom on his own, out of his own forces.[19]

Or in the words of Rudolf Steiner:

> The soul is widowed. Humanity is thrown back onto itself. It must find the light of truth within its own soul in order to act as its own guide. Everything of a soul nature has always been expressed in terms of the feminine. Therefore the feminine element—which exists only in a germinal state today and will later be fully developed—this self-directing feminine principle, which is no longer confronted by the divine fructifier, is called by Mani the "Widow." And therefore he calls himself "Son of the Widow."[20]

Humanity became increasingly fragmented as it gradually descended

---

19 Christine Gruwez, *Mani and Rudolf Steiner*, p 47.

20 *The Temple Legend*, p. 62

into the material world, relying ever more on the senses to connect to the surroundings in order to make sense of the world. Slowly we have to find a way to return to the whole, which is only possible through a unifying spiritual element—the Isis-Sophia.

Apart from the legendary Parzival, there existed a historical-physical Parzival, who was the first to truly trailblaze the *consciousness soul* path, as depicted poetically and more fully in the character of Wolfram's *Parzival*. It is the path of the contemporary human being. It allows us to go forward without being held back by traditions, customs, and rigid rules and norms of the past—vital to a humane development within the context of the globality. Though the Parzival individual was an initiate—towering above the others—he had to *start from scratch*. He had to enter and get to know the physical world and find his way to the transcendence of the Grail "out of his own forces." It is a search and renewal of the old wisdom, which has been lost. Parzival is unable to initially tap into his past accomplishments, having to develop everything out of his own resources, a journey that takes him from dullness and darkness, through doubt and suffering, into *sælde*—joy and enlightenment. Nothing is given. Even the smallest step had to be regained out of his own Self. Consciousness is hard earned, with blood, sweat, and tears. In the words of Steiner: "Everything that comes from Mani is an appeal to man's own spirit light of soul and at the same time is a definite rebellion against everything that does not come out of man's own soul, out of man's own observation of soul."[21] Walter Johannes Stein, after much research, came to the conclusion that the historical Parzival is based on the figure of Liutward of Vercelli, counselor to Charles the Fat and his wife Richardis (who, according to Stein, can be identified as the historical Jeschute).[22]

This individuality has accompanied humanity from the most distant past, incarnating many times, also since his Parzival incarnation. And, as Lutters writes: "The reason for giving attention to the historical Parsifal in a contemplation on the karma of the Waldorf school movement is the

21 *The Temple Legend*, p. 62.

22 *The Ninth Century*, p. 113.

expectation that this same individuality will now, at the beginning of the twenty first century, be able to have a new essential influence on the development of human culture."[23] Presently we see that the problems of the world are caused by the embodiment of the extremes—far to the right and left. What is missing is the middle, already pointed out by Buddha and practiced by Parzival, as a path to unite humanity in the future—consciously. The middle path is the *only* way forward, and it can only be achieved through the gift of freedom and love in all spheres, without exception.

Ehrenfried Pfeifer, who discussed the incarnations of Mani with Steiner (between 1919–1921), relates that the Mani individuality, according to Steiner, would not incarnate in the twentieth century, but in the early twenty first century, on the condition that an appropriate body can be found. Furthermore, a normal mainstream education would give no opportunity for the development of Mani, only a Waldorf education. If, however, the conditions are met, he will appear as a great leader of humanity, especially in the area of art and religion. He or she will act in accordance with the Grail Mystery, and through the Grail Light, lead humanity forward—and encourage people to decide for themselves in regard to good and evil.[24]

After first reading this, I was profoundly moved, thinking about the immense responsibility we have as teachers. Hardly anything has humbled me more than reading those lines in regard to the effects we as teachers can have on students and the future. So many questions arise: What kind of Waldorf School is needed to fulfill an initiate's conditions? What does it demand and require of us as teachers? How ought teachers to be trained? How much love, patience, gentleness, kindness can we muster and shower the children with? I began to look at every child as a potential Parzival, as a great initiate to be—and in essence, it's what all children deserve, no matter if you are an initiate or not, and in a way, we are all initiates of sorts,

---

23 Frans Lutters, *An Exploration into the Destiny of the Waldorf School Movement* (AWSNA, 2011), translated by Philip Mees, p. 85.

24 Steiner, *Zur Geschichte aus den Inhalten der ersten Abteilung der Esoterischen Schule: 1904-1914*, GA 264, p. 240. (In English: see page 161)

for every human being has the ultimate highest within them. But what if we fail? What if we, as a movement, forget the founding principles, the ideals and spiritual underpinnings of Waldorf education? Ultimately, however, the task fills me with the greatest of hope. The thought that a lofty initiate would want and need the best that a Waldorf education can offer is a confirmation of a kind. It is quite likely, in my opinion, that this individuality might incarnate in the Americas or in Asia and as a woman or a person of color from a diverse social and cultural background, where the emphasis is on the universal human element.

Discussion Topics, Questions

- When is it time to talk and when is it better to keep silent?
- Have you experienced "synchronicities" in your own lives?
- What keeps us connected to the spiritual source?
- What does it mean to find one's voice?
- How many times do we suffer grief through our own arrogance?
- Why must we continuously prove ourselves to the world and ourselves?
- Do you or have you spoken up when you have observed an injustice?
- Is there such a thing as "Love at first sight"?

Illustrations:

1. Parzival crossing the swaying bridge (Julia M. Davis)
2. Condwiramurs (Rosabell Mongan)
3. Knight with sword and crest
4. *Parzival* main lesson book cover (Alexander Madey)

BOOK FIVE

I APPROACH THIS chapter of "marvels unparalleled" with the greatest reverence. Though eleven more chapters follow, it is the epic's most pivotal, and Parzival's true quest is only about to begin now.

Le fils du roi Gahmuret achieved his initial quest of becoming a knight with the greatest of ease, largely due to his impressive heritage. Though he made stark mistakes on the way, he received lucky breaks. He was tutored in knighthood, "won" a wife beyond compare, achieved renown and wide recognition, and gained a vast kingdom. The story could end there. Outwardly he has everything that a person could desire, yet Lady Adventure has more in store for him—as she does for us all. Fame and fortune mean little if the inner life is left wanting. It is a symptom of our age, amply exemplified all around us. Our modern age demands more. We might be successful in our job, but what is our calling?

The Angler

"What makes night within us, may leave stars." ~ Victor Hugo

For the third time, Parzival sets out on his charger that he churlishly won from Ither of Gaheviez, and once again the horse takes charge, galloping along unrestrained. He is wholly preoccupied with thoughts of his beloved Queen Condwiramurs, more so than when he first left Gurnemanz, with sweet Liaze on his mind. And his unguided horse with the dropped reins rides even faster this time round: "[A] bird would have been hard put to it to fly the distance he rode that day" (p. 120).

In the evening, he looks for lodgment. He comes across fishermen anchored in a lake. One of them is richly attired, "wearing clothes of such quality that had he been lord of the whole earth could not have been finer" (p. 120). It is a strange and striking scene that conjures forth vivid images: a young knight at dusk, hungry and tired, coming across opulently clothed men sitting quietly in a boat on a lake. There is something incongruous and mystical about the image.

Once, I took a late afternoon stroll with my wife to the alleged Lake Brumbane near Arlesheim, Switzerland, at dusk, which, according to legend is the very lake in question—though it is now called the Öleweiher, and is much reduced.[1] On that particular evening, while imagining the scene, it came alive like never before. There were no other people around and dusk had turned to night. I could almost see the Angler's peacock-feathered headdress that suggests the stage of imaginative insight, as well as pride. Seeing those peacock feathers must have been like a prompt for Parzival to find the way to imaginative vision. He needs that vision in order to fulfill the task he does not know is his. However, it is also a warning against pride, which creeps in everywhere, especially into the souls of seekers.

When Parzival asks about accommodation, the Angler makes it clear that there is no lodging for thirty miles around in this wilderness, but if he

---

1 Werner Greub, *Wolfram von Eschenbach und die Wirklichkeit des Grals*, (Dornach, Switzerland : Philosophish-Antroposophisher Verlag, 1974), p. 336.

carries on straight along the path, he will come to a castle nearby. "Ask them to lower the drawbridge and open up the road to you" (p. 120). He adds that he must remain on the path for one can easily be led astray.

We are reminded of the first time Parzival asked a Fisherman for accommodation just after he left Sigune. Yet, the two scenes, though analogous, could not be more dissimilar in quality. In both it is evening, he has ridden all day, he's tired and hungry, and he asks for accommodation. In some translations, the Angler is referred to as a Fisherman. However, the first Fisherman is boorish and a churl, whereas the other is regal and garbed in finery. The first answers, "I'd not give you half a loaf in thirty years" (p. 82), underscoring the fact that he would never be generous without some reward. The Angler on the other hand, says, "I shall take care of you myself this evening" (p. 122). It's interesting that the number thirty appears in both descriptions. During this block I do partially touch on the symbolism of numbers, and it's worth noting that the number thirty is also mentioned in regard to the fortress's unassailable position: It would "not have ruffled its defenders once in thirty years" (p. 121), followed a bit later with, "the inhabitants of thirty lands could not have wrung such a flood from their eyes" (p. 124). Apart from meaning a great number (as in "many-many"), thirty is also associated with cycles and circles, symbolizing completion, suggesting the fixed and continuous nature of life. One only has to think of the thirty days in a month. However, there is also a definite relationship to Saturn, which takes almost thirty years to orbit around the sun (29.4 Earth years). In Book Five, the forces of Saturn play an important role, forces which delve deeply into the *past*, in connection with a person's karma, and how it interweaves and connects with others and transforms into future impulses. His horse—the unconscious intelligence within his will—has led Parzival to this nodal point of his life. "The whole working of the Saturn sphere is conditioned by the fact that in all the Beings of this sphere there is an intense, all-pervading consciousness of the past, and more or less unconsciousness of the immediate present."[2] Parzival certainly

2 Rudolf Steiner, *Karmic Relationships: Esoteric Studies*, Vol. VII (London: Rudolf Steiner Press, 1973), p. 52.

is not conscious of why he has been led to this particular place, which will determine his entire future. Often it is only in retrospect that we recognize these pivotal points in our lives, as Steiner suggests in the above quote.

Parzival rides on, making sure to stay on the path. When he arrives at the formidable castle, he tells the page in attendance that the Angler has sent him. Forthwith, the drawbridge is lowered and he is welcomed into the castle.

Where is the Grail Castle? It is a question that scholars have asked for centuries with no conclusive answers, though a tremendous amount of literature has been written on the subject. Rudolf Steiner makes it clear on numerous occasions that the Grail castle was in the remote areas of northern Spain, and that the first two Grail castles were in the Sierra de la Demanda,[3] located in the mountains through which the Camino de Santiago winds in the north. Steiner told Ilona Schubert that a later castle "was at Montségur in south-west France," [4] giving specific indications about its location. Werner Greub in his book *Wolfram von Eschenbach und die Wirklichkeit de Grals,* places Munsalvæsche near the Hermitage in Arlesheim.

The one does not necessarily exclude the other, as the Grail does change its location. Furthermore, though outer locations existed, well-hidden and off the beaten track, they should be considered in a more internal sense. At the end of the epic, it is intimated that the Grail will disappear once more from middle Europe and move to the East, to the realm of Prester John. In the end it must be found in our own hearts.

Parzival's Welcome

"We are made to tell the world that there are no outsiders. All are welcome: black, white, red, yellow, rich, poor, educated, not educated, male, female, gay, straight, all, all, all. We all belong to this family, this human family, God's family." ~ Archbishop Desmond Tutu

3 *See Paths of Christian Mysteries* (section four).

4 Ilona Schubert, *Reminiscences of Rudolf Steiner and Marie Steiner-von Sivers* (Temple Lodge Press, 1991), p. 60.

Parzival's growth, stage of development, or task can be gleaned from the various receptions he receives at the respective castles: ridicule and amusement at Arthur's court; disbelief and curiosity at Guernemanz's; rejection, indifference, and finally hope on entering Belrepeire; and an exceptionally courteous, warm, and generous welcome at the Angler's fortified stronghold. I ask the students to think back and share examples of how they were received when they arrived at a new place, such as a school, sport's team, summer camp, or even at a party. What did they notice? Were they welcomed with warmth and interest, or with hostility and antipathy, or simply ignored, left to their own devices? Could they get a sense of how their welcome would affect their stay? How did they comport themselves, based on their surroundings and treatment? These conversations, in conjunction with Parzival's development, can help to make the students more aware of their own lives and take note of significant details that otherwise might have escaped them.

What Parzival does not immediately perceive is their grief and sorrow, just as the famine in Belrepeire did not fully register with him initially. His faculty to read what is unfolding in front of him is still underdeveloped and will continue throughout his entire sojourn at the Grail castle. The inhabitants hide their sadness behind their warm and eager treatment, as they help him dismount, show him to his chamber, take care of his horse, unarm him, and hand him Princess Repanse de Shoye's precious purple cloak, still warm from her body (a touching detail). They explain that his clothes have not yet been cut for him, which suggests that he was expected, just not quite so soon. In short, they take care of all his needs while putting on a sincere and friendly front. Parzival is shown honor and respect, except for one occasion.

At the appointed time a gentleman, known for his jests and wit, summons Parzival in a belittling tone of anger and arrogance to join his host. Instinctively Parzival feels for his sword, but not finding it, clenches his fist so tightly that blood seeps from underneath his fingernails into the cloak, which causes a blemish. Likewise, he will stain the entire company at the court of the Grail King by the end of the evening. It's a small but telling scene. It shows us that he is still impulsive though he has learned to restrain himself, barely. Parzival is still slow to read social cues, for the man who mocked him is "licensed to jest" (p. 122). Discussing the reading of social cues in class can offer some amusing anecdotes from the students. The scene is a warning and admonition to not only be and remain awake but to act and respond accordingly. Jesters of the Shakespearean ilk are often prophetic, speaking words of truth. If we listen to life, we are often given signals, which, however, are easy to miss. They come in all forms, such as premonitions of things to come and subtle signposts, stirring us to be prepared. All too often we only recognize them in retrospect. We've all had them. Nevertheless, they can make us more aware in the future, even if we've overlooked the "wake-up" signs in the past. In Parzival's case it was meant to tell him that the Angler is now ready to receive him, and the jester is basically saying, "Don't screw this up! You've been warned." His anger and scorn are nothing compared to what will confront Parzival later because he did not heed the "welcome" sign—the call to act fittingly.

The Grail Ceremony

"Every moment of light and dark is a miracle."[5] ~ Walt Whitman

Every aspect of the Grail ceremony is choreographed down to the last detail. Everything counts, nothing is arbitrary. It is obvious that this ritual, observed before by the others, gains in meaning and is fraught with implications during Parzival's presence.

Parzival is led *up* the stairs to a spacious hall, hung with one hundred chandeliers, each one holding many candles high above their heads, like a firmament of gleaming stars. The scintillating light is enhanced by innumerable crystals and lit candles in sconces along the walls. A hundred couches, decked out with costly quilts, fill the hall, evenly spaced. Each couch seats four knights. Three large fireplaces burning aloe wood give off warmth and fragrance. The lord of the castle, Anfortas the Angler, in

5 From Whitman's poem "Miracles."

painful repose in front of the central fire, beckons Parzival to sit beside him. Though the hall is a picture of riches and lavish luxury, sorrow pervades the air, underscored by a page running in bearing a lance from whose steel point blood gushes down along the shaft—a conscious allusion to the centurion Longinus who pierced the side of Christ. This poignant rite sharpens the prevailing grief, causing a weeping and a wailing from hundreds of throats in the great wide hall, stilled only at his departure. Parzival does not understand what he sees: *What does it all mean? Why the magnitude of sorrow in this palace? What place is this? What is the source of this all-pervading grief?* He has questions but does not ask.

The choreographed observance continues with groups of fair maidens entering the wide hall through a steel door thrown open: two maidens, holding golden candelabras, followed by two more maidens carrying ivory trestles, which they place in front of the lord—all four dressed in gowns of *brown-reddish* wool; eight ladies in two groups of four, dressed in *green* samite robes from Azagouc,[6] carry in a garnet stone slab for a table top that they set on the trestles, as well as more candles; six ladies, two of them carrying a pair of knives, the others candles; six more maidens wearing gowns of *gold* enter. After the entrance of the twenty-four ladies, Princess Repanse de Schoye enters, bearing the *thing* ("*dinc*") called the Grail, this perfection of Paradise, beyond anything found on earth—vision and manifestation of the deepest and most profound wish ("*Wunsch*") in a human's heart. Radiant Repanse de Schoye places the Grail before the ailing Anfortas. Parzival observes it all, yet his gaze is on the Grail Bearer rather than on the illimitable and unfathomable Grail, thinking only that he is wearing her cloak. Sometimes, like Parzival, we don't see what is of true import. We miss the most essential elements that confront us—the core of what is right in front of us. The cloak, that which is an outer garment meant to dress and enclose, has more power over Parzival than the Grail. His own is not yet made. Parzival is not yet worthy of wearing the earthly sheath, the costly veil of one as sublime as Repanse de Schoye, chosen to bear the inscrutable

6 An allusion to the African kingdom once ruled by Isenhart and won by Gahmuret.

unearthly perfection. He is wearing borrowed perception. True insight is not yet his. He lacks the necessary inner maturity.

Often, we hear secrets, but do not understand or recognize them as such. We might be in the proximity of the greatest treasure but fail to acknowledge it for what it is worth. The mysterious Grail is within his reach, yet his mind is on the Grail bearer instead of the "thing" itself. How many times do we bypass the most notable and precious moments of our lives? How many times do we miss the miraculous, including the small daily miracles that would leave us in awe if we pondered them? Parzival, when he was still a dull fool could not gauge the worth of Jeschute's priceless brooch, thus letting it slip from his hands. Now he cannot fathom the greatest of miracles displayed right in front of him. Repanse is the "Spreader of Joy" as her name indicates, but through his inactivity he will become the "Spreader of Sorrow." As yet he is unable to recognize that which transcends "all earthly perfection" (p. 125).

The crowned Princess then takes her place at the center of the maidens, twelve on either side of her. She radiates like the sun shining on the earth. The plants and the starry firmament are expressed in the color of their gowns. Parzival, though he misses another cue, is given a few more opportunities to *see* and *respond.*

The beardless youth becomes a witness to the consecrated unfolding of the otherworldly splendor surrounding the Grail and the nourishment that it offers to all, each person receiving the victuals they most wish for: "whatever one stretched out one's hand for in the presence of the Grail, it was waiting, one found it all ready and to hand—dishes warm, dishes cold, newly-fangled dishes and old favourites, the meat of beasts both tame and wild. . . " (p. 126). The Grail supplies all the nourishment one could hope for in this world and in the "Heavenly Kingdom." Parzival absorbs it all, how the "noble company partook of the Grail's hospitality" (p. 127). Though he recognizes the wonder of the transpiring display, he refrains from asking questions, remembering Gurnemanz's counsel not to ask too many questions. He is still adhering to outer authority. However, he rationalizes, thinking that answers might reveal themselves, especially if it turns out that his stay will last as long as it had with Gurnemanz.

At this point a student once interrupted angrily, stating, "Gurnemanz didn't say he should *not* ask any questions, just not *too many*". He's again taking things too literally, just like he did with his mother. Aaagh!" I agreed and ensured her that we would get back to discussing the theme of *questions* at length.

At that very moment, a page comes running up holding a magnificent and priceless sword in his hand, the hilt adorned with a ruby (a poetic and pictorial response comparable to the outrage of the student). Anfortas presents it to Parzival, extolling its virtues in battle: "Whenever you put it to the test in battle, it will stand you in good stead" (p. 127). Anfortas, who has not said much till now, clearly states how he took it to battle before it was God's will to wound his body, adding that he hopes it will make amends for any want of hospitality he might have endured. Eschenbach cannot resist a comment at this point, which underscores the gravity of Parzival's lapse: "Alas, that he asked no question then. . . . For when he was given the sword, it was to prompt him to ask a Question" (p. 127). Not only concerning Anfortas' suffering—the foremost question—but many more: regarding the Grail, the splendor around him, the ceremony, the procession of maidens, the castle in the wilderness, the grief of the people, the bleeding lance, the ruby hilted sword, on and on. Eschenbach's statement reinforces the student's perceptive outrage.

Parzival's silence—his non-responsiveness—puts an abrupt end to the ceremony. It marks the turning point of the entire story. He has just added to his culpability without knowing what he has done—or rather, not done. For all his knightly excellence, he remains dull of heart when it counts the most. From now on, he will consciously have to deal with the consequences of his actions. He is about to cross a major threshold of his development, leading him to a series of self-confrontations, where he will be forced to wake up to himself and consciously choose his subsequent courses of action.

From then on, everything transpires in *reverse* order, which, for him, will continue beyond his time in the castle, and lead him to witness the effects of his actions. However, just before the door closes and the maidens complete carrying everything from the hall, Parzival catches a glimpse of the most beautiful old misty haired man he has ever seen, lying on a couch. Wolfram promises that he will reveal the identity of the person at a later and more appropriate time. As a storyteller, timing is everything, especially in regard to important aspects of the narrative. It also suggests that Parzival is not yet ready or worthy to know the identity of this person who left such an impression on him.

Forthwith, Parzival is ushered off to bed in his chamber, where he spends a night riddled with nightmares that foreshadow future suffering, analogous to his mother's nightmare that presaged her own insurmountable suffering. Parzival does not yet have access to his own *inner* fire, which would have prompted him to freely ask the Question—out of himself—symbolized by the red ruby hilt. This dimness of heart unleashed the torturous nightmares. The young knight might be able to wield a sword better than the best of them, but his skills with the *inner* sword of the word are sorely lacking. He needs the help of the fiery East to kindle his heart with tongues of flames. We recall Belacane's fiery ruby crown of ancient wisdom.

He wakes in a sweat, and finds himself alone and untended. Succumbing to a few more hours of restless sleep, he finally gets up, still alone, though his armor is laid out for him. Confused, he questions what is going on,

whereas the night before he was unable to ask even one question. These questions come across as angry complaints rather than a real interest for the place and what it might mean. He is still too self-absorbed. He senses that something is amiss and has changed, but he has no idea that he is the core cause of his own present predicament. While Parzival is forced to dress and arm himself without any help, he thinks presciently, "I fancy there is toil in store for me today, now that I am awake" (p. 130). Little does he realize how true that is. Before leaving, he runs through the castle, screaming his indignation at being abandoned, and is furious when he observes the trampled ground, the tracks leading from the castle. Clearly, he has been left behind, which he experiences as an insult, especially as he considers himself a knight of superior skills. Anger, we know, is an emotion that can have an awakening quality, but it tends to be deflective, pointing the finger outwards instead of inwards—the true source of his rage.

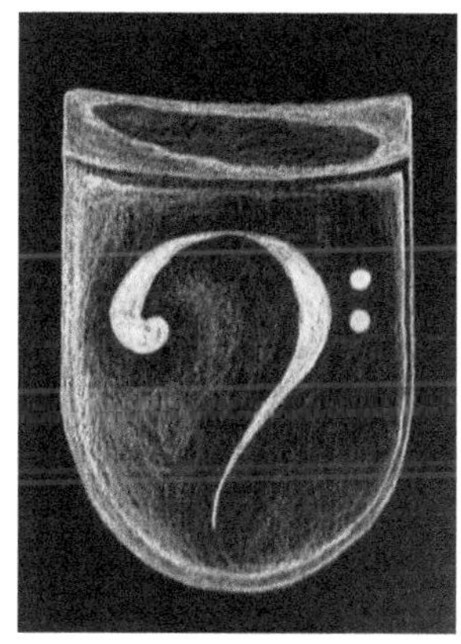

Finding the gates wide open, he rides out, hoping to catch up with the army. As he trots briskly over the drawbridge the page pulls it up sharply, almost causing his horse to topple, shouting after Parzival, "Damn you, wherever the sun lights your path . . . You silly Goose! Why didn't you open your gob and ask my lord the Question? You've let slip a marvellous prize" (p. 131). When Parzival wants to know the meaning of his words, he's answered with silence. He's got to answer that question himself. Parzival's life has unequivocally taken a turn. His chance of witnessing the Grail has now left him bereft of happiness. "If trouble is now rousing him to wakefulness, he has so far been unused to it, he has not known much sorrow as yet" (p. 131). By not asking the Question, he has precipitated his own Quest. The true *journey into the interior* has begun.

The event at the Grail Castle needs to be digested, discussed, and given its full due before continuing. Ideally, one should let the students sleep on what they have heard, allowing the mystery of the ceremony to sink in. I might pause at the end of class and ask, "Have you ever experienced anything remotely like this before? What can we make of it? Why does the asking of the Question play such a weighty role? Can you glean its significance? What do you make of the Grail ceremony? Is there anything in your life that you can recognize as having Grail qualities? If yes, how would you describe them? Think about these questions and we'll discuss further tomorrow."

Over the years the general sentiment from the students has been: *What's the big deal about Parzival not asking the question?* Even Richard Wagner, who wrote the opera *Parsifal,* had the same sentiment, finding it silly that Anfortas could be healed by a mere question. It comes up without fail and we proceed to look at the theme of "questions" from many different angles. What kind of questions are there? Can we differentiate between important and trivial questions? When is it appropriate to ask questions, when not? What attitude prevailed during the Middle Ages or ancient cultures in regard to questions? The Catholic Church, for instance, rejected questions. Science lives off questions. Yet, science also rejects or dismisses certain questions, especially in regard to the spirit, which science tends to relegate to the sphere of religion, or, at best, psychology. However, if there is the science of matter, then logically speaking, there ought to be a science of the spirit, with its own underlying laws. These types of perspectives and questions are the lifeblood of humanities classes, and I thrive on seeing the students come to life during these deliberations and dialogues, which can burst into dramatic debates. The students often include what they have read and heard from cultures from around the world. Over the years, without fail, I have found that the students largely believe in some form of spirituality or higher power, though there are only a few who claim to adhere to a specific religion, even when I know that some of their parents are religious and belong to certain denominations. The students are remarkably open, tolerant, and accepting. Questions open the doors to the inner life of the other. In turn, the depth of the question depends on the inner life of the one asking. A question is always seeking the *source* of something.

I might repeat the question of the previous day: "Have you ever experienced anything remotely similar to such a Grail ceremony?" If there is a silence, I might provocatively add that they all partake of something analogous on a regular basis, which garners quizzical looks. "The Grail gives sustenance, to each what they need. You too receive that. The Grail supplies the food—remember the food imagery throughout the epic." Now they usually begin to come up with suggestions: soul food, spiritual sustenance, offering examples like good conversations with friends, discussions, insights, "food for thought," and so forth. And then, with some further prodding, someone may suggest *sleep*. And, in a manner of speaking, sleep can be compared to the properties of the Grail. In his book *Why We Sleep*, Matthew Walker goes into great detail about the "mysteries" of sleep and "the historic failure of science to explain why we need it," adding that the "physical and mental impairment caused by one night of bad sleep dwarf those caused by an equivalent absence of food or exercise."[7] A discussion on sleep and its manifold mysterious elements also points to the dreamlike quality of the entire ceremony, hinting at its otherworldly essence. "What happens to us when we sleep? Where do we go? Why do we feel so nourished? What aspect of sleep solves our problems?" Questions along those lines not only elicit more questions, but they make the students more aware of their own sleep life, its importance (especially all those aspects that deter and keep us from sleep—and the dire consequences thereof). Of course, we don't or cannot answer all the questions, letting them echo on so that they might ponder them on their own.

Other examples students have mentioned include celebrations of a cultural or religious nature: community events, weddings, centennials or anniversary parties, even a school functions like the various fairs, a well-choreographed graduation, a play, or a meaningful concert—whatever gives soul-spiritual nourishment and where people have gone to great lengths to create an embracing, welcoming, and light-filled atmosphere.

After the discussion, we focus again on Parzival and his egregious error

7 Matthew Walker, PhD., *Why We Sleep: Unlocking the Power of Sleep and Dreams* (Scribner, 2017), pp. 6-7.

of not asking the question. The splendor of the ceremony underscores his failure to ask, which occasions the turning point in Parzival's destiny. He could have saved the Grail King but he squandered the opportunity, just like he squandered the brooch with the first Fisherman. He didn't know and could not assess the worth of either. This overarching theme of "Questions" runs throughout the block, to be focused on from different angles at different times. Many questions can be put on hold till we arrive at specific segments of the story. It allows the unanswered or unformed question to ripen within us.

After finishing this section of Book Five with a class, I once asked, "When you think back on what we've just covered so far, what has impressed or touched you the most?" We went around and everybody had something pertinent to contribute. One girl mentioned how interesting it is that Parzival thought he was seeing God when he first saw the four knights in the forest of Soltane because their armor shone so brightly in the sun—pummeling them with questions. But then, when he sees the Grail—something truly sublime and godlike, shining brighter than the sun—he does *not* ask any questions at all. She went on to say how, in the first instance, he misconstrued what he saw, but it triggered his quest to become a knight. Conversely, at the Grail ceremony, he recognized that something mystical was happening, and though he lacked the capacity to understand, it gave birth to his quest to find the Grail.

I love it when the students have these "ping" moments and truly discover something significant.

Sigune in the Linden Tree

"To love is to hold the wound always open." — Novalis

The picture of Parzival leaving the Grail Castle alone, angry, and forsaken hints at what is about to come toward him. For a while the valiant warrior follows the multiple tracks of the knights, all the while fancying himself fighting courageously in their midst, bringing them honor and proving himself worthy, a bit like a child dreaming of becoming a basketball or soccer star. However, the tracks weaken, grow faint, and finally disperse in different directions till he loses them altogether and he finds himself deserted with no outer tracks to guide him—an apt metaphor for certain aspects of our lives. The image of the tracks further suggest that we are meant to experience the episode at the Grail Castle as a waking dream. It depicts the loftiest aspects of our night life when the soul and ego ("I" consciousness), enters the mysterious realm of the spirit, which we call sleep, the place of inner nourishment. On waking, the remnants of our nightly life quickly scatter and fade—a frustratingly common experience when we try to recall and recap complex and convoluted dreams. Chasing the tracks of the Grail knights is like chasing the contents of dreams.

Instead, Parzival hears a lamenting woman's voice, and he guides his horse through the dewy grass toward the source of the sounds of woe. The sight he beholds is in strong contrast to the unbelievable splendor of the Grail Castle, though no less strange: a grief-stricken lady ensconced *in a Linden tree*, holding a reclining and embalmed knight ("*vor im ûf einer linden saz . . . ein gebalsemt ritter tôt*")[8]. It is his cousin, though he does not immediately recognize her. Interestingly enough, it is, once again, a woman's suffering that has moved his heart to speak, whereas the suffering of the Angler had left him silent.

I make a point of emphasizing the peculiar pictorial element of this scene: a woman sitting *in* a Linden tree, cradling her dead and embalmed lover. It is strange indeed and has a fairytale quality. I've been surprised at the discussions that this scene has generated. The loyalty ("*triuwe*") of her love towards Schionatulander impresses them—that she wouldn't part with him and that she goes to all the trouble of embalming him and hauling him up a tree. We have come across the Linden a number of times: his first meeting with Gurnemanz, who was sitting under a Linden tree, followed in chapter four, when he is led to a "walled in" Linden tree just before

8 Lachmann, V, 249, 14-16, p. 124.

his meeting with Condwiramurs (suggesting Condwiramurs' besieged situation of her heart and her castle). The Linden tree is a favorite of the poets from around the world and across the ages, mostly in association with romance, faithfulness, fidelity, friendship, prosperity, healing, truth, but also destiny. And Parzival's destiny is given sound direction through each of his impactful encounters with her. However, the Linden's associations with love, in the fullest sense of the word, stands out the most, pictorially confirmed by the heart-shaped leaves. The Linden is a magnificent tree, and exudes a most delicate fragrance. I recall the Linden tree in my father's backyard, with its fine scent ("*Duft*") of heaven, which the bees from his hive loved so much. The Linden or lime tree, named after the Baltic Goddess Leima, is also associated with marriage and death, which, in this case, fits Sigune. It is evident that Eschenbach is not content to have Sigune merely *under* the tree, but embraced fully within its loving boughs, forms, and fragrance. The German original word is "ûf" or "auf," which confirms that she is consciously meant to be placed *in* the tree.

It is Sigune who once again recognizes him through his *voice*. Due to grief, she is now almost bald and robbed of youth's luster. Parzival perceives and absorbs this wretched panorama of loyalty, fidelity, and uncompromising love. Compared to their first encounter, it is a bleak and unadorned pietà that he is confronted with. However, this enhanced portrayal of loyalty will serve him well as he continues on his journey, a signet impressing itself on his heart to safeguard against the possibility of falling into restlessness like his father. This metamorphosed pietà image is like a consecrated cautionary prayer: *May you be true to Condwiramurs as Sigune is true to Schionatulander. May you remain loyal to your quest—the one that soon will spur your horse.* Schionatulander, even in death, or because of his death, will accompany Parzival through his travails and serve him as Schionatulander once served Gahmuret on his second excursion to the Baruch of Baghdad. The potent image will be like a portal through which the being of Schionatulander can support Parzival. Though Sigune talks to him and sets him on the right though painful course, Schionatulander's influence will be ongoing through the inner picture of him resting in her devoted arms—a vision of steadfastness. Through her undying love, his spirit is near and nourishing, and can act as a guide to Parzival from the beyond.

Sigune partially clues him up on the secrets of the Grail Castle, its history and significance. In their first encounter, she gave Parzival his name, and this time she gives Parzival the names of the Angler, the castle, and the surrounding territory, putting things in context for him. Knowing the names of things is empowering. What was generic becomes specific. It lets one identify with the outer world more consciously. Though Parzival hears, he does not understand the full import of her words. Not yet.

When Sigune sees the gift of the sword, she assumes he has asked the Question. She relates to Parzival the special attributes of this sword: that it "will stay whole for one blow but at the second it will fall apart" (p. 134), explaining that it must be taken to a spring, named "Lac," before dawn and "wetted" by the water in order to make it whole once more—and far stronger than ever before. The sword, like the Grail, has renewing power. They belong together as do the tree and water of life, yin-yang, anima-animus, straight and curved, light and dark, vessel and lance—the polarities. The Grail has a more yin like quality—rounded and feminine—and the sword has the masculine yang attribute.

Sigune's words regarding this precious sword are especially pertinent to teachers. We might have a successful class, where every word is absorbed and well-received, leaving an indelible impression. However, the exact same lesson on another day with another class might be an utter flop. We always have to return to the "Lac" and reforge our sword. It's what the sword of the *word* demands. Only then will our lessons hit their mark. I have taken this lesson to heart. A student once suggested that the sword could represent pride and the need for humility: "The sword needs to break to prevent the person becoming too prideful." She'd made a pertinent point. Teachers, too, have to guard against pride—it's easy to become glib, relying too comfortably on past achievements and our accumulated personal knowledge. If we do not renew our presentations, if we do not sufficiently prepare, then the lesson can fall flat and we are in danger of becoming stale, dull, outdated. Sometimes, we get too attached to an idea, and are unable or unwilling to let go, to reimagine and present the material in a new and fresh manner. Sometimes we don't even recognize our failure. Each lesson we teach is a bit like a meal, and after each meal we need to wash the dishes before reuse—every time!

Curiously, Sigune adds that it must be accompanied by a magic spell, which she intuits he does not yet know ("left it behind"), though when he has learned it, "good fortune abounding will grow and bear seed with you forever." It intimates that he will learn it, and that it may even become a prerequisite for his success. (For me the spell is an invocation that allows the inexplicable to take place—Grace). A magic spell will never work with the mere parroting of the words. It needs the power of life and heart behind it. Parzival's power of speech is, as yet, sorely underdeveloped, which becomes clear moments later when she talks about the wonders, marvels, and splendors that will be his *if* he has asked the question, which she presumes he has. However, he answers, "I did not ask it" (p. 135).

This spoken admittance changes everything. It is the pivotal *outer* turning point, the very moment when he is made conscious of his failure. The Question would have served as the magic spell. The whole morning was filled with clues, cues, and signs, which did not quite register within him. Now he becomes aware of the *crisis* of his own making. Medically speaking, it is the "critical" (Greek: *krisis*) turning point in the development of a disease—for better or for worse. Crisis denotes the change that must come, indisputably. Crisis separates (Greek: from *krinein*) and sifts out (*krei*, to sieve, to distinguish). Crisis, like catharsis, always signifies purification, and for Parzival it is the beginning of his long journey to consciously purify himself, which calls for decisive actions. No one can attain self-knowledge without purification. The ancient mystery centers demanded it from without; now it must come from within. The developmental path of purification is a free choice.

At once Sigune chastises Parzival in no uncertain terms, her language harsh, merciless, and as sharp as the most lethal sword—every word piercing through his heart. She calls him dishonorable and accursed, stating outrightly that he has "failed so abjectly to ask," adding, "You should have had compassion on your host . . . and inquired about his suffering. You live, yet as far as Heaven's favor goes, you are dead" (p. 135). Parzival tries to defend himself, but she dismisses him, refusing to talk to him anymore. Her words are words of truth. Truth can harm, but ultimately heal. No doubt: *He has failed.* Her incisive and peremptory words have launched him headlong into a *crisis* of no return. The crisis ushers in a renewed departure along the untrodden road to the "Self," though he will only succeed if he has the necessary will and courage to find and redeem himself.

Failure is painful. Failure is a ubiquitous human shortcoming. No one can escape the curse (or cure) of failure. Failure wakes us up to our own deficiencies, our weaknesses, our errors, our unconscious selves. Failure leads and thrusts us inward. Failure is an I-bending self-confrontation. We fear failure, yet it's a necessary, irrevocable, and inescapable part of life. Failure is an infallible companion. Failure is a directive, a corrective, a dictate from destiny. We avoid failure but need failure in order to not fail in the future. Even the gods fail. It is only now that his true initiation begins. His separation from his mother and Soltane was more like an instinctive drive, a subconscious desire to become a knight, a deeply ingrained hereditary impulse, though essential for his individual destiny. Now, however, it becomes an experience. "Initiation itself is separation from a state of continuity, of everything familiar and secure into a state of disruption, uncertainty, and dilemma."[9]

Discussing failure with the students can be profound, both in quality and content. Writing poems about failure is an artistic way of introducing a discussion, in groups or singly. Often the poems lead to unexpected and surprising insights on the topic—with enhanced effects when read aloud. It can be reassuring for students to know that failure is a part of life, that we all suffer the pangs of failure and that failures can be overcome (especially for the melancholics).

9 Bishop, p. 27.

Jeschute and Orilus Reunited

There lives in me an image
Of all that I should be.
Until I have become it
My heart is never free.
~ Angelus Silesius

PARZIVAL HAD LIVED very much in the moment during his time in Soltane, which initially determined his behavior at the outset of his quest to become a knight, especially in regard to his mother, Jeschute, and the Red Knight, where it was a matter of "out of sight, out of mind." His memory was triggered by his surroundings as were his actions and his speech. However, we observe a gradual internalization in Parzival, effecting a marked change in actions and speech, which gives birth to reflection that gradually leads to the faculty of thought. It's a painful path that necessitates loss and self-confrontation. We saw it revealed in his yearning for Liaze, followed more strongly by his love pangs for Condwiramurs, and thirdly, when Sigune chastises him for not having asked the Question.

Alone again, after his outright dismissal from Sigune, he is caught up in self-reproach: "It was a cause of great remorse to the warrior that he had been slow to ask the Question as he sat beside the sorrowing king" (p. 135). His failure makes him think and it is no longer a matter of "out of sight, out of mind." His failure occupies his mind, weighs on his chest, and sits like undigested food in his stomach. The students, of course, know Parzival's state of mind all too well. It is especially poignant when we are not used to these kinds of self-reflections. With Cunneware he had witnessed someone suffering because of him, though he had not done anything, nor was expected to do anything. Now he is suffering himself because of an action he was expected to fulfill, but did NOT. As far as his inner life is concerned, he is still a fool—or a "silly goose," in the words of the page—even though he has successfully graduated from Gurnemanz's school. True thinking must go beyond the parroting of someone else's lessons, codes, or creeds.

It demands true understanding and not merely the adoption of someone else's dogma or belief system. Instead of listening to an outside authority, he himself must become the author of his decisions and actions.

His self-reproach is accompanied by the heat of the day that forces him to remove his helmet, leaving his head exposed, clearly indicating his detached thinking faculty. It is more difficult to think in hot weather. We are once again reminded of Gahmuret and how he met his end when he removed his helmet in the heat of the day (and fray), or how Ither of Gaheviez had met his end through the opening of the vizor. In order to overcome his inner dullness, he is required to "make good," and redeem his thoughtless actions. Students recognize this dilemma. In life we are always given the opportunity to redeem ourselves, yet we often miss our chances, or fail to recognize the moment when it comes, or simply lack the integrity or will power. The tracks are there if we look for them.

Parzival lost the tracks leading from Munsalvæsche (not ready to ride with the Grail Knights), but finds new tracks, meant for him, co-inciding with the path he now finds himself on. He first has to sort out his own mess before he's worthy to join the ranks of the Grail knights. As mentioned, from the moment he failed to ask the Question, things have been moving in a *reverse* order, starting with the Grail Bearer and the ladies leaving the Great Hall, followed by Sigune, and now his second encounter with Jeschute. Sigune and Schionatulander gave him an image of loyalty and steadfastness, and now he is confronted with a heartrending image of the consequences of his actions.

Eschenbach goes into great detail about her pitiful outer appearance to make his point. Parzival does not recognize her immediately, like he had not recognized Sigune. And like Sigune, Jeschute is first to recognize him—by his voice, the instrument and vessel of speech. Surprisingly, she does not chastise him for his past actions and even tries to protect him from possible death, should her husband Orilus see him. She is depicted as absolutely pure, innocent of any ill will, which only serves to emphasize the uncouth *thoughtlessness* of Parzival's deed in the pavilion, which he has forgotten. Initially, he firmly denies her accusations—"[No] woman has been put to

shame by me" (p. 156)—and claims not to know her till she reminds him. How often have we denied something, possibly with great vehemence, before realizing with shameful shock that we are indeed guilty? It's a topic worth discussing with the students and is sure to sink in.

The meeting with Jeschute is a test for Parzival, for though she is described as a wretched victim of abuse, she is nevertheless depicted in an openly sensuous manner—partly naked, exposed breasts of the most exquisite shape, dazzling skin, red hot lips—just as in the first encounter. She is compared to a swan, which puts her on the initiatory level of the "Swan," one below the "Pelican"[10] (Belacane). This time Parzival takes pity on her, offering his surcoat so she can cover her humiliating nakedness, which she declines. Instead of taking any advantage of her state, which he once did, he now displays knightly chivalry, ready and eager to fight Orilus who is approaching. Her inner devastation is conveyed through the description of her tattered and torn shift and the pathetic nag she has been forced to ride.

Eschenbach describes Duke Orilus as a most formidable knight, making allusions to Gaheviez, describing his costly armor, highlighting his strength and achievements, making him appear as an almost invincible foe. Orilus is recognized through the heraldic emblem of the rearing dragon, portrayed on his shield with ninety nine more rearing dragons on his surcoat and all over the embroidered cloth that covers his charger. Fighting Orilus, Parzival is fighting the dragon within himself as well as the outer dragon.

10 According to the alchemist Basilius Valentinus

He is fighting to redeem himself for his shameful deed against Jeschute. Moreover, though he does not know it, he is also avenging the death of his uncle Galoes, and the slaying of Schionatulander at the hands of Orilus. Orilus has met his match in Parzival. After a fierce and prolonged battle, the dragon-knight is defeated, bearing in mind that Parzival himself was associated with the dragon from the moment Herzeloyde had that awful nightmare on the eve of Gahmuret's death.

Almost every year we have students from China or the East in our class, and for them the dragon has a completely different meaning. The dragon is seen as a divine being that represents ancient paradisal wisdom, reminding humans of their celestial origin, spurring them on to pursue knowledge and wisdom. In the West the dragon has different connotations, though its power, wisdom, and knowledge has never been doubted. The West's dragon not only represents the loss of ancient wisdom, but the uncontrolled urges and desires arising from the soul's depths. The rise of individualism all too often succumbs to self-centered arrogance and self-absorption. And this dragon-fire all too easily results in chaos, destruction, suffering, and devastation. With the rise of independence, the lower urges tend to dominate, which is an ingrained characteristic of our scientific and enlightened age. This dominating trend will persist if it is not curtailed by a shared consciousness to nurture humanity through the warmth of love, rather than the heat of devastation. In the imaginative depiction of Saint Michael or his earthly counterpart, Saint George, the need is reflected. We *all* carry that dragon within us, both the Eastern or Western, the destructive dragon needing to be transformed into the other. Once transformed the dragon will again represent wisdom. With Cunneware, we have an individuality who has achieved the taming of the dragon. It will take a lot more for Parzival to transform his own dragon, but his conquest over Orilus is a start.

Parzival, through his victory, is able to reunite Jeschute with Orilus. In the rocky cell of a hermit—which will prove to be the place of his most profound transformation in the future—Parzival swears that Jeschute is an innocent woman, admitting that he stole the ring and brooch from her when he was a "young fool—no man—not yet grown to years of discretion"

(p. 141). Through his confession, Parzival convinces Orilus to forgive Jeschute and she gladly returns to him. It takes courage to confess and own up to one's offenses.

Many students voice their outright indignation that Jeschute would return to a man who has treated her with such blatant disrespect. Though I try to soften the picture by suggesting that it could be seen in a more symbolic and mythical sense, I too am irked by her swift acquiescence. The students point out that so many women return to their partners even after years of domestic violence and abuse.

The impression we are left with is that from now on their relationship will be harmonious, loving, and trusting. Parzival has accepted his guilt and matured, but at a steep price—the suffering of an innocent victim. He'd caused harm and hurt. He'd reached out, which is a start. However, even with the best of outcomes, there is always a loss, indicated by the fact that though Parzival could give back the ring, he'd squandered the brooch. Growth and development come at a cost, leaving scars. Relationships go through difficulties and misunderstandings happen, as do false accusations. They have to be worked through. Jeschute and Orilus are a couple who were able to forgive each other and transform and strengthen their relationship.

Moreover, there is something moving about the change of heart in such a proud and unlikeable character as Orilus. Parzival avenged Orilus for his ill treatment of Jeschute and the killing of Galoes, but simultaneously redeemed him. Yet, without Jeschute's honesty, truth, and power of forgiveness, none of the change could have transpired. She recognized the higher, nobler selves in both Parzival and Orilus. And that is the essence of this scene. Through seeing their potential to change, she frees aspects of themselves, allowing them to glimpse an inkling of their true and authentic selves. She was willing to accept and literally ride out the soul sacrifice in order to help others onto the next step of their development. Her spirit fortified her soul in order to endure the indignities that her body had to endure.

Parzival parts ways with the reunited couple, taking a checkered lance with him that had been forgotten in the hermit's cave. Jeschute and Orilus ride off to King Arthur's court, where Orilus has promised Parzival to serve Lady Cunneware, his sister. She, in turn, frees him of his submission, saying that he would always come to her service if need be. He is the last of the knights Parzival sends to Cunneware, the lady who guards the spring. Through sending the knights to her, he has kept in touch with the source—the memory of her umbilical laughter keeping him on the path to honor.

Who Are Sigune and Schionatulander?

"Everything visible clings to the invisible—the audible to the inaudible—feeling to the impalpable. Perhaps the thinkable in the unthinkable."[11] ~ Novalis

The historic personalities behind Sigune and Schionatulander are not known, nor are there any extant documents about them.[12] However, some brief verbal indications by Rudolf Steiner regarding these legendary chaste lovers throw light on their karmic background, as well as some elucidations in his lecture series on karmic relationships.[13] Though their lives were cut short, they play an essential role in *Parzival*, and, in context of their previous and subsequent incarnations, a significant part in world history. Rudolf Steiner is identified to have been the legendary character of Schionatulander in a previous incarnation, and Ita Wegman as Sigune. Exhaustive research on the series of incarnations of these two individuals has appeared in book form, published initially only for members of the Anthroposophical Society, but now readily available to all. It clearly outlines how Rudolf Steiner and Ita Wegman are linked to Schionatulander and

11 *Wunderworte: Mit Novalis durch das Jahr*, Hrsg. von Florizn Roder (translated by the author) (Verlag Freies Geistesleben), p. 23

12 Stein does suggest that Sigune's name is Elisabeth, based on Schionatulander calling her Elisabeth, her guardian Saint, which was often the baptismal name in the Middle Ages.

13 In 1924 Steiner gave over 80 lectures on the theme of karma, published in eight volumes called *Karmic Relationships: Esoteric Studies.*

Sigune respectively.[14] In the interim, other authors have written extensively about Steiner's various incarnations and his connection to Ita Wegman (a close colleague of Steiner and leader of the Medical Section of the School of Spiritual Science). Going backwards, their joint incarnations include: Thomas of Aquinas and Reginald Piperno; Schionatulander and Sigune; Aristotle and Alexander the Great; Kratylos (student of Heraclitus in Ephesus) and Mysa (his student and member of the Mystery Center of Ephesus); and Enkidu and Gilgamesh. In this series of earthly lives, we see how they have profoundly contributed to world evolution in both thought and deed.

In their short incarnation as Schionatulander and Sigune, they are able to internalize through their connection to the Grail the wisdom they carried over from the East. Parzival starts off getting to know the world through the senses, but slowly suffers *internalization* pangs. He is guided along by the directives of Sigune. Schionatulander, in turn, guides him from the beyond. We could also call Waldorf education the pedagogy of internality, or the art of becoming inward. Only when we look out into the world and bring it into ourselves, and only when we look into ourselves and let it shine out into the world, can we become free, by controlling how we choose to act and react in the world.

When their karma led them down again [Aristotle and Alexander] on the earth . . . they lived, unknown and unheeded, in a corner of Europe not without importance for anthroposophy, dying at an early age, but gazing for a brief moment as it were through a window into the civilization of the West, receiving impressions and impulses but giving none of any significance themselves [regarding world history]. That was to come later.[15]

14 Margarete and Erich Kirchner-Brockholt, *Rudolf Steiner's Mission and Ita Wegman (*Rudolf Steiner Press, Reprint Edition, 2016).

15 Rudolf Steiner, *Karmic Relationships: Esoteric Studies* Vol. VIII, lecture of August 14, translated by D. S. Osmond. (London: Rudolf Steiner Press ,1975).

Discussion Topics, Questions

- Give examples of how you have been welcomed in various places, such as schools, institutions, gyms, parties, jobs, etc. What does it say about the respective places?
- Discuss the benefits of an imaginative understanding of the world, and how all cultures around the globe learned through stories and mythologies.
- Talk about dreams and the benefits of *Sleep*.
- What is your deepest and most profound wish?
- What nourishes us in our lives? What keeps us going?
- Discuss the reading of social cues.
- In what instances do we squander opportunities?
- Have you ever been accused of a failure of which you were not aware?
- Why does failure have such a bad reputation in our age?
- Why are people afraid of their inner reality?
- What does it take to confess and own up to a prior offense? Is it worth it?
- Examine the nature of ceremonies. What ceremonies have you experienced and how did you relate to them? What qualities did they have? What did they represent and what were they in aid of? Did you enjoy them? How were they arranged? What went into them? Who was behind them? What effect did they have on you?
- Discuss the theme of Questions. Why is it so difficult to come up with meaningful questions?

Illustrations:

1. The Öleweiher near Arlesheim, the alleged Lake Brumbane where Parzival met the Angler
2. "Why didn't you ask the Question?"
3. The unasked Question
4. Orilusfelsen or Orilus rock near Arlesheim, where Parzival and Orilus allegedly fought

BOOK SIX

PARZIVAL INITIALLY SET out on a quest to become a knight at King Arthur's court. By now Parzival has gained great renown as a knight, having sent some of the best knights to Arthur's court in Briton to surrender and serve Cunneware. Now King Arthur is the one "riding in quest of him," wishing to "invite the Red Knight to the Table Round as a companion" (p. 147). Not only is Parzival on the threshold of fully attaining his initial quest, but a reversal has taken place. Clearly, Cunneware's laughter is proving prophetic. Parzival, who has begun redeeming himself, is drawing King Arthur toward him. The name Arthur is Celtic and derived from "Art-hu." "Art" means "to plough" and "hu" means "Sun" or the "Sun God."[1] "Ar" also means "royal": Thus, Arthur, means the "Ploughman of the Sun God" or "Royal Sun." Parzival went in search of the royal sun—or the one ploughing the earth in the name of the Sun God—and is now drawing the

---

1 Richard Seddon, "The Matter of Britain, Arthur, The Grail, and Parzival," in *The Quest for the Grail* (Floris Books, 1994), p. 14.

Sun force toward him, just as in the end, he will draw the force of the Grail toward him. The other derivation is from the Welsh: *Arth Gwyr*, which suggests "Bear Hero."[2] Scholars generally associate Arthur with the Big Bear, better known as the Big Dipper—part of the northern constellation known as Ursa Major.

Parzival knows nothing of this and continues on his journey to see how his mother is faring. In that respect, Herzeloyde's wish for him to return to her is fulfilling itself. However, to truly find and reconnect with Herzeloyde, he would have to enter the invisible world and lift the myriad veils of the material world, one by one.

Wolfram reinforces and augments his various points through contrasts. Whereas in the preceding scene with Jeschute and Orilus, Parzival had to contend with the heat of the day, he now has to endure cold and unseasonable snow that has fallen heavily during the night. According to Walter Johannes Stein[3] and both the Penguin and Vintage translations of Parzival, it takes place around Michaelmas in late September. Other authors place it during May, based on King Arthur's association with that merry month, which, however, does not mean it necessarily takes place in May. Irrespective of the season, Arthur is always connected to the sun forces of springtime. Aside from the calculations that are given in both the above translations, the symbolic significance of Michaelmas makes sense, as it heralds the shortening of days—the light giving way to darkness—and the encroaching winter. Michaelmas is associated with courage, healing and justice. Furthermore, Parzival's fight with Orilus, bedecked with a hundred dragons, fits the image of Saint Michael fighting the dragon. This fiery archangel is known as the spiritual warrior fighting evil—evil in the form of a dragon. Though Parzival will imminently meet King Arthur and his retinue, it will prove not to be a time of fulfilment, blossoming, and happiness that is usually associated with spring. "Thus, the tale is of contrasting colors here, it is chequered with that of snow" (p. 147). It corresponds to the gaily colored lance that Parzival took from the hermit's

2 Christopher R. Fee, *Arthur: God and Hero in Avalon* (Reaktion Books, 2019), p. 9.

3 See "The Chronology in Wolfram's Parzival" in Stein's *The Ninth Century*, p. 306.

cell and heralds the checkered experiences he will have to endure till he once again returns to the place where he first found the painted lance.

Three Drops of Blood

As we Wander the World
We become Wounders of the World
Until we discover the Wonders of the World
~ Elryn Westerfield

THE SCENE LEADING up to and including the three drops of blood has always struck me as sweetly melancholy, sentiently romantic, and filled with tender longing and dreamy adoration, to which the students respond with deep empathy. The image of a knight in armor riding along a path "snowed under," having to maneuver randomly through rough terrain of boulders and fallen trees, conjures forth an inner world that corresponds to feelings of loneliness, yearning, confusion, obsession, and preoccupation—feelings that young people know all too well.

As Parzival rides along, he receives companionship in the form of a falcon from Arthur's camp, both having spent a night in the freezing cold. As the trees begin to thin out, he arrives at a level clearing where a thousand geese have settled. At once the falcon flies in, wounds a goose who barely escapes, seeking refuge under a solitary log, but not before letting fall three drops of blood in the fresh new snow. The goose is "too badly hurt to seek the heights" (p. 148), which perfectly encapsulates Parzival's state of mind, his pained condition of soul, and his failure

and rejection, both from the Grail Castle and Sigune. He was called "Silly Goose" by the page, and he has become the wounded goose, unable to seek the heights, which was not only Gahmuret's pursuit, but Parzival's ardent yearning from the moment he heard the singing of the birds in Soltane.

Parzival had arrived at the Grail castle unprepared, unready, and ignorant of what was asked of him. Yet, life expects things from us, even if we are not ready, especially the fast-changing modern world. These failures are wake-up calls to practice readiness for future tests and trials. Parzival proved himself to be a "goose uncooked" like so many of us in various life situations. The spirit vision of the falcon, associated with independence, speed, acute sight, light, and swift thought, is lost to a goose, which is a more earthbound bird (the falcon is often used interchangeably with hawk, and hunting with a falcon is called hawking). The goose, in contrast to the swan, represents the loss of the soul's ancient wisdom. They both have white feathers but are polar opposites. The goose embodies earth-consciousness, which is also important in the evolution of humanity, and which, through the intellect, can glitter with cleverness, but is also subject to deceit, cunning, and inner coldness.

The three red drops of blood on the pristine white snow form a powerful and transporting image, reminding the Red Knight of Condwiramurs, his wife, his love—her fair skin, the red blush of cheeks and chin, and the black hair. The vision turns his gaze from an outer world into an inner one. It is generally interpreted as Parzival's inability to master the pangs of love—succumbing to his feelings rather than overcoming them. Granted, he loses himself entirely in her visage, mesmerized by the contrasting image of the red blood on the white snow, surrounded by the black tree trunks. However, it is more than a sentient memory; the image serves as a connection with her spirit and thus offers sustenance. He is deeply hurt and in need of comfort. Losing himself in the vision of Condwiramurs gives him the consolation he needs. Through the red trinity, she becomes the supportive conduit of love, even from a distance, functioning as a healing salve for the wound of his own making. Outwardly, he is the unconquerable knight, but inwardly he is defenseless and wounded. Inner vulnerability is new to him, just as it is for many 11th graders who tend to withdraw and hide within themselves. Parzival's knightly heritage is a gift, but his soul-spiritual capacities are in a state of conscious development and strengthening. It is like the sixteen-petaled lotus, where eight are a gift from the past, and eight are in need of development, which takes effort. He is dependent on Condwiramurs' soul-sustenance, for he has not the strength to ease himself, not yet. Mistress Love can lead people into violence and conflict, but also supply an image that is filled with the soul-nourishing power of love to alleviate the pain, at least for a while. Parzival, as yet, still lacks the forces of independent thinking. He failed because he adhered too strictly to Gurnemanz's advice. Condwiramurs' love assuages his loss and alleviates his pain, similarly to an anesthetic, induced, in this case, by the administering of the three drops of blood.

Fairy tales often make use of blood imagery, and in "The Goose Girl" retold by the Brothers Grimm, we have a number of pertinent parallels (see also "The Juniper Tree"). Like Herzeloyde, the mother of the Goose Girl is also a widow. She cuts herself and lets three drops of blood fall onto a white cloth, which ensures that the connection to the most sacred forces of her lineage is kept intact, and that her daughter is protected and can call on her mother in times of duress. The same can be said for "Snow White and the Seven Dwarfs," where the Queen pricked herself with the needle while sewing, causing three drops of blood to fall upon the snow. Taken by the beauty of the blood in the snow, the Queen wishes for a daughter that would be as white as snow, as red as blood, and as black as the wood from the ebony window frame. Soon after she gives birth to a daughter who has those features. The colors refer to inner conditions of thinking, feeling and willing. Each snowflake is a crystalline star from heaven; thus, the crystalline thinking is mirrored in the snow, endowed with divine essence. In the blood we have the sphere of the heart, filled with the purest emotion of love. And in the black window frame made of ebony, we have the strength of will, allowing thoughts and feelings to be put into action, especially here on earth. We see the three main colors of *Parzival* mentioned in the most positive and essential light: the polarity of black and white, balanced out by the red that reaches into white and black. Together they form the whole human being. Of course, the purest form of these three attributes is attacked and poisoned, just as we are throughout our lives. Our thinking gets dulled, our feelings easily succumb to temptations, and our will is paralyzed or goes rampant. The three drops of blood serve as the connection to the royal home. Both the fairytale princesses have to endure loss and are separated from the celestial source. Both, in their own way, are able to reconnect and become whole. Like the *Parzival* epic, they are, as Kofi Edusei would say, "separation tales."

Likewise, the three drops of blood in the snow allow Parzival to have a holy connection to Condwiramurs, a source of inspiration and soul sustenance. Yet, the blood is also the carrier of the ego, the I, and it is exactly that strength of individuality that Parzival, like the Goose Girl, has to develop. The time of blood connections, as experienced in ancient times, such as in the royal families of Egypt, which insured ongoing clairvoyance where the blood was kept pure, is now over, once and for all. Hence, the Goose Girl loses the white cloth with the three drops of blood, and Gawain (as we shall see) frees Parzival of the hypnotic effect.

Parzival, the dragon, becomes *lost in thought* till he falls into a trance to such an extent that he lacks all awareness and is closed off to his surroundings. It's almost as if he is feeding off the blood like Dracula ("Dragon" from the Latin: Draco). He has entered into a cocoon of sorts, a waking sleep, without any control over himself or his thoughts. But the cocoon is made of secreted silky love-strands, fondly woven by Condwiramurs, surrounding Parzival's wounded and numbed heart, conjured forth by the red triad. Having lost control, letting himself sink into the mirrored image of her love—a love he trusts—will give him the foundation he needs to once again *find himself in thought*, thereby empowering him to control himself out of himself. If his love were based on physical desire alone, the entrapment would be more oppressive, but the red droplets mirror Condwiramurs, and at this moment he needs her, even if it is only born out of his own dependence on her.

It is the third time that he has lost himself in such a manner. The first two times he was preoccupied by Liaze and Condwiramurs respectively, while riding along on his unrestrained horse. In both those trancelike instances, his unleashed horse took over and brought him to where he needed to be. During this third and most potent vortex of longing, his horse stands perfectly still, letting him drink from the well of the entrancing vision—or holding him captive. Outwardly and inwardly, he had to come to a complete *STOP*, a state of sleep, before reawakening and coming to himself.

In the discussions we have around this scene, the students bring up the significance of *blood*, the number *three*, and *love*. The mood is usually imbued with poetic reverence. They understand his hurt, since they have all gone through various states of suffering caused by rejection and failure. One student wondered what Parzival would have done had he not met someone like Condwiramurs, suggesting that he would maybe have longed for something or someone else to take her place, to fulfill his ideal love, to ease his pain. Another student wondered if there was a connection to the trinity of God, the Son, and the Holy Ghost. Judging by the tenor of the discussions over the years, the students find comfort in knowing that he couldn't just do everything by himself, that he needed someone to depend on and trust, and that it is fine to show one's vulnerabilities. At that moment, Parzival is held by the protective calyx of her care. Conversely, they also recognize that love can be a like a trap, robbing one of the abilities to act and function in normal life, that the dependency on love can be debilitating to one's sense of self. It highlights that he has not yet mastered love. Who has?

Parzival's stock-still state is contrasted with the hubbub he arouses in Arthur's court, who have taken note of this unknown knight standing motionless up on the hill near to where they are encamped. Cunneware's squire thinks the knight is desiring to joust, egging on the other knights to fight. When Parzival first arrived at Arthur's court in Nantes, he was seen as a fool, and this time as an outlaw, an enemy. Both times he is initially not recognized for who he is. Segramors is the first to ride out to meet the inert knight, filled with the urge to battle, bloodlust surging through his veins. Upon being charged, Parzival's horse turns around, freeing Parzival from the blood's spell. At once "Mistress Reason restored him to his senses" (p. 151), casting the proud Segramors into the snow, after which Parzival immediately returns to the three red drops, leaving him once again detached from his senses.

Sir Keie is next to ride out, finding the love-engulfed knight in sullen silence, oblivious to his taunts and threats, until Sir Keie beats him across his head with a mighty "thwack" that makes his helmet ring, calling him to "wake up" (p. 154). And that is exactly what Parzival needs to do—wake up: to himself and the world. In life we are continuously called upon to "wake up," and often it takes repeated blows of fate, literally and figuratively, to return us to our wits. Like Parzival, humanity grows slowly wise. The first time that Parzival was thwacked over the head was by Gaheviez, when Parzival had so rudely demanded the knight's armor.

Once again, when Sir Keie charges, Parzival's horse is forced around, freeing Parzival of the "bitter-sweet pain, the image of his Queen Belrepeire" (p. 154). Sir Keie, to his utter humiliation is thrust from his horse onto the fallen tree under which the wounded goose has sought shelter. Sir Keie's horse is killed outright and he breaks his right arm and left leg. Parzival has avenged the beating of Cunneware. Once the threat has been taken care of, he returns to the red triplet.

When finally Sir Gawain rides up to Parzival, he comes without sword, and after addressing him and being met with stolid silence, he spots the drops of blood and realizes that the knight is in the hold of love, having known the oppression of love himself. At once he covers the offending drops with a yellow cape of silk, which restores Parzival's reason, though he does not realize that he has jousted with two knights, which shows that his ability to fight is instinctive, like a reflex. Even unconsciously he can do what must be done when challenged. It is the observant eye of Gawain, who could deduce Parzival's affliction. He has the bird's eye view of a hawk, which Parzival still lacks but seeks, which is fitting since a hawk has generally been associated with Gawain's name ("May Hawk" of Celtic and Welsh origin). A bird of prey had wounded the goose while "hawking," and now a "hawk" has freed Parzival from the mists around his senses, which presages their future relationship. When Parzival says that "I shall gain from being well received by you" (p. 158), he is speaking prophetically. Gawain, through his own forthcoming adventures, will help Parzival to lift the veils that had shut off his senses; he will help him gain the inner strength needed to never again be held captive by Mistress Love. For now, Gawain, the one swift of flight and sharp of eye, leads Parzival to Arthur's Court, where he will be honored.

Cundrie, the Sorceress

Failure

I have somehow managed to fail again
I have taken back what I value now
Fallen from the height of expectation
I pick myself upwards toward the light
Yet something keeps weighing me down
I can see light as it shines through my eyes
But it is so easy to just lie here.

~ Lila Porcelly (Student)

Imagine you've pursued a goal and after much hard work and countless challenges along the way, you are finally publicly recognized for your stellar accomplishments. Maybe you're about to receive a Grammy, Tony, or an Oscar for outstanding achievements in the entertainment industry. Or you become a director or a CEO of a large corporation, achieve success as an author, receive an honorary doctorate for work in a special field of expertise, maybe a military decoration, an Olympic medal, or a sport's trophy; perhaps you are about to be knighted. And imagine then, how you would feel if you were to get publicly shamed on that very special day of distinguished recognition. That is what happens to Parzival.

He is asked by King Arthur to join the Round Table, the ultimate honor for Parzival who has desired such an esteemed place from the moment he encountered the four knights galloping through Soltane. Outwardly,

Parzival has proven himself worthy, and he is welcomed by all. The snow has melted, warmth has returned, and a circular silk cloth from distant Arabia is spread across a flowery meadow. Parzival is held in high esteem and all admire his beauty—he's even compared to an angel.

The induction ceremony is barely underway when in rides a most hideous lady on a large, pitiful mule. However, she is fashionably attired with costly and exquisitely tailored garments according to the latest French and London fashions (even then). Wolfram goes to great lengths elucidating on her loathly appearance, which include an array of animal images, yet highlighting her great knowledge and learning—known to speak all languages. This lady of contraries enters the festivities and the news she bears is compared to a bridge that carries "grief across joy," that snatches "away the merriment of the company there" (p. 163). Her name is Cundrie, which is derived from the German word "Kunde" meaning "news." This messenger is also known as *La Surziere, the Sorceress*, and the news that she carries will pierce Parzival through the heart. On this day she is the bearer of suffering and sorrow.

I make a point of having some students read Wolfram's description of Cundrie, the details of her hideous appearance, together with her unparalleled erudition. Once I had a storyteller relate the scene with Cundrie. We also read her blunt words to King Arthur, how his Round Table has proven to be deceitful, dishonorable, and that the once so glorious and renowned Round Table has been destroyed by letting Parzival join its ranks: "The mighty reputation of the Table Round has been maimed by the presence at it of Lord Parzival, who moreover wears the insignia of knighthood" (p. 164).

After ruthlessly discrediting King Arthur, she turns to Parzival and delivers a thrashing of curses that could not be more severe. "You think me monstrous, yet I am less monstrous, far, than you" (p. 164). She wastes no time to get to the point, asking him to explain why he did not ask the *Question* when he witnessed the suffering of the Angler in the presence of the Grail and the entire Grail company, the grief of which was made apparent to him in no uncertain terms. She tells it straight: "*You ought to have had compassion on his sufferings. May your mouth be as empty—I mean of your tongue—as your heart is void of feeling*" (p. 165. My italics). Cundrie does not give him time to explain himself, relentlessly continuing to shame him, questioning his manly valor, that he is beyond all cure, that no man on earth could be more duplicitous, and comparing him to a viper's fang. The torrent of accusations accumulates, clearly spelling out his errors, one by one. No question in her mind: he messed up! "Had you thought of asking there at Munsalvæsche, your Question would have brought unparalleled wealth" (p 165). At this point she mentions Feirefiz, his African half-brother, mottled black and white. Not only did Parzival not know about him, but Feirefiz is portrayed as vastly more courageous, noble, and successful. To rub it in, she states his father's multiple attributes, and that compared to Gahmuret, Parzival's "renown has now proved false," adding, "Alas, that it was ever made known by me that Herzeloyde's child has strayed thus far from the path of fame" (p 166). The Angler had warned Parzival that it was easy to *miss* the path to Munsalvæsche, which could also have been a warning that even if he makes it outwardly, he could be led astray inwardly, which happened by not asking the Question. Munsalvæsche means "Mount of Salvation," and salvation was not granted—remained unfulfilled—because Parzival failed to ask. In that sense, the unasked Question remained unanswered and came across as "savage"—another interpretation of Munssalvæsche: "Savage Mountain."

Done upbraiding Parzival, Cundrie abruptly dismisses him and turns to King Arthur, delivering a new message, concerning the Castle of Wonders in which four Queens and four hundred Ladies reside: "Compared with what one could achieve there, with its noble prize of lofty love, all other adventures are vain" (p. 166). She departs without giving any more information, leaving the remaining knights to ponder the fame and renown they might gain from seeking out this *Schastel marveile*. It also suggests a task that must be completed *before* Parzival can fulfill his next goal, which is mounting within him as a result of her merciless rebuke.

Her last words to the disrupted Table Round are, "Acme of sorrow, ah Munsalvæsche! Alas that none will console you" (p. 166), the words leaving their mark on Parzival, which will precipitate his next Quest, which is rising up from the depths as he copes with the public shaming that has slashed, reopened, and deepened the wounds of his failure. He is left speechless and inconsolable. Instead of the joy and pride of joining the fellowship of the Table Round, he has to digest and bear not only personal humiliation and shame, but the shaming of Arthur's entire court because of him. On Parzival's first visit to Arthur's court, he left them in sorrow after killing Gaheviez, and now he has plunged them into sorrow once again.

Cundrie never ceases to impress. The students are quite taken aback at the severity of Parzival's defamation and public disgrace. Just like after Sigune's severe chastisement, they once again wonder why he is treated with such severity, simply for not asking a simple question. It is another opportunity to probe deeper into the theme of failure. Mainly, we are moved to inquire: Why did Cundrie have to appear and curse him with such vehemence? Attendant questions arise: Who is Cundrie? How does it affect Parzival? What will he do now? What can we learn from this? How relevant is this potent imagination in our modern times? What must it feel like to be brought down at a highpoint of your life? She comes across as Parzival's visible conscience. By awakening our conscience, we wake our intelligence.

In life we are mostly slow to learn. A child has to be shown numerous times how to do this or that before the lesson is learned and becomes a habit. Parents and educators are acutely aware of this. Any kind of consciousness-raising takes time. Waking up to oneself, one's errors and mistakes, is painful and takes time. It is true for the little things and the big issues of life. Humanity, for instance, has been grappling with injustices for millennia, yet we are continuously struggling to arrive at solutions that uphold human dignity, always adjusting to the times. And we all have our personal struggles and issues which need to be dealt with, each person in their own specific way. Furthermore, we all have our goals and tasks in life, and we can easily be led astray in our endeavor to achieve them. Do we have a sense for our true goals, or are we led awry by outer trappings? Or having achieved outer goals, do we rest on our laurels, thereby foregoing new goals, possibly the most consequential ones?

These kinds of questions are important to eleventh graders who are beginning to think of their futures and what they want to do with their lives. Will it have meaning, fulfill them? And sometimes, like Parzival, we need to be pushed into the right direction. His desire to win knighthood from King Arthur was only a stepping stone, not his true destiny. That goal alone would be shortchanging the scope of his abilities, his talents and inner capacities. Especially when one is young, it can be incredibly difficult to determine the paths one should follow in life, taking into account the manifold choices, coupled with the interests one might have, especially when one has received a taste of what's out there. One's destined path in life is not at all linear or straightforward. One needs to listen to the inner voice, which easily gets drowned out or submerged by distractions.

Parzival initially did not realize that he had failed. He was a person of unlimited promise and potential, and he learned quickly, mostly due to the generous gifts of his heritage, even though they were kept dormant and left untouched in Soltane. But he could not continue to ride that wave. At Munsalvæshe he was led to the point where he was expected to act out of himself without any prodding, and that's where he failed. If you need to get nudged, then it does not truly arise out of yourself. Then the nudging and prodding will come in a different form—as a consequence of the inner lapses. The Page's anonymous rebuke and Sigune's strong and *personal* shaming

was not enough. At Arthur's Court he accepted his induction to the Round Table, without another thought of his still fresh failure. But some things cannot be forgotten or cast aside. Failures have their consequences. Parzival could not afford to put his destiny on hold by becoming a knight of the sword for King Arthur. To really prove that he is worthy of receiving the honor of Cunneware's laughter, he has to fully transform himself inwardly, and go beyond the ultimate *outer knight* which his father was. He has to figure out what it truly means to serve the highest. And serving King Arthur clearly does not represent the highest—not for him, at any rate. The time of the *Sword* is waning, making way for the Knight of the *Word*. Cundrie, in her public shaming, has silenced Parzival. He is sentenced to silence, an inner removal from society, banished to an inner Soltane.

With some of my classes, I have asked the students to close their eyes and imagine their own failings as objectively as possible, free of remorse or regret, purely objective. I might prod them a bit, reminding them of little failures like unfulfilled promises, forgetting something, or messing up on a project or homework assignment. I avoid examples of overwhelming failures in case it might trigger painful events. Next, I ask them to imagine a portrait of themselves, not the way they look physically, but an inner picture of their feelings, which would include all the faults and foibles, like anger, jealousies, greed. What would such an inner portrait of their "Doppelgänger" look like? What forms would those emotions take on, what colors? "Imagine, as fully as possible, a depiction of yourselves, warts and all." The first few times I went through this imagination, I had them volunteer to describe their portraits in words, with as much detail as possible. In other classes, to put it down on paper (as poems or in prose), which they were free to include in their main lesson book or not. In my last few *Parzival* blocks, I provided colored chalk and asked them to spread out to the three blackboards available and draw their inner life, which they did, spending much more time on them than I ever would have thought, with some of them insisting on making even the "ugly" parts beautiful. There were also some group efforts. Afterwards we went around and honored the drawings, with each student talking about their portrayal or answering questions.

The students got a sense of their own "double"—aspects of themselves that need inner discipline and work, facets of their personality or character that they wish to overcome or develop. Parzival, in his encounter with loathsome Cundrie, is experiencing self-confrontation, seeing the unadulterated truth about himself, with all the ugly aspects brought to the surface. She tells the truth he needs to hear. And hearing home truths is never easy. Cundrie, for his sake, did not "tell it slant" as Emily Dickinson advised. There was no time to "dazzle gradually," for Parzival was on the verge of failing his true destiny, thereby forfeiting his true goal, which would have dire consequences beyond his comprehension. Cundrie knew he would not be "blinded" by the truth. She acted as a guardian of his true destiny. We all need people like Cundrie in our lives to push us in the right direction, whether we like it or not. It's sometimes referred to as "tough love." The *Cundrie effect* can come in different forms, but hardly anybody escapes some such experience where we are met—painfully so—by a certain truth thrust upon us, forcing us to look at ourselves in an unmitigated manner, thus shocking us to the next step. Cundrie knocked the dullness out of Parzival, allowing light to enter through the wound so that he may see the ramifications of his actions. She personified his "bad conscience," which is reminiscent of a description from the Zend Avesta, the Holy Book of the Persians, that describes what happens to evil people after their death. The person who has committed evil is confronted by a hideously repulsive woman who declares: "I appear before you in this repugnant and ugly state because you created me through your evil actions, thoughts, feelings, and words." It is likely that Wolfram or Kyot the Provencal would have known this, given the Manichean underpinning of *Parzival*. Being plagued by a bad conscience is a premonition of *kamaloka*.

Be it as it may, becoming a knight for Arthur would only have been a short-term solution, a temporary gratification, and Cundrie, like Sigune, helped him remain true to his destiny.

⁂

As soon as Cundrie leaves, another knight, Kingrimursel, arrives at Arthur's court and accuses Gawain of having slain his lord, demanding that he defend his honor by doing battle with him in Schanpfanzun in forty days' time. Like Parzival, Gawain is shamed, called a traitor, his name slandered publicly. However, there is a difference: Gawain is innocent of the charge, whereas Parzival is *guilty*.

By having the shamings presented back-to-back, it shows that Gawain and Parzival's destinies are entwined, which was already made evident when Gawain freed Parzival from his trance.

Ekuba, Queen of Janfuse

Black is the color
where everything goes;
the place that no one knows,
the great mystery of life.
~ Goni (Student)

Parzival accepts the shaming without retaliation. After Cundrie and Kingrimursel leave, the ceremony is forthwith ended and people walk over to Gawain and Parzival to console the pair. Ekuba, the puissant African Queen of Janfuse, is amongst them, consoling him by telling Parzival more about his half-brother whose "skin has a most marvelous sheen" (p. 171), which sets him apart from all other people in that he is dappled both black and white. She forms a link for Parzival to his African connection, forging awareness of Gahmuret's marriage to Belacane. Ekuba vouchsafes and confirms Cundrie's revelation of his brother, and what a great influence he has in Africa and far beyond in Persia and other realms. She conveys that his lands are beyond compare, save for the wealth of the Baruch and the riches of Tribalibot.[4] Ekuba goes on to relate that Feirefiz wooed her while she was traveling to King Arthur's court, though she rejected him because

4 Feirefiz will acquire that realm as well through his union with Secundille, Queen of Tribalibot in India.

she was after *new* experiences "and to learn about Adventure" (p. 171). Moreover, they are cousins, she being the daughter of Belacane's sister.[5] Ekuba's connection to Belacane is significant in that it shows the ongoing wish to have a connection between East and West. Without that mutual respect, understanding, and bond of love, global peace and freedom cannot flourish.

Ekuba,[6] though she plays only a small role in the epic, is intriguing. One of the main reasons for her travels to King Arthur was to form a link between the realms that are still separated, and thereby paving the way for Feirefiz's journey later on. She is self-determined, seeks new experiences and adventures, and is sensitive and awake to the needs of others. That she, as a black woman unaccompanied by any man, had the courage and vision to travel on her own volition to white Europe during the Middle Ages, is unheard of and beyond impressive. What fortitude and vision must that have taken? I like to think of the "Ek" to mean "I," referring to her self-reliant strength of ego.

Though she is referred to as an "infidel," it should be taken in the most positive sense, as in a person who adheres to a different belief system—not worse or inferior, simply different. In that way, all people of different belief systems are infidels to one another. Both Parzival and Ekuba are not only mutually accepting of each other's beliefs, but show high regard for one another's spiritual heritage. She is a true "gift of God" as one of the meanings of her name suggests.

Her words offer nothing but the highest praise for Feirefiz, which bolsters Parzival's mood. "May God reward you, madam, for consoling me so kindly" (p. 171). What is most striking, however, is that he proceeds to open up to her, entrusting her with his heavy and oppressive thoughts, finding in her an unbiased and empathetic listener. "I cannot show my pain as it makes itself known to me when many a one, ignorant of my griefs, misbehaves towards me and subjects me to mockery too" (p. 171). More notably, she is the first to hear of his new quest, the one that he is meant and destined to follow:

5 According to some scholars.

6 Possibly a reference to the Kuba kingdom in Africa.

> I shall never know myself happy till I have seen the Gral, whether the time be short or long. My thoughts impel me to that goal, from which nothing shall sever me till the end of my days. (p. 171)

Whereas it was his mother whom he told of his initial quest to become a knight, it is now again a woman, but one from a different country, continent, and race, who becomes the recipient and bearer of the seminal news, which will have vast consequences for him and the world. It births a bond to the people of Africa and the East. The idea of being impelled to search for the Grail is passed on to the son of Belacane via her niece. It underscores the human relatedness between the peoples of different cultures and races—the synchronicity. It suggests a harmony between the polarities: East and West, black and white, Saracens and Christians—and everything in between, for the polarities are all inclusive, just like colors are the offspring of black and white. In that sense, the literal meaning of the name Feirefiz, based on the old French *vers* and *fiz,* which translates as "colorful son," is broadened. In other words, *humanity*, no matter what skin tone, is united.

Parzival does bring up the cause of his indefensible failure, for which Cundrie so severely cursed him. His confession to dynamic Ekuba indicates that he is waking up the source of his painful omission:

> If, having followed the precepts of my education ..., then Gurnemanz's schooling may have had some flaws. For the noble man had instructed me that I should refrain from asking questions over-freely and to be always on my guard against unmannerliness. (p. 171)

The above quote confirms that Parzival was only trying to be a good student, to listen and follow the advice of his elders, the wise people with gray hair (Gra-harz, "gray hair" or "gray heart," according to Wolfram's love for word play), as his mother had said. There was not a shred of ill will in Parzival. He became "Pure Failure" through ill advice, or advice taken too literally and on authority. Both his mother and Gurnemanz got him into great trouble with undesired consequences. It is a critique on the education, it's unintended flaws. Every parent, guardian, counselor, and especially teachers need to take this deeply to heart. What we say to children and students has potentially great effect. The smallest comment can have the greatest outcomes, positively and negatively. And our present educational system is materialistic in almost every way. Its god is the intellect. We might have people who proselytize against racism, intolerance, and so forth, but continue to uphold the academic intellectual rigmarole, based on people such as Darwin, Newton, Francis Bacon, and others, who created the foundation of our mechanical and intellectual worldview—a far cry from the mythic, spiritual, pictorial, ancestral worldviews of the vast majority of cultures. Do we, as teachers, subconsciously uphold the materialistic reductionist worldview, or do we begin to truly offer a curriculum that supports globality and self-examination, that questions what it means to be human, while bringing our history into context by including a soul-spiritual component that has existed from time immemorial? Do we offer a balanced curriculum that has equality of mind, body, and soul? What we say to students also depends on *how* we say it, *when* we say it, and *why* we say it. And that takes hard work, consciousness, and great humility. There is no place for self-righteousness or proselytizing. Truths have the greatest effect if they are imparted out of *who* we are. And who we are depends on daily endeavors to our ongoing self-growth and transformation. Unfortunately, many people try to do the proper thing according to societal laws of the day, rather than following their heart. It's a bitter lesson that Parzival will have to learn.

After this thoughtful admission, Parzival then turns to those around him, stating that "execution" has been accomplished with *words*, which expresses his feeling of having inwardly died, just like he caused a kind of death through *not* giving breath to any words. He adds that he is now in great haste to take his leave, which demonstrates the same forceful drive that Parzival had exhibited from the get-go: his determination to get things done. As the old Bible proverb goes: *What must be done, do soon.*

Doubt and Departure

"Thinking is difficult, that's why most people judge." — Carl Jung

One by one, Parzival bids farewell to all, but not before absolving them of their fellowship to him till he has set things right: to search for and attain "that thing the lack of which has seared my verdant joy" (p. 172), referring to the Grail, thereby making his quest public.

Gawain's subsequent parting words to Parzival are significant. "May God then grant you a favorable outcome" (p. 172), wishing the same for himself. Parzival's response is as surprising as it is shocking, coming from someone in medieval times, where everybody was so deeply entrenched in Christianity:

> "Alas, what is God?" asked the Waleis. "Were He all-powerful—were God active in His almightiness—He would not have brought us to such shame! Ever since I knew of Grace I have been His humble servitor. But now I will quit His service! If He knows anger I will shoulder it. My friend, when your hour of combat is at hand, let a woman join issue in your stead, let her guide your hand." (p. 172)

What mind-shattering words, sounding almost displaced in the context of his time. Parzival, through the horrendous shaming, feels dead inside, and because of his verbal "execution" has excommunicated himself from God. For Parzival, *God is Dead*, a widely quoted Nietzschean statement that epitomizes the prevalent attitude of our current times. However, Nietzsche found humans guilty of the murder: *Gott ist tot* because we have killed him. His words are Macbethian in their might, describing how nobody can wash the blood away, that no water and no atonement or sacred rite will accomplish that cleansing. The execution of God is too great a crime that we humans have committed. Nietzsche intimates that we, as humans, have to become gods ourselves to make good the bad.[7] The students literally sit

7 The famous quote by Nietzsche appears in *Thus Spake Zarathustra*, as well as his explanatory analysis.

up and lift their heads when we come to this turning point in the story. It reflects the materialistic attitude of our scientific age where God is dead and has no place in the pursuits of science. The topic deserves a full discussion and review in class. Nietzsche is stating the naked truth of our age, not dressed in the pictorial frills of fairy tales. The statement depicts the dead-end of our age. All we can do now is turn around, look at what we've been separated from, and reconnect, which marks the quest for the Grail. Parzival, as the trailblazer of the modern age, killed God within himself. The search for the Grail is to find God in himself again—in freedom, out of himself, and on his own terms. It is wonderfully paradoxical.

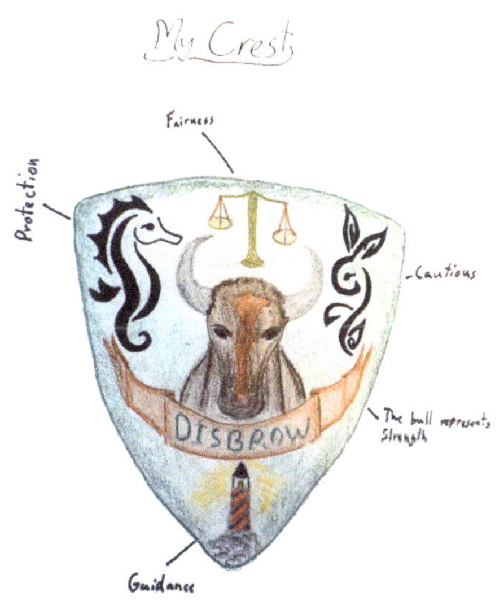

After this potent disclosure, Lady Cunneware takes Parzival to her pavilion on top of which the dragon emblem hovers, and calls for his new armor to be brought, proceeding to arm him with her own soft hands, as a way of thanking him for serving her, restoring her honor, and helping King Clamide's request to win her hand in marriage, thus also making amends to the loss he endured through Parzival (even though he was in the wrong for trying to force Condwiramurs into marriage in the first place, and causing so much pain, suffering, and death). Parzival's special bond to Cunneware and his servitude to her can be seen as the quintessence of "*hohe Minne*" (courtly love in its most refined and ethical form that strives for the purification and perfection of the higher self, which usually includes an element of sacrifice).

It is worth noting that when Parzival had first entered Arthur's court in Nantes, Cunneware had gifted him with prescient laughter, whereas this time she was immediately moved to mantic tears on witnessing Cundrie's scolding, showing her compassion and prophetic knowledge for the grief he will have to bear. The two of them are kindred spirits. She is a source of strength to him, recognizing the transformative and taming potential of this wild "dragon," implied by her dragon emblem and the fact that her pavilion is situated over a *spring*, which connotes renewal, healing, and rejuvenation. It is the "spring" or "well" of inspiration where the broken Grail sword could be reforged. Cunneware, the guardian of the spring, is like a Sybil or Pythia, breathing in the Apollo-transformed snake-like vapors from the earth's depths in order to voice the oracle through her cathartic laughter or tears.

Up till now Parzival has uncovered and mirrored the qualities of his heritage, but from this moment onwards, the real work of crafting his new self can begin. It's no longer a mere matter of conquering the dragon, but of tempering its power and divining its wisdom for the sake of all, the wisdom submerged in the subconscious. Through Parzival sending the vanquished knights to her, he has kept in touch with this renewing source, and the strength he gained through that will help him in the next phase of his development. Sensing the name Cunneware poetically, we find hidden the German word "Wahr," "die Wahrheit," or "das Wahre": Truth. And in "Cunne," we sense the word "Kühn," meaning "bold" or "brave": "One who bears truth boldly or bravely" (apart from "Kunde" or "message" as mentioned earlier).

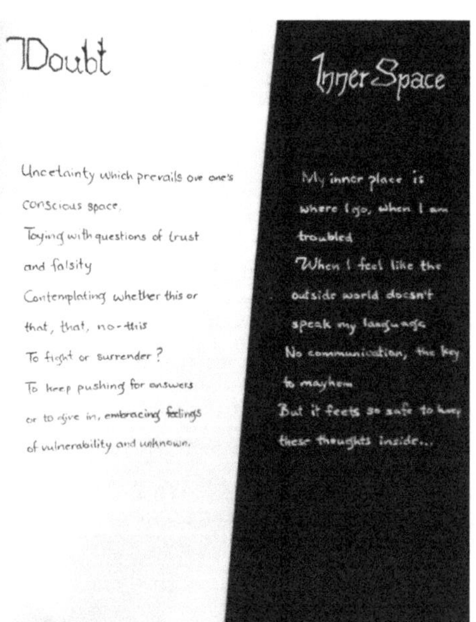

The new stage of his life is about to begin, and his "war-horse" is readied, foreshadowing many struggles, troubles, and jousts, each battle signifying another step in his development, another confrontation with himself, another opening of the mind, a softening and massaging of the heart, so that it may open when the time is ripe, all the while sharpening his life of thought.

Gawain, too, readies himself, albeit with a large entourage and fine costly gifts of gems, gold, and silver, bestowed by King Arthur. Moreover, apart from wealth and weapons, Gawain chooses seven chargers in case of battle, and acquires twelve lances. This little detail of twelve and seven, shows that he too is bound for an adventure that will take him on a zodiacal journey, subject to planetary ups and downs. Gawain's fortunes are now also "trundling towards cares and perils" (p. 174). While Gawain sets out in one direction, Parzival departs in the other—alone, silent, and determined. Heart (Gawain) and mind (Parzival) separate in order to gain experience, knowledge, and deepened insights, so that they may merge once more in the future, to mutually fructify the heart and mind for the sake of the whole.

Parzival started out as a *Pure Fool*, then proved himself as a worthy knight, only to fail in the presence of the ailing Anfortas and the Grail at Munsalvæache, after which he is reduced to a wounded goose. Instead of questing after the Grail immediately, he forgets his failure and accepts the invitation to join the Table Round. He's saved from that short-term satisfaction by Cundrie, the loathly lady, who shames him to his senses. The sense of shame is held in the highest of esteem in the chivalric code. It becomes one of his most important resources, for "a sense of shame . . . reigns supreme over all his ways" (p. 166). The momentum of shame will drive him forward, similarly to his refusal to return to Arthur's court till Lady Cunneware's beating was avenged and redeemed. However, the pain of having been cast down is experienced as a death, and with that inner death, he falls into the depths of *DOUBT*, in effect closing the door to something higher, to the divine, the heavenly, while simultaneously having made it his new ardent quest to search for the Grail, which is exactly that which he has rejected. He rejects God to find God. He rejects that God which was given to him through his surroundings in the context of the time. The previous idea of God must be cast off so that he might arrive at a new and living experience of God, arising out of his own free will, through his own resources. Rejection of God leads to his greatest self-confrontation by running into the wall of himself. Steiner relates how *doubt* played an essential role in the Irish Mystery Center of Hibernia. His portrayal of an initiate's experience in Hibernia clearly mirrors Parzival's development, through which he has to go in order to find the Grail:

> The aspirant of Initiation had first to experience every kind of doubt that can arise in the human soul concerning the great truths of existence. The pupil was actually taught to doubt, to be utterly sceptical of everything, especially of the highest truths. And only when he had undergone all the suffering, the sense of tragedy, dejection and inner despair, which accompany such doubt, only then was he guided to a full comprehension of truth, first of all as an Imaginative, pictorial experience and then as an experience of spiritual reality. Thus everyone who attained Initiation in the Hibernian Mysteries had learned not only to believe in the truth but also *not* to believe in it. Only so could his fidelity to truth prove itself a potent, unshakable force in life.[8]

Parzival's immense suffering is encapsulated in the above quote, making it more understandable. It also reflects our contemporary situation. Modern human beings cannot evade having to go through this state of doubt on their way to arrive at truth—a dark state that seeks illumination. We constantly find ourselves confronted by extremes, where we can easily be swayed this way and that by exceedingly cogent arguments.

Discussion around spirituality, diverse religions, and atheism finds fertile ground at this point in the story. The students strongly identify with this stage of doubt, for they have many unanswered questions regarding the truth of things, visible and invisible. Parzival has graduated from a fool to a *doubter*. He becomes an outcast. In Soltane he was an outcast without

8 Rudolf Steiner, *Karmic Relationships: Esoteric Studies Vol. VII*, Lecture 4 (Rudolf Steiner Press London, 1973) (GA 239), pp. 59-60.

knowing it, removed from the norms and traditions of courtly life by his mother. Now the circumstances have pushed him into an *inner* Soltane—place of isolation, a place of silence, a place of loneliness. He's always been a loner, but now he will suffer true loneliness, which will wake him up to himself. The ideal of being "Alone" is to become "All One," an individual, grounded within him or herself. Only then will he feel ready to rejoin the wider community, transformed. He feels misunderstood, but only because he does not yet understand himself. Loneliness and silence go together. He has been shamed into silence. He has to find his voice again for which silence is a prerequisite. Mahatma Gandhi did not speak on Mondays. Such controlled moments of silence make one more aware of what one does say. Are my words really necessary? Will they contribute or take away from the moment? The spoken word has more weight if it is offset against silence. Silence can be healing, just like chattiness can make one feel polluted.

At this stage, he no longer feels he can remain part of the courtly life, represented by Arthur. However, he is driven to find the Grail—to serve the enigmatic highest—without knowing what exactly it is, but sensing that it exists with unwavering conviction. Thus, Parzival now consciously withdraws himself, as once Herzeloyde withdrew him from courtly life. This time it is to preserve and protect his inner life, for he would surely die inwardly if he chose to stay. It's less a choice than a necessity, which eventually will guide him back to community.

It's important to underscore that Doubt is related to the double nature of things—doubling: looking at things from two sides. Similarly, the German word for doubt is "Zweifel," ("zwei" meaning "two")—the polarity of things. Everything can be approached from two sides with cogent and persuasive arguments made in both directions. It forces us to THINK. It guides and prods Parzival to think. It strengthens our capacities to think a thought through to the very end, which, unfortunately, very few people do. It takes effort, and people easily get caught up in their own emotions which clouds any clear thinking, as do urges and compulsions. And when emotions get in the way, then it stokes the fires of division. We see so much of that in the political and social sphere. "Doublethink"[9] is ubiquitous. True understanding, however is light within the darkness of doubt. In the words of Orland Bishop: "Understanding is light and as we are lighted we become a light unto others."[10] As of now, Parzival has a long way to go before he can become a light for others.

Book Six completes the first large arc of Parzival's development from fool to knight to failure to shaming, and finally to doubt. In this chapter the reader's gaze is directed both backwards and forwards. Parzival has slipped into error, is quick to learn outer lessons, wakes up through witnessing others' grief caused by him, and slowly gains in consciousness. He has become judicious, proven himself a true leader, and found a conduit or guide of love through Condwiramurs. However, he now needs to strengthen his own forces of love, sans dependence on Condwiramurs' "guidance," but finding that source within, while remaining steadfast. The road inward is more arduous than traversing outer paths. His lack of compassion of which he has been harshly accused cannot simply be switched on. It's not a matter of, "Now I will be compassionate." Compassion is "suffering with" ("*compatio*," from "*com*" meaning "with" + "*pati*" meaning "suffering"), similar to the German word *Mitleid* ("*mit*" meaning "with" + "*Leid*" meaning "suffering"). The journey from knowing to compassion is lengthy and includes internalizing the experiences of the world in a living manner, which, in turn, requires practice and time. Parzival must find the world within himself, which he can only achieve if he discovers himself in the world. Cundrie cursed him into silence, and now he begins his second grand Quest as a *Pure Mute*, as a listener in the making: listening to others, the world, and himself.

When Cundrie and Ekuba mention Gahmuret and Belacane's son, Feirefiz, heaping praise upon praise on his older brother, our attention is

---

9 "Doublethink," coined by George Orwell in his book *1984*: holding two contradictory or opposing ideas at the same time, and believing both to be absolutely true.

10 Bishop, p. 169.

taken right back to Book One, while simultaneously intimating the future. It forges the brothers' mutual connection, just as Parzival's life's path has now crossed and become intertwined with Gawain's. Our development is never isolated, though we might be forced into isolation or have come from isolation. The saying "It takes a village to raise a child" holds true for Parzival, though it is more like "a world" than "a village." It is approximately the halfway mark of the book, if one considers only the chapters devoted to Parzival.

All the main players are mentioned, and it is not without significance that Wolfram ends Book Six by honoring the prominent women in this epic, highlighting their virtues and strengths. They form the warmth body of the community by their overarching embrace; they ensoul the story, give it spirit, and usher it forward. They are like the matriarchal singers of ancient chants from misty antiquity who guided and directed their people, immersing them in tonal spiritual sustenance. Wolfram is deeply concerned that women receive their due. Already in his "Apology" at the end of Book Two (which completes the section on Parzival's hereditary background), he makes his point by stating: "If any speak better concerning women than I, he may do so without my resenting it" (68), meaning that he wants all people to honor, respect, and recognize the importance of women, even if their words are better than his. It's an ongoing theme and must be mentioned often, today and through the vista of tomorrows, for we are a long way from having anything close to equality of the sexes (in the widest sense of the word). We are reminded how the ladies he names suffered, how they endured, and how they showed empathy and forgiveness, and above all: strength of conviction and determination. They bared their inner lives and lived the compassion, which Parzival can only emulate. Parzival will learn to suffer like they have suffered. May he learn from their example, may he comport himself as seemly. It marks an end and spurs a new beginning.

Discussion Topics, Questions

- Do you distinguish between religion, spirituality, and atheism?
- Do you think that what has happened to you are clues to who you are?
- What makes a person civilized or barbaric?
- Do we want to change others more than ourselves?
- Discuss the concept of shame.
- Why are we mostly dissatisfied with our lives? Are we?
- Why is it so difficult to convey what one truly feels?
- What are the consequences of seeing oneself as a victim?

Illustrations:
Three drops of blood (Violet Middlebrook)
Falconry. Wounding of the goose (Gabriel Lopez)
Blackboard drawings of the students' "doppelgänger"
Personalized coat of arms (Carly Disbrow)
Poems on "Doubt" and "Inner Space" (Goni Ronen)

BOOK SEVEN

Pure Knight

"I'm startled . . . when people walk up to me and . . . inform me that they are Christians. My first response is the question 'Already?'[1] ~ Maya Angelou

CLOSE TO HALF of *Parzival* is devoted to the adventures of Gawain: "For this tale takes friendly note of many beside or beyond its hero Parzival" (p. 176). Their close connection is already indicated in Book Six. We have to pay careful attention to Gawain's development, for he represents another aspect of Parzival. They are one, which gradually clarifies itself.

These Gawain chapters have an entirely different mood, yet they are intimately linked. I ask the students to compare and contrast these two heroes, and in their role as literary sleuths and detectives, to find the multiple clues dropped along their respective paths of development. What are the differences and similarities between them? What is the main focus of the Gawain story? What can Gawain's adventures teach Parzival? What are Gawain's challenges? What does he have to learn? How do his

1 Maya Angelou, *Letters to my Daughter*, "Keep the Faith," p. 165.

encounters parallel those of Parzival? Why would Wolfram choose to pay such close attention to Gawain? What aspect within ourselves does Gawain represent? The answers are found within the descriptions, the plot, the characterizations, and the smallest of details in the story. There are many correspondences, and every year there are a few students who thrive on paralleling these two knights whose life trajectories are so different. However, the divergences have a crossing point.

In some schools the chapters on Gawain are left out entirely or only marginally addressed, due to lack of time or because they might not be considered as important. However, without considering the progression and fruits of his adventures, one cannot get a full and complete picture of Parzival. Gawain is integral to Parzival, whose growth only makes sense through Gawain's developmental journey.

The first couple of paragraphs of Book Seven serve as a brief prologue to Gawain. He is straightway depicted as "one who never did a shameful deed" (p. 176), and further described as an upright, valorous, and circumspect knight of courage and fame, held in high esteem by all, earning respect by friend and foe alike, as he pursues honor. On the battlefield, his "heart was a stronghold which loomed high above the fray" (p. 176).

We see, therefore, that in many respects Gawain is the polar opposite to Parzival. He is the epitome of a knight and anything but a fool. He has grown up in Arthur's court, received the best education of the time, and has proven himself. He is the perfect knight, known for his balanced disposition and stability. Knights from all around emulate Gawain.

Gawain now sets out into the unknown on his own personal adventure. He, too, needs to experience homelessness, where his honor and character will be sorely tested. It is one thing to be successful and revered within the context of one's home territory, and quite another to have to prove oneself in the outside world, away from the familiar context. Whereas Parzival had low status when he first left Soltane, Gawain's high status is undeniable as he leaves Arthur's court to meet Kingrimusel and uphold his honor. As of now, Gawain is the "pure knight" as Parzival was the "pure fool."

It is a good time to remind the students that the initiates, leaders, and wise people of antiquity were expected, urged, and asked to travel and learn about other nations, foreign customs and cultures. Leaving home was part and parcel of the old mystery schools where the neophytes or disciples were taught and prepared for the stage homelessness—homelessness as a prerequisite for the soul's awakening. Through the travels, the wise individuals would be able to use their innate powers for the good of others. Homelessness is a precondition of attaining inner freedom because all connections to one's family, clan, race, language, and religion are severed, and have to be renewed and found again from within. One's home-identity is broken down, which subsequently has to be rebuilt, stage for stage. Gawain is on the threshold of becoming homeless, which will enable him to serve others from a higher spiritual vantage point.

Weighing the Options

"Why? Why am I writing this essay? Why are we here on this Earth? Why do we human beings constantly question and search? Why?"
~ Jae-Yeon Yoo (Student)

Time blurs, and many days elapse, confirmed by the fact that Gawain comes to an unfamiliar area to which his fame had not spread. He is now removed from his customary and regular context, entering unknown territory where rules and customs are different. The foundation of who he is will be tested.

Encounters once again play a vital role, but they are not as straightforward as they were with Parzival. The story picks up when Gawain steps out of a forest with his retinue to cross a valley where he espies a "fearsome sight" in the form of an approaching army. He wonders whether he should escape back into the forest, but instead he musters his courage, and rides out toward them on his charger Gringuljete, thinking, "when a man loses heart and turns tail before he is attacked, it is too quick for his good name, as I see it" (p. 177). It is the first of many examples of him weighing out his options, in contrast to Parzival who simply rides from one adventure into the next—

alone, unconscious, and with happy-go-lucky abandon. Gawain could have retreated back into the forest, but that would have been cowardly. He is also concerned about his good name and honor. He cannot lose heart, which is key to understanding Gawain. In the soul realm of the *heart*, we weigh and balance things out continuously. It is a feeling-knowledge that rises up and becomes conscious within us: this or that? In weighing out the alternatives, we feel *into* the one or the other option, wondering which route to take. In one way or another, they become moral questions. In those moments of indecision, we are temporarily in doubt: This or that? Yes or no? Now or later? Too much or too little? Should I stay or should I go? To avoid the one clashing against the other, they need to be consciously addressed, but in a more sentient manner. Predominantly, these choices rest and depend on the given situation and the present moment. What does the *moment* demand? The weighing of the heart reminds us of the Egyptian *Book of the Dead*, where the heart—seat of intelligence, memory, and feeling—is weighed against an ostrich feather, which represents truth, justice, and order. With Gawain, this weighing of options is to avoid any wrongdoings in order to maintain his honor at every turn. As we continue with Gawain's adventures, we will encounter this warm heart-intelligence numerous times from different perspectives, in contrast to the cold intellect.

Gawain, though he is acutely aware of feeling like a stranger, observes the impressive army carefully. He does not recognize any of the crests and heraldic designs, but sees that the army is comprised of many different types of people, from nobles to tradesmen to riff-raff, and a welter of mules and wagons laden with armor and provisions. Many of the women are "ladies of the road" rather than of any chivalric court. This motley crew, drawn from all ranks of society, convey an "indescribable confusion" (p. 177), yet, they ride proudly, filled with esprit. Wolfram's colorful description is another key to Gawain's realm and mission. He functions fully in the greater *social realm*, and the heart must keep afloat and hold its own in the turbulences and confusions of the great social diversity. The social sphere is like an ocean, always in motion, always in transition and always needing constant adjustment. Like the passing army, the social realm contains all types, drawn from every stratum of society. There is something mercurial about the social life. How does one bring order and clarity into the social instabilities? There are clues. One of them is Gringuljete, the charger on which he rides, described as white with red ears. It is a Grail horse from Munsalvæsche, which connotes something divine. The red ears, like two hearts on the head, suggest empathetic listening: listening with the ears of the heart.[2] I imagine Gringuljete's ears pricked forward while Gawain weighs out what he hears or observes. In "Celtic lore heroic horses are white with red ears, and of divine origin."[3] This holds true for most animals from the Otherworld (or the land beyond death) in the Celtic tradition. It suggests that Gawain is a good listener and that matters of the heart need two listening ears, in order to truly weigh out the worth of the words and deeds.

The first person he encounters is a squire (in contrast to Parzival meeting the four resplendent knights in Soltane). He listens to the squire who explains what is going on, discovering that there are two armies riding toward Bearosche, all because the advances of the young lover, King Meljanz, were rejected and mocked by Obie, the daughter of Duke Lyppaut who had raised him after Meljanz's father died. Angry over the rejection, he is now set on avenging the rebuff and intent on seizing her by force. Interestingly enough, Meljahkanz, the knight who had abducted Imane, and had been chased by the four knights, is riding in the first army. It is another example of forced love. The squire says it plain: "He has succumbed to pride and anger and acted for no other cause than misconceived love" (p. 178). Obie's words have whipped up Meljanz's emotions. It is the prime motivation behind this entire chapter. It highlights how quickly the emotions can spin the senses into disarray, how they can blind rational thinking, and how easily the balance of the heart can be thrown off kilter through self-centered pride. If there is one thing young people know and have experienced, it is this overwhelming feeling of confusion in the realm

2 I like to point out to the students that "ear" is hidden within the word "heart."

3 Wolfram von Eschenbach, *Parzival: A Romance of the Middle Ages,* translated by Helen M. Mustard & Charles E. Passage (Vintage Books, 1961), footnote on p. 183.

of love, caused mainly by hurt pride, insecurities, feeling disrespected, and low self-esteem. Wolfram's description of Meljanz's act of revenge is long and convoluted, which underscores the intricate nature of the heart. *"It's complicated,"* as people like to say regarding any lover's tiff. "Thus anger plays so prominent a part in this affair that these two kings plan to besiege Bearosche, where ladies' favours will have to be striven for by the breaking of many lances" (p. 180). Matters of the heart, when out of control, create much pain and confusion for many involved. It never remains a private matter. It's happened before and will happen again. The tabloids are full of these types of stories. It's the stuff of movies and binge-worthy TV shows.

Having heard the situation, Gawain again has to weigh his options: What to do? His indecision is emphasized. Not being rash, he decides to take a closer look. His quandary of the heart mirrors the mental doubt of Parzival. "With anguish for blade, Gawan's indecision cut him plane-like to the heart" (p. 181).

Obie and Obilot

My inner place is
where I go, when I am troubled,
when I feel like the
outside world doesn't
speak my language...
it feels so safe to keep
these thoughts inside.
— Goni (Student)

Most of us have been falsely accused at one point or another in our lives. It is unpleasant, and for some people it can have devastating effects, especially if it lands them in prison, or if they suffer great injury, even execution. No matter how small and seemingly insignificant, it leaves its mark. The false accusations are a leitmotif in Gawain's story, to which we have to pay attention as it reveals something about his task and inner development.

Gawain sets up camp below the well-fortified walls of Bearosche, above which Lyppaut's wife, his two daughters and a profusion of women observe him.[4] Obie, the older daughter, immediately accuses Gawain of being a merchant—an oft repeated accusation. However, the younger sister Obilot—her polar opposite—comes to his defense at once, saying, "'You are accusing him of what never happened" (p. 182). Just as Gawain was falsely accused by Kingrimursel, he is now again suffering that same fate of shameful words. And similarly to the way a merchant might weigh what prices to charge for his wares, Gawain weighs his actions according to his heart. There is a correlation of sorts, but it is inner and relates to morals, to truth, to right and wrong, and not to outer material things. Yet, a warning is sounded for Gawain who is eavesdropping into their conversation, hearing every word. Desire or selfishness, no matter how well fortified we might be, can easily enter and color our emotions. Obilot, however, is so sure of herself and of Gawain's integrity that she decides to have him for her knight. "He can serve me and ask for my reward, and I'll give it him, seeing that he pleases me" (p. 182). Whereas Obie mocks and maligns him, Obilot straightway recognizes Gawain's true essence. They are bound together by destiny, even as the son of Lot finds himself fused to her name, Obi-lot.

In Obie and Obilot, Gawain experiences contrasting aspects: he is mocked and reviled by the older daughter of Lyppaut, and revered by the younger. How he deals with them will determine his future encounters. Obie continues to insult and offend him, which he bears with patience and grace, like he bore Kingrimursel's calumny. Obilot, on the other hand, eventually comes to him and asks him to become her knight-servitor. This is a touching encounter. She, a little girl, at least five years too young to have a relationship with a man, vies for his love—in all innocence! It is the epitome of innocent love, yet rendered powerful through her innocent purity. No untoward or lower feelings color her love, and Gawain responds in turn (how different to Parzival's first encounter with a woman, with Jeschute).

Meanwhile, there is a great deal of back and forth with ongoing discussions

4 Women play an important role in all of Gawain's adventures.

about "how to cope with the harsh situation" (p. 184), as Lyppaut laments, while seeking advice from those who have joined him. It is a situation fraught with doubt about how to proceed. Solving social problems is never easy and always involves discussions and endless dialogue. It's hardly ever clean and straightforward, and resolution usually comes after much loss, pain, and sacrifice. Most of Book Seven deals with aspects of this social conflict, which has grown totally out of proportion. After all, the whole debacle arose out of Obie's proud rejection of Meljanz, and his angry, impulsive, and proud response. Furthermore, Obie exacerbates the situation by her persistent attempt to discredit Gawain, calling him a swindler and a counterfeiter, even sending the Burgrave to seize all of Gawain's goods without payment, which tests his patience and inner equilibrium.

The voice of reason in this disorientating bewilderment comes from little Obilot, who ends up solving the conflict through her resolute action.[5] The episode adds new meaning to Christ's words, "In truth, I say, unless you change and become like little children, you will not enter the kingdom of heaven" (Matthew 18:3). What a determined, courageous, and self-reliant girl she is to approach an imposing knight, surrounded by his retinue, and ask him to fight for her, knowing that he has already refused Lyppaut's request. Her "speech" is truly the "outer garment of [her] mind" (p. 190). Her words are music to his ears, and though she is still at least five years too young for marriage, he remembers Parzival who "placed greater trust in women than in God" (p. 191), the advice of which entered his heart, moving him to accept her request and fight for her. "People will see *me* doing battle there, but it is *you* who must be fighting for me" (p. 192). Her response is profound:

> "I shall be your shield and your defence, your heart and your firm faith, how that you have *freed me from doubt* [my italics]. When misfortune threatens, I shall be your guide and friend, the roof

5 Students always ask how old she is. Eschenbach does not give a specific age. I imagine her around 10 years of age, but some scholars claim she is as young as seven (making the marriageable age 12, which even for medieval times seems young).

> sheltering you from hail-storm, affording you sweet repose. My love shall fence you about with peace, and bring you luck when you are faced with danger so that your courage will surely defend you." (p. 191)

These words are like a magic spell that will hold true into the future, when he will be faced with much greater trials and tribulations. They become power words, alive with the force of love. Obilot's love is effective through its innocence, free of any desire, infatuation, or self-interest. It rests in the truth of true love, based on recognition of a soulmate, worthy of her being, though she is still so young, or because of it. All well-rounded love relationships, no matter how passionate, would do well to have a pinch of innocent love in the blend.

Just as Obilot's love is future-bearing, so is Obie's scorn for Gawain. Nonetheless, Wolfram asks the reader to "*not reproach Obie*" (p. 189), for her anger springs from her hurt.

> Whether in man or woman, heartfelt Love often impairs a lofty understanding. Obie and Meljanz's love was so true and entire that the young man's anger deserves your sympathy. Obie was hurt so deeply by his riding away in a huff that she lost her composure and flew in a passion, too! Thus Gawan, though in no way to blame, had to bear the brunt of her displeasure, together with others who had to endure the siege with her. (pp. 188-9)

Ah, how easily we misunderstand each other, how we misjudge outer actions or words. Thus, we have true love clothed in thorns, in the form of Obie (experience) and Obilot (the epitome of innocence): polarities with which the heart has to contend, that have to be weighed out and discerned, that have to be understood, perceived, received, and endured—above all, met with compassion. These two daughters bestow an immense gift on Gawain that will stand him in good stead in the trials that await him. They form a unity like yin and yang.

However, as of yet, the snowballing conflict is without a resolution.

Battle for Bearosche

Will these words
ever find a way out?
Will I have the courage
to spill them out?
And if I push them out...
maybe they won't come out right—
So, I might as well
stay silent.
— Student

The ensuing battles between the armies in the name of (misconstrued) love get off in a spirited fashion with the "ear-splitting sound of shattering of lances" (p. 195), mirroring the inner emotional turmoil of the lovers, who fight each other with thorns of pride instead of the rose's beauty, fragrance, color, and form. The name Bearosche implies "beautiful rose," though "rosche" has also been interpreted as red, or purple, and even as a cliffside, all of which is fitting to the conflict. This particular battle exemplifies the antithesis of knightly conduct, overrun by anger and bloodlust, where both lovers have succumbed to their lower natures, which ignore or defile all of the *codes of chivalry*: The battle shreds the lesson of shame, giving in to the unworthiness of both deed and speech. There is a blatant disregard for the poor and innocent involved, and a blindness to compassion, while yielding to rude, ill-mannered behavior, in place of opening paths of communication through thoughtful questions and answers, guided by the senses that lead to circumspect resolution. Concealing the faithful voice of love is a form of lying, which can never serve love. Instead of the lovers uniting as one under the sun, they cede their dignity and submit to strife. However, how are Obie and Meljanz—the cause for the excessive tumult—to understand what marriage or true union means? The outer battle becomes a battle of the soul. If a resolution is found, it will have served as a battle *for* the soul.

Gawain enters the battle because he fights on the side of *innocence*, protecting those who are suffering an attack, just as Gawain is repeatedly accused of something though he is innocent. On the other hand, we hear of "Sir Nameless," a knight dressed all in red, who has joined the cause of Meljanz, the attacker, who we can immediately identify as Parzival. We might wonder why he and Gawain are fighting on opposing sides. It becomes understandable when we recall that Wolfram asks the reader not to judge Meljanz too harshly and that he deserves our sympathy. Parzival, who has become culpable himself, and experienced the pain of his failings, chooses the side of the guilty. Just as he aches for and seeks redemption, he joins forces with those at fault in order to redeem them. In this light, the redemption of Orilus and Clamide that Parzival helped to facilitate makes more sense. Gawain's fight, as mentioned, is in the name of *innocence*, represented by the pure power of young Obilot, and by doing so, helps to restore Parzival's innocence, which he lost due to his dullness of mind and emptiness of heart.

It is clear that Gawain and Parzival outshine all the other knights: "These two took the palm above all others beyond question" (p. 199), Sir Nameless fighting for the "Outers" and Gawain for the "Inners." The polarities continue to be ever present in *Parzival*, as they are in life.

Eventually, Gawain confronts Meljanz, defeating him solidly, wounding him in the arm and taking him prisoner. When the word of his defeat reaches Parzival, he releases all his prisoners with an oath to surrender themselves to the Queen of Belrepeire, to offer their servitude to Condwiramurs, and to make sure that they "tell her that the man who fought Kingrun and Clamide for her sake is consumed with longing for the Gral and of course again for her love" (p. 200). This lets Condwiramurs know that he still loves her, that his fidelity is intact, and that he is in search of the Grail. The fact that he no longer sends knights to Cunneware shows that he has ended that stage of his development and is on to the next. Condwiramurs's love has now become his source.

Before he leaves, Parzival picks a new horse because the horse he had won from Ither was badly wounded. The choice falls on Ingliart of the short ears, one of Gawain's horses that had wandered off, almost as if he was seeking Parzival out, transferring a message. The exchange of horses, hints at a change and growth of intelligence, facilitated through Gawain's deeds. The "short ears" of Ingliart suggest that Parzival's capacity for independent *listening* is starting to sprout. Furthermore, it is fast and sturdy as Ither's horse had been.

Meanwhile, Gawain meets and jousts with Meljahkanz, who had abducted Imane in Soltane. The misogynistic knight now suffers inglorious and public defeat, witnessed by the ladies looking down from the palace (foreshadowing his combats at Shastel marveile). Thereby, Gawain avenges and redeems Parzival's youthful inattentiveness to someone else's plight due to the naïve ignorance of his Soltane days.

Gawain, up in the palace of Bearosche, gives over King Meljanz to Obilot, so that she may choose his fate. She, knowing that Meljanz and Obie truly love one another, orders them to reconcile, which they do to everybody's relief and delight, especially the lovers, though it's not "all's well that ends well," since so many people have suffered and died through their cumulative pride. There is always a costly price to pay for pride, anger, and egotism.

When Gawain leaves, Obilot wants to accompany him. Though unable to grant her wish, he assures her that he will never cease to be her lifelong servitor. Thereby, she will always be with and part of him—as one in spirit.

Gawain has witnessed how relationships, obscured by selfishness, pride, and anger, can create confusion, sorrow, and pain. Obilot acted out of the wisdom of innocence, the direct insight of a child that is still close to the divine, untainted by lower emotions and desires. Now he will have to prove his strength in another realm of the heart. Sorrow awaits him, for all relationships in the social sphere take place in the heart's domain of joy and dolor.

Discussion Topics, Questions

- What throws us into emotional turmoil and why?
- Characterize innocent love.
- When have you had to navigate unknown situations or places, such as a foreign country? What was that experience like? What do we learn?
- Is the love between Obie and Meljanz believable? Is their behavior understandable? Are there contemporary examples?
- It makes sense standing up for the victim, but how do we understand Parzival fighting for the aggressor?

Illustration:
1. Personal Crest (Magdalen Garrity)
2. Knight on Horseback (Grace Burfeind)

BOOK EIGHT

ANTIKONIE

"Young men's love then lies not truly in their hearts, but in their eyes."
~ William Shakespeare (*Romeo and Juliet*, Act II, scene 3)

GAWAIN NOW RIDES toward Schanpfanzun with his entourage to make good on the promise of the contest, a potentially hostile environment, since he has been accused of killing Kingrisin, King of Ascalun. The route leads through a forest, broad and long, overgrown and uneven, followed by high mountain ranges and swampy moors, which suggests an inner terrain that he has to navigate. Without his steed, Ingliart, he is slowed down, for it could gallop like hardly any other horse, which suggests Gawain's own gradual fall from knightly perfection. Parzival, on the other hand, having claimed Ingliart, can increase the pace of his inner progress.

Eventually, the splendid castle appears before Gawain, rising up above a wide plain and the open sea. An army of five hundred knights rides toward him, headed by Vergulaht, King of Ascalun, son of the slain Kingrisin. Furthermore, he is Parzival's cousin, and mention is made that he is of the fairy race. It implies a different realm to what Gawain is used to, not without its dangers, already foreshadowed by the circuitous journey.

An episode reinforces the danger zone for Gawain. Falcons hunting a heron are brought down in a swamp, pursued by Vergulaht who endeavors to rescue the hunting birds, though he loses his horse and is drenched. Unable to welcome him properly (or reluctant to), Vergulaht sends Gawain to the castle, ensuring him that his beautiful sister, Antikonie, will take good care of him. Wolfram asks the reader to take note "how a clear mind [is] muddied by other's duplicity" (p. 207).

The imagery is clear. The falcons who are brought down into the swamp represent Gawain, who is in danger of losing his bird's-eye view and his dignity. Furthermore, the heron is universally associated with balance, tranquility, and calmness, suggesting that those qualities are threatened. Both the hawk of the heights and the crane of the level environs—of swamps, wetlands, and mudflats—are in danger. It is a pictorial portrayal of Gawain's path of development that calls for the purification and internalization of soul capacities. The name Schanpfanzun indicates Gawain's forthcoming experience or trial. In the original Middle High German "*Schamfanzûn*," we have the word "Scham," which means "shame," as well as a poetical allusion to a "swamp" in "Sumpf."

After the servant relays Vergulaht's message, Antikonie says to Gawain, "Now command and instruct me. For if I am to entertain you, it must be just as you say. Since my brother has commended you to me so favorably, I will receive you with a kiss. Now bid me kiss you or no, as you judge fit" (p. 208). He takes her offer literally and there is an immediate erotic spark between the two, already hinted at by Vergulaht's promise that she would entertain him so well that he would not even want to see his host. This is entirely different to Gawain's meeting with innocent Obilot. Gawain is struck by her beauty from the moment he sets eyes on her, and the attraction is mutual, confirmed by the welcome kiss: *"ir munt was heiz, dick und rôt,*

/ dar an Gâwân den sînen bôt."[1] Gawain, inflamed by her hot, voluptuous red lips, went far beyond the customary greeting kiss between strangers ("*kuss ungastlîch*"[2])—a kiss with "the inside lip" as Shakespeare might have quipped. They sit down and he seeks her love with passionate appeals that only fuels his desire. The others in the room, aware of the amorous talk and energy between the two young lovers, conveniently leave the room. "Seeing the whole company gone Gawan reflected that a very small eagle may take the great ostrich" (p. 209). What he does not consider is that the ostrich could bring down the eagle as the heron brought down the falcons in the swamp only a short time before. He loses the clear view of the heights, and driven by the prize, he cannot help but "thrust his hand beneath her cloak," proceeding to stroke her "*hüffelîn*," which is usually translated as "thigh," though could also refer to her private parts, as some translators and scholars have suggested. Either way, it serves to arouse them both: "The man and maid were so hard-pressed by desire that if malevolent eyes had not espied it a thing would have been done that both were intent on" (p. 209). At this juncture of accelerated erotic culmination, they are interrupted by a white knight in the form of an old grey-haired man, who immediately sounds the alarm, accusing Gawain of rape.

Once again, Gawain is accused of something of which he is innocent, for it is clearly as consensual relationship. The scene has overt erotic overtones from the moment King Vergulaht invites Gawain to let himself be entertained by his sister, reinforced by her welcoming words that she would do his bidding, a clear invitation for him to follow his amorous desires. They are instantly attracted to one another, leading each other on, their desire-enflamed bodies mutually intent on satisfaction. The uncontrolled desires of this otherwise so perfect knight are laid bare. One cannot help but think, however, that Gawain was lured into a trap by Vergulaht, who suspected that Gawain would be enticed by his sister, thus creating the ideal opportunity to take revenge on his father's alleged murderer. The grey-haired man who interrupted them at the height of their passion is a

1 Lachmann, VIII, 405, 19, p. 197.

2 Lachmann, VIII, 405, 21, p. 197.

counter-image to the type of grey-haired men that Herzeloyde had meant Parzival to seek advice and wisdom from, such as Gurnemanz or Trevrizent. What Vergulaht did not anticipate is that Antikonie would listen to her heart and choose Gawain over the rights and laws of the clan.

Chess Gambits

"What is the hardest task in the world? To think . . . "
~ Ralph Waldo Emerson

Every class has a few chess aficionados and I usually ask the students to describe a typical chess game. The answers are similar: it's a highly competitive game of strategy and stratagems, a game of opposites, requiring envisioning, remembering, and maneuvers, while gauging the opponent. It is outwardly a quiet game of conquering the other through tactics and calculated critical thinking—except for the occasionally vociferous exclamation of "checkmate."[3] It requires a calm mind and self-control, always keeping the inner feelings at bay, lest the opponent gain the psychological upper hand. Most of what is going on is unseen, played out in the minds of the opposing players. There is nominal movement and sound. It is played under strict rules, yet there's freedom within the boundaries with an infinite number of moves at one's disposal. The rules are known and agreed upon by both parties, and in that regard the game of chess can be considered as a reflection of a healthy social life. The chess board lies horizontally between the two players and the lawfulness provides an element of order and harmony. Chess, which has its origins in India and Persia, has hidden within it a hint of the great laws of the universe, as Steiner intimates. The "Adepts have known how to introduce the great cosmic laws, so that, even in play, people have at least a smack of wisdom."[4] It is a game of consequences. However, the upcoming chess contest will prove to be anything but quiet, calm, and thoughtful.

3 The German translation of "checkmate" is "Schachmatt," which comes from the Persian "Shah Mat," which means "the king is helpless."

4 Steiner, *The Temple Legend*, p.129.

As soon as the alarm is sounded, Gawain, who is swordless, puts himself into her care. "Madam, what shall we do?" (p 209) Antikonie, in her leadership role, immediately comes up with the idea of climbing up the tower by her room where they strategically defend themselves. She stands fully by her man, which demonstrates her affection and loyalty, proving that the accusation of rape is false. In Antikonie we have another example of a strong and self-determined woman, willing to stand for the truth and the convictions of her conscience, even if it means siding with the "enemy" and going against the clan.

People come running from all around, knights, merchants, and the rabble from the town. The accusation has spread like wildfire, and nobody questions whether the rumor of rape is true or false. It is not unlike the celebrity scandals today that take front and center stage, receiving more air time than wars, famines, and natural disasters combined. Emotions run high, and the status quo is accepted and believed without inquiry. The couple defend themselves as best they can from their turret lair, Gawain ripping off a door bolt and Antikonie scurrying around looking for weapons till she finds a large chess set. She begs the unleashed horde to stop, but her pleas are lost in the noisy tumult. She hauls a massive chess board from the wall and hands it to Gawain who uses it as a shield, while she proceeds to hurl the heavy chess pieces at the enemy, each one hitting the mark. She fights like a knight at Gawain's side. "As she fought she shed copious tears. But she showed clear proof that affection between lovers is steadfast" (p. 210). However, even in battle there is an erotic nature to the scene, as Gawain cannot help but be impressed by the spirited manner of her attack, in between looking up and admiring her body, how "neatly shaped" she is, her eyes, mouth, nose, her slender waist. She continues to "kindle love's desire" (p. 210) and instills renewed courage in him.

This scene can be compared and contrasted to the previous chapter. In both we have a great escalation of confusion that leads to battle and death. In the first, it is the pride of the lovers that gets out of hand, where hurt feelings on both sides hemorrhage into misunderstandings, hiding the truth of their love underneath it all. In this instance, the couple respond to their mutual attraction, and the misunderstanding and accusation comes from the outside. With Meljanz and Obie the rift is borne between them, their inability to really see and recognize each other, a consequence of their immaturity, where they are still caught up too much in themselves. In contrast, Gawain and Antikonie get caught up in each other, wanting to live out their mutual but rampant desires without even knowing one another, thrust along by instinctive physical compatibility and bodily recognition. Love relations are always tied into the community in one way or another.

Confusion, tumult, and rampant disregard for life, civility, and the codes of chivalry overshadow both chapters, highlighting the obfuscation that underlies so much of the social life. Using the game of chess as a symbol of chaos is a potent picture. What should be a quiet battle of the minds is turned inside out—has become outer. It is the antithesis of a refined meeting place between two people or different cultures. Thoughtful tactics are thrown overboard. It is no longer a sophisticated dance of opposites, but a full-scale battle. The polarities are at odds. The hierarchy of knights, bishops, kings, queens, rooks, and the riff-raff pawns is thrown into disarray. All rules and regulations are out the window, or—in this case—down the tower. Gawain and Antikonie are up in the turret but lack the clarity of vision from up on high—the bird's-eye view. Everything is topsy-turvy, and it only gets worse. Nor is it white against black, but all the chess pieces are cast helter-skelter into the mob. And the societal hierarchy is just as chaotic, with kings, bishops, and knights behaving like uncultivated thugs.

Vergulaht arrives on the scene and instead of bringing it to a stop, he joins the fray. As host he should have the foresight to end it, especially since he sent Gawain to Antikonie to be entertained, knowing his sensual sister's charms full well. He does not stop to ask questions, to get any clarity but even goes so far as to order the tower ripped down. It is almost humorous, if it weren't so tragic. Yet, we know ourselves from experience how ridiculous some social strife can become. Furthermore, Kingrimursel, who had promised Gawain safe passage and protection until the appointed time of the duel, joins the two lovers to uphold his promise, which means that Vergulaht and his men are now essentially fighting one of their own.

Luckily, through a chosen spokesperson, Vergulaht is persuaded to enter into a truce "till he had taken further counsel as to how to avenge his father" (p. 212). It is as if a curse has fallen on everybody in the entire kingdom of Schanpfanzun. The social sphere, which is easily swayed by emotions, needs to be brought into a state of rest. The storms must subside for clarity of thought to resume and solve the conflicts.

Conflict Resolution

"The most useful piece of learning for the uses of life is to unlearn what is untrue." — Antisthenes (Greek Philosopher)

It's an opportune moment to discuss conflict resolution, to describe and rethink how conflicts—local and global—are handled, and how they could be solved. The Gawain section of the epic can teach us a great deal about social conflicts and how to best overcome and deal with them. Nothing is simple in the social sphere. It's a theme that students feel strongly about.

In both of these Gawain chapters, the outer battles are followed by endless discussions, with many people voicing their personal opinions. Nevertheless, home truths are aired, such as Antikonie scolding her brother for his shameful behavior as a host. "I have always heard it said that whenever it chanced that a man sought refuge with a woman, the gallant pursuers if bred to truly manly ways, should call off their attack. Lord Vergulaht, the flight of your guest to me in fear for his very life will bring deep disgrace to your name" (p. 213). Kingrimursel also upbraids him. This causes Vergulaht to recognize and *wake up* to his dishonorable actions, seeking to make amends without loss to his self-esteem. He realizes that hasty judgements got in the way. Through the process he could reflect on his behavior. He got caught up in the heat of the moment—all because of one small false accusation. Everything has consequences, as does every move in chess. The whole episode brought shame to all. It's almost as if the fairy heritage had blinded them in order for them to wake up and recognize their own stupidity.

The discussions go on for hours (in contrast to the accusation of rape, which took seconds), while Antikonie takes Gawain by the hand and leads him to a place of rest. It allows Vergulaht, with the help of others, to "weigh up what is best to be done" (p. 216). Here we again have the image of weighing things up—finding balance, looking at the situation from different angles in order to overcome the *doubt* of not knowing what the best solution might be, what *move* to make. However, if the intention is good, then we can have confidence that the right resolution will avail itself. That takes listening, effort, and a touch of something else: the *spirit* that can enter into the group. I have been in enough meetings to know, without doubt, that deep heart-listening can invite something higher and inscrutable to enter which allows all involved to arrive at the right solution. When that happens, it feels like a blessing. In moments like these, the group becomes a vessel, a Grail, lit up by a spark of insight that helped to solve the problem.

In the interim, Antikonie "courteously entertained Gawain, for whom she cherished tenderest feelings" (p. 217), though she worries that Gawain's life is in danger. However, all's well that ends well, and it is ultimately decided that Gawain should take on the search for the Grail for Vergulaht, because the Lord of Schanpfanzun had lost a battle with a certain red knight. Gawain agrees, which means he has to set out *alone*. The duel, for now, has been postponed for a year. Antikonie and Gawain are forced to separate. A solution has been found. Gawain will not suffer execution. However, their love is not meant to be, just like their lovemaking was interrupted minutes before consummation. Wolfram leaves it open whether something might still have transpired between the lovers: "Overnight, so I am told, the warrior was given the most comfortable quarters" (p. 218), and the next morning she leads Gawain in, hand in hand, wearing a garland.

Before the general parting, Vergulaht asks Antikonie for advice and forgiveness for his wrongdoing that has "swooped between me and Nobility and driven me from Reputation" (p. 219). She, like Kingrimursel, forgives him, and Book Eight ends with a general feeling of levity and happy resolutions, except for the parting lovers. "Deep attachment found vent in bitter sorrow" (p. 220) at the parting between the two lovers. Like with

Obilot, he will carry her in his heart forever. "I shall be bound to devote my knight-errantry and chivalric aspirations to the service of your womanly virtue always. A happy fate has taught you to vanquish falsity, so that your honor outweighs all other" (p. 220). There is no *Hohe Minne* without some pain and sacrifice.

Students often ask whether Antikonie has any connection to the Greek Antigone, immortalized by Sophocles (often covered in 9th or 10th grade). It is highly likely that he knew the story. It is surprising how well-versed Wolfram was in ancient mythology and history, based on the myriad allusions and comparisons he makes to antiquity, considering that the Middle Ages did not have easy access to most works from the past.

The Greek Antigone is a strong-willed woman who follows the laws of the gods over the laws of the city state, burying her brother with all the appropriate burial rites. She is arrested but remains defiant against her own flesh and blood—her father, who has imposed the city's law. Similarly, Antikonie stands by her man and for what is right and honorable against her brother, King Vergulaht. It therefore seems likely that Wolfram, who chooses his names carefully, did have the Greek Antigone in mind. Dauntless Antikonie stands by her convictions, and justifies her actions by speaking out convincingly and rationally, which, in the end, sways the decision in Gawain's favor. The Greek Antigone is often recognized as one of the first feminists. Likewise, Antikonie stands up for herself, in a time when women were still under the dominance of men. She follows her heart and conscience, instead of the rule of the land and the patriarchy, represented by King Vergulaht. Furthermore, she advocates her rights through fierce actions and through right speech.

When we discuss relationships, the students admit that they are initially attracted to others by their looks: *outer* attributes, such as facial features, body, the clothes they wear, how they move. Inner qualities often come later, though the outer aspects offer clues to the inner life. Physical attraction in relationships is important, even though one is all too often deceived by looks, which can lead to hasty decisions, which are often regretted.

The love between Gawain and Antikonie is sparked by a mutual physical and sensual attraction, as much as by an immediate and instinctive kinship. It is consensual and it immediately pulls them together. The sensuous urges rush to the fore, take over, and the couple succumbs to sexual desire. Rational thinking is dimmed, yet it is a natural human drive they both share and are ready to give to one another. They want to get to know one another, and in this case, it is first through the intimacy of touch. And from the first deep kiss they feel their bodies mutually uniting. They are physically compatible—an important attribute between lovers. In the hasty and fragmentary speech between them, they admit that they barely know each other. But it is not important. Their bodies know. Wolfram, who makes many asides, never once makes any moral judgements against either one of them, which, given the times, one might expect. On the contrary, Wolfram goes to great pains, assuring the reader of Antikonie's virtues, admonishing those who might slander her name. According to Rudolf Steiner's study of the twelve senses, he connects and relates the sense of touch to the sense of ego, which is fitting, for they get to sense each other's higher selves, their respective egos, through touch. The quality of a handshake, for instance, can say a great deal about the other person. However, a dimming of the mind can occur through arousal, if it only remains sexual, but a lifting of hearts to the essence of the other can also take place in an enhanced manner. Gawain, uncharacteristically, is clearly impatient and wants immediate gratification, which hints at an inner dimming and lack of control, which partly leads to the interruption and the false accusation of rape.

It is this very interruption that highlights their mutual love. Antikonie is not only the one who is determined to stand by Gawain (*heart*), but comes up with a solution (*thought*). Furthermore, she is actively involved in the fighting (*deed*), but later on in reprimanding her brother and voicing her mind (*speech*). It is all a profound expression of her strong ego, all of which Gawain observes and absorbs. Their love starts with an intense physical attraction, and it intuitively embraces the other attributes and thus becomes an expression of goodness. In this respect, it is in direct contrast to the chaste love of Parzival and Condwiramurs who spend three nights together before their love is consummated physically. Then again, Antikonie is not the woman destined for Gawain. Their relationship prepares him for the one to come, for Orgeluse.

If bodily love remains purely sexual, then it remains in the dark realm and has weakened staying power. If the ego of the other is not fully recognized, then the body becomes a commodity and the person might not be respected or revered in the long run. If it is one-sided, it can become manipulative and exploitive. If it is forced, it becomes harassment and abuse. Sex is simple, relationships are difficult, as is often said.

With their lovemaking interrupted, they are forced to practice restraint and their relationship becomes a public event. The entire community is drawn into the fray. Had Gawain been more circumspect and not so pushy—driven by desire and self-satisfaction—the resultant confusion could have been avoided. His urge-driven impatience brought death, injury, and sorrow. Vergulaht did save his falcons that got pulled into the swamp by the heavy heron, but he lost his horse, got drenched, and was waylaid. Gawain is saved by Antikonie, but was dragged into a social swamp. The realm of desires and emotions are like an ocean, and seafarers need skill to weather the storms, to maintain control and steer the boat to safe shores. We all need to become mariners of the heart. Parzival was stopped by the three drops of blood, which took hold of his heart, dimmed his senses, and darkened his thinking. Gawain was stopped by the old grey-haired man when his body was aflame with lust, which dimmed his mind.

Their true, honest, and sincere relationship is essential for their personal growth. The lesson of restraint—though forced—prepares him for the encounters that still await him, when he will have to exercise restraint by using his own forces of soul. The heart's realm needs direction through the mind's clarity, while thinking needs the warmth and balancing power of the courageous heart. Most people can identify with the Antikonie scene. Many high school relationships are based on mutual, sexual attraction. However, after sexual gratification (if it comes to that), couples often realize that they are not really meant for one another, that their interests do not necessarily coincide, and that they are not soul-mates but enjoyed each other as "body-mates." As swiftly as they came together, as swiftly they drift apart, often leaving pain in their wake. The interruption by the old man, in one way, helped Gawain and Antikonie to go their separate ways. Their relationship, though not meant to be, is mutually enriching. Antikonie, like with Obilot, will be an important part of Gawain's life, both contributing to his advancement and the outcome of the upcoming relationship.

Discussion Topics, Questions

- Discuss social issues and different ways of dealing with conflict resolution.
- What are the different types of love relationships?
- Consider desire nature versus restraint.
- Describe the ceremonies and rites of passage in various parts of the world.
- Why are ceremonies around relationships or sexuality so widespread?
- What attracts you initially to another person?
- What are the responsibilities in a consensual relationship?
- How do you differentiate between head and heart intelligence? Can we characterize the difference? Can we feel the difference?
- When have hasty judgements exacerbated a situation or created social turmoil?

Illustration:
Knight bidding farewell to his lady (Jae-Yon Yoo)

BOOK NINE

The Return

"There is nothing like returning to a place that remains unchanged to find the ways in which you yourself have altered." ~ Nelson Mandela

In Book Nine we are reunited with Parzival. It is a chapter of inner transformation and change, clearly indicated by the first word of the chapter: "*Open*," followed by:

> 'To whom? Who is there?'
> 'I wish to enter your heart.'
> 'Then you want too narrow a space.'
> 'How is that? Can't I just squeeze in. I promise not to jostle you.
> I want to tell you marvels.' (p. 222)

It Is Lady Adventure and she wants to *enter* our hearts, suggesting an inner space. She has been leading us through all of Parzival's quests. A prescient, omniscient Lady who withholds judgement, yet speaks the truth. It behooves us to listen to her intermittent words, for they guide our understanding. They serve as a bridge from the Gawain section that deals with his developments of the heart, which have a direct effect on Parzival, the shamed knight who left Arthur's court with a closed heart and mind. The adventures will have a different quality to the others in that they turn inwards.

11th graders have the tendency to retreat within themselves and become ponderous and contemplative, reflecting more deeply on what transpires in the world and in their personal lives. Everything is reevaluated and it can be a trying and confusing time. However, it can also be accompanied by beautiful moments of self-discovery and profound insights that can serve as helpful signposts, precipitated by certain events or encounters, which are reflected in Book Nine.

Many years have elapsed and Parzival has traversed through many lands on horseback and on ships, taking part in wars and jousts, always coming out the victor. He has won great renown, like his father before him, yet he is unhappy, for his main quest of finding the Grail has remained unsuccessful. The sword given to Parzival by Anfortas "helped him in winning fame" (p. 223). It did get shattered but was reforged by the "virtues of the well near Karnant and known by the name of Lac" (p. 223), which shows that Parzival took heed of Sigune's advice and learned how to make the sword whole. Each one of his battles can be seen as a trial and a step in his development, where one hurdle after another is conquered along the long road to self-knowledge. One could equate them to the tradition of the Journeyman years ("Wanderjahre"), where Parzival travels the world, gaining experiences as a knight, even though he is no closer to the object of his goal. Nor would the constant fighting ever help him to return to Munsalvæsche. More is needed. However, each battle, coupled with his ongoing suffering, does loosen his hardened soul, readying him to *open* his heart. Gradually he has become more receptive, occasioning his return.

His extensive travels have another aspect. Parzival is undergoing a nature initiation. Whenever he travels through forests and fields, through valleys, over mountains, across deserts and oceans, he not only leaves his mark but moves through his own soul. It was already evident during his boyhood in Soltane, and continues along the different stages of his journey. He experiences the elemental forces and the movement of the planets through the zodiac. Parzival is, it must be remembered, a great sun initiate, and when he moves through nature, he not only feels nature within his own body, but he leaves his imprint on nature. Each footstep, imbued with his quest to find the Grail, leaves its mark, heard and absorbed by the beings of nature.[1] One could say that Parzival was on a pilgrimage, similarly to those on the Camino de Compostela, his soul in a constant state of battle with inner trials taking place.

Sigune the Anchoress

"Real knowledge is to know the extent of one's ignorance." — Confucius

Parzival, riding through a thick forest and rugged terrain, comes across an anchoress who is none other than Sigune, enclosed in a newly-built cell, through which a swift stream flows. He asks, "Is anyone inside?" (p. 224). It is really a question to himself. She answers in the affirmative. Ashamed, Parzival dismounts and ties his horse firmly to the branch of a fallen tree—a picture of his fallen self. Sigune is still together with her deceased lover Schionatulander, now entombed within her cell. Parzival and Sigune both suffer the pangs of separation: she from her lover Schionatulander, and he from the Grail and Condwiramurs. Her cell, devoid of happiness, mirrors Parzival's own inner life. When Parzival first met her, she appeared like a Pietà, but now she looks more like the Lady of Sorrows by Christ's tomb. This is their third encounter, and every time he sees her, he also sees death. Parzival has to come to terms with the little deaths, embodied in the disappointments, failings, and rejections—as we all do. But he also sees loyalty and love—sustaining forces.

Parzival shows compassion for the anchoress even before recognizing her, wondering how she can nourish herself.

1 *Paths of the Christian Mysteries,* p 97.

She tells him that Cundrie, the Grail messenger, comes every Saturday to bring her food. These two women who had shamed him so thoroughly now reenter his life. It shows that he is on the threshold of another stage of his development after a timeless phase of unsuccessful searching, and that the time is now ripe for him to continue from where he left off. It is Saturday evening, which is regarded as the beginning of the first day of the week for Jews. With the mention of Saturday (Saturn), the element of time reenters. Saturn has manifold associations, especially in regard to creation and time. The Greek equivalent is Cronos, the god of time. Saturn's ancient hidden power has to do with change and the shift from something old to something new: death and rebirth. Parzival, who has been oblivious to time, is slowly being drawn back into the realm of sequential development. Every encounter, however, that takes place during this chapter is according to *kairos* time—a favorable opportunity for change, the change he now is ready for.

Sigune is no longer angry with him, realizing how much he has suffered for the lack of asking the Question. She forgives him, repeating his failure, but this time with care and kindness and not to chastise. He fully acknowledges his offence, and now consciously *asks* for advice, but not before inquiring how she is faring. This shows that his interest and empathy for others has grown. She, in turn, makes him aware of the fresh tracks Cundrie has left behind after dropping off the nourishment. She advises him to follow them, which might lead to Munsalæsche. This gives him temporary hope and feels like a blessing. Again, she directs him and again he is following tracks. Like Parzival, we all have to become trackers and learn how to read them. Parzival leaves at once, motivated to catch up with Cundrie, glad to be in the vicinity of the Grail Castle. Unfortunately, he once again loses the fresh tracks and has to forego the Grail a second time. Consequently, "his happiness [is] utterly dashed" (p. 227). However, his meeting with Sigune has proven pivotal. It shows that there is a chink in his armor, that he is more *open* and ready to receive what he has rejected up till now. He has entered the spatial realm of Munsalæsche and is waking up to the time of reckoning for which he was not strong enough earlier on. He is a step nearer to his goal but still not ready to return to Munsalæsche quite yet.

This can lead into a fruitful discussion with the students about "readiness." When are we ready for what is needed from us? When is the right time to right a wrong? What does it take to confront one's failures? What is really at the bottom of all his suffering? Is it his conscience? What is conscience? When can we look at our shortcomings objectively without our emotions coloring them? However, we have to be sensitive to the timing in regard to these questions. Maybe one needs to take a few more steps into Book Nine.

Grail Horse

"Time is inner space – space is outer time." ~ Novalis

Losing Cundrie's fresh tracks leaves him disappointed and unsure of how to continue. However, when the next step does not show itself from within, it comes from without, as often happens. In Parzival's case, it emerges in the form of a knight who says, "Munsalvæsche is unaccustomed to having anyone ride so near without fighting a desperate battle" (p. 227). This confirms that he is very close to his goal—the Grail. They joust and

both lose their horses. The knight pummels into a steep ravine and Parzival's horse, Ingliart, plunges over the edge to his death, leaving Parzival hanging from a cedar bough, in a decidedly unknightly and compromising manner.

This moment is reminiscent of Odysseus, when the vortex of Charybdis almost swallows him up, and he saves himself by hanging onto a fig tree, which shows how far Odysseus, the great hero and leader of the Trojan War has fallen in status, hanging onto life by a proverbial thread. Though not as dramatic, Parzival is also alone, hanging on for dear life, so close to Munsalvæsche. Still, it's an apt metaphor: Parzival hanging loose with no solid ground beneath his feet—a picture of his inner state , and another stage of his initiation.

Wolfram chooses the cedar tree at this juncture of the story. The spiritual associations regarding the divine wood of the cedar have been well known and documented in many cultures. The cedar tree is not only mentioned in the important holy books of the world's main religions, but the timber has been used for holy artifacts, buildings, boats, and hallowed relics. It is said, for instance, that Solomon's temple was built from cedar wood. Many societies around the world attribute spiritual associations with the cedar tree: faith, support for mystical quests, and inner healing, amongst others.

The cedar bough reaches out to Parzival as much as he reaches out for it. Though the Grail still remains out of his reach, its convenient placement serves to reassure him that he can succeed with endurance and persistence. He does not hang for long, quickly regaining his foothold on the hard rock beneath him, allowing him to climb back out of the steep gulley, while his opponent saves himself on the far side. On top of the gorge, as if waiting for Parzival, stands the Templar's sturdy warhorse, which Parzival forthwith mounts. Parzival has lost Ingliart and his lance, but gained a Grail horse—a priceless exchange. With the Grail horse he gains greater receptivity and new ears to hear, though he first has to untangle the reins around its feet, symbolizing his own tangled thought life. Though the intrepid knight still has no idea where he should be heading, he is now riding a surefooted Grail horse, suggesting that he is now endowed with Grail intelligence that can serve as a guide to what the future might bring. He has crossed another significant threshold.

The Grey Knight

"We turn not older with years but newer every day."
— Emily Dickinson

To hear about Parzival going through such intense suffering, doubt, confusion, spiritual rejection, and loneliness is a source of comfort for the students of the 11th grade. They realize they are not alone, that others before them have gone through similar experiences of estrangement, of feeling adrift, or of yearning for something greater beyond themselves. They can identify with his position and inner disposition. Not knowing where exactly one is headed is a normal part of growing up. Even with a set goal in mind, the road often includes many twists and turns. But, "The Long and Winding Road," as Paul McCartney sings, will eventually lead to that desired door, as long as one persists.

Weeks pass and Parzival continues with his adventures, roaming this way and that, losing track of time and space once more, though never of his quest to find the Grail and of his love for Condwiramurs. Then, on a chilly day with the ground covered with light snow he encounters an old knight and his wife, both grey haired, wearing coarse grey cloaks over their bare bodies, accompanied by two fair daughters, all barefoot, "on a pilgrimage to and from confession" (p. 229), and a retinue of knights and squires following behind. Parzival greets the noble knight dressed in humble attire, who gently reproaches Parzival for riding fully armed during this holy season. Parzival answers:

> "I have no knowledge as to when the year begins or the number of passing weeks or of what day of the week it is. – This is all unknown to me. I used to serve one named 'God' till it pleased Him to ordain such vile shame on me. Told to look to Him for help, I never failed Him in devotion: yet there is no help for me there." (p. 229)

This clearly shows that Parzival is still caught up in the endlessness of doubt, uncertainty, and loneliness. He is again standing in front of a grey-haired person and subconsciously Parzival must be thinking of the parting words his mother gave—to heed the wise words of a grey-haired men. The pilgrim tells him that it is Good Friday, which draws Parzival back into the sequence of time.

This prompts me to ask the students about the meaning of Good Friday. It is not a given that they all know about Easter. Nature herself expresses the themes of death and rebirth, which takes place in the spring time, going back into pre-Christian eras, as far back as the beginning of creation. The dance of life and death is as archetypal as it gets and the discussion often includes religious festivals as they are represented in various cultures and religions. Though there is a strong anti-Christian sentiment amongst some students, especially among the more liberal-minded households from which many of them come, it is important that they understand and know about the various religious traditions in an objective manner. It teaches diversity, inclusivity, and equity in regard to religious streams.

The grey-haired knight suggests that Parzival should seek out a nearby hermit who will be sure to give him helpful advice. The two daughters, on the other hand, chastise their father for being too unfriendly, suggesting instead that they invite Parzival to warm himself at their home. They recognize how cold he must be on this snowy day, which mirrors the true state of Parzival's inner life, coinciding, as it does, with the sorrow of Good Friday and the day of Christ's crucifixion. It points to the nadir of Parzival's sorrows. It is exactly this warmth of human companionship and community that Parzival has been missing and for which he desperately longs. But Parzival is still feeling like a victim, thinking: "It would be more fitting if I left them, seeing that I am at feud with Him Whom they love with all their hearts and look for help but Who has shut me out from His succor and failed to shield me from sorrow" (p. 230). Apart from the overt religious connotation, Parzival is still blaming his sorrow on someone else instead of himself. He does not yet realize that his search for the Grail is really a search for his true and higher self, for knowledge of who he is, which includes his culpability. The truth of oneself and the world does not have to be within the parameters of any religion or church. It has a spiritual element either way, even if we do not label it as such. Truth goes beyond the physical and the visible. Humanity has lost the big picture, but reaching for it and lifting the veils that exist in the outer and inner world, will inevitably lead to something that is true. Parzival is at the threshold of another profound turn in his life. But it needs to come from himself. Just like in life: nobody can or should force a worldview onto another. It would be a violation of freedom. The students understand this perfectly. Young people are by nature "spiritual," though many of them do not adhere to any denomination. They have a feeling for the elusive beyond, for the "moreness" within and around them.

Parzival takes his leave, bearing the brunt of Herzeloyde's suffering within him. He has become *Parziloyde*—steeped in "pure suffering." As he rides away, he feels remorse and begins to ponder how the world came to be, wondering about the Creator, "how mighty He must be" (p. 231) to have created everything. It is an enhanced version of Herzeloyde, when she questioned herself after having ordered the killing of the birds back in Soltane, which led to her brief description of God and the devil. Students who have trouble accepting the term "God" or any religious overtones, readily accept the concept of a "creative force"—the force that goes into the creation of the tiniest flower, the highest mountain, nature, and the universe.

Parzival, through his deliberations arrives at the question: "'What if God [the creative force] has such power to succor as would overcome my sorrow" (p. 231)? There's an opening to new possibilities, to his closed off inner self. The thought alone is a ray of light, or at least a foot in the doorway. "'If this is his Helpful Day, then let Him help, if help He can!" (p. 231) He is *open* or *opening* to the possibility. There is a slight inner shift, possibly because he is riding a Grail horse. He immediately returns to the pilgrims. With them as witnesses, he says, "'If God's power is so great that it can guide horses . . . let it guide my Castilian to the best success of my journey" (p. 231), and he drops his reins over his horse's ears (listening quality) and spurs his horse. We are reminded of the times he rode in a preoccupied manner after leaving Gurnemanz and Belrepeire, when he was deeply lost in thought and caught up in the pangs of love for Liaze and Condwiramurs respectively. This time he *consciously* drops his reins and *consciously* spurs his horse. He knows what he is doing. He is not preoccupied but knowingly cedes control over to his horse's Grail intelligence, putting his trust into something higher. It shows that he is beginning to become more aware of his own destiny. Let go and let God, as they say.

Trevrizent

"I pluck golden fruit from rare meetings with wise men."
~ Ralph Waldo Emerson

The trusty Grail horse leads Parzival straight to Fontane la Salvæsche, the fountain of salvation, Trevrizent's humble abode, who invites him in and is willing to listen, receive, and offer him deliverance from suffering through the confessional dialogue. Parzival arrives in a state of ongoing crisis. From the moment of his failure at Munsalvaesche, the double shaming and scolding of Sigune and Cundrie, Parzival has sought a way to free himself from that vicious circle of crisis. The German word for crisis is "Krise," in which we detect the word "Kreisen," to go in circles. He is about to enter a sacred space, which will help him find his way out of his personal crisis.

> Personal crisis always has three elements. First, you feel you can't go on like this, that you're up against a wall. Then you feel as if something has to be sloughed off if you are to go on. The third and most important element in that process is guidance. We need guidance; otherwise, we do not know what to slough off and how to get to the other side of this impenetrable wall. This guidance is what I have called the life force or blessing.[2]

He is about to find his guidance and his blessing in the hermit Trevrizent. "Trêvre" in French means "truce," (a cessation of fighting, peace), which is

---

2 David Steindl-Rast, O.S.B., with Sharon Lebell, *The Music of Silence: Entering the Sacred Space of Monastic Experience* (SanFrancisco: Harper, 1995), p. 83.

based on "trust" or that which is "true." The German word "treue" means "loyalty." Teutschmann interprets Trevrizent as "treve rezem, he who regains or restores peace."[3] A variant spelling of Trevrizent in the old German is "*Trefrizend*," which suggests various further interpretations. The name's first syllable, "tref," makes one think of "trefflich," which alludes to something good and admirable; or "treffend," which means apt or appropriate; or "treff / treffen" that translates as "meeting." Hence: a wonderful, well timed and appropriate meeting. The word "Zend" in the Persian means to translate or paraphrase, as in the *Zend Avesta*, the sacred Zarathustrain text from Persia, where the "Zend" comments on and explains the "Avesta." From Wolfram's intermittent indications, we know that there is an intimate and conscious connection to the Zoroastrain faith, the followers of which still exist to this day, mainly in India amongst the Parsis.[4] Similarly, Trevrizent will comment, interpret, paraphrase, and impart insights into the secrets of the Grail, Munslavæsche, and the Grail community. Through their increasingly intimate discussions, more is revealed, which will lead to Parzival's inner awakening and gradual self-transformation. The destined encounter with Trevrizent is indeed vital and enlightening for Parzival on many levels.

The students get a sense for the crucial significance of Book Nine, particularly Parzival's meeting with Trevrizent. They respond to the growing relationship between the old Hermit and the young knight, their developing interactions, the place-based implications of the setting, and how Parzival's inner growth is fostered; less so with the quasi-religious overtones of the latter part of the chapter. Yet, though most students do not necessarily read through all of Trevrizent's more in-depth explanations on the source of the Grail and all the talk of Lucifer and God, I rarely receive overly critical or hostile commentaries on that section, though I always expect it. The students have surprised me in their tolerance and open-mindedness. Nevertheless,

3 Teutschmann, p.182.

4 In the name Parsi-val we can also detect a connection to Parsis or Parsees, the followers of Parsiism.

though there is much one could study and penetrate, we usually only have time to focus on a few of the essential aspects that contribute to Parzival's development. And as a teacher I bear in mind that every one of them is on their way to becoming a Grail King, or rather, a Grail Sovereign—rulers over themselves and their respective realms of responsibilities. I have found the students to be most accessible and amenable to the following sections of the encounter between Parzival and the hermit.

First, however, in response to Wolfram's earlier admonition regarding the revelations of the Grail: "Kyot asked me to conceal it [the Grail] because his source forbade him to mention it till the story itself reached that point expressly where it has to be spoken of" (p. 232), I pose the question again: When is it appropriate to reveal something? When is it the right time to disclose or divulge a truth? Do we have examples from life—your own lives—where something has been revealed to you with positive or negative effects? We discuss "hidden knowledge" and how it could be dangerous, hurtful, and debilitating. I remind them of the secret spiritual knowledge of the ancients, Greece and beyond, or the story of Cleve Cartmill, mentioned at the beginning of the block. I give examples from different cultures including the revelations of Credo Mutwa from South Africa whose writings in *Indaba, My Children* almost got him killed for revealing the hidden secrets of the Sangomas. Or Rudolf Steiner, who suffered assassination attempts for revealing esoteric knowledge.

I remind the students about Wolfram's source for the epic, referred to as Kyot the Provencal. He has never been definitively identified by scholars, who usually look for him during Wolfram's lifetime. However, there is no reason to doubt Wolfram's word, given the architectural genius of the epic, and the great learning and knowledge—both exoteric and esoteric—found in this medieval masterwork. Many scholars, including Heinrich Teutschmann warns against confusing the two Kyots.[5] However, Werner Greub, in his exhaustive study on the historical background to *Parzival*, does link the two personalities. First, he identifies the mysterious master

5 Heinrich Teutschmann, *Der Gral: Weisheit und Liebe* (Philosophisch-Antroposophischer Verlag am Goetheanum, 1984).

Kyot as the hero Willehalm in Wolfram's eponymous epic *Willehalm*. In *Parzival* this personality appears again as Kyot of Katelangen, the uncle of Condwiramurs. Thus, according to Greub, the two Kyots are one and the same. Greub's arguments are cogent, well-developed, and make sense.[6] In time this mystery will reveal itself conclusively.

Master Kyot's source, in turn, was the "heathen" Flegetanis, which gives a broader, more global scope to this medieval epic, going far beyond the strictly European borders but includes East and West (the known world at that time), and focuses on the shared ideals of humanity, specifically the shared development of each person, irrespective of gender, religion, class, politics, or economic background. Having introduced this information at the beginning of the block, I briefly bring it back at this juncture of the course, thereby fostering the values of a collective humanity, freely experienced by the individual. One can reinforce the fact that Flegetanis (*Felek-Thâni*[7]) was a highly educated person, son of a "pagan" father and Hebrew mother. His name means "familiar with the stars." He has also been referred to as the "Star Sage."[8]

So, we see that Wolfram is pointing toward the merger of the great world religions, as far as they were known at the time. Often, "heathen" is interpreted by the scholars as referring to Muslims, but it could also point towards animists, Zarathustrians, or adherents to the ancient Egyptian sun-centered beliefs connected to Ra-Osiris. Naturally, decadence has entered into the practices of all religions. Christianity, for one, is riddled with decadence, abuse, inner decay, and corruption. I am grateful that we teach books like *Parzival* that gives opportunity to talk about these thorny topics, in order to heal some of the wounds of old—but more: to bring the topics into the right context, appropriate to our times, rather than avoiding them or only criticizing them from a one-sided perspective.

Of course, it is a matter of timing. Linda Sussman in her book, *The Speech*

6 See also Ueli Seiler-Hugova, *Das Grosse Parzival Buch* (SchneiderEditionen), p. 359.

7 According to scholars such as Dr. Paul Hagen, Pierre Ponsoye, and others.

8 Also see: "Kyot and the Stellar Script of Parzival," by Ellen Schalk. https://sophiafoundation.org/wp-content/uploads/2017/04/kyotandthestellarscriptofparsifal.pdf

of the Grail, talks very eloquently on this subject. For Parzival, the timing is aligned to his inner readiness to receive, a time when it will be able to grow within him, a time when his heart has opened enough to let the words enter like cleansing and revivifying waters. We note that Sigune has a river run through her cell, and that Trevrizent has a fountain in his cave: waters that heal, nourish, and cleanse. After Wolfram's aside on the source of the Grail, he returns to the initial meeting between the Hermit and Parzival.

Parzival's Grail horse follows the fresh *tracks* in the snow, left by the grey-haired knight on his pilgrimage. This little detail is noteworthy, for in the past, Parzival had lost the fresh tracks on numerous occasions. But now, having ceded over his own intention to the horse, it's no longer a matter of trying to stay on track or fearing to lose sight of them. Rather, the tracks are drawing him on and in. On the way, he recognizes the place where he had met Jeschute and fought with Orilus, so he knows he is once again not too distant from Munsalvæsche. It shows that he is reconnecting with his destiny, the people he has harmed and redeemed. His path is leading him back to the juncture from where he can start afresh. Time and space are intersecting. He does not tarry but rides on to find Trevrizent at home in his spacious cave, where once Parzival had confessed his misdeed, and Orilus and Jeshute had reconciled, proving Jeshute's innocence. The Grail horse has led him straight to where Parzival needs to be. Another circle is completed, which starts a new cycle.

Trevrizent directly admonishes Parzival for his pride of riding in his armor but invites him in to warm himself beside the fire. Parzival dismounts and says, "'Guide me now, I am a sinner" (p. 233). In the original it has a slightly different connotation: "*nu gebt mir rât:/ ich bin ein man der sünde hat*,"[9] which translates as "now give me advice: / I am a man that has sin." Hatto's translation, "I am a sinner" has a judgmental tone, whereas the original is more objective, free of guilt's oppressiveness. One could also read it as "I am a man that has *division*," which we all feel in one way or other. Parzival is consciously asking Trevrizent for help, guidance, and advice. It comes from deep within, from the recognition that he really needs it. That is a change from the past, where it was given to him, first by his mother and then by Gurnemanz—apart from the advice that rained down on him in the form of scathing reprimands from Sigune and Cundrie.

Trevrizent agrees and their conversations begin. Still, it does take a bit of overcoming for Parzival to give himself over into the care of another, indicated by his initial reluctance to give the horse's bridle to Trevrizent. In order for him to truly receive guidance, he has to put his trust in the hands of the hermit. "And so Parzival yielded the bridle to his host, who then led the horse beneath the overhanging rock where the rays of the sun never came—a wild stable indeed" (p. 234). There is a parallel to his arrival at Gurnemanz' Court where he initially refused to get off his horse. From there Trevrizent leads Parzival into a well-protected grotto where Parzival removes his armor and can warm himself by the glowing coals. He's finally feeling safe enough to let down his guard, to remove the hard protective shield. Trevrizent lends him a coat to wear, which is an allusion to the Repanse de Schoye's robe he was allowed to borrow. For Parzival, the hermit's grotto serves as a humble and private version of Munsalvaesche. Parzival first needs to find his own inner space before he is ready to reenter the public life, just like he first had to endure Sigune's private shaming, before Cundrie's public scourging. The hermit leads him to another grotto where Parzival immediately recognizes the altar in front of which he had sworn the oath in the presence of Jeschute and Orilus, admitting to Trevrizent that he had removed the colorful lance on that day in a moment of obliviousness, having lost his self-awareness, while engrossed in thoughts

9 Lachmann, IX, 456, 29, p. 220.

of Condwiramurs. This bit of information prompts Trevrizent to reveal that it was exactly four-and-a-half years and three days ago. However, in the original it says five-and-a-half years: "*fünfthalp jâr und drî tage / ist daz irz im namet hie.*"[10] Johannes Stein also adheres to the longer period, though most scholars do not. Only now does Parzival realize how long he has been wandering the world "with no sense of direction and unsustained by any happy feelings" (p. 235). It is exactly this "sense of direction" that the students are looking for during this time of their lives when they are waking up to their inner selves.

There are numerous indications by Rudolf Steiner that the area around Dornach and Arlesheim are closely connected to the Grail story. Werner Greub in his well-researched book *Wolfram von Eschenbach und die Wirklichkeit des Grals* goes into substantial and credible detail regarding the geographic background of *Parzival*. Other scholars have different ideas regarding the placement of the various scenes and their respective historical backgrounds. Though I focus predominantly on the literary aspects of *Parzival* with the students, I have studied the various viewpoints, which I sometimes voice in class, such as Trevrizent's cave, its historic significance, confirmed by Rudolf Steiner. I cannot imagine a more authentic place than the "Hermitage" outside Arlesheim, close to See Brumbane (now known as the Öleweiher), where Parzival first encountered Anfortas on the lake. Farther up on the hill is a little hut, which marks the place where Sigune's cell allegedly stood. The vicinity is filled with legends of hermits and holy people, who have lived in these caves over the centuries, including Saint Odilia, who fled and

10 Lachmann, IX, 460, 23, p. 222.

hid from her father in a fissure of the Hohlefelsen (Hollow Rocks) high above the place where Parzival fought Orilus. Hence, it is also known as *Orilusfelsen* (Orilus Rock). Both places can be viewed from Castle Birseck located above the Hermitage at the top of the mountain. It is fascinating to walk through the caves, grottos and overhangs, that clearly show remnants of hermit life from times gone by. Steiner called this area "Grail territory."[11] Greub firmly believes that a Grail castle made of wood did exist in the Swiss Jura not too distant from the Hermitage.

While living in nearby Muttenz for a few years as a child, we often went for walks in that area and I would play around in those caves with my brother, running through the tunnels and up and down the ancient steps, hewn into the rock. Since then, I have made it a point of visiting the area whenever I sojourn or pass through Basel. I urge the students to visit the Hermitage in Arlesheim should they ever travel to Switzerland. I am glad to report that a number of them have done just that. One student, while on an exchange in Germany went to Trevrizent's grotto with his whole class during their visit to the Goetheanum in Dornach.

Parzival is now ready to "open up" his heart and receive Trevrizent's guidance. The inside space of the heart is mirrored by the inside space of the cave, the words coming from the warmth space of the mouth, to enter the listening space of the ear—the hearing space, making space for the inner meaning of what is revealed and what is confessed, deep from within the chambers, the grottos of the heart. Trevrizent will guide him through the darkness of his doubt-filled suffering to the inner light of understanding. [12] The turning point for Parzival is that he has now chosen to listen and be listened to. Without that conscious decision, it won't have the same effects.

Oftentimes, when we discuss these intimate cave-conversations between the old man and the young man, one can feel something akin to a reverent and holy mood emerge in the class. The students can relate to the intimacy

11 Ilona Schubert, p. 60.

12 See Linda Sussman, *Speech of the Grail*, Chapter Five.

between the two. Trevrizent is not some world-removed holy man, but a knight who has known life, who has fought many battles in the name of love, made mistakes, had his share of failings, traveled the "highways and byways" of life, and experienced pain and suffering, knowing what a long road it is to pursue enlightenment. Trevrizent becomes the perfect conversation partner for Parzival, in that he knows what Parzival is going through. Trevrizent has paid his dues, has gained insights through experience, contemplation, and *prayer*—in the original sense of the word: asking for greater understanding, echoed in the Spanish word *pregunta* (question), or the Latin *precari*.

The hermit leads and guides the discussions with the intuitive wisdom of a spiritual mentor, a counselor, or a psychotherapist. For any change and receptivity to occur, Trevrizent first needs to draw out what is troubling Parzival. Near the beginning of their counseling sessions, Trevrizent relates the years and weeks that have passed since Parzival removed the lance, by the reading of the psalter—"if you care to listen" (p. 235). The mirroring of time helps pull Parzival back into the present moment, allowing him to reenter the stream of time more consciously. Consequently, Parzival does reflect on the time spent in the relentless pursuit of battle which had been the downfall of his father, Gahmuret. Furthermore, it names the source of his suffering. "All I sought was battle. I am deeply resentful of God, since he stands godfather to my troubles. . . . If only God's power would succor me, what an anchor my happiness would be which now sinks into sorrow's silt" (p. 236). Parzival is aching to be "anchored," which Gahmuret never achieved, indicated by his having reverted back to the crest of the panther. To be truly anchored in the inner life is a conscious decision in how one leads one's life and the values one chooses. What Parzival is still rejecting is the willingness to confront himself, accept culpability, and enter into a dialogue with *Truth*. Our scientific age holds little stock in God, though it does pursue Truth *relentlessly*, albeit in a one-sided manner. If one exchanged the word "God" for "Truth," the text would immediately be more accessible to the contemporary mind, without having to deny that there is a greater creative power behind Truth—the Truth which continues to be a "hard nut to crack." One could also use the word "Love." However, the epitome of Truth contains Love, which in turn, contains Goodness and Beauty. So, in this case, we will use Truth to represent the Creative Spirit. Trevrizent's words would sound like this: "[I]f you have any sense you will trust in [Truth]. [Truth] will help you, since help [Truth] must. May [Truth] help both of us." After these words, Trevrizent urges him to tell his story. "You must give me full account.... Tell me soberly how your anger began so that [Truth] became the object of your hatred" (p. 236). His anger and pride have caused him to project his hatred away from himself to God, the Truth about his own failings. It is the same kind of anger that fueled Meljanz's fury against Obie, though deep down, he loved her. Parzival, deep down, loves God, loves Truth, loves Love.

Our materialistic age does embrace Truth, just not the whole Truth and nothing but the Truth. How often have we heard the statement, "I believe in the science," during the pandemic? Science has taken the place of God, though most people have no understanding of the science they "believe" in. The same could be said for "the force" from Star Wars. All people in our time recognize the forces of nature, or that there are forces behind nature—the energies. When people say, "May the *force* be with you," its religious overtones are more readily accepted, as George Harrison from the Beatles once allegedly quipped. A little later, Trevrizent says, "Anyone who sees you hating [Truth] would think you weak of understanding" (p. 236). And that exactly mirrors our time in regard to science. However, in the future, which has already begun in a seminal manner, the Truth in the science of the Spirit will not only be just as important as outer natural science, but will far surpass and supersede it, bringing it all into context. Natural science and spiritual science will coincide, become one, just as it once was, but with full consciousness. We are not there yet, but anybody with the slightest sensitivity for the Zeitgeist will recognize this. It will become the new imperative. Talking about the concept of Truth with the students, which happens from numerous perspectives in almost all classes and disciplines, is always rewarding. Parzival, after all these years is now strong enough to hear the truth, which leads to having the strength to confess one's mistakes—to own up.

Trevrizent, as mentioned, bids Parzival to tell his story. This, as all counselors and therapists know, is essential in any healing process. The late Desmond Tutu saw it as an essential criterion in the Truth and Reconciliation Committee (TRC), where the victims of apartheid told their stories, which helped South Africa to become a free democracy (not without its ongoing challenges). In *The Book of Forgiving: The fourfold path for healing ourselves and our world*, Desmond and his daughter Mpho Tutu give a fourfold path to forgiveness: *tell the story, name the hurt, forgive, move on.*[13] These steps perfectly describe Parzival's inner journey with Trevrizent, starting off with *Telling the Story*. Through telling his story, Parzival will be able to form a different picture of himself. It will help him to let go of the old and make room for what wants to become. It begins the healing.

Wolfram does not shy away from going into lengthy theological and metaphysical detail about the interchange between the two. The pious language used in this section is foreign to most modern students and can be off-putting, yet I welcome it for that very reason. If it comes up, one might ask the question: why is the language disconcerting for the contemporary mind? I refrain from going into the minutia of scriptural discussion with the students, but am always ready for questions should they come from those who actually take the time to read the entire chapter. I always expect more voices of protest or rejection, given the religious content, but mostly they are remarkably tolerant. If discussions do arise on religious themes, it's mostly because they really want to know more about figures such as Lucifer, Adam, Cain, or concepts such as Hell. Are we as teachers equipped to talk about these topics in an objective, non-religious manner? It behooves us to constantly deepen our understanding.

The time spent with Trevrizent is also a schooling in clear thinking, the essence of Parzival's development. All that he has experienced so far now

13 Desmond & Mpho Tutu, *The Book of Forgiving: The fourfold path for healing ourselves and our world* (William Collins, imprint of Harper Collins Publishers, 2014).

receives the light of understanding through Trevrizent's words (still using Truth for God):

> [Truth] that passes through men's thoughts bears such Grace. Thoughts keep out the rays of the sun, thoughts are shut away without a lock, are secure from all creatures. Thoughts are darkness unlit by any beam. But of its nature [Truth] is translucent, it shines through the wall of darkness and rides with an unseen leap. . . . And when a thought springs from one's heart, none is so swift but that it is scanned ere it pass the skin—and only if it be pure does [Truth] accept it. Since [Truth] scans thoughts so well, alas, how our frail deeds must pain Him." (p. 238)

We clearly see that Wolfram does want us to distinguish between the mere intellectual thought process, the dead thoughts of the sense-based intellect, and the living-thinking, immersed in the spirit. Parzival realizes that his suffering is really a reward imparted by God / Truth. "Sir," says Parzival, "I shall always be glad that you have taught me about Him Who leaves nothing unrewarded, whether virtue or misdeed" (p. 238).

One thing that the students understand full well is that all of us are in need of counseling. We all need a listening ear every now and then, someone to talk to, someone to tell our stories to, our pain, to help us make sense of life, receive advice that we could not come to or give ourselves—or just to vent. We all need to retreat into some "cave," some inner space, and gain *in*-sight to that which has driven us into doubt, ignorance, and confusion.

When Parzival starts to *name the hurt*, to divulge the source of his pain, he mentions the Grail for which he pines, as well as his wife. This elicits almost a rebuke from Trevrizent. "You foolish man—this I must deplore! For no man can win the Gral other than one who is acknowledged in Heaven as destined for it" (p. 239). In other words, he's declaring that it is a futile endeavor, and that it cannot be fought for. This leads Trevrizent to explain the history and source of the enigmatic Grail. The students, especially those from China, relate enthusiastically to the *Phoenix* reference, the queen of the birds. In Chinese legends the *fenghuan* symbolizes the virtues of heaven, good-fortunes, and happiness. The phoenix (yin) is also brought into an intimate relationship with the dragon (yang). Here we see a picture of Parzival's possible renewal, the dragon's renewal: his suffering and pain burned to ashes, only to reemerge anew like the phoenix—a rebirth of the inner more female element. Alternatively, the Chinese phoenix was originally regarded as two birds: feng (yang) and huan (yin) before they became one and were regarded as feminine. The multi-colored plumage of the phoenix or *fenghuan* is an apt picture of the multifaceted inner soul-spiritual aspect of the human being. Though there are differences between the Chinese fenghuan and the Greek phoenix, there are significant similarities (as there are with the *Bennu*, the mythical Egyptian bird that periodically renews itself). They both symbolize new beginnings and the divine. It is telling that the phoenix is brought into close association with the Grail, as the phoenix is an immortal bird and is known to represent the striving spirit as well as heralding a new ruler. Phoenix, the bird of rebirth. Parzival, the future Grail King, whose spiritual striving and outer sovereignty pairs within himself the dragon and the phoenix, the yin and the yang. Parzival, the promise of societal renewal, breaking old norms so that the light of the spirit may enter.

Trevrizent goes on to relate the wondrous attributes of the Grail, its life-sustaining and healing qualities. The Grail as the eternal becoming of the human being. "Such powers does the Stone confer on mortal men that their flesh and bones are soon made young again" (p. 239). The phoenix is not the only bird that is mentioned. Trevrizent relates how once a year, on Good Friday, a white dove descends to place a wafer on the stone, "from which the stone receives all that is good on earth of food and drink, of paradisal excellence" (p 240). The dove is universally recognized as a symbol of love, peace, and new beginnings, as was exemplified at President Biden's inauguration, when lady Gaga wore a gilded dove carrying an olive branch, sending the message of peace to the world.

Calmly, Trevrizent conveys further attributes of the Grail, the Grail Castle, and the nature of the inhabitants. Parzival is now receiving the answers that lived in the form of unuttered questions while he was in the presence of the Grail. Many are summoned to the Grail. Their names appear as an inscription on the top edge of the stone for a short while, and they are called from all around the world, rich or poor, irrespective of race, gender, or social standing. Munsalvæsche represents the people of the world. The Grail does not discriminate. The Grail is the epitome of inclusivity and equity, its loving arms of light embracing all of humanity. The Grail is an always-womb of concealed wisdom that wants revealing constantly. But the "*dinc*" needs people to develop faculties in order to see, hear, and experience its ever-creative source—the essential but fathomless beingness of the Grail. The Grail is the riddle of the I. The I secret. The Grail needs to be asked for; it gives and reveals when the wish to fathom its depths arises from the immeasurable depths of one's inner being, which takes time, years, a lifetime—as illustrated in the story of "Singing Stone" (as referenced on pages 35/6).

When Parzival details how he has fought many a battle for the Grail, Trevrizent admonishes him for his pride, causing him to relate the story of Anfortas' wound, which he received because of his pride. The name Anfortas indicates his suffering, which is derived from *infirmitaz* (Latin) and can be detected in the words *enfermo* (Spanish) or *enfertez* (French), both relating to infirmity. While talking about the name's meaning, a student pointed out that it could also mean "unfortunate," to which another student added, "or someone who has lost fortitude." Richard Wagner calls the Grail King Amfortas. "Am" means "at" (and to a lesser degree "on," or "in"), which suggests "at the fort." However, "fortas," apart from sounding like a fort, also sounds like "Pforte," a "portal" or a "gate," which could indicate "at the portal" or "gate"—someone who has not crossed over; in this case, impeded by his own pride.

Trevrizent continues by relating that "Only one man ever came there [Grail Castle] without first having been assigned" (p. 241). Once again Parzival has to relive the moment and hear about his shameful failure of not asking the Question. However, Trevrizent does not know that the one sitting right in front of him is that very person. It is only after this disclosure that Parzival truly tells *his* story, though he does not reveal his greatest failure—not yet—preferring to start off with his father Gahmuret, followed by the slaying of Ither, the Red Knight while "dull of understanding" (p. 242). Parzival is opening up; he is confessing. He is laying bare his own wound, brought about by his ignorance and lack of thought. He is *naming the hurt.*

Trevrizent is shocked and saddened at the news, especially since Parzival, in killing the Red Knight, slew his own flesh and blood. "May God have pity on it that you were ever the cause of such distress" (p. 243)! The admission leads to news that Parzival is not expecting, which puts it all in context: "Add to that your mother, my sister Herzeloyde, died of anguish for you!" (p 243) Trevrizent spells it out to Parzival, "You were the Beast she suckled, the Dragon that flew away from her" (p. 243), going on to explain the family connections. Herzeloyde was Trevrizent's sister, as was Schoysiane who died while giving birth to Sigune, as well as the Grail bearer herself, Repanse de Schoye and his brother, Anfortas. Parzival's Grail heritage is made clear. Trevrizent, who is revealing Parzival's "sins," goes on to disclose how Anfortas was summoned to be Grail King after Freimutel's death, the previous king. Like Parzival, Anfortas was not ready for the profound task. "Love assailed him, as is her way with striplings—she presses her friends so hard that one may call it dishonourable of her" (p 243). For a Grail King, any love that is not destined (i.e., written on the Grail) will cause suffering and sorrow. This underscores that Anfortas, too, was not ready. As modern people we are all too often not ready to take on the huge tasks assigned to us (or those we assign ourselves), which consequently cause much grief to ourselves and others. Yet, we have to carry that weight and persevere through it. It is the modern way, which wakes us up to be ever more truthful and vigilant in the face of the challenges we are confronted with. The pain prods us awake.

Trevrizent relates how Anfortas came to his wound while fighting for Amor, and getting pierced in the scrotum during a joust, the spearhead remaining in his testicles, leaving him in pain ever since, drained of strength, even when the offending part, including a splinter of the bamboo shaft, was removed by the physicians. (There is a parallel to the splinter that remained in Gahmuret's head after Ipomidon's lance thrust. The piercing of the head and the scrotum respectively, points toward the different aspects of the human being that are in need of development: head and heart, thinking and feeling). It is the reason why Trevrizent chose to become a recluse, giving up all luxuries, especially the eating of meat and drinking of wine, in the hope that it might heal Anfortas. Yet, no sacrifice could stop the wound from festering. Anfortas is only kept alive because he is brought before of the Grail. At this poignant point in the story of Anfortas' ailment, Trevrizent relates that they even tried to cure him with the blood of a Pelican, because in times of need, it feeds its starving chicks by piercing its own breast and letting them feed of her own blood, after which it dies. All to no avail. It is a poignant reference to Belacane.

This backstory, as it is told to Parzival, finds its highpoint in the prophecy which was written on the Grail, that a young knight would appear who would remove all sorrow and heal the king if he were to ask a Question. Yet, all were forbidden to prompt him. "If he omits the Question on the first evening, its power will pass away. But if he asks his Question in season he shall have the Kingdom, and by God's will the sorrow shall cease. Thereby Anfortas will be healed, but he shall be King no more" (p. 246). Had they alerted him, it would not have come from his innermost self, in freedom. This too, Parzival has to hear and bear once again, the detailed revelations piercing right through his soul, especially the words:

> All that he had achieved there was shame, for he saw all the marks of suffering yet failed to ask his host "Sire, what ails you?" Since youthful inexperience saw to it that he asked no Question, he let slip a golden opportunity. (pp. 246-247)

At this point I might ask the students to imagine all the golden opportunities that we let slip by, simply because we are either not awake enough or because we lack compassion and cannot live strongly enough into someone else's pain. Parzival does not immediately reveal that he is the culprit.

They continue to talk for a while, until Trevrizent suggests they go out and look for food, "if only the snow would let us," adding "God grant that it soon thaws" (p. 247), suggesting that Parzival's heart will hopefully soon thaw. With the foraged food, they share the humblest of meals, yet "Parzival shrewdly judged that he had eaten with greater contentment here than when Gurnemanz was tutoring him, or when so many dazzlingly beautiful ladies had passed before him at Munsalvæsche where he was feasted by the Gral" (p. 247), which shows how profoundly he is moved and that he is arriving at a greater understanding of the Grail, its meaning to the world and himself.

Only after their humble meal does Parzival admit the truth: the "man who rode to Munsalvæsche and saw all the marks of suffering and who nevertheless asked no Question was I" (p. 248). Finally, he has confessed, acknowledging his failure in a safe space to a person who understands and who has compassion, but most of all—can listen! Trevrizent's tough but honest response, however, is also a lesson that Parzival, in this moment of baring his soul, can take to heart. "The five senses that God gave you shut off their aid from you—how they betrayed your compassion then, when faced with Anfortas' wound" (p. 248). I ask the students: How can the senses be a genuine bridge to the world, to the other person? Do we use them with enough awareness? Do we care for them and sharpen our senses enough to gain the most subtle of insights? Are we awake enough to what our senses can reveal? Or are we stuck too much in our heads, the intellect, which keeps us from our hearts?

When Trevrizent talks about his own life, we learn how far and wide he traveled, all across the continents of Europe, Asia, and deep into Africa, similarly to Gahmuret and Parzival. Furthermore, Trevrizent relates that he met Gahmuret, who recognized him as Herzeloyde's brother. He is a man of experience, who has erred, done penance for misdeeds, and knows that outer achievements must be balanced and brought into context through inner work and insights. During their conversations, Trevrizent reveals the secrets of the Grail community, how Parzival is connected to it, and that he owes his Grail heritage to his mother (inner life), whereas, up to his sojourn with Trevrizent, he owed his knightly heritage to his father (outer life). During this cocooning in the cave of Trevrizent, Parzival discovers his own heritage, based on the emergent strength of his own individuality, where outer and inner strengths merge. That crossing point is a sacred and holy point; it's where the polarities meet—light and the dark. It is the reason why we find the cross as a symbol in so many cultures. It unifies the opposites in the *middle*—pierce through the middle, as Parzival's name signifies. Pursuing the middle path is not easy, for humans are multi-layered beings, easily pushed to this or that side in their bumbling pursuit of independent judgement.

After that first day with Trevrizent, Parzival stays with him in his humble abode for another fortnight, fifteen days in all. It mirrors his fourteen-day stay with Gurnemanz, though Trevrizent's counseling focuses on the development and nurturing of an inner life that helps to guide his judgement, so that he can understand how and when the knightly rules should be applied—the ability to listen to one's own inner voice rather than blindly following outer commands learned by rote, as Gurnemanz instructed. Parzival has gone through a transformation. It has brought him a huge step forward in self-knowledge. The number fifteen shows that he is close to achieving his quest. Sixteen is the number that represents "Attainment" in this epic, culminating in the sixteenth book.

Outwardly, not too much happens in Book Nine. Parzival has "opened up," thawed his soul, and let the nourishing words of the hermit enter his heart. Parzival was able to tell his story, name his hurt, *forgive* others and himself (the source of his pain and sorrow), and now he is ready to *move on*, to go forward. The life-experienced Trevrizent, through his *deep listening*, his pointed and well-timed questions, could heal the painful divisions of the questing knight and forgive him for his failure. Parzival gains more than life-lessons from the aged and wise Trevrizent, but a *blessing*. The time spent with Trevrizent is more like a consecration—the honoring of the inner life as something sacred, which holds true for all honest exchanges of thoughts, insights, and human sharing. Something sublime enters into the space between people, becoming soul-spiritual nourishment. The doubt with which Parzival was afflicted has lifted and he can ride away feeling inwardly strengthened, rejuvenated, blessed, purified, and reborn.

A rather shy student, and new to the class, once compared Trevrizent to Cundrie. I'd never thought or come across that assessment before and I was intrigued. "Cundrie and Trevrizent have similar functions." She paused, trying to find the right words. "They both tell him the truth, but with Cundrie it comes across as a *curse* which wakes him up, and with the hermit it is like a *blessing* that gives him new hope to continue in his quest. Both move him forward." Ah!

What is blessedness? I ask the students. Have you ever been blessed? Have you felt its effects, its power? What does it feel like? These are intimate questions, so they mostly remain rhetorical, yet I sense sharpened listening when we broach the subject. The word blessing or blessedness usually has religious connotations. The word bless comes from an old English word, *bledsian, bletsunga*, or *bloedsian*, that refers to blood—blood that was sprinkled on altars, consecrating them, blessing them. Later, holy water began to be used. We can also think of the blood that flowed from Christ on the cross, that was said to be pure like water, blessing the earth.

Blessing, this "gift from the gods," goes beyond a feeling of gratitude or praise. Some people in specific situations are endowed with the gift of blessing. Blessing is something we offer and receive more often than we might think, though we might not always be conscious of it. Think of Mother Theresa walking through a crowd, both hands outstretched letting people touch them. Similarly, devotees and followers want to get a glimpse or touch of their holy person. There's power in the touch of certain people. The celebrities, too, like to run along the edge of the stage, letting adoring fans touch their hands.

When we say "take care," or "all the best," it is a form of blessing if we say it earnestly. Children want their parents' blessing for what they do or are wanting to do. It's a form of approval. Warmth from one person to the other can take place with a quick look, a kind word, a nod of the head, a slight touch on the shoulder, a smile, or a subtle gesture—a thought. They can all be blessings, quickening the blood as it purifies the soul. It does not take much. There is power in blessings.

Older people, especially those who have given selflessly of themselves, and spread kindness and love, or have striven toward something higher, have an enhanced power to bless. Our good thoughts toward others are a form of blessing. It's the opposite of a curse, which we know can create a lot of sorrow and harm. Rudolf Steiner mentions that a feeling of reverence which children experience can transform into the power to bless in old age.

Recently, when I asked my youngest son which scene in *Parzival* had left the most poignant impression on him, he answered without hesitation: "Oh, without a doubt Parzival's encounter with Trevrizent." He went on to say that he's thought about that particular scene on numerous occasions, especially in regard to his last cello professor in college, who reminded him of the old hermit. All of what he had to say went beyond the cello to include the big questions of life. But even more than his words, it was his being and overall bearing that made the difference. It was WHO he was. There was a metaphor in everything he said, even his excursions of the most technical aspects. Timothy Eddy, the cello professor, became his Trevrizent. We all need a Trevrizent in our lives. If we are lucky, we might have more than one: a person who can give advice, relieve us of our burdens, anxieties, and sorrows, lift us up, make us feel worthy, recognize our potential, guide us to the next step, and help us to find the means and power to transform ourselves. That is a true blessing.

Who Was Trevrizent?

"The stars had only one task: they taught me how to read. They taught me I had a language in heaven and another language on earth."
— Mahmoud Darwish

Walter Johannes Stein, who taught the first *Parzival* block in January, 1923, to the 11th graders at the Stuttgart Waldorf School, had already begun an in-depth study of the epic in 1922. Throughout the next few years, he worked closely together with Rudolf Steiner on the topic, seeking advice, asking probing questions, and receiving confirmation of his findings. These comprehensive discussions only ended with Steiner's death.

Rudolf Steiner must have recognized the essence of Johannes Stein from the moment he met him, appointing him as a history and literature teacher at the first Waldorf School in Stuttgart, though Stein had studied mathematics, physics, and chemistry and had fully expected to be teaching the sciences. In fact, it is ironic and almost amusing how it transpired, karmically speaking. Stein recalls the moment well: "I still remember my despair when Rudolf Steiner told me, at two o'clock one night that I should have to take a history lesson the next morning. 'But I do not even know in what century Charlemagne lived,' said I. Dr. Steiner was not perturbed. 'Begin by teaching what you know,' he said."[14] It's notable, because Stein chose the historical personality of Charlemagne randomly, unaware at the time how intimately he was connected to that leader in a past lifetime.

Frans Lutters, in his carefully researched book *An Exploration into the Destiny of the Waldorf School Movement*, in which he examines the lives and karmic connections of the core teachers of the Stuttgart school, writes: "In 1924 [Stein] went through a remarkable experience. He began to experience prior incarnations, which Steiner was still able to confirm to him. In the historical time of the Grail, the ninth century, he recognized

14 Walter Johannes Stein, *The Death of Merlin: Arthurian Myth and Alchemy* (Floris Books, 1990), p. 63.

himself as a knight at the court of Charlemagne, Hugo van Tours."[15] Lutters goes on to quote a letter from Daan von Bemmelen to Werner Greub in which Stein had told Bemmelen that Hugo of Tours is the same person as Trevrizent. This, too, according to that letter, was confirmed by Rudolf Steiner. No wonder that Rudolf Steiner urged Stein to teach a Medieval epic and enthusiastically supported him teaching Eschenbach's *Parzival.* Steiner himself had delved deeply into spiritual and karmic research on the topic and had lectured widely on the Grail theme for many years already.

Johannes Stein, in his book *The Ninth Century*, elucidates extensively on the historical background of Hugo of Tours, who was one of Charlemagne's closest and cherished counselors. Furthermore, the intimate connection between Stein and Steiner in a previous incarnation is solidified in Stein's book *The Death of Merlin*.[16] The contents are from a lecture that Stein gave on Trevrizent, which deals with a young knight coming to visit the old hermit, seeking shelter and rest. In this case, the young knight is not Parzival but Schionatulander. Their discussion focuses on *education*, specifically the seven liberal arts. As mentioned earlier, Schionatulander has been identified as Rudolf Steiner. The exchange takes place in the grotto near Arlesheim (the Hermitage), where a few years later Parzival would go through his cathartic meeting with the hermit.

The hermit says, "If you want to understand reality you have to learn to see through the appearances. . . . Something makes the grass grow. To discover what it is, you have to pass from the observation of external appearances to interior listening."[17] The emphasis is on "interior listening." During Schionatulander's short incarnation, the emphasis is on internalization; internalizing the outer world, and letting it live anew within. It, too, is a lesson for Parzival, as it is for all of us, dealing with the outer world in our intellectual scientific age. Trevrizent brings it in connection with music—the sounds we listen to. If we *listen*, everything will begin to resound. Trevrizent finds beautiful words to express the grandeur of music

---

15 Frans Lutters, *An Exploration into the Destiny of the Waldorf School Movement*, p. 115.

16 *The Death of Merlin*, Chapter 16 (Floris Books, 1990).

17 Ibid., p. 219.

and how the whole cosmos is music. With these introductory words, Schionatulander asks to be the hermit's pupil, to which the hermit answers:

> "I cannot teach you anything," the old man replied. "Your soul is much richer than mine. But I can teach you who your teachers are."
>
> "And who are my teachers?" the youth asked in surprise.
>
> "The cosmos itself," the old man told him. "The only reason you met me was to recognize the poverty of the people of my century. You will enrich them."[18]

Schionatulander stays a while with the hermit. One day he has a dream where their situation was reversed: he saw himself as old and the hermit as young. He had become Trevrizent's teacher, which became a riddle to Schionatulander. And, indeed, the situation is reversed when Rudolf Steiner becomes the teacher of Johannes Stein. To get a clearer idea of Hugo of Tours (the historical Trevrizent), I suggest reading the section in Chapter Two of Stein's *The Ninth Century*.

This scene between Schionatulander and Trevrizent has left a deep impression on me as a teacher, for as teachers we never really know who the students are in front of us. However, what I do know is that all of them are incredibly gifted, each in their own way, endowed with remarkable faculties. Karmically speaking, we might be teaching some of the most advanced initiates the world has seen. A humbling thought. It is our duty to draw out what lives in them. We become facilitators.

---

18 Ibid., p. 220.

Discussion Topics, Questions

- How can we ready ourselves for the tasks that we might encounter?
- Do we hide behind our metaphorical armor? What forms can this "armor" take on?
- What does it take to confront one's failures?
- When can we look at our shortcomings objectively without our emotions coloring them?
- Examine the different types of senses.
- Look at the theme of being blessed—its power, its source. Give examples.
- Why are so many of the important characters in Parzival related?
- What's the difference between forgiving yourself and forgiving others?
- Do you have the needed patience and drive to achieve what you really want and quest after?
- Pick a theme to counsel one another on, either in pairs or in small groups. If the weather allows, go outside, find an appropriate setting to converse.
- Portray the different stages of Book Nine in a pictorial manner.
- What components would an ideal religion need to have? Discuss in small groups, take notes, and report the findings to the whole class.

Illustrations:

1. Hermitage near Arlesheim
2. The site of Sigune's Cell at the Hermitage
3. Two knights jousting (Goni Ronen)
4. The rock arch at the Hermitage, Fontane la Salvæsche; entrance to Soltane forest according to Greub
5. Trevrizent and Parzival at the Hermitage (Odin Esty)

BOOK TEN

One Year Later

"May your shadow never grow less." ~ J.R.R. Tolkien

A YEAR HAS gone by and we "are approaching strange tales such as can empty us of joy and bring high spirits: they have to do with both" (p. 256). This tale of polarities now takes us back to the "ever-blameless" Gawain, who is forever blamed, though remaining innocent of the accusations, such as the slaying of Kingrisin, a deed that was actually perpetrated by Count Ehkuna. Eventually, Gawain's name is cleared and he is absolved from the duel. Through bearing the brunt of blame, he helps to heal and resolve issues and misdeeds, thereby ending the confusion and aiding the transformation for *others*. It is the realm of the heart that is easily besieged by false blame, resulting in confusion, but calling forth strength of endurance. Gawain's noble bearing invites attacks on his integrity, similarly to shadows that intensify with light. It's a matter of coming into the right relationship with one's own shadow and those of others. The "shadow side" of things is usually seen negatively, yet there is so much to cherish and learn from shadows. For example, on a sizzling hot day we seek "shade," a word that has positive connotations. This shade offers relief from the blinding light and the heat. It's protective. It offers balance to the one-sidedness of the outer elements. Laurens van der Post writes that the Africans have the greatest of respect for shadows, that it would be improper to step into someone else's shadow. An African he once spoke to called his shadow, "the person at my side," adding: "When I die, I go into the earth, but *he* goes up there."[1] It's not so much a matter of rejecting the darkness, but coming to terms with the shadow side of things—ourselves. Thereby, we become more conscious.

Parzival has made himself guilty, but Gawain endures the guilt of others. Both have to undergo great suffering, but from different ends. Parzival started life from scratch without any previous guidance and education in how to behave in the social realm, thus falling into error and making himself culpable. Gawain grew up, surrounded by the best that civilization could offer and a refined lineage he could emulate, uphold, and surpass. He suffers because of his relentless pursuit to help those who suffer or have made themselves culpable. It causes him to be pulled into the depths, where he has to rely on his own resources and resilience to withstand the onslaughts. The epithet "ever-blameless Gawain" is fitting, though he is not spared a descent into despair, shame, and suffering.

Gawain, as he now journeys forth in the pursuit of the Grail, comes across a wounded knight under a tree, resting in the lap of a maiden. It immediately reminds us of Parzival's first encounter with Sigune and Schionatulander, yet there are differences, some subtle, others obvious. The parallel encounters reinforce the intimate connection between the two heroes. Almost every year I have students who love to discover the parallels, pointing them out and how they differ, such as Gawain having to go *around* the tree to see the knight lying in her lap, or that Parzival was indirectly guilty of Schionatulander's death, whereas Gawain was innocent and could immediately assess the situation and offer a cure. "His wound is not a fatal one, it is simply the blood pressing on his heart" (p. 257), an apt metaphor for the imbalances we find regarding matters of the heart. All of Gawain's

---

1 Laurens van der Post, "*Intuition, Intellect, and the Racial Question*," transcript of a lecture at the Waldorf School, Adelphi University, October 2, 1963.

actions and adventures have to do with the realm of the heart, underscored once again, lest we forget.

Gawain relieves the pressure by inserting a tube of bark into the lance-wound and asking the lady to suck out the blood, which frees the knight's heart, helping him to regain the power of his speech. Similarly, Parzival's heart is freed during his stay with Trevrizent and he returns from silence into regained speech, which will need further cultivation in order for his word to be imbued with the power to ultimately ask the Question. All of Gawain's actions flow into Parzival, for the one is a different aspect of the other. We all know that the heart and the mind work best if they are unified and working in harmony.

Gawain intends to pursue Lischois Gwelljus, the knight responsible for the lance-thrust. Thus, the healing is a stepping stone to his most significant encounter, but also a step toward greater suffering. The knight, however, tries to deter Gawain from such an endeavor, just as we are often deterred from following what we know is right and must be done, even though we might suffer humiliation, be discredited, or suffer pain and shame. Instead, Gawain speaks a charm (power of the word) and follows the tracks of blood that lead him to Logroys—in contrast to Parzival, where the tracks fade and lead him to other encounters.

Orgeluse

"Proud people breed sorrow for themselves." ~ Emily Brontë

In Logroys he comes across a most splendid castle. Its path ascends in spirals that makes it look like a spinning top, a fitting image that describes how easily we can spin out of control in our emotional life, affecting clarity of thought. An unkind word, a slight rebuff, an angry gesture, and already our feelings start to spin. And Gawain will have to muster all his strength not to spin out of control when he comes face to face with his next encounter.

As Gawain makes his way up the path, he sees the most beautiful lady—equaled or surpassed in beauty only by Condwiramurs—residing next to a fresh spring. Her name is Orgeluse de Logroys and she is described as a "lure to love's desire, sweet balm to a man's eyes, windlass to his heartstrings" (p. 259). In other words, the proverbial *femme fatal*. It is love at first sight for Gawain, and he immediately offers to serve her. However, unlike with Antikonie, where the attraction was mutual, she rebukes and discards him, telling him that he will only bring disgrace upon himself if he consorts with her, which does not deter him one bit. Every word to him is spoken in a hurtful and condescending manner. Though she tells him to leave her, she adds, "you are near my heart, but right outside, not in! If you desire my love, what have you done to deserve it of me?" (p. 259) In contrast to the "opening heart" of chapter nine, her heart is still closed, but she does say that he is "near" her heart, which shows that there is potential for it to open. Essentially, she speaks the truth, based on all the knights who have sought her love so far, for they have reaped nothing but pain and dishonor, including the wounded knight that Gawain had tended to. Yet, he will not be dissuaded. "[Y]ou *do* tell me truly, my eyes are a danger to my heart . . . I must truthfully declare I am your prisoner" (p. 259). However, he must find a way into her heart in order to be freed, which will not be easy. His pursuit will eventually help Parzival achieve his quest. Gawain has recognized her higher self, which stands behind the veil of her beauty. He knows that love cannot be forced, the way Meljanz tried to force Obie's love—Obie, whose mocking words are reminiscent of Orgeluse's sharp words. Gawain, who has learned restraint through the interrupted love with Antikonie, is willing to be her prisoner in love until she herself chooses to release the pressure of the blood against his heart. The name Orgeluse means pride, which we can also detect in *Orgullo*, the Spanish word for pride, or *Orgueil* in the French. In becoming her servitor, he will have to endure, suffer, and persevere without complaint. She, too, is a widow, like Herzeloyde, and Belacane, though, as yet, he knows it not.

Their fraught relationship can lead to fruitful discussions in class: How much are we willing to endure in a relationship? When does it become abusive? How do we know it will not be futile? What might cause someone like Orgeluse to become a shrew and treat others so badly? One thing the students usually agree on: we all carry a certain amount of pride within us that needs to be worked through.

Seeing that Gawain will not be deterred, she allows him to accompany her, warning him it will be the source of trouble. She orders him to fetch her horse. To oblige her, she must hold his horse for him. It indicates that Gawain is putting his intelligence in her care, just like Parzival did when Trevrizent took hold of his horse. Similarly, when Gawain untethers *her* palfrey, he is loosening her knotted, tied-up intelligence. Students always like the part where she says, "I see you are a fool . . . Your hand has rested there! I'll not lay hold of it" (p. 260), as if he might infect her with the *cooties*. When Gawain goes down to the village to fetch her horse, the villagers in the orchard all look sad and try to dissuade him from serving her, having seen it all before: young men driven to their demise because of her "deceitful" ways. Gawain, unlike Parzival, ignores their words and those of a grey-bearded man, and untethers the horse. He does not take the old man's advice but follows his heart, and leads the horse back to the mistress of his heart who is also the lady of the land. On his approach, she says, "'Welcome back you goose. If you are set on serving me no one will ever have lugged such a load of folly around as you" (p. 262). Gawain has now been brought down to the same level as Parzival when he left Munsalvæsche and was called "goose" by the page for not asking the Question. She will bring much suffering to Gawain, though he seeks refuge in her.

In one way or another, we all experience much heart suffering. It is our lot and cannot be escaped, arriving either from within or from without. How we deal with it—that is the question. Before setting out, she mocks and upbraids him ceaselessly. Not one kind word leaves her lips. He endures the abuse, confident that he will win her love in the end.

At this point, Wolfram comments that nobody should judge or think ill of her. "Let nobody's tongue run away with him till he knows the full charge, and has learnt the state of her feelings. . . . I exonerate her on all accounts" (p. 262). This can give rise to an important question regarding how we judge people, based on their conduct, which, of course, we do all the time. What has caused that behavior? What pain lies behind it? How can intolerable behavior be redeemed? So much of *Parzival* is about redemption. It's about lifting the veils that obscure the truth. Once again, it all comes down to the question of truth: understanding the full picture, which is so inexhaustibly difficult in our time of extreme divisiveness. Wolfram, in his way, is asking us to accept the outer appearance that presents itself as a shadow—to see beyond it to the reality. We are called, like Gawain, to enter the dynamic intermingling of the dualities of life. It is an ever-recurring theme of the epic, which cannot be overlooked, as it holds the answers to the problems of our modern times.

Malcreature and Urjans

"What would life be if we had no courage to attempt anything?"
~ Vincent Van Gogh

As they make their way, Gawain digs up the root of an herb that will heal the wounded knight, which garners more mockery from Orgeluse, comparing him to a quack and a merchant hawking his wares (another parallel to Obie, who accused him of being a merchant). Though she scorns Gawain, she takes note. She herself is in need of healing. The Greeks saw Hermes as the god of merchants and of healing (amongst others)—known as Mercury to the Romans. We can see the duality of Mercury in the Caduceus, his healing staff, which symbolizes the spinal column, around which the two snakes curl, keeping the body in balance, connecting the wise snakes to all the organs of the body (the Caduceus is the popular symbol of the medical profession, though the staff of Asclepius is recognized as the official logo of the medical profession). Hermes or Mercury is also the guide of the soul. Gawain incorporates all of these qualities: the healer, the merchant, and the soul guide.

Directly, a squire rides up with a message for Orgeluse. It is Malcreature, the equally ugly brother of loathly-looking Cundrie. He too comes from Tribalibot, the realm of the beautiful Secundille, mistress of Feirefiz. These two "wild and outlandish" creatures allude to a distant time of humanity's development, representing the intemperance of the soul in physical form, which populate fairy tales, legends, and folk stories around the globe. It's another manifestation of the theme of dualism: that necessary part of creation which ultimately helps to lead humanity to self-reliance and freedom. We all share aspects of the loathsomeness in our soul, of which we need to become aware, the corruption within, the *ill-timed Good*. Secundille, having heard of the splendid Grail, and wanting to have more knowledge of the man in whose care it was, had sent him Cundrie and Malcreature as a gift, together with illimitable treasures. He, in turn, gave Malcreature as a gift to Orgeluse.

Malcreature, like Orgeluse, calls Gawain a "fool," and says, "You will win high praise if you can fend off the correction in store for you. But if you are a man-at-arms, staves shall so tan your hide for you that you might well wish it were otherwise" (p. 264). Though the loathly creature's words are insolent and sound disrespectful, they bear truth, as did Cundrie's words with Parzival. However, he is more a representative of Orgeluse's double, rather than Gawain's, depicting aspects of her pride which Gawain is endeavoring to redeem through his enduring devotion and recognition. But his heart-intelligence will be tested—as prophesied by Malcreature—more than he can fathom at this moment. Cundrie can be seen as the double within oneself, and Malcreature as the double in others, those whom we choose to redeem.

Gawain, though he weathers Orgeluse's insult, will not suffer his. "[I]t is you alone who will have to enjoy what you will rightly call my anger" (p. 264), summarily throwing Malcreature off his horse, causing him to look up at Gawain "most timidly," though the creature's bristles slash Gawain's hand in the process, leaving it bloodied, to the vindictive delight of Orgeluse.

Shortly after, they arrive at the site of the wounded knight, where Gawain administers the herb to the injury. Gawain finds out that Orgeluse had been the cause of the knight's hurt. He, too, advises Gawain to abandon Orgeluse: another voice added to the chorus of those who try to distract Gawain from his quest to win Orgeluse. But his *heart* is made up. He will not be discouraged, though he has much to endure still. It again raises the question: How much are we willing or able to bear for someone else, and under what conditions? In many instances, people are not able to change, no matter how much the lover tries to rehabilitate them. Girls especially relate to this question. Many have suffered in their futile attempts to help their partners mend their ways. "How do you know if it is worth sacrificing yourself for a guy, or someone else?" one girl once asked during such a discussion. There is no easy or prescriptive answer, though it helps to look at the relationship from various perspectives.

The all trusting and well-meaning Gawain is tricked by the wounded knight, who jumps on Gawain's Castilian the moment the lady mounted her palfrey, leaving Gawain without a horse and once again exposed to Orgeluse's mockery: "I took you for a knight. Soon after, you turned surgeon. And now you are reduced to footman. If anyone can make a living you certainly trust your wits. Do you still desire my love?" (p. 265) It is another example of his path to humility, an essential component for any form of initiation. And indeed, he needs to trust and have faith in his "wits," and not let himself be tricked, which means reading a situation with greater awareness. He must trudge through the muck of her mockery. Yet he still desires her love, no matter what. He is practicing and strengthening the art and soul quality of steadfastness, which Gahmuret had lacked. Gawain's perseverance is essential to Parzival's growth.

The wounded knight turns out to be Urjans, who had once raped a woman and was sentenced to death by King Arthur. Gawain had stepped in and won the King's pardon, able to commute Urjans' (another name for the devil, or "unwanted guest") death sentence to a four week stretch of living with the hounds and being stripped of knighthood. Urjans had not forgiven Gawain for this degrading shaming. No good deed goes unpunished, as they say. It is yet one more example of Gawain taking the brunt for other people's mistakes, let alone their baseless accusations. Once again, he is dragged down by the mistakes of others. His destiny is to gain strength by weathering the storms in which he finds himself.

Nevertheless, the story makes an impression on Orgeluse, and she ensures Gawain that Urjans will be punished while he is in her domain, though she lets Gawain know that it is still highly unlikely that she will ever show him favor. She no longer dismisses Gawain entirely. She's getting to know him, peu á peu.

With Malcreature sent back to her Castle (a sign of progress) but leaving the nag for Gawain, they continue their journey alone. Gawain does not initially mount the old nag, seeing how frail it is. He has descended to the level of the "fool," similar to Parzival when he first left Soltane on his nag of a horse. It exemplifies Gawain's vulnerability, having to make do with very little, a far cry from what he has been used to. How do we fare in life without the benefits of what we are accustomed to? Often, we don't even realize to what extent our identity is not really of our own making, but a given through circumstance. We can so easily be misled into a false sense of security, strength, and self, based on our heritage. But how strong and confident are we really when stripped of all those aspects that make up our identity, such as race, economic and social standing. Gawain, who has been depicted as an impeccable knight, has to prove himself, even without all the trappings of knighthood. In this case, he is stripped of his charger, an essential part of any knight. Can we find examples of this in our own lives?

Gawain has been called upon to use a different or expanded "intelligence" while serving Orgeluse. He cannot rely on his traditional, customary, and familiar intelligence. He first has to lose it all and feel the helplessness of not possessing the inner and outer accoutrements of the past, indicated by the loss of his horse Gringuljete. Through the experience, he is forced to adapt to the resultant conditions, directing him toward altered ways of navigating the circumstances as they play themselves out, so that he will have to work out of his own resilience and resources. That said, it does not help having Orgeluse laugh at his "cruel ordeal."

Throughout the epic, the respective knights have to go through "ordeals," which comes from the German word *Urteil*, which means "judgment," and leads to a "verdict." It used to entail a physical test, a trial. Initially, the trial was believed to have been delivered by the gods. "Ur" refers to the macrocosmic "All" (or archetype) and "teil" means "part." Thus "*Ur Teil*," also points to a "division from the whole"—that which has been divided (Indo-European root *da*, to divide). Gawain's greatest ordeals (judgements) are still ahead which will determine his character's mettle.

All along, Gawain has not condemned Orgeluse's faults. Instead, he is trying to *understand* them, which is exactly what Parzival must do: to understand his own misfortune, which put him into such a deep state of doubt and gave him so much pain and suffering. "It is absolutely correct that we *cannot learn* by condemning a fault, but only by understanding it."[2] This is exactly what Gawain also has to do—to understand why Orgeluse is behaving the way she is.

His ordeals have reduced him to a footman with a peasant's horse, but he bears his shame and looks beyond it to what it might hide, what it could reveal about himself. He does not like it, but he certainly does not try to escape or conceal it. Thus, it allows him to see other aspects of himself, which ultimately allows Parzival to accept himself.

> Shame . . . is a force that impels us to conceal something within us and not allow it to become outwardly perceptible. ... However, this hidden feeling ... prevents a person's innermost being from appearing to that person as a perceptible image. If this feeling were not there, we would confront a perception of what we are in truth. ... This feeling conceals us from ourselves, and at the same time it conceals the entire world of soul and spirit.[3]

---

2 Rudolf Steiner, *An Outline of Esoteric Science*, Anthroposophic Press, 1997, p. 344

3 *Esoteric Science*, p. 358.

Lischois, Ferryman, and Bene

"Good can exist without evil, whereas evil cannot exist without Good."
~ Thomas Aquinas

While traversing through a forest, Gawain does mount the nag, though it slows him down even more. They arrive at a vast clearing in which Gawain beholds a most magnificent castle with four hundred ladies at the windows looking out. Approaching this looming Castle of Wonders, the *Schastel marveile*, Orgeluse commands him to fight a knight who they see on the jousting meadow. "Now defend yourself, if you can," adding, "you will be embarrassed because of the ladies sitting up above and looking on. Supposing they were to glimpse your shame. . ." (p. 271) And with that she leaves him to his own devices, having to prove himself and uphold his honor. The further along we are on the path of development, the more challenges we have to bear.

The knight is Lischois Gweljus of high repute. On seeing Gawain, he charges. Again, Gawain weighs out his options, wondering whether he should meet him on foot or on the feeble nag—the ongoing leitmotif in Gawain's character. In determining the best outcome, he orders his thoughts based on his present predicament and decides to remain on his horse. In the realm of the heart, we must act in accord to the pulse of the moment. Though Lischois is a formidable opponent, Gawain conquers him, twice. He lets him live for Orgeluse's sake, though the proud knight refused to surrender. He too has fought to win her love, and it was Lischois Gweljus who wounded Urjans.

Through his victory, Gawain is reunited with his beloved Grail horse, Gringuljete, and he is invited to spend the night in the home of Plippalinot, the Ferryman. Initially, the Ferryman wants to claim Gawain's horse, but Gawain persuades Plippalinot to take Lischois instead, which he accepts. I wonder whether the name Plippalinot is a modification of Pippa or Phillip, which means "lover of horses," which also could indicate the wise horse intelligence that Plippalinot seems to have, based on the sound advice he gives to Gawain on several occasions. The conquest has restored his honor, though his love for Oregluse still pains him. The Ferryman, hearing his love woes, says,

> "Sad today, glad tomorrow'—this is the rule here below, both out in the meadow and in the forest, and everywhere where Clinschor is lord, and neither courage nor cowardice can contrive to alter it. Here is a thing for which you may well be unaware. —This whole land is one great marvel, and its magic holds night and day!" (p. 277)

This is important because it alludes to the fact that the entire land is under the spell of Clinschor, the representative of evil; a forcefield that holds sway over all that happens in that area, even to the best of knights. "Clinschor" holds sway in our time more than ever. We only need to look at the forcefield that social media has, which the students understand all too well. Our modern lives are locked into it. The question is: How can we free ourselves from that all-prevailing influence? Can we? (See "Clinschor" in Book Thirteen).

At his host's abode he is introduced to Bene, who will play a crucial role in the story.

> "See to the comfort of my lord here' he at once commanded his daughter. 'You two go together. Now see to his every need." (p. 277)

This is a direct parallel to the situation with Vergulaht and Antikonie, which almost led to Gawain's downfall. Bene is beautiful and willing, and they are even ushered up into a bedroom where they can be alone. The insinuations are clear, but it is a different situation entirely. She too, like Antikonie, has been told to take care of Gawain and do whatever Gawain desires, yet Gawain is now embarrassed that she was *ordered*, though she assures him that she only wants to win his favor. However, Gawain does not succumb, remaining true to his love for Orgeluse, though it is very likely that he otherwise would have yielded to her charms. It shows another stage of his development and inner growth. He does, however, honor her, asking that she dine with him. The Ferryman agrees, adding, "Daughter, do everything he asks, I give my full approval" (p. 278). This is the second clear signal that he can sleep with her, which reinforces the invitation to have his pleasure with her, which she seems willing to give.

There is, however, a brief but telling vignette with the three larks, caught by the host's merlin. The merlin (sparrow hawk) represents Gawain who is learning to fly again, to regain his high status. The larks are wonderful birds that rise up from the fields and fly high into the sky, their songs of praise reverberating over the meadows, symbolizing hope, abundance, balance, and the achievement of one's goals. Bene asks Gawain to give one of the larks to her mother, which he readily does, saying "that he would gladly do her will in this or any other thing she might ask him" (p. 279), thus leaving her free of the command of her father. He is honoring her as a woman and as a free human being. It is clear, he will not take advantage of her. "Had he desired anything from her, I [Wolfram] fancy she would have granted it him" (p. 279). It would have been consensual, but unlike with Antikonie, he had learned restraint, was not driven by uncontrollable desires, and was devoted to Orgeluse. Bene, which means "good," "well done," or a "blessing" is a bit like a nightingale or a lark herself.

Discussion Topics, Questions

- To what extent are we blinded by appearances?
- Why is it so difficult to distinguish between appearances and reality?
- When in life did you pursue something, though you knew you would be mocked, shamed or discredited?
- Discuss shaming on social media and how people's lives are potentially harmed.

- "No good deed goes unpunished." Is that really true?
- Can we recognize and admit to our own pride? Do we recognize the pride in others as our own?
- What has given us a feeling of confidence and strength?
- Discuss the importance of humility in one's development and its subsequent effects in the social sphere?

Illustration:
Poem: "*On Yearning*" (Violet Middlebrook)

BOOK ELEVEN

Gawain's Questions

"You can tell whether a man is clever by his answers. You can tell whether a man is wise by his questions." ~ Naguib Mahfouz

The next morning, Gawain questions Bene about the many ladies in the castle whom he saw the day before and again that morning through the window when he first got up. Though Bene is willing to serve him in any way he wants, she bursts into tears, unwilling to tell him anything because it would only bring sorrow and grief. "Though I know, I am bound to silence" (p. 281). It contrasts starkly with Parzival, who did not ask any questions at the Grail Castle, though he should have, and where the people wanted him to ask but were forbidden to prompt him. Gawain asks a second time, but Bene only weeps all the more. At that moment Plippalinot, her father, enters and assumes she is crying because there had been some "rough and tumble," saying, "Don't cry, daughter . . . When things of that sort happen in fun, though at first they may arouse anger, it is soon forgiven and forgotten" (p. 281). This is also in stark distinction to what transpired in Schampfanzun, where the old greybeard accused Gawain of intended rape. Here, the Ferryman gives his consent, though Gawain assures him that nothing happened.

Gawain, persisting, now asks the Ferryman the same question for the third time, regarding the grieving ladies in the castle. His reaction is even stronger than Bene's. "In God's name do not ask. . . . My Lord there is anguish surpassing all other there!" (p. 281) But Gawain presses on until the Ferryman relents. Gawain has seen the women's suffering and cannot help but do something about it, which is a hallmark of a healthy social future, one in which Parzival failed so miserably. It comes from the depths of Gawain's being. He *must* know. He *must* act, and that's why he insists: "You must tell me" (p. 281), saying that he will anyway find out one way or another, which causes Plippalinot to relent and not only tell him but *advise* and help him, though it might cost Gawain's life. Gawain continues to display perseverance, consistency of action, confidence, and faith that things will turn out right because *it is the right thing to do*, no matter what the consequences might be. Gawain's resolve and relentless questioning in the face of witnessed grief is going to flow into Parzival. Questions are keys that unlock, though there's always the risk that one will not be sufficiently prepared for what one might have to face. In this case, Gawain follows Plippalinot's instructions and heads for Schastel marveile, the Castle of Wonders, to ease the suffering of the imprisoned women.

In the ongoing and relentless fight for freedom, the oppressed and sidelined people of the world should not have to fight for their rights and liberties alone. They rely on help from others who are willing to battle on their behalf. Too often, however, the fight for social justice or racial equality manifests itself as token activism—often referred to as "slacktivism."

Gawain is in a position to help, and he has been forewarned that it will presumably end in failure, yet he does not retreat. It is vital to recognize that it's more than a knight wanting to free women. It represents the inner determination to liberate an element within us that is held captive, thus rendered inactive, like suppressed talents, goals, ambitions, ideals, and so forth. Humans are beings of illimitable potential but hampered or rendered useless for any number of reasons, which are not always clearly defined or understood—as if a spell has been cast, in this case by Clinschor, who is the embodiment of lies, corruption, and temptation. Gawain recognizes this: "I should be very sorry if I were to ride away from these ladies in comfort without exerting myself, . . . and without trying to learn more about them. . . . [F]or their sakes I shall not shirk the challenge" (p. 282). His "comfort," like any privileged circumstance, should not cause someone to remain a couch activist. In our time it is essential that we get to *know* the other, to understand their respective situations, and to act accordingly. The emancipation that is vital in the world demands that we get out of our comfort zone. Gawain displays the tenets of a true and empathetic leader (what the DEI movement of today needs). He probes into a situation, recognizes the need, and acts on it—in this case, the plight of the four hundred ladies. It is tragic, for example, to see how the women of Afghanistan are once again forced into the medieval mode of servitude, their fledgling freedoms taken away by the Taliban. They would do well with a leader like Gawain who would recognize their predicament and set out to liberate them from their situation. It presupposes a specific education and inner development.

Terre Marveile, Lit Marveile, Schastel Marveile

As long as you do not attain
From out of death: rebirth
A gloomy guest you will remain
Upon a dismal earth
~Goethe[1]

Before leaving, Gawain hears that Parzival came by the day before,

1 Goethe, *West-östlicher Divan*, last verse of "Selige Sehnsucht," Translated by John Barnes.

though he did not ask any questions about the castle, which indicates that he's still not ready to find the Grail and ask Anfortas the healing question. Then again, it is not part of his destiny. It simply did not occur to him. "If it had not occurred to you to ask *of your own* accord [my italics] you would never have been apprised by me, of what's to do here—mighty sorcery fraught with terror" (p. 283). Anybody who has confronted evil, who has experienced the worst that humanity has to suffer through, will know that evil is not easily understood, that the inexplicability feels like sorcery, like a foreign entity, an anti-force to humanity, a riddle.

Armed with Plippalinot's advice and shield (with which he must never part during his upcoming ordeal), he rides off toward Schastel marveile. As advised, he makes a stop outside the castle at a singular Booth that is filled with priceless treasure beyond anybody's imagination. He finds out from the trader that no other knights have come to purchase anything from him in all the years he has been there, explaining further that should Gawain be successful, he will inherit all the treasure. We are reminded of the many accusations and allusions to Gawain being like a merchant, especially by Obie and Orgeluse. In the realm of emotions and the heart—so easily vulnerable to pride—we are often a bit like traders, trying to get the best deal (or steal), desiring this or that in selfish ways. Yet, if we can purify our feeling life, cleanse our life of the soul, transform it into the "Golden Fleece," then we will gain the greatest treasure of all: the treasure of inner freedom. The Booth refers to the inner treasures we can gain, a recurring and common theme in fairy tales and mythology. The trader offers to look after his charger while he enters the castle.

Gawain observes that the roof of Schastel marveile resembles colored peacock feathers, symbolizing pride, but also the realm of imagination, essential for the artist. The ordeals that await him are clothed in alchemical images taken from the outer world—the transmutation of baser metals into gold, representing the gradual transformation and purification of the human soul. Pride, from the most ancient times, has caused the gradual downfall and imprisonment of our soul life. And Gawain's battle is a battle for the rehabilitation of the soul. Pride, in its multifaceted aspects, lies at the core of our contemporary problems. The epic offers many opportunities to discuss this theme from various perspectives.

Gawain enters. The castle is deserted. It is magnificent. He is alone. Nobody greets him. He is fully armed. He does not know what to expect, yet his life is in danger. He has to remain vigilant. In all ways, it is the polar opposite to when Parzival entered the Grail Castle. The hour of peril is indeed at hand, as the trader had voiced. The only thing he can rely on now is trust and faith, not blindly, but based on his belief in himself, his resilience, and knowledge that it is the honorable thing to do. After all, he has prepared himself for moments like this throughout his life. I tell the students that we all have moments like these in our lives. Gawain has to remain receptive and prepared for what he is about to encounter. Not knowing the nature of the challenge necessitates inner openness and flexibility. He knows from the trader that he would have to face the *Lit marveile*. He enters a chamber and within it he sees the marvelous bed—the Lit marveile. We are in a fairytale landscape, which is nothing less than a picture scape of one's own interior. Different rules apply, but rules, nevertheless. Soul rules.

The level floor is as smooth as glass and he can barely get a sure footing when he tries to approach the bed, which moves away on its four swiveling casters of ruby balls with each step he takes—each one like a little heart, over which he needs to gain control. Realizing the futility of giving chase, and weighed down by his armor and heavy shield, he takes the opportunity, while the bed comes to a complete stop in front of him, to leap on top of the bed. At once it starts to dash around the chamber with incredible speed, bashing into all four walls with an ear-splitting din, on and on, as if he was riding a bucking bronco, or getting pummeled by high-powered bumper cars. He rides umpteen jousts. With all this thundering and relentless clashing and banging he strains and battles to retain consciousness: He must remain awake!

Gâwân muose wachen
Swier an dem Bette læge[2]

2 Lachmann, XI, 567, 26, p. 268.

Often students ask: "What's with Gawain fighting a bed?" True. In literature and in life there are hundreds of different types of battles, but battling a bed!? What do we associate with beds? The students come up with some of the answers themselves: most obviously it is the place of rest, where we lie down to sleep, but also the birth bed, death bed, and the lovers' bed, where desires, passions, and lust find their fulfilment. Often, it is the place where we fight our internal battles, where we fend off torments of the soul or nurse our pain.

I ask them what they might experience if they could fall asleep consciously, a sheer impossibility for most, which has led to discussions around lucid dreaming and the meaning of dreaming as such. We discuss how sleep is really a protection from what we might encounter if we did remain conscious. Over the years, I have noticed that a growing number of students suffer from insomnia: lying awake for hours thinking about their troubles, their fears, anxieties, their wishes, desires and yearnings, which repeat themselves ad nauseum, a drain to their life forces. And that in itself can feel like a battle. In this case they *want* to fall asleep, but cannot. The question is: Are there times when we need to remain conscious, when we cannot afford to *fall* asleep? Parzival went through a battle of the soul in Munsalvæsche, and Gawain is going through a different sort of soul battle in Schastel marveile. What we have here is an imagination of a person who gradually overcomes sleep and can stay awake while sleeping, which is the pursuit of an initiate. If the initiate can consciously cross over into the realm of sleep, which contains the beings and workings of the spiritual world, then the initiate can return—fully conscious—to daily life, enriched with the experiences of the night. Gawain, on his path of development—initiation—has consciously crossed over into the realm of death, the place we enter every evening when we fall (or lift) asleep.

Gawain must remain *awake* in order to conquer the unrecognized desires, the impure thoughts, the drives and urges that he has not yet *consciously* recognized—all that he is still in denial about. Furthermore, it takes immense *courage* to confront oneself, including the different levels of intensity, which Gawain will have to contend with. It is maybe for that reason that a movable bed also appears in the fairy tale "The Story of the Youth Who Went Forth to Learn Fear" (Brothers Grimm).

Realizing that the bed will not stop and that he is helpless to do anything about the cacophonous ride around the chamber, Gawain gives himself up to providence or fortune. He puts his trust in a "higher power"—consciously. "What did the warrior do? He was so overwhelmed by this clamor that he put the shield up over him. . . . He asked Him to Whose power and goodness he had always ascribed his own renown, to watch over him now" (p. 287). It parallels the moment when Parzival consciously dropped the reins and spurred his horse, trusting that his horse would lead him to where he was meant to go—Trevrizent. There is power in trust, in faith. It is not easily given and it must arise genuinely from the heart, from one's own center, not like a selfish prayer or passing wish, but from a grounded point of certainty. At that point-zero moment, the bed stops its movement, coming to rest "at the very *center* of the pavement equidistant from the four walls [my italics]" (p. 287). Yet, it is simultaneously the start of the next peril, coming in the form of five hundred slingshots that pound into the shield, the hard stones piercing through in places.

The students of today recognize this torment of the soul. It can drive them to the brink of death, and often leads them to assuage their pain through drugs or drink. Like Gawain, they have to shield themselves and endure the onslaught that comes from the outside. How much can one bear? How strong do we have to be? Is it even fair to have to deal with such excruciating torments? These are the kind of questions that might come from the students. How do we as teachers respond to these questions? How have we ourselves dealt with such inner agonies? Do the students recognize in us a person worthy of emulation? Do they see our strengths? They certainly see and sense our weaknesses. I have noticed that more gets said and answered in the silences than through words.

Yet, the ordeal is far from over. Next come five hundred crossbows that are aimed right at the bed on which he lies. Once there was a student who made the connection to Cupid's arrows and the lovers' torments that inevitably ensue. The stones and arrows have left him "cut and bruised through his chain-mail" (p. 287). Gawain, on his perilous path of initiatory development, has consciously crossed over, into the realm of death, the place we enter every evening when we fall asleep.

Just when Gawain thinks it's over a huge burly man dressed in fish skins and carrying a mighty cudgel enters. He does not attack, just takes stock of Gawain's situation, promising him that worse is yet to come, which will surely kill him. "That you are still alive is due only to the power of the Devil, but even if it has saved you, nothing can prevent your dying" (pp. 287-8). The reference to the Devil is not only ironic, but another false accusation, for it is the very opposite of the Devil that has saved him; and ironic because Gawain is in *Terre marveile*, which is under the rulership of Clinschor, the representative of evil. After the burly hulk of a man departs, a mighty lion enters, as tall as a horse and ravaged by hunger, accompanied by a roar that sounds like the ferocious beating of twenty drums.

Here we come to the *heart* of it all. The lion stands for courage (cœur / heart). The heart-forces of the lion (endowed with a huge physical heart) need to be brought under control. No matter how much we think we are in control of our emotions, it is always only the tip of the iceberg. Beneath the surface, protected within our subconscious, the bulk of the molten emotions are waiting for us to consciously bring them under our control and rulership. The story of Parzival, like all the other great epics, is a story of initiation, and nobody enters the higher realms or achieves enlightenment without the most severe trials of courage. It is a global cultural maxim, a virtue to be striven for out of necessity. We find it in all tribal cultures where trials of courage are integral to the rites of passage. In our modern age, beset by fear, it holds truer than ever. True for each individual—though no longer held in the same way by the traditions and customs of the tribe or clan as in past ages.

Gawain dismounts at once and, standing as firmly as he can on the slippery ground, faces the opponent who is "trained to kill good people." A vicious fight ensues, the bed, meanwhile, dashing back and forth, creating a terrible din. Gawain is able to hack off one of the lion's legs, splashing the chamber with copious amounts of blood, which, however, gives him better foothold. Eventually, he manages to stab the lion deep into his chest, killing the beast. In this hectic moment, he again weighs his options: "What is best for me now?" (p. 288) From his manifold wounds, however, Gawain is losing his senses and his blood, as well as his strength and intelligence. He collapses, his head cushioned by the lifeless lion. "Both Gawan and the lion seemed dead" (p. 289).

Queen Arnive comes to check on him, and she, too, fears he has died, recognizing that his "loyal heart" had prompted him to act. Though his life is in doubt, breathing is detected and he is ushered back to his senses with driblets of life-giving water, which revive his senses.

He is brought to a comfortable bed and given medicine, which Old Queen Arnive has received from Munsalvæsche's wise Cundrie—the messenger between the realms—who also tends to Anfortas. Gawain, hearing the mention of Munsalvæsche says, "You have got my senses back into me that had taken leave of me, ma'am" (p. 292). With that, he falls into a needed and well-deserved sleep.

Human growth and development depend entirely on inner transformation, which necessitates numerous experiences of death and rebirth. In the above imagination, Gawain goes through a traumatic death experience, holding on to life by a thread—and possibly would not have made it without the help of Queen Arnive. Gawain's exhibited selfless courage, prompted by the grieving and sorrowful women—the imprisoned soul life—who stand in striking contrast to the grieving and sorrowful men from the Grail Castle. The two castles highlight the separation between the gender polarities, in need of being brought into harmony, consciously—both within society at large and within the individual human being, for we are made up of feminine and masculine aspects like the phoenix/fenghuan. There is a definite lawfulness in how the dualities of universal Taoism live within us and around us.

The battle with *Lit marveile* within the chamber of *Schastel marveile* in the land of *Terre marveile* has to do with the confrontation with evil, which is an unavoidably part of self-development. We live in a noisy and impatient rat-race culture of immediate gratification, where everything is looked at through the lens of materialism, including spirituality. As long as we remain steeped in materialism, catastrophes and the sheer magnitude of seemingly unsolvable socio-political issues will continue. It can only change when enough people work on themselves to defeat their "double," which means attaining inner strength and confidence out of their own internal resources. And such soul-striving can be symbolically recognized in the trials of Gawain. Gawain's trials become our trials if we become activists of the temporal and spiritual worlds.

Gawain needed the Ferryman's shield to guard himself against the multiple onslaughts. In our modern world, we are in existential need of such shields, carried with courage. These shields take on the following forms: the shield of *logical and living thinking*, the shield of *emotional control*, the shield of *faith and trust*, the shield of *tolerance*, and the shield of *inner calm and equilibrium*. These are acquired soul attributes, which determine one's actions and their outcome. We fall short, for we are human, and humans fall into the spectrum of imperfections. Gawain entered the unknown when he crossed into Terre marveile, where his "perfections" were put to the test. Unlike the fool Parzival, he initially ventured forth as a nigh-perfect knight, but in the land dominated by Clinschor's forcefield, he began to encounter imperfections within and around him. And these destructive and life-sucking forces needed overcoming. "Good people" (which is most people at their core) need to train their own inner lion's strength and courage. Gawain lacked the power to entirely transform the hungry lion, hence his lethal sword thrust.

When Gawain awakes, he is a different person. He has reached a new stage of his development. He has new capacities. We all do after we have gone through trying ordeals. Initiations never leave us the same. And we never attain initiation without the help of others. Going backwards, Gawain could never have succeeded without Queen Arnive, the maidens, the trader, the Ferryman, and Bene, not to mention those who came before them in previous adventures. However, new strengths will be needed to meet the forthcoming adventures in store for him to test his skill and valor.

Discussion Topics, Questions

- What habits do you have that you would like to change?
- What happens exactly when you try to give something up that you are attached to, like checking your phone, social media?
- Discuss the difference between "activism" and "slacktivism."
- Would you describe yourself as having an addictive personality?
- Pride is at the root of many socio-political problems. True or false? Discuss.
- How can we shield ourselves from the onslaughts of life?
- Have you ever done something that takes great courage?
- Does honor still have a place in our time and in our lives?
- Gawain's ordeal in Schastel marveile has fairytale qualities: discuss.

Illustration:
Castle by the ocean (Alexander Madey)

BOOK TWELVE

Mistress love
A question begins it —
a search, a desire;
once the yearning is lit,
it ignites a great fire.
~ Student

Gawain is resting in bed having barely survived the threats. Eschenbach underscores the severity of his perils, by elucidating on a number of perilous adventures by other heroes, all of which put together would not equal what Gawain has had to endure. Nevertheless, Orgeluse is the cause of his greatest suffering. Even while asleep, she enters his "inmost thoughts," and through a narrow path enters Gawain's *heart*. But how is "it possible for a woman of her stature to be hidden in so small a space" (p. 294). It parallels Book Nine, where Lady Adventure wants to enter that narrow space to tell of Parzival's journeys. "[W]hat does it mean? —It is Mistress Love venting her ill humour on one who has covered himself in glory" (p. 295). The connection at the outset of these respective chapters is important for it suggests that both heroes have reached a critical and cathartic stage of their development.

Gawain and his ancestors have all lived in accord with Lady Love's commands, recognizing her authority all the way back to Mazadan, whose passions were aroused by the Fay Terdelaschoye. All of Mazadan's descendants have suffered Lady Love's power, including Ither of Gaheviez, who lost his life at the foolish hand of Parzival. Gawain and Parzival both share common ancestry, though their different streams have a different focus. Each stream has its challenges, and Gawain's line has "often been assailed by heartfelt anguish because of love" (p. 295). Nor has Parzival's stream been spared, as Eschenbach reminds us, giving the example of how that Red Knight was so tormented by the three drops of blood in the snow. The mind and the heart belong together. The one lives in the other as the yin dwells in the yang, or the heart in the head of a lettuce.

Gawain is recovering from the wounds inflicted by the bed, but now the bed "has redoubled [his] thoughts of love" (p. 296), and he is unable to stop thinking about Orgeluse. Thinking is brought into Gawain's heart, while heart is brought into Parzival's thinking.

The Pillar

"Yes, you can do the impossible – what else is worth doing?"
~ D.N. Dunlop.

Eventually, Gawain gets up and walks around in a desultory manner till he comes to a splendid castle hall, where he sees a winding staircase leading up to a high tower, which he follows, coming upon a sturdy and splendid pillar on top, which hails from the land of Feirefiz. A great panorama appears to him in the pillar and he sees people walking and running around. At that moment, Queen Arnive arrives, accompanied by her daughter, Sangive, and her two daughters, Itonje and Cundrie (not the Grail messenger). They are all women. It is his family, though they know it not: grandmother, mother, and two sisters. In contrast, Parzival also met family members at Munsalvæsche: his uncle Anfortas, his aunt Repanse de Schoye, and Trevrizent in a cave nearby. Gawain asks Arnive about the splendid pillar. The wise Queen Arnive answers: "[E]ver since I came to know it, this stone has shone out day and night over the countryside to a distance of six miles on all sides. All that takes place within that range can be seen in this Pillar, whether it be on land and water" (p 298), adding that it was taken from Queen Secundille in Thabronit, *without* her consent, which suggests that it has not been used in the right way in Clinschor's realm, rather for self-serving and fraudulent purposes. Once again, we have a reference to Feirefiz and the East, to the ancient wisdom of Queen Secundille and her realm in India.

At this moment, Gawain sees Orgeluse and a knight, the Turkoyt, appear in the Pillar. At once the "Duchess stung his eyes as she pressed through to his heart" (p 299), which clearly reveals that he is still not free of her and that his *eyes continue to be a peril to his heart.* He turns around and sees them through the window, riding toward the castle on the field of battle.

The last time that Gawain was up in a tower was with Antikonie, after he was accused of rape. It was a scene of chaos and upheaval, sheer survival, where clear thinking had given way to wild action and confusion. In this present scene up on the tower with the magic pillar, the scene and mood are entirely different. The tower and the pillar, expressing verticality over horizontality, suggest that Gawain is once again rising up to regain the bird's eye view, foreshadowed by the serving of larks. In terms of initiation, he is gaining second sight, spiritual in-sight. It is not yet entirely his own but helped along and supported by the Pillar that represents ancient wisdom and is brought into motion through self-development. Whenever one works out of one's own resources to strengthen and gain new ways of thinking and feeling, one always stirs and brings to light whatever is hidden within one's subconscious. If brought back to consciousness in the right way, it can harmonize the old and the new.

Gawain's gaze is caught by what he still needs to accomplish and overcome, by what still keeps him in bondage—his love for Orgeluse. Once he can love freely, he inevitably will free others. The Pillar shows him what still needs to be done.

As a teacher I sometimes find myself having to be a Pillar for my students, so that they may see beyond their immediate horizons, to become far-sighted, to become more aware of their surroundings, especially their own actions in the world, or the actions of others. In essence, we are all a Pillar for each other. So often we need someone else to "show" us what is going on or happening around us. To be Pillars of uprightness for one another is to care for one another, to *look out* for one another, to help extend each other's views, to reflect the *truth* of the world. We need to become "seers" in order for our students to "see." In that way, we can be true pillars of support.

Knowing that the book is comprised of "mystery knowledge," filled with secret insights that were once taught in the Mystery Centers of Greece and Egypt and beyond, we have to take the number *six* seriously. Gawain's task is to purify the heart forces, as alluded to earlier. This relates directly to the twelve petaled heart chakra, where one has to develop six of them, which can then bring the other six into motion. The basic exercises, which are straight forward, practical, and make sense (common sense) are: Control of *thought*; control of *will*; *equanimity*; *positivity*; and *open-mindedness* or *tolerance*. And lastly, bringing them all together in a *harmonious whole*.

The realm of the emotions has always needed purifying, as exemplified in the myth of Jason and the Argonauts. Emotions are easily roiled, spreading confusion. Attaining the Golden Fleece represents this purifying, harmonizing, and clarifying element. 11th graders understand this, as they have to contend with multiple confusions. The theme of "confusion" is prominent in popular music. It is not enough to just talk of confusion, which can easily be an indulgent wallowing in that emotion; one needs to find ways out of that odorous maze. Confusion obscures. The Pillar, on the other hand, can be a "lighthouse" that shines into this cloudy, dense, and murky night, a guide to the sailors out in the stormy oceans of their own emotions. The solid symbol of the Pillar can offer solace and perspective, if approached without malice and pride.

As high school teachers, we are—to some extent—guides for the students. At a reading of his book *Teacher Man* (predominantly attended by teachers), Frank McCourt (*Angela's Ashes*), in answer to a question whether it is still worthwhile becoming a teacher, said: "Who else in their lives is going to tell them the truth, when they are confronted with so many lies around them."[1] To echo McCourt's words: *teachers need to be truth tellers*, even if it hurts, we need to be Pillars of truth and support, we need to hand them Ariadne's thread so that they may find their way out of the labyrinth of lies. The Minitaur is alive and well, demanding his sacrifices.

There is so much that weighs people down, especially young people. They themselves need to become *pillars of strength*, but we need to supply the exercises and the time to practice. We need to be representatives of Pillars of Hope. Or, to quote the Dalai Lama: "Love and compassion are the pillars of world peace." And world peace cannot be attained without Love. And *wisdom* is a prerequisite for love. Both love and wisdom are never achieved without much suffering and pain. There are many types of battles, but one of the greatest battles takes place in the *Soul*, which demands self-confrontation. And in our time, the age of the consciousness soul, it takes place *within* us. In essence, Gawain battled with himself. To truly love and know what love is, we have to know it within us, irrespective of any blood relation, of any family ties, tribe, nationality, or race. A love that transcends all—all the boundaries, a love that is truly inclusive in all of its splendid differences. This new love "is the result of wisdom that has been reborn in the I."[2] The Gawain path shows us the way. It shows Parzival the way.

---

1 Personal notes from "an evening with Frank McCourt" in Albany, NY.

2 *Esoteric Science*, p. 397.

The Leap

"We are very near to greatness: One step and we are safe. Can we not take the leap?" ~ Ralph Waldo Emerson

THROUGHOUT OUR LIVES, we get a great deal of advice. It comes in many forms: information, instructions, suggestions, guidance, recommendations, and so on. How do we react to the advice? Are we able to discern between the various offerings? How does it change over the course of our lives? How much advice do we give others? Is there a pattern to the advice that comes our way? What feelings does the advice arouse in us?

Gawain, unlike Parzival, tends to reject or simply discard much of the advice he receives, even if it seems to make complete sense. This is also true for the counsel he receives from Queen Arnive, who vehemently dissuades him from fighting against the Turkoyt, who Gawain sees in the far-seeing Pillar, riding in the company of Orgeluse. "You must avoid battle with this formidable man now, for it is much too early for you to fight, you are too badly wounded" (p. 299). He refuses, saying that his *honor* is at stake. Honor is another recurring theme that helps Gawain weigh out his options, which he has done throughout. It comes from a deeper place, transcending his upbringing and the codes of honor he was exposed to from his earliest years—deeper than his experiences, which confirms the foundations on which his honor rests. Gawain's honor is a force that comes from beyond, which has not only entered his heart but continuously keeps spreading in the circulation of his blood, renewed with an ever-rhythmic pulse and accompanying breath. It comes from the past, enters and centers in the ever-present heart, only to surge into the future—death transformed into new life. Honor is a form of conscience but is in constant danger of losing its balance, succumbing to reckless *pride*, which leads to egotism, or closes itself off against the world—a hardening and fear-inducing element. Honor guides Gawain with more certainty than any advice from the outside, for it is lodged deep within his I. Although Gawain is not free of pride, he has the integrity to keep it at bay. A well-developed sense of honor defies all odds. It is something one can trust like the unconditional love of a mother. How much in life do we do because we simply "know" it is the right thing to do and we *have* to do it, led by some inscrutable inner voice? It is a good question to pose to the students. Sometimes, if I remember, I suggest they ask their parents whether they have ever done something because they were impelled by some inexplicable reason. Maybe it is only something apparently small or minor, yet one would have felt inwardly dishonorable not to have acted. Our honor depends on our inner standard we have developed over time. It rests on the extent we have outgrown our pride, selfishness, and egotism. Attaining honor is a process. Many high school students are acutely aware of the changing issues going on and they are ready to get up and stand up for these rights because it is the honorable thing to do.

Gawain mounts his faithful war-horse and sets off to his host, Plippalinot the Ferryman, in the house of goodwill, who arms him with a lance and gives him some sound advice about how to fight against the Turkoyt. In this instance Gawain listens and takes the advice, as he did with the gift of the shield and the advice to never let go of it before entering Schastel marveile. Gawain's pattern is to reject advice that tries to dissuade him from an action but to accept the advice of how to succeed in a venture.

Gawain, mounted on Gringuljete from Munsalvæsche, rides out to meet the Turkoyt. It is a reminder that Gawain's task is closely connected to the Grail stream. Releasing Schastel marveile of Clinschor's spell is intimately connected to Munsalvæsche. They are connected like Parzival is connected to Gawain.

They charge and their lances both land in the head region: Gawain gets struck where the laces of the helmet are knotted together, and Gawain catches the Turkoyt's helmet through the visor, carrying it off on his short spear, almost like a trophy. One can say that Gawain's clarity of thought has gained in strength, whereas the Turkoyt's is left vulnerable (a pictorial decapitation), thus defeated. Gawain's victory is another step forward in his quest to fulfill his task as Orgeluse's faithful and steadfast servitor. It shows that he has gained spiritual strength after his victory at Schastel marveile.

Orgeluse, who keenly observed the battle, still mocks him, belittling his achievements, saying that he got off lightly. She goads Gawain on by scorning him, insinuating that he would not be able to endure more pain than what she has already caused him by calling him a goose. Yet, he assures her that he is ready for any challenge, that "there would be no danger so formidable but that I would not be found serving you in despite of it!" (p. 301)

She concedes and lets him ride with her, as if she is doing him a favor. The ladies weep at seeing Gawain ride off with her, fearing that after his victory in Schastel marveile, he might ultimately succumb, which would reverse all his achievements so far. This causes Queen Arnive to lament, "The man on whom we have pinned our high hopes has chosen a lady who is balm to his eyes yet a thorn to his heart" (p. 302). In other words, the senses still overpower the forces of the heart, thus leaving him unfree. Yet, paradoxically, though his senses have a hold on him, they also drive him on in his pursuits. Orgeuluse's radiance also serves to remove any agony Gawain is suffering from his wounds. Clinschor gains his power through the allure of the senses, to which people easily yield at the expense of their strength of self. Gawain is in Clinschor's world, a dangerous terrain that leads people astray. Even Anfortas, the Grail King, succumbed.

However, in the end, the purest expression of love manifests itself when the heart is *freed of the thorn* and is no longer subjected to the senses' domination. It is a common experience for most people, yet so difficult to overcome. It is not a matter of rejecting the pleasures of the senses or submitting to any form of self-flagellation, but rather one of connecting to the senses so deeply and with so much gratitude that, instead of wanting to possess and immediately acquire and seize hold of the desired object for oneself, one lets it exist freely. Being free of something in the sense-perceptible world does not mean we are losing it. On the contrary, the whole experience is vastly enhanced when one is no longer burdened by the heaviness of self-gratification. Fear of loss is transformed into something freely given, or simply: Love—with no strings attached.

As they ride along a wide road and into a forest, she tells him that if he fetches a wreath from a tree branch, she will be his. It sounds almost anticlimactic, given all the other tests he has had to endure. "If you will give it me, I shall praise your exploit and then you may ask for my love" (p. 302). Finally, he has received a concrete promise. His goal is within reach. End is in sight. One way or another.

Orgeluse points out the tree at the other side of the escarpment, within easy reach of his eyes, but separated by a wide and steep ravine through which a strong current of water roars. She warns him that the tree is guarded by a man who has robbed her of all happiness. All he has to do, she says, is to urge his horse to a mighty leap across the impassable abyss.

Gawain spurs his trusty horse and takes the perilous leap, but Gringuljete only lands with his forelegs, causing the horse to be dragged downstream by the force of the torrent. Luckily a whirlpool pushes the horse to the shore. Gawain, holding onto a branch of a tree, pulls himself onto the other side and with his spear is able to prod and guide the horse till he can grab the bridle and haul it ashore. Orgeuluse, witnessing the fall, breaks into tears, which reveals or at least hints at her true feelings for Gawain. One can ask the students whether they have ever taken a leap of faith, consciously or unconsciously, big or small? "Every day, when I get out of bed," one student joked.

We are reminded of Parzival when he hangs on to a branch after jousting with the Grail knight. Both the heart and the mind have to take leaps of faith. Furthermore, the allusion to Odysseus hanging on to the fig tree is emphasized through the image of the vortex. It is a Charybdis moment.

Life inevitably presents us with potentially perilous decisions of uncertain outcome. Gawain has to struggle to keep his wits, his intelligence afloat. He cannot afford to lose his mind (horse) because of his heart's desire. He was placed, so to speak, between Orgeluse and the *Li gweiz* prelljus. He is left to his own devices and resourcefulness. The difference here is that Gawain consciously *chose* to serve Orgeluse (Scylla), and consciously spurred his horse in order to leap across the torrential ravine,[3] in contrast to Odysseus, who could not avoid the twinning trials.

Gramoflanz

"A proud man is always looking down on things and people; and, of course, as long as you are looking down, you cannot see something that is above you."
~ C.S. Lewis

The moment Gawain breaks off the twig and puts the garland on his helmet, King Gramoflanz comes riding up: a handsome but arrogant knight who only battles against two or more knights, the very reason for dismissing Gawain as a worthy opponent. He wears a peacock-feather hat, which underscores his pride, and he is carrying a sparrowhawk, sent to him by Gawain's sister, Itonje, a surprising and inscrutable coincidence. After taking one look at Gawain's dented shield, he knows that Lit marveile has been conquered by him and that this knight is now the lord of Terre marveile. He goes on to tell Gawain about his enmity with Orgeluse, whom he had *abducted* for a whole year, offering her the crown and all his lands, which she rejected, admitting, "[I] failed to win her love, I must tell you with deep sorrow. It is clear to me that she has offered you her love" (p. 305). However, he declares that his heart now belongs to another, to Intonje, though he has *never* set eyes on her. This is interesting in that it contrasts Gawain, whose "eyes are a peril to his heart." It indicates that true love lives beyond the senses, which is a lesson Gawain needs to heed, though it seems

3 A parallel to Parzival consciously spurring his horse that led him to Trevrizent.

to contradict everything about Gramoflanz. For all his pride, Gramoflanz has something to teach Gawain—he models a destined love that is free of the senses. The pride that Gramoflanz projects also reflects the residue of pride that still lives in Gawain.

Gramoflanz, though he realizes that the knight in front of him has become the lord of Terre marveile, he does not know *who* he is—let alone that he is Itonje's brother. Thus, he asks Gawain to deliver a ring as a love token to her, to help him win her heart, which he agrees to do.

Before Gawain leaves, he finds out that the only person Gramoflanz would deign to fight in single combat would be Gawain, since he has heard him greatly praised. Gramoflanz explains that "[Gawain's] father treacherously slew my father in the very act of greeting" (p. 306). We see that Gawain's father, King Lot, was also falsely accused, something which Gawain once again has to bear and set aright. At this news, Gawain reveals himself. "To shield him from calumny I will stake in single combat any honor life has brought me!" (p. 306) King Gramoflanz accepts, but insists that they fight on the field of Joflanze in *sixteen* days and that the battle must be a public event, witnessed by all four great armies: Gramoflanz's army, the company of Schastel Marveile, Orgeluse's army, and the knights and ladies of King Arthur. Having agreed to the terms, Gramoflanz invites him to the town of Rosche Sabins, which, however, Gawain refuses, deciding to return to Orgeluse the way he came—across the Sabins river.

Eschenbach references the Rape of the Sabine Women through the naming of the river and town connected to Gramoflanz. The term "Rape," from the Latin "raptio" refers to abduction or kidnapping, which is exactly what King Gramoflanz did to Orgeluse, keeping her against her will for an entire year (though there is no indication that he slept with her). It is another example of bringing awareness to the egregious practice of forcing women against their will into marriage or sexual slavery. The Books devoted to Gawain underscore that love, if deserving that name, can only be given and received freely. Love needs to be pure on all levels, which means prevailing over any urge to possess another human being in any way whatsoever. There are tremendous unconscious biases in this realm that most people need to grapple with.

Having achieved what he came for, Gawain, wearing the wreath like a crown on his helmet, feels light of heart for the first time since encountering Orgeluse. He spurs his horse, gives it free rein, and leaps across the gorge with confidence and without mishap.

Orgeluse Divulges

To suffer without release
It gnaws and grows within my chest, like a beast
Constricting my heart till it bleeds
Through my body this virus feeds,
Either I live or die, there is no in between,
This feeling within me, what does it mean?
~ Student group poem

Orgeluse rides up and says, "Truly, your trials afflicted me with so much heartfelt suffering as a faithful woman must feel for her dear friend" (p. 307). Gawain, however, thinks that she is still mocking him, and says, "If I am to be the butt of your mockery I would rather be without love" (p. 307). The statement clearly confirms that he is no longer dependent on her love. He has exhibited honor and done what he promised her, but enough is enough. She has lost her hold over him. His freedom allows her to open up to him, and she confesses the source of her great sorrow, which has caused suffering to so many others. One of the roots of her sharp and venomous tongue is the fact that Gramoflanz was the one who killed her husband Cidegast.

> "My Lord, if I have used you ill it was because I wished to put to the test whether you were of such worth that I should offer you my love. I am well aware that I said things which offended you; yet it was to try you out.... I compare you to gold that has been purified in the fire—your spirit has been purged. The man whose harm I sought through you and whom I still hope to harm has done me mortal wrong." (p. 308)

Orgeluse represents all the women of the world wronged by men. Women whose happiness has been immorally snuffed, who have been forced into situations against their will. Orgeluse's trust was broken and only a man of exceptional worth could rectify that—someone who could see beyond her façade. Her trust in men through Gawain has been rectified, but it needed sacrifice, labor, and a purified heart. It is the alchemical process of the soul. Through the "adventure" with Orgeluse, Gawain has gone through a soul-purging process, bearing all the hardships, till he could free himself of her hold on him—no longer a peril to his eyes. His soul, "purified in the fire," has turned to gold.

Recognizing that her words are truly genuine, he immediately pardons her ill treatment of him, and—in true Gawain style—wants to make love to her right there on the spot, which she gently defers for a more suitable time and place.

On their way back to the castle, she divulges the other root cause of her grim discontent. This second confession puts the entire story of Parzival into context. It underscores how significant the Gawain saga is in the totality of the thematic content of the epic, for it was Orgeluse who had accepted the services of Anfortas, the Grail King. Anfortas was wounded while fighting for the love of Orgeluse. Realizing the immense and far-reaching scope of his wounding, gave her even more grief than she had already suffered under the loss of Cidegast, her husband. Anfortas had gifted the priceless merchandise of Thabronit to her. However, to be left in peace by the wicked Clinschor and his powerful spells, she had given the merchandise to Clinschor—with one condition:

> "Of all the worthy people on whom his eye falls not one does he leave without trouble. And so I gave him my precious Merchandise in order to be left in peace, and on these terms: that I should seek the love of the man who had faced and achieved the Adventure; but that if he would not favor me the Merchandise would revert to me. ... As matters stand it shall be our joint possession. I was hoping to bring Gramoflanz down with this

> ruse, but unfortunately this has not yet come about—had he gone for the adventure he would have met his death." (pp. 309-310)

It is clear that any dealings with a Mephistophelean type of character like Clinschor would only escalate trouble for all. Yet, Mephisto's answer to Faust's enquiry about his identity also holds true for Clinschor, for he is indeed "Part of that force which would / Do evil evermore, and yet creates good."[4] Through Gawain and his encounter with Orgeluse, Clinschor's endeavor to sow evil does ultimately create good for all. (It is another foreshadowing of the *Faust* block in the senior class.)

Orgeluse discloses that she could have had the service of every man who had set eyes on her, except for one who wore red armor. Not only did he defeat five knights in her retinue, but plainly rejected her when she rode after him to offer him her lands and herself. He replied that he already had a more beautiful wife and that he had no desire for her love, revealing himself as Parzival (Ouch!). His rebuff was a huge blow to Orgeluse's pride, but it shows Parzival's steadfastness not only to his wife Condwiramurs, but to his pursuit of the Grail. It underscores that the freeing of Schastel marveile and Clinschor's power was not part of Parzival's destiny. Gawain assures her that the incident does not diminish her worth in his eyes.

When they approach the castle, Gawain asks her not to reveal his name and identity. Some students have found this strange, but I ask them whether they have ever consciously avoided revealing their identities, and why that might be a good idea. At that moment they see knights approaching them. First Gawain wonders whether they mean to attack, but Orgeluse assures him that they are Clinschor's men who are welcoming him, filled with joy to receive Gawain. We see that Gawain has not only broken the spell for the women imprisoned in Schastel marveile, but also Clinschor's former troops and the men locked inside the castle.

The Ferryman and Bene meet them on the meadow, and Bene, this mysterious messenger woman who represents ultimate goodness, unarms Gawain and offers him her own cloak to wear, which is again an allusion to

4 *Goethe's Faust*, p. 159.

Parzival's receiving Repanse de Schoye's cloak. Bene is a selfless servant of Goodness, just as Repanse is a selfless servant of the Grail. True and selfless Goodness has Grail powers. There is an endearing line that exemplifies her sacrificial humility and modesty: "[S]he kissed [Gawain's] stirrup and foot and then welcomed the Duchess" (p. 311). Her kiss of the stirrup feels almost like a blessing and a moment of gratitude that Gawain had remained steady and balanced on the horse, thus helping him achieve his goal—a kiss paying homage to grace. And similarly, her humility comes through in the kiss on Gawain's foot, that lowest limb on the human body that is connected to the earth and enables us to move forward through the joys and sorrows, the beauty and grime of the world.

The lovers are invited to sit at the bow of the boat where for the first time Orgeluse can look straight at Gawain and study his face. She is beginning to see him for who he is, instead of an object to use for personal vengeance. She sees and takes him in, no longer caught up in her own story. How many times in our lives do we get too deeply entrenched and stuck in our own story?

At that moment Bene serves some well-deserved food, and notably larks are served for the second time, caught by the merlin. The first time, before Gawain set out to Schastel marveile, he had to share the larks with Bene's mother. This time the two lovers share the larks. In their hearts Gawain and Orgeluse can *sing* again, similarly to the larks that shoot up from their earthly nests and fly heavenward like arrows. The lark gives its song to the cosmos and in the ensuing silence, it listens to the song's reverberations, now imbued by spiritual forces. In the words of Steiner: "The larks send out their voices into the cosmos, and the divine-spiritual element, which participates in the forming and shaping of the animal realm, streams back to earth on the waves of what had streamed out from the songs of the larks."[5] Like the larks, Gawain and Orgeluse need to *listen* to what comes toward them from the divine world so that they can achieve and accomplish the complex social

5 Rudolf Steiner, *Der Jahreskreislauf als Atmungsvorgang der Erde und die vier großen Festzeiten* (Rudolf Steiner Verlag, Taschenbuch Ausgabe 1990), GA 223, p. 62 (translated by the author).

sorting out that lies ahead of them. "The song that streams out from the throat into cosmic expanses returns again to the earth as a blessing, infusing earthly life with the impulses of the divine-spiritual."[6] This "listening" to what needs to be done, and how, is crucial. It is noteworthy that Gawain, who has to renew the heart forces, first had to conquer the lion, which is then followed by a serving of larks—once he retrieved the wreath and attained Orgeluse's love. This connection between the lion and the lark can also be found in the wonderful fairy tale "A Lilting, Leaping, Lark."[7] The youngest daughter asks for the gift of a lark, in contrast to the sisters' wish for pearls and diamonds. The lark represents the consciousness soul, which seeks to go beyond the physical—it seeks to wake up and be free. To gain victory over the heaviness of the sense world and wake up to the world of truth—the spirit—requires courage and sacrifice, the attributes of the lion. In his book *The Wisdom of Fairy Tales*, Rudolf Meyer writes,

> In the human heart, when a force begins to be liberated by dispelling despondency and accepting destiny, there appears the picture of a bird that flies up rejoicing. It means that the liberating forces are beginning to work in the heart. And the bird that longs to fly in thanksgiving, lilting and leaping free from the dust of the earth, is the lark.[8]

We see these liberating forces mirrored in the hearts of Gawain and Orgeluse, and the larks represent the the triumphant joy against all the odds and hindrances.

Further bird imagery is introduced when they ransom two knights—Lischois and the Turkoyt—for *Swallow*, a harp that once belonged to Queen Secundille and which Anfortas gave to Orgeluse. Swallows and larks are songbirds and symbolize the flight of thoughts, but not just any thoughts; thoughts that are divinely infused. It suggests that Gawain,

6 Ibid.

7 Also translated as "The Singing, Soaring Lark."

8 Rudolf Meyer, *The Wisdom of the Fairy Tales*, translated by Polly Lawson, Floris Books, Anthroposophic Press, 1988, p. 125.

through mastering his travails, has opened his heart to free such liberating thoughts, as they liberate the two knights.

Gawain and the Duchess repair to the castle where they are welcomed and he is led to a chamber where his wounds are treated. Secretly, Gawain sends a messenger to King Arthur and Guinevere, requesting that they arrive at Joflanz with their retinue of knights and ladies, to witness him defend his honor in combat, stressing that the adventure he had won at Schastel marveile would otherwise be worthless.

Discussion Topics, Questions

- Do you have a personal sense of honor? Is honor important to you?
- Have you ever taken a leap of faith?
- Why was it important not to reveal Gawain's identity?
- Discuss the theme of identity in our time.
- When is it appropriate to hide one's identity?
- Do you ever do something because you feel it is the right thing to do?
- Discuss leadership in class, and how poor leadership affects society.
- What bird or birds fit your character?

Illustrations:
Dubbing Ceremony
Parzival main lesson book (Odin Esty)
Excerpt from a main lesson book (Violet Middlebrook)

BOOK THIRTEEN

Secrecy and Sorting Out

There is one quest that encircles us all in life,
And one question that has always been asked.
The quest is for the balance of the material and the spiritual,
And the question is, "Who am I?"
~ Solomon (Student)

Secrecy pervades most of this chapter, underscoring the importance of keeping significant information hidden until the right moment is at hand. There is also a very practical reason to keep things quiet, because things first have to be sorted out, planned, and prepared. It is common practice before any major event: in business, politics, the arts, education, and religion. Threads have to be connected and nothing can be left to chance. Everything worthwhile needs a gestation period.

We are approaching the end of the epic and things are slowly coming together. What was very private is becoming public. It's part of the lawfulness and breath of life. It relates to the symbolism of the rounded wreath. Things are coming full circle. Both time and space are cyclical, and the circle represents completion and the birth of something new. Yet, so much can still go wrong. The circle that aches for completion is vulnerable and can be broken in many places.[1] Secrecy is essential. There are many rings that require coordination. There is much that needs to coincide: *coincidere*, that which must fall together or into place so that the disparate circles can "occupy the same space."

Arnive, the crone Queen, is eager to know. She tried to gain information from the squire sent to King Arthur, but failed. Now she is questioning the Duchess, but she, too, remains mum. Arnive still does not know Gawain's identity, that he is her grandson. To keep things secret takes restraint and strength. And in the case of Queen Arnive, she needs to wait her time, remain patient. It requires trust on both sides. There is movement on the way. Contrasting and incongruent streams are slowly finding their way and place, and it must happen fluidly and freely, but also well guided, and Gawain is trying to see to the success of the great public event: his culminating battle with Gramoflanz. There is potential for larger conflicts at this late stage, and it must be avoided at all costs. That requires wakefulness and ongoing consciousness for things to fall into place—peaceably.

The preparations of the event and the people involved include right clothing, for clothes represent who we are, symbolizing spiritual aspects. They can highlight inner transformation or lack thereof. The clothes offered, for instance, to Lischois and the Turkoyt are precious, imported from distant countries, such as China and the East, known for their unsurpassable quality. Once again, Secundille's country is mentioned in regard to a cloth of gold called *saranthasme*, which, according to the footnote on page 316 of Hatto's *Parzival*, refers to a tissue with six folded ornamentations (again, the reference to six, and the purity of gold). Though we never meet Queen Secundille, she represents not only ancient secret wisdom, but a great and sophisticated culture with riches far beyond what the West has ever seen. The East is represented as a stimulus to the West so that it may come into its own and not succumb to the death forces of intellectualism. Mutual

1 See Linda Sussman, *Speech of the Grail*, Chapter Seven, Book XIII.

renewal and revitalization thereby can occur between the East and West. As mentioned earlier, it is important to remember that the East-West dichotomy is more cultural and religious, rather than geographic.

Gawain, to fulfill his promise to Gramoflanz, seeks out Itonje, with Bene's help. Bene, the good messenger, asks Gawain to be discreet, for she knows about Itonje's pangs of love. In questioning Itonje, he finds out that her love for Gramoflanz is real, though she has never set eyes on him—a love born beyond the senses. Itonje, too, asks Gawain to keep her love for Gramoflanz secret. Her love is as true as it is innocent, reminiscent of Obilot's love for Gawain, for Itonje has barely come of age. The relationship, which could easily disrupt the peaceful coming together of the four powerful armies, needs careful tending. At one point she confesses and says, "I shall never be fully reconciled for those who bear unrelenting hatred towards King Gramoflanz" (p. 318). Further secrecy is needed. What is stalling and retarding the process? It is the residue of pride, based on self-importance, egotism, and arrogance. For things to run smoothly in the social sphere, self-centered pride needs to be offset by the recognition of what is good for all parties involved, which calls for the willingness to think things through clearly to the end. Itonje, like Gramoflanz before her, asks Gawain to help her. "May your help and God's blessing take charge of our love so that I, wretched woman, can bring his sorrows to an end" (p. 319). Gawain agrees to be of assistance, though he does not divulge that he is indeed her brother, her flesh and blood, who is set to fight her love, Gramoflanz. It is an impossible situation.

All the turmoil, wars, and disagreements between people, since Gawain set out, involved love relationships. Thoughts of love have to be sorted out, which means the feeling-life needs to be clarified, calmed, and settled. Once resolved, the wider and disparate communities that are affected can move forward harmoniously. Effective resolutions demand effort, which necessitates communications between different parties till all can be revealed. It is the horizontal plane of all social life, which is so well articulated by Linda Sussman in her book, *The Speech of the Grail.*

Meanwhile, the preparations for a great feast are going ahead. The ladies and knights sit on opposite sides as is the custom of the day (still practiced in many places and cultures around the world today), but will soon be encouraged to mingle. Up to this point, the men and women were kept separate in Clinschor's realm, forbidden to communicate with one another. Eschenbach highlights the joyful occasion by describing in detail the fabulous dishes served. This feast celebrates the breaking of Clinschor's spell, bringing happiness to all those who had been unnaturally kept apart against their will—men and women living together behind the same gate. For the first time, thanks to Gawain, they can get to know one another during the course of the festive evening.

At this point, one can discuss what divides and keeps people apart, especially in regard to the sexes. In our time that would include the social taboos regarding gender inequality as such, which are receiving much more attention and are gradually beginning to disintegrate. However, there are still shockingly many places around the world where same sex love is condemned, punishable by death.

As night sets in, a tremendous number of candles are brought in, placed in splendid chandeliers and lit, bringing light to the festal occasion. And with the light comes an overriding sense of joy. For the first time, the knights and ladies can see each other and exchange longing glances with the promise of getting to know each other. Once the fiddlers strike up, the dancing can begin and those who have been kept apart for so long can now, at last, intermingle.

Following the universal merriment, the dancing ends and Gawain and Orgeluse are led to their chambers, and after a few well-meant words by Queen Arnive, she bids them goodnight with the words, "Now go to it with a will." At last Gawain and Orgeluse can consummate their love. As Eschenbach quips: "Let decorum be the lock that guards Lover's rites" (p. 322).

Meanwhile, the squire has reached King Arthur's Court and delivered the message, first privately to Queen Guinevere in the chapel, then publicly to King Arthur. That he must first seek out the queen also hints at the waning power of King Arthur. The Arthurian stream of ruling by the *sword* is gradually giving way to the Grail stream's rule by the *word*. Their meeting takes place about five weeks after Parzival's visit to Trevrizent. The squire is successful in persuading King Arthur and his retinue to travel to Joflanze to witness the combat.

On the squire's return, Queen Arnive once again tries to press news from him, but he remains true to his oath and reveals nothing. Gawain is happy at the outcome. Once again, Gawain forbids the squire to breathe a word of what has transpired, keeping King Arthur's arrival a secret.

Clinschor

Despair!
This feeling is too big
For any of us to handle
I'll sink like all things taken
Into the blue of it
Into the helpless blindness of it
Releasing...
Healing...
Blooming.
~ Student group poem

One morning Gawain and Queen Arnive find a moment to sit alone together in an alcove overlooking the river, where they fall into conversation. He thanks her for all the help and support she has given him, admitting that he would have died of love and his manifold injuries without her care. Then he comes to the point: "Now tell me, most felicitous of ladies, about the magic that was and is here, and why subtle Clinschor has devised such cogent spells, since but for you they would have cost me my life" (p. 328). Gawain wants to know the *secret* of Clinschor that has been kept hidden from him. The wise-hearted crone answers, "[T]he enchantments he has here are mere curiosities compared with the mighty spells he has cast in other lands" (p. 328), and she goes ahead, informing him about Clinschor. Foremostly it is about desire, temptation, deceits, and divisiveness, but the above statement intimates greater evils in the world and those yet to come from Clinschor's widespread and growing realm—in which the contemporary world is presently caught.

Clinschor's influence in Terre marveile can serve as an introduction to the deeper influences of the dark arts. In the Middle Ages, the riddle of evil was not grappled with in the same way as it must be today, the age of the consciousness soul. We cannot rely on the church or politics to take care of the overriding evils. On the contrary, these bastions of power are often at the very root of the greatest manifestations of evil, through their lies that result in so much widespread corruption, suffering, and discontent. No question, all of us today need to deal with evil in one way or another. Nonetheless, evil, in all of its embodiments, plays a major role in the epic, offering sound and carefully structured solutions to the dissolution of evil. The focus centers on the soul-spiritual development of the human being, with all the disparate characters playing a distinct role. What is laid out in *Parzival* gives the modern human being the essential steps needed to deal with the evils of our time the evils of our time, no matter how the ills manifest themselves. It's literally in our faces, daily. We confront evil within us, without us, around us, and between us. To counteract these forces, we have to change ourselves, which means working intentionally on our own self-development. Self-development is soul-development, is social development, is human development, and cannot be sidestepped.

Queen Arnive, when she talks about Clinschor is referencing a historical and extremely powerful person of legendary proportions who once lived in Sicily. Clinschor's land is known as Terre de Labur and she describes him as a descendant of the poet Virgil of Naples, who was associated with magic and prophetic capacities, as was his stock. Duke Clinschor was held in high esteem till scandal caused his downfall. Clinschor had an affair with Iblis, wife of the King of Sicily. When King Ibert discovered the affair, he had him castrated. This humiliation happened in "Kalot enbolot," better known today as Caltabellotta, the Castle or Fortress of the Oak (p. 329).

Rudolf Steiner talks of Clinschor and Iblis as one of the evilest unions in the history of humanity, and that one can still sense the echoes of their vile effects to this day in Sicily. He adds that their malevolent influence that radiated out from Sicily was only balanced out by great people such as Empedocles who also lived on that island. Caltabellotta certainly embodies an eerie and uncanny atmosphere. One summer, a few years back, while traveling along the coast of Sicily on the tracks of Goethe, we spotted Caltaballotta from the road and immediately veered off the highway and ascended the narrowing road to the little Sicilian town endowed with so much diabolical history. The castle is unlike any I have ever witnessed, clinging to the steep and sheer cliff faces of the rocky narrow mountain that juts like a colossal fissured tooth into the air. It exudes a palpably repellant mood, as if all sorts of unsavory deeds have been committed in that pinnacled edifice. Maybe it was only coincidence, but all of our cameras ceased functioning while there. We only have some grainy photos from a distance. If Neuschwanstein in Bavaria is the archetypal fairytale castle (as depicted in Disneyworld), then the castle of Caltabellotta could easily be seen as the archetypal devil's castle, or a representation of Sauron's evil fortress, as imagined in Tolkien's *Lord of the Rings*. The "etheric" space of the entire place, including the fissured, craggy, weathered, and rocky nature around the castle, was suffused by murkiness, even the church on the outskirts of the village with a distinct view of the fortress, left us leaden and deadened within. It is said that certain groups still consider it as a center for their "dark" arts. Some scholars claim that Schastel Marveile is based on Clinschor's Castle at Caltabellotta. However, Wolfram's description of the Castle's surroundings does not match Caltabelotta. Rather, Caltabelotta could have inspired the initial depiction of the impressive castle that ascends like a "spinning top," when Gawain first meets Orgeluse in Logroys. That image is certainly more fitting.

"Because of the dishonour to his body he [Clinschor] no longer bears good will to man or woman, . . . for it gratifies his heart to deny them any happiness he can" (p. 329). King Irot, father of Gramoflanz, to be left in peace, gave him land for eight miles all around, including the almost inaccessible castle that has many marvels and enough provisions to last thirty years (parallel of Munsalvæsche). "Clinschor has power over all those beings that haunt the aether between earth's boundary and the firmament, the malign and the benign, except those under God's protection" (p. 329). Queen Arnive assures him that the wicked enchantments are now broken and that Clinschor will never again bother himself with the Castle or the surrounding lands. Though evil, he "has publicly declared—and he is a man of his word—that whoever passed through this Adventure should be free of his molestation, and that the gift should rest with that person" (p. 330). She explains that the Castle has many men and women from *many countries and religions*, all of whom were forced to live in the castle. She urges Gawain to let all these people return to their homes. Clinschor's realm must be taken as a microcosm of the modern world, where all of us are affected, in one way or another.

Gawain, who withstood the Adventure of the Lit marveile and took the perilous leap to attain the wreath from the well-guarded tree, now has the power to free all those held in captivity—soul captivity—by Clinschor's dark forces. Gaining ever more consciousness over oneself and one's inner growth has *freeing* power, not only for oneself but for others. Gawain's adventures supply us with a potent imagination of how we can work toward freedom, each of us in our own small way, but only *if* we choose to work on ourselves—to fight Gawain's battles within us.

Greetings and Meetings

"In a gentle way, you can shake the world." ~ Mahatma Gandhi

On the day of Arnive's disclosures regarding Clinschor, King Arthur, as well as the Duchess' army from Logroys, arrive with pomp and grandeur. As yet, Queen Arnive does not know that her husband Utependragon died during her imprisonment. Gawain sends Bene to Plippalinot to prevent the army crossing over that day, and he gives her "Swallow," the magnificent harp from the wondrous Booth, shaped like a wing of a swallow. It befits her. She flies like a swallow back and forth, here and there, the winged messenger between people, each flight a melody, to achieve harmony for all. Her will to resolve the conflict between Gramoflanz and Gawain—with Itonje stuck in the middle—quickly gains in strength and significance. So much depends on her. Bene's feathery words soar as she flies between the adversaries, cleaning and clearing the air of the last vestiges of Clinschor's lingering effects.

The Duchess and the inhabitants of the castle do not recognize the banners and escutcheons of King Arthur. Unfortunately, both armies, on their way to Joflanze fall into battle, with losses on both sides. We see that there is still much that needs sorting out before agreements are made and situations are recognized for what they are. As Eschenbach remarks: "Truly, my Lord Gawan ought to have informed the Duchess that an ally of his was in her territory! Then there would have been no fighting" (p. 333). Gawain still has a few vestiges of self-importance lingering within him. He did as it suited him, for the sake of creating a more powerful effect, thereby crossing the tipping point. Furthermore, Gawain and Orgeluse also still need to practice open communication. Gawain has a touch of Gramoflanz's pride in him, also desiring the duel to be witnessed as publicly and widely as possible. For the sake of a grand entrance, Gawain withholds the greeting all day, though it is not easy for him.

Only the next morning, when King Arthur sets out to battle the army under Gawain's command, does Gawain choose to reveal the truth. Gawain says, "Matters have reached a point at which I must name their lord for you all to know who he is. He is my uncle Arthur, under whose roof and at whose court I was reared since childhood" (p. 333), and with that he makes his grand entrance, his companies crossing the river, an impressive cavalcade of knights and ladies. Greetings of spectacular breadth take place, with much kissing and affection. Introductions are made and revealed. Agreements are carried out, and the knights that have been captured on Arthur's and the Duchess' side are freed. All is forgiven and there is much happiness.

Early next morning before sunrise and in secrecy, Gawain arms himself and rides out to exercise himself and his horse Gringuljete in preparation for the duel with Gramoflanz. While riding out over the plain, Gawain sees a motionless knight, waiting and ready for battle.

Discussion Topics, Questions

- Discuss gender issues and what separates and unites men and women.
- What builds healthy relationships, what hinders them?
- What is at the core of the East-West dichotomy? How can it be understood?
- Discuss the importance of joy. What are its qualities? What is joy?
- What is the modern equivalent of Clinschor's forcefield?
- Is there truth to certain places radiating negative or positive energy? If so, can we influence our physical surroundings? What form would that take? Give examples.
- When in life have you had to rely on trust and faith?

Illustration:
Two knights jousting (Goni Ronen)

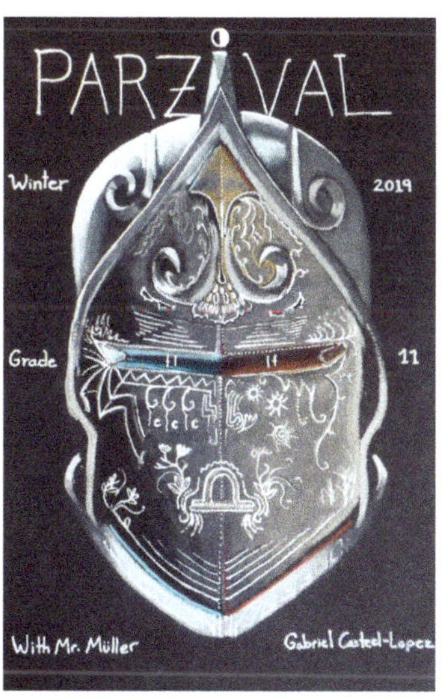

BOOK FOURTEEN

Parzival Revealed

"No matter how gradually you go, as long as you do not stop." ~ Confucius

Gawain notices that the unknown knight, clad in armor from heathen lands, redder than ruby, is wearing a wreath plucked from Gramoflanz's tree, which causes Gawain to think that it might be King Gramoflanz. Without further ado the two stalwart knights charge and a battle ensues without a soul to witness it.

Meanwhile, Arthur's messengers meet King Gramoflanz on a meadow between two rivers running to the sea. We note the mention of water, which is life-giving, and the streams which merge into the sea, not only uniting but becoming one with something greater and all encompassing. It is an image of hope. The messengers see many foreign knights, who have arrived from many diverse countries, all eager to ride to Joflanze to witness the duel. The messengers have come to dissuade King Gramoflanz from pursuing the battle, yet this proudest of men refuses. Bene, who is sitting next to Gramoflanz, has, as yet, no issue with the duel. Having come separately by boat, she has her own message to convey: to confirm Itonje's constant and unwavering love for him. The news pleases Gramoflanz and he proceeds to don his most splendid armor. Once he is fully armed, he kisses Itonje's ring and is ready to set out toward Joflanze.

Arthur's messengers leave disappointed, and on their return-journey come upon the two knights in the throes of bitter fighting. Recognizing Gawain and the perilous plight he is in, they call out his name, which causes the strange knight to cease fighting immediately, flinging his sword far from him. The stranger breaks into tears, crying, "Accurst and contemptible! . . . To think I have been attacking noble Gawan here! So doing I have vanquished myself" (p. 344). It is the moment in which *Parzival reveals himself*, ushering in his grand and forceful reentry into the main story of the epic. Simultaneously, he chastises himself for battling against Gawain—another aspect of himself. Gawain realizes their inseparable bond as clearly as does Parzival:

> "Two hearts that are but one have shown their strength in fierce enmity. Your hand has overcome us both. Now regret it for our sakes. If your heart be true, you have subdued yourself." (p 345)

This fierce battle, in which Parzival is seen as the clear winner, shows that there is still a great deal of smoothing over that needs to happen. The timing is still off, but it helps to shift things into place. Not only is the social sphere fraught with misunderstandings, mistakes, and plain ignorance, but it needs the extra push of imperfections and failings to bring things to light. It caused kindred spirits to fall into unwanted discord. The armor prevented them from knowing who they were really jousting against. How often do we hide behind metaphorical armor with opinions, principles, attitudes, or judgements? Moreover, we are quick to react out of misplaced pride or plain habit. Maybe we should make a point of removing our metaphorical "helmets" before entering into conflict. It could change the whole tenor of the encounter.

By now, the other armies have arrived, including King Gramoflanz, who is distressed to see Gawain's feeble condition and that he is in no state to endure another battle. He suggests they fight on the following day. Parzival immediately offers to stand in for Gawain, but Gramoflanz will have none of that.

It is only now that Bene realizes the truth and extent of the prearranged duel. Not for a moment had she suspected that the highly anticipated joust was to be fought between Gawain and Gramoflanz. The true, noble, and courageous nature of Bene now shows itself in full measure. She speaks up to address King Gramoflanz head on. She does not mince her words:

> "You treacherous cur," are the words her sweet lips uttered. "Your heart is in the hand of that same man whom your heart is hating! To whom have you surrendered yourself in Love's name? She has to live by that man's favor! You have pronounced your own defeat—Love has lost her rights in you! For if ever you loved, it was in bad faith." (p. 346)

Bene, who, up till now, has always shown herself amenable and compliant, continually aiming to serve and be there for the needs and well-being of others—almost to the point of submissiveness—now shows her mettle, the unadulterated strength of her convictions. She is no meek and mild lass. In this moment of need, she rises to the occasion, becoming a formidable force in the name of unequivocable goodness. She berates Gramoflanz—the epitome of pride—trying to bring him to his senses, to recognize the illogicality of his stubborn insistence on fighting Gawain. She is a guardian of sorts, guarding the well-being of Itonje and Gawain, even of Gramoflanz himself, though he does not realize it yet. In truth, she becomes the guardian of all those gathered to witness the duel—all four armies. Gramoflanz tries to placate her. He still does not see the absurdity of it all. Pride certainly is a deep-rooted weed. Nevertheless, it is true to life, because it often takes a long time before we wake up to our own deep-seated incongruities. His feeble and stubborn words only confirm the travesty for her, and she retorts: "Out with you, you cursed man! . . . Loyalty is a thing you never knew" (p. 347).

Gramoflanz rides off, as Parzival, Gawain, and Bene ride back to their own army, where Parzival is welcomed with great honor, even though he gave Gawain a beating. Everybody is talking about him, praising his valorous achievements and good looks. Gawain sees to it that both are robed in new clothes, which are identical and of equal preciousness, solidifying the idea that they are as one. The four queens welcome Parzival, though Orgeluse can barely hide her embarrassment when she has to kiss him, the only man who has spurned her love. It is a humbling moment, but is also part of the sorting out process. Nobody is spared some humility, even beautiful Orgeluse, who has never known rejection. Parzival, too, has a painful recollection when he thinks back to his public shaming five years earlier by Cundrie, wondering whether some ladies would find it offensive to lay eyes on him. The shame smarts him still. But he sees that his misgivings are unwarranted, and he is relieved.

Itonje, during the midday meal, wonders why Bene is present because she had sent her to Gramoflanz to convey her love for him. Itonje notices that Bene is crying to herself and senses that something is amiss, though unaware of the reasons behind Bene's sorrow. Gawain explicitly told Bene not reveal anything of the upcoming duel between Gawain and Gramoflanz. Unfortunately, Itonje misinterprets the situation, thinking that Gramoflanz has rejected her love. The students in class understand this all too well—those times when situations are misread or misinterpreted. It's a side-effect of the social realm, not just in love, but in all spheres where people work, live, or have dealings together.

After the meal, Arthur is sitting together with Parzival, surrounded by a ring of people—Christians, Saracens, and many strangers from disparate lands of which Clinschor's army was comprised. Wolfram says it would be a lengthy business to name them all, their names and dominions. They represent humanity. And all these diverse peoples are in agreement that Parzival is beyond compare. This prescient recognition by such a variety of people bodes well for the future Grail King: a ruler, loved by all, who has the strength and vision to unify the greatest diversity of people in his realm, where all are treated with equality. As the people are gathered together, joined by Gawain and Orgeluse, Parzival stands up and says that he was once parted from the Round Table, but that he now has a request to be inducted and to rejoin: "I ask those who were once my Companions, by exerting their companionship, to help me back to it" (p. 350)!

Reconciliation

"There is an extremely powerful force that, so far, science has not found a formal explanation to. It is a force that includes and governs all others, and is even behind any phenomenon operating in the universe and has not yet been identified by us. This universal force is LOVE" ~ Albert Einstein[1]

King Arthur graciously accepts Parzival's request to join the Round Table. Parzival consciously wants to complete his original quest. It strengthens the will to follow through on ideals.

Stepping aside, he asks for a second request, namely, that Gawain lets him fight against Gramoflanz, explaining that he had explicitly picked the wreath from the tree to provoke a fight with Gramoflanz. This shows that Parzival had already *consciously* planned to fight Gramoflanz, not for Orgelus' sake but out of his own intention. And indeed, he thought he was when he fought against Gawain that morning. Gawain, however, declines, not wishing to go against his word.

Parzival nevertheless examines his armor, repairs his straps, and procures a new shield. Satisfied with the order of the armor and the grooming of his charger, Parzival lies down to rest. It is clear that he intends to follow through with his intention of fighting Gramoflanz, for his own sake as much as for Gawain. And as they have already professed: they are one.

Gramoflanz, having been cheated out of the glory once, also prepares himself, riding out early the next morning, making sure that no one would fight Gawain in his stead. Likewise, Parzival rides out unseen toward the designated place of the duel where he sees the King waiting. Without a word, they charge and thrust their spears through each other's shields. The

1 From a letter to his daughter, Lieserl.

fight has begun. Gramoflanz has no idea who he is fighting and that he is about to experience a humiliating drubbing.

Around mid-morning, as Gawain prepares for battle, he hears that Parzival is missing. Instead of bringing about a reconciliation, as could be assumed, Parzival is in the midst of battle. When Gawain, Arthur, and the entire army finally ride out to the designated spot, they witness two knights loudly hacking away at each other. King Gramoflanz is not faring well. For a knight who scorned fighting with only one foe, it now feels as if he is attacked by six. It is a cathartic lesson in humility, one only Parzival could give. Never again would Gramoflanz make such arrogant claims about only fighting two men or more. One way or another, humbleness must be attained on the path to self-knowledge and initiation. When Gawain and the others appear, it is obvious that Parzival has all but won the contest. They decide to end the battle. Like the day before, Gawain offers to postpone the battle to the next day, seeing that Gramoflanz is in no shape to fight. Parzival, in fighting Gramoflanz, knocked the pride right out of him. Simultaneously, he overcame the last vestiges of pride within himself, for nobody can become the Grail King who still harbors even a smidgen of pride, based in self-glorification. Gramoflanz represented the deep-rooted pride that had clung itself so fiercely to all who lived or entered Clinschor's realm. It was not enough for Gawain to conquer the Castle of Wonders. It needed the combined effort of Gawain and Parzival—of the heart and the mind, of feeling and thinking, and of the multiple stages of development expressed in the adventures of Gawain and Parzival.

As they ride back to camp, Arthur gently reprimands Parzival for riding out "like a thief" to fight Gramoflanz. Nevertheless, Parzival has won high merit, especially since he has distinguished himself through his jousts with Gawain and Gramoflanz. Wolfram used the same turn of phrase when describing Gahmuret's covert and faithless *departure* from Belacane. In this similarly furtive act, Parzival redeems his father and reinforces his exceptional *return* into the main part of the story, underscoring his peerless worth as a warrior.

Gawain is happy about Parzival's high acclaim, even though he begins to recede and fade into the background. It is plain that he does not want to fight against Gramoflanz, but feels that he *must*, though he says, "If the King would release me from it I should account it very reasonable on his account" (p. 353).

The ordering and straightening out continues in the form of negotiations between the parties, endeavoring to bring the duel to an end in an honorable manner so that nobody has to lose face. A great deal of back and forth happens behind the scenes, between Gramoflanz and his people, and those surrounding Itonje, with Bene serving as the key element, flitting back and forth between the various parties like a swallow.

Gramoflanz's people ask him to send messengers to King Arthur to ensure that nobody fights in Gawain's place, to avoid a repeat humiliation. Gramoflanz, in turn, asks the envoys to note how the woman sitting next to Bene conducts herself, handing them a letter and a ring which they must give to Bene to pass on to Itonje. Itonje, on the other hand, finally realizes the full import of the impending duel, and that her brother and Gramoflanz, her love, cannot be dissuaded to fight one another, a source of grievous torment. Itonje asks King Arthur to settle the issue. He agrees, recognizing the authenticity and purity of her love for Gramoflanz.

If we think of what has happened since Gawain agreed to fight Gramoflanz, all the strife and loss of life, the battles and the grief, one wonders if it could all have been avoided. Pride, the root cause of so much upheaval got in the way, and pride is a manifestation of egotism. Gramoflanz desired the glory of battle, to be witnessed by as many people as possible; apparently for the sake of love. Yet, the mutual love between Itonje and Gramoflanz is true and unquestionable. It does not need verification through the glory of battle. It is misplaced honor and glory. Much time is spent on trying to ascertain the genuineness and legitimacy of their love. What can we do in our own lives to avoid unnecessary troubles and conflicts? How can we practice social interactions so that we can sense what needs to be done without undergoing so many sacrifices from so many people? Can we find modern examples of that? Much can be achieved through the practice of open and true communication. And yet, there will be setbacks if even a hint of pride gets in the way, which it inevitably does.

Again and again, it is emphasized that Gramoflanz and Itonje have never seen each other before, but that their love is a *given*. It remains almost a mystery. King Arthur, convinced of the power of the love between the two, vows to put an end to the duel, though he too wonders how they fell in love without any physical contact. Itonje reveals that the engineer behind their love is Bene, and that Bene is the one who can arrange a meeting between the two. And thus, it is organized that Gramoflanz and Itonje meet and that he looks around to see if he can *identify* her, though he has never seen her, as a proof of his—their—love. In order for that to happen, a truce from the Duchess Orgeluse must be obtained, for the whole pain of the situation goes back to the unfortunate occurrences between those two. Orgeluse agrees, finally. Yet, she has conditions: that Gawain withdraws from the duel for her sake and that Gramoflanz withdraws his accusations against King Lot. After much back and forth, the conditions are met and Gramoflanz enters the pavilion and is able to identify Itonje, partly because he recognizes her features in those of her brother Beacurs, who had accompanied him. With that, the need for a duel is averted.

Earthly antipathies are set aside in order for purity of love to emerge and thrive. The duel would have stained the love affair because of its "Catch 22" nature. Arthur says it well: "Where love is tinged with hatred, happiness is denied entry to the constant heart" (p. 362). In this situation, King Arthur shines, more than in any part of the epic, where he often appeared weak. His help in averting the duel is critical. But the greatest credit goes to Bene. Bene is the true hero of Book Fourteen. Without her, it would have ended badly. In her quiet, unassuming manner, she leveled out the inconsistencies. She is the Queen of sorting, resolving, and working things out. She has the prescience of someone who personifies Goodness. She works her magic behind the scenes, yet is not afraid to voice her opinions when needed, rooted in truth.

And so, "for affection's sake rancour was put aside" (p. 363). In this moment of solemn peacemaking, Arthur invites Queen Arnive, Queen

Sangive, and Cundrie into his circle. Even Orgeluse overcomes herself and kisses King Gramoflanz when he comes over in the hope of winning her goodwill, which is followed with Gawain and Gramoflanz exchanging a reconciliatory kiss. And finally, King Arthur gives Itonje away in marriage, to the joy and satisfaction of Bene. Cundrie receives Lischois, which renews his happiness. And Arthur gives Sangive and the Turkoyt to each other. Of course, these arrangements were all discussed before the ceremonial "giving," which is a blessing rather than a giving. Orgeluse takes this moment to formally announce to all the union between her and Gawain, and that Gawain—who faithfully served her—is now the rightful lord of Schastel marveile. Itonje and Gramoflanz, in the care of Arthur and Guinevere, celebrate a splendid wedding feast of surpassing grandeur. The weddings not only seal the personal unions of the respective knights and ladies, but also new won peace between the four great armies. The social complexities were cleared up and worked through, resulting in a festive culmination, based on mutual *forgiveness* between the former adversaries.

All these love alliances cause Parzival to think of his lovely Condwiramurs. With so many around him finding love, he misses her even more, refraining from offering his service to another, remaining steadfast to Condwiramurs. While others rejoice in the happiness of their new love, he feels the loss of love, which enhances his sense of isolation. Pensively, he muses, "May fortune guide me for what is best for me to do" (p. 364). He must have trust in his own destiny. He feels cut off from the merriment of others around him, and he is beyond caring about what might happen to himself. He is resigned to his position. He is no longer angry or defiant at his misfortune. He accepts his lot. It is often this very moment, the moment of tranquil acceptance, when something new can happen. It is a private moment. I tell my students that when they go through life, they should look out and become aware of these "letting go" moments, should they arise. In the moment of inner acceptance, something new can enter. It's a hallowed moment, if consciously acknowledged. Parzival is happy for the others in their joy—but as for himself? "I shall ride out from amid these joys" (p. 365). Fully armored, he sets out at the break of day. Though he is ready to take on new hardships, he is at the cusp of change and of receiving his deepest heart's desire.

Discussion topics, questions

- When do we react, based on habit?
- Why are social cues or situations often misinterpreted? What are the consequences of misreading or misunderstanding people's words or actions?
- Are you able to accept a difficult situation?
- Is it possible to love a person that you have never seen before? How can the love between Gramoflanz and Itonje be understood?
- Do you trust your destiny?
- To what extent do sympathy and antipathy play into social relationships? Should these contrary feelings be overcome?

Illustration:
Helmet (Gabriel Lopez)

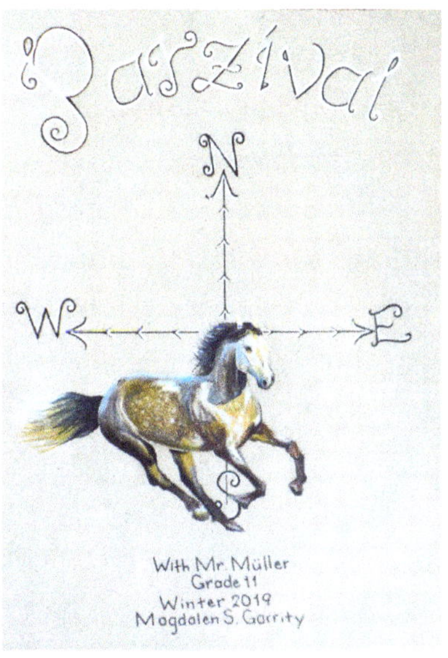

BOOK FIFTEEN

The Strange Knight

Face to face they fight.
Unmatched by all, equal only to each other
Grappling, gasping, with might
Helmets cast aside. Finally, he sees his brother.
~ Student (Dezjuan Smith)

The last two chapters of *Parzival* complete the story of the Grail, left unfinished by Chrétien de Troyes in his original version. "I shall now withhold it no longer . . . of how gentle, handsome Anfortas was made well again" (p. 366). We must remember that Wolfram's version was published approximately 30 years later, which amounts to a long wait for a sequel, clearly acknowledged by the author: "Many people have grown impatient at the Sequel's being locked away from them" (p. 366). We remember that Wolfram also added the first two introductory chapters. Only the twelve chapters in between run parallel to Troyes' story of the Grail. Wolfram was aware of the symbolic significance of the extra four chapters that frame the book:[1] The twelve-petaled lotus flower of the heart is in harmony with the sixteen-petaled lotus flower of the larynx—of speech. It is an epic of self-development for the individual and for communities, but it also supplies clearly outlined steps toward initiation. The circular motif, popular in medieval times, is used consciously by Wolfram, connecting the introductory chapters to the concluding chapters, bringing the epic full circle—a finale that hints at the next cycle. It clearly sets Wolfram's story apart from Chrétien's.

At this point, Wolfram emphasizes that whatever toil and trouble Parzival has had to contend with so far is nothing—mere "child's play"—compared to what he is about to encounter. He is setting the stage for Parzival's greatest and most significant battle. Wolfram is asking his audience to take heed of this singular encounter. Thematically speaking, it is possibly the most important for our present time, our global age, which encapsulates the matrix of the twenty first century. For whatever we do, no matter how small, has to have global reach in one form or another if humanity is to resolve its multilayered problems.

Parzival's culminating opponent is introduced in the grandest of terms, before Parzival even sets eyes on him. Wolfram refers to him as a stranger and a heathen, but foremostly as a pure and noble knight. Not just any knight, but a leader of twenty-five nations with riches beyond compare, unequaled by any, making King Arthur appear like a pauper in comparison. The number twenty five is filled with symbolism, often associated with the overcoming of obstacles and of change, especially in regard to the choice of people you want to be close with. It is clear: this stranger is a paragon of knights and Wolfram is "afeared" for Parzival's safety.

Parzival, having set out alone, meets him in a forest, and immediately their eyes light up on seeing each other. Both live for adventure and jousts (chip off the old block). Though they both rejoice at the chance of fighting, Wolfram adds: "Each of these unblemished men bore the other's heart within him—theirs was an intimate strangeness" (p. 368).

---

1 However, some scholars claim that Wolfram did not initially divide the epic into 16 books.

"Intimate strangeness" is a fitting description of how our *heads* relate to our *hearts* or to our *limbs*—our *thinking* to our *feeling* to our *willing*. Nowadays it is easy to think one thing, feel another, and act in utter contradiction to either of them. As modern people, we tend to be dismembered in regard to these three foundational aspects of our human selves. In earlier times they formed a whole, but the loss of our inner "royalty," our sense of our "higher selves," our connection to the truth behind the maya has rent us apart, the cause of so many of our mental health concerns. Alone, the strength of our individuality can unify this sacred trinity, and for that to happen requires self-development, the effort to work on ourselves, stage for stage.

Once we recognize the humanity in all people, then almost everybody, in a way, becomes "intimate." However, we are a long way from this grand form of "intimate strangeness." To reiterate, our thinking, feeling, and willing are often at odds with one another. There are many examples, such as people preaching peace but waging war; spouting high morals and acting lowly; condemning drugs or alcohol while indulging. Oftentimes people realize their own hypocrisy, yet cannot overcome themselves, as exemplified by addictions (drugs, media, or sex addiction). It is a truth battle. It does not take much self-examination to acknowledge the dilemma.

Nothing prevents the two stalwart knights from coming to blows, and they immediately recognize that their opponent is unlike any other they have ever encountered. The stranger's helmet is adorned with an Ecidemon, a creature that kills poisonous snakes—suggesting that the vestiges of poison will possibly be snuffed in Parzival (similarly to when Parzival fought against remnants of pride while fighting Gurnemanz, or the dragon in himself when he conquered Orilus). The stranger's war-cry "Thasme" and "Thabronit" gives him uncanny power, allowing him to advance. He fights in the name of Queen Secundille, who gave him the land of Tribalibot, a source of immense wealth, wisdom, and culture. No doubt, the stranger is gaining the upper hand, forcing Parzival to his knees—a first. Up till this moment, "Parzival had been a stranger to defeat, never having suffered it, though many had got it from him" (p. 369). Though they are two, yet they are one, as Wolfram once again declares. Whenever the stranger shouts "Thabronit," he is invoking Secundille's love, her spirit, in whose favor he lived. Trabronit is the place where Queen Secundille resides at the foot of the Caucasus mountains, which most likely refers to Hindu Kush, also known as Indian Caucasus. Historically the Caucasus were applied to two areas: the above-mentioned one and another further west (Russia, Georgia, Ukraine), thus alluding to one of the cradles of civilization. The pure beast Ecidemon is the minder of her love.

Still, Parzival does not think of calling on his inner strength which resides in Condwiramurs' love. And still, he suffers stroke after stroke, heavy blows that hail down on him without pause. The stranger's font of power lies in the constancy of his love that he cherishes in his heart, symbolized by the gemstones of his armor: "precious stones which with their pure and noble virtues gave him spirit and enhanced his strength" (p. 370). Gemstones represent "solidified light" in all of their different manifestations and connections to the various planets and their respective powers, which exude healing properties. It is well known that stones balance the body, soul, and mind. Stones, along with the themes of birds, food, clothes, colors, numbers, and so forth, play a significant role in this medieval epic. They are mentioned throughout *Parzival*, often in great detail, and with direct allusions to their power.

Just in time, Parzival answers the stranger's cry of "Thasme" and "Thabronit" with "Belrepeire!" "And now from four or more kingdoms away and just in the nick of time, Condwiramurs came to his aid with the power of her love" (p. 370), and immediately new strength pours through him. At this moment, the stout sword of Gaheviez shatters across the stranger's helmet, bringing him to his knees. The sword of Ither has served him all this time, but he had stolen it from a man—a kinsman—he'd killed in a dastardly manner. In Parzival's development, as in all of our developments, every detail needs to be resolved, every transgression, every mistake, failure, and misdeed must be balanced out. It is all part of redemption and closure. This is Parzival's last battle before becoming the next Grail King, and the last vestiges of his past mistakes need to be paid off, erased. Life itself is a Mystery Center, and life presents us with the disciplines that must be practiced. And similarly to the Mystery Centers of old, the modern neophyte cannot advance before certain terms have been met. We are charged to take on our own development of feeling, thinking, and willing—from the inside out, rather than directed by the high priests or the gods. The Age of the Consciousness Soul demands it.

The Stranger is in a position to put a quick end to Parzival, but his good breeding and education comes to the fore. Instead, he says, "But what honor would I gain from you then? Refrain valiant warrior, and tell me who you are" (p. 371). The Stranger does the right and honorable thing. A quintessential moment has arrived in their relationship: the revealing of their identities! Not only have they already divulged something essential about themselves, but they needed to fight in order to spark an interest for one another. The "heathen" commends Parzival for his fighting skill, wanting to know his name and lineage, which would make his whole journey worthwhile.[2] When Parzival is reluctant to disclose any information, the stranger insouciantly volunteers to go first. "Then I will name myself first. . . . I am Feirefiz Angevin with such plentitude of power that many lands pay tribute to me" (p. 371). After some moments of consternation (Parzival considers Anjou to be his personal inheritance), they realize they are brothers, confirmed when Feirefiz removes his helmet to reveal his marvelously dappled skin. Parzival immediately remembers Queen Ekuba's

2 To underscore: Wolfram never uses the term "heathen" in a derogatory manner. What matters is the character and the inner worth of the respective person.

description of his brother, while Feirefiz throws his sword into the forest to make things equal between them. They seal their union with a kiss. Feirefiz gives praise to Juno and Jupiter for leading him to his brother, son of Gahmuret, a union long in coming. It is a significant moment, for it links the beginning of the epic to the end. The students are inevitably moved by this unification scene.

It initially struck me as strange that the Roman form of the Greek gods was chosen for this son of an African Queen, though, admittedly, northern Africa and the Middle East is a melting pot of a multitude of tribes, nationalities, races, and religions. The term "Saracen," often used in the epic, cannot solely be equated with Muslims. During the Crusades, a Saracen was considered synonymous with a Muslim. However, the story of Parzival refers to the ninth century where a broader view was still associated with the Saracens, which included a looser concept of geography. The Saracens have a long history and they were an independent people with a polytheistic worldview, including a variety of gods. Nevertheless, we can glean something from Feirefiz's mention of Juno and Jupiter, which relates to the planets and their influences on the course of the quest story. Juno (Hera) is the daughter of Saturn, who is associated with the *beginning of things*. She is married to Jupiter (Zeus, ruler of the gods on Mount Olympus) and her son is Mars (Ares). These planetary qualities are also associated with Feirefiz. He gives credit to Jupiter, giving praise to its light under which he set out on his adventure and which guided him to Parzival. The planet Jupiter, in contrast to Saturn, contains the promise of the future.

Without hesitation, Feirefiz exhibits his generosity by gifting two countries to Parzival: Zazamanc and Azagouc, the two countries acquired by Gahmuret after he married the dazzling black Queen Belacane after the death of Isenhart. It serves as a lead-in to talk about Gahmuret. Feirefiz makes it clear that he felt abandoned by his father. "I have not forgiven my father this wrong" (p. 373). Not only did Gahmuret leave him fatherless, but also motherless, for Belacane died shortly after from grief. Belacane, too, was a "Herzeloyde," sharing the similar fate of a grieving heart (as so many women did). Then he reveals the purpose for his voyage: *to seek his father!* Parzival reveals that he has not met him either, and relates the sad news that Gahmuret died many years ago in "heathen lands" fighting for the Baruch of Baghdad. It is noteworthy that Feirefiz left Secundille to look for his father and that Parzival left Condwiramurs to search for his mother, both goals thwarted, though it led the brothers to one another and to the Grail—the future. Understandably, Feirefiz is saddened and disappointed, though thrilled to have found Parzival, his long-lost brother.

As they talk, Feirefiz expresses sentiments similar to what had been exchanged between Gawain and Parzival after their battle.

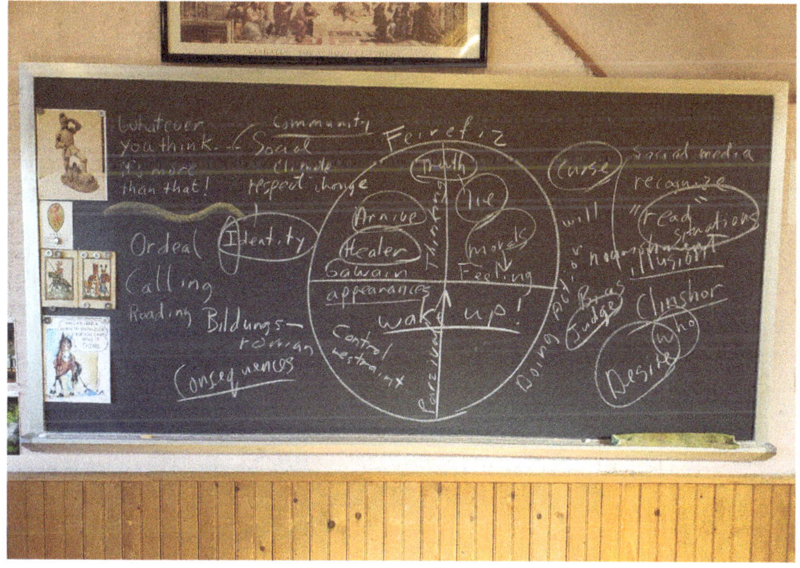

> "On this field you were fighting with yourself. I came riding to do battle with myself and would gladly have slain myself. By fighting on so doggedly you defended my own life from me. Jupiter, record this marvel: thy power succored us by coming between us and death!" (p. 374)

Not only are Gawain and Parzival connected as one, but also Parzival and his brother Feirefiz. Thus, they make a trinity. We have repeatedly alluded to the polarity between head and heart, thinking and feeling, as represented by Parzival and Gawain. Feirefiz can be seen as the *will* element. The three of them make up the whole human being, each one representing one of the human capacities. Earlier on, Feirefiz described to Parzival how they, together with Gahmuret, are like one. If we exchange the name "Gahmuret" for "Gawain", we have the perfect wording for the relationship of Parzival, Gawain, and Feirefiz: "If I lay hold of truth, both [Gawain] and you, and I, too, were but one, though seen as three distinct entities" (p. 374). There are other places in the book where Wolfram points out the unity between people (as one), such as the relationship between man and wife, or Obilot's description of her relationship with Gawain. However, out of these examples, the unity between Parzival, Gawain, and Feirefiz is most pronounced and significant. It makes perfect sense to the students when we discuss it. Up to this point, I consciously focused on the polarity between head and heart, adding the *will* element only when Feirefiz enters the story.

Legend tells that Parzival was greater,
But in fact, it was Feirefiz who cast aside his blade
And with it fear and jealousy, abated
And it was he who hugged his kin, and forgave.
~ Student (Dezjuan Smith)

The dramatic entry of Feirefiz is the perfect moment to show how the *will* streams throughout everything. It is the subterranean force without which there can be no control of thinking or feeling. Feirefiz, so to speak, has been intimately connected to both Gawain and Parzival from the get-go. That is why he also appears at the beginning of the epic, resurfacing again and again, though only through the words of others, such as Cundrie, Ekuba and Queen Secundille, his wife (or mistress). If we imagine Parzival to represent the vertical sphere, and Gawain the horizontal, we can imagine Feirefiz as the circle around the cross—resulting in that most archetypal and ubiquitous of religious symbols, found in the Celtic cross, or in the symbology of Native Americans (First Nations). It represents unification between the spirit and the earth, the invisible and the visible, matter and the divine, light and darkness. This sacred solar cross that unifies all that is separated is found globally, from prehistoric times through to the present. The swastikas are a variation of this sun sign, found throughout Europe and Asia, but also in the Americas. The cross within the circle divides the circle into four. I ask the students what *quaternities* they can come up with, and they quickly respond with the four cardinal directions, the four elements, and the four seasons. One student brought up the preponderance of the number four throughout the epic, such as the four queens; the four hundred knights of Munsalvæsche; the four hundred ladies of Schastel marveile; the four weeks Urjans spent with the dogs; the four encounters between Parzival and Sigune; the stages of inner development depicted by the crow, peacock, Swan, and pelican; and many more. The number four also stands for the earth, in contrast to the trinity that represents the divine (and the evolutionary sequence of Saturn, Sun, and Moon). In this case, the quaternity is born out of the trinity of the three knights. Furthermore, we have the connection between point and the periphery—rest and movement. There are unending meanings to the circle and cross. It has a universality that one cannot overlook, where the disparate elements are kept in fluid balance. "Everything visible in creation stands in the sign of the four. . . . Four is, therefore, the number of the cosmos or of creation. With the entrance into the fourth condition, a being becomes fully visible to eyes that can see external things."[3]

Feirefiz's power is made evident when he invites Parzival to view the finest of his armies. Parzival is amazed at the power he wields over his legions: "Have you such control over your people that they will wait for you today and for as long as you are away from them?" (p. 375) Instead, Parzival invites him to Arthur's court, of which Feirefiz has heard a great deal. He considers Arthur as his relative. Parzival confirms that Feirefiz will

3 Rudolf Steiner, *Occult Signs and Symbols* (Anthroposophic Press, 1972), pp. 41-42.

find "our own true race, people of whose blood we are born" (p. 375). This "race" is not connected to skin color but to kinship, to kindred spirits, to the human race that will one day be united—the transmuted blood, free of prejudice, hatred, and odious discrimination, based on the striving after the highest ideals.

Parzival retrieves Feirefiz's sword for him from the forest, and they depart as friends and brothers back to Arthur's encampment.

Welcoming Feirefiz

"Colors are the deeds and suffering of light." ~ Goethe

The great battle, observed in the magic Pillar up in the watchtower, was described as a battle beyond compare. When the two brothers enter the multi-ringed pavilions, Feirefiz is welcomed in a grand fashion, leaving all amazed at the riches of his armor and the "Infidel's" unique skin texture, mottled like a magpie. Luxurious clothes are brought and much joyous time is spent on welcome kisses, after which the talk turns to the epic battle the two of them fought.

Parzival praises Feirefiz, saying that he has never fought a harder battle, relating with what honor and fearlessness he comported himself. This battle has mythic qualities, almost like an archetype of all brotherly rivalry. One might be prompted to think of that earliest of rivalries between Cain and Abel, which continued unresolved throughout the ages, manifesting itself over and over again. All wars are manifestations of that earliest shedding of blood. As humans, however, we are all "brothers," we are all siblings to one another. Especially in our time we have to learn and consciously work at the mighty task of uniting the streams that for millennia have been flowing separately. It will not happen by itself. Crossing points are needed. They become junctures, meeting and connecting points, enabling us to cross over into peaceful terrain.

As of this writing, I heard the United Nations Secretary Antonio Guterres, while visiting Kiev, say on the evening news, "The war is an absurdity in the twenty first century. The war [Russia invading Ukraine] is evil."[4] And indeed, it is a sentiment most modern people share. In the same vein, India's Prime Minister Narendra Modi told Russian President Putin: "I know that today's era is not an era of war."[5] Wars of this nature are outdated. In our global times, we should know better. There is no excuse anymore, especially since we rely on each other like never before for natural resources and so much more. But the change starts small and with ourselves. This battle between Feirefiz and Parzival can serve as a helpful imagination. Fighting will continue, of course, but every effort needs to be made to diminish and decrease the tensions—ruled by clear thinking rather than instinct and nationalistic riled up emotions. Conflict cannot be eradicated, just as evil will continue to test humanity. It remains and wakes us up, but we can minimize the destruction and horrific suffering, especially of the innocent. Worldviews clash and the fight goes on—but how and with what means. As Gawain says so aptly, "Nevertheless, having fought, you know each other all the better for it. Now be friends where you were enemies" (p. 378).

In the true Manichean tradition, the light enters the darkness to punish it with goodness. It is a leitmotif that runs throughout this epic; therefore, we find very little overt discrimination or prejudice. Tolerance and acceptance are surprising for a book coming out of the medieval period, epitomized by the mutual acknowledgement and respect between the four armies encamped at Joflanze, ring within ring, that once were bitter enemies. On this expansive field, Gawain is once again in the horizontal sphere, the social sphere, over which he must preside with a birds'-eye view, which he has now regained.

King Arthur and his company are the last to enter the lofty "rings," arriving with great fanfare, rejoicing in the return of Parzival, but mostly to honor the exalted company of Feirefiz from Africa and the East. "Feirefiz Angevin

---

4 The above is an excerpt of his comments which were reported in various news outlets such as https://www.washingtonpost.com/world/2022/04/28/united-nations-sec-gen-guterres-ukraine-kyiv/

5 Meeting between the two leaders, Friday 16, 2022. https://www.nytimes.com/2022/09/16/world/europe/modi-putin-ukraine-russia.html

was quick to understand from them that he was among good friends" (p. 380). Arthur, seated next to Feirefiz, declares, "No man ever came from the Infidel lands to those of the Christian rite whom I would more willingly serve in any way you wish" (p. 381). This alludes to Gahmuret who chose to serve the most powerful ruler of the world, the Baruch of Baghdad. The emphasis, always, is on the person, not the race, the religion, or the politics. It is a matter of not only finding the crossing points, but seeking them. Worldviews in our time need to merge, so that something more and greater can emerge. We still see a great deal of vilification going on, where the left and the right, the liberals and conservatives , both claiming to be absolutely right, instead of putting effort into understanding one another and finding common ground.

King Arthur wants to know how Feirefiz came to the West. In answer, Feirefiz first tells him of the immense power of his army, asserting that the defenders of Troy and the besiegers combined would be no match for his army. But then he gives credit its due, speaking in the highest of terms of Queen Secundille, this mysterious goddess Queen of the East, his taskmaster, and the *source* of much of his mighty wealth and inspiration.

> "Whatever she wishes is my wish too. She has given my life direction. She commanded me to give open-handedly and so recruit good knights.... In return, her love rewards me. Wherever I was in peril and as soon as my thoughts were on her, her love has come to my aid, giving me far more encouragement than my god Jupiter." (p. 381)

This reminds one of Parzival, who put his trust in women rather than God, after his life-defining shaming, which he also conveyed to Gawain. Secundille, similarly to Parzival's Condwiramurs, guides Feirefiz in his ways and helps him in times of need through her love. Secundille is Feirefiz's third woman (after Olympia and Clauditte), following the pattern of Gahmuret, Parzival, and Gawain, all of whom had three important love interests, each one signifying an important step in their development.

Secundille is the most mysterious of all. She remains in the background, yet she is the driving force behind Feirefiz. With prescient knowledge, she leads Feirefiz not only to the West and to Parzival, but ultimately to the Grail, that heavenly "Dinc" that was already "seen" by the pagan Flegetanis. Secundille, with all her gifts to Anfortas over the years could foreshadow the connection that was destined to happen, almost like an evolutionary law. Just like Flegetanis saw the Grail in the stars, Secundille comprehended the Grail's migration to middle Europe, from where it was tasked to radiate into the future—the "new" taking the place of the "old," having outlived its time; simultaneously intimating that the Grail would once again return to the East—after the West would cease to be worthy of its essence—from where the ethereal holy blood of light would seep into people's souls and spread throughout the world, far beyond the limitations of our present age. Thus, gradually its soothing power will rise from the shadowy subconscious into higher perception—a shared inner globality that will reap mutual outer understanding. There is much in Secundille that reminds one of the Queen of Sheba, another Black Madonna, representing the soul of the East.

Arthur asks both Feirefiz and Parzival to name all the lands that they came to know through their battles. Each mention twenty to thirty countries, though they battled many more knights whose names have been forgotten. Each battle represents a trial, a step in their development, a nodal point of growth. What is important is the breadth and depth of their travels through the known world at the time. It calls to mind a well-known quote by Mohammed: "Don't tell me how educated you are, tell me how much you traveled." All outer traveling parallels inner journeys, inner growth. Through dealings with other people and the respective geographies, one becomes increasingly global, expanding one's views and worldviews. One builds tolerance and realizes that there are many ways of looking at the world and the universe. It stimulates continued reevaluation of oneself and the world. One becomes a true cosmopolitan. And the more one gets to know the world, its cultures and people, the more one harbors a love for all, fueled by the diversity which enriches everybody. Feirefiz goes on to name those who command his knights, each one coming from a different place, which shows that the opponents were incorporated into his growing empire as equals. The impressive list emphasizes the might of his territory and vast dominion. Parzival's encounters are more private, personal, one on one, though they include some of the most reputable knights, kings, and dukes across immense territories, adding that many were fought in tourneys while riding in pursuit of the Grail. The quest gave rise to these confrontations, whereas Feirefiz's might has been attained through outer conquests that added to the strength of his army.

Meanwhile, his magnificent armor was brought for inspection, admired by all, especially the rare and precious stones adorning the helmet, their worth and meaning reaching back into distant antiquity with the mention of mighty heroes such as Hercules and Alexander the Great, alluding to outer conquests. Wolfram makes a strong point of underscoring the metaphysical knowledge which the stones represent and their ongoing influence, emphasized by mentioning Pythagoras, "who was an astronomer and beyond dispute so sapient that no man since Adam's time could equal him in understanding, he could speak of great knowledge of precious stones" (p. 384). Wolfram consciously goes all the way back to Adam, the name given to the "first" human being (Adama—formed from the soil, earth, both male and female). Feirefiz, through his armor, characterizes the power of the ancient ways of life, its spiritual supremacy and influence, which has been *lost*, even to Feirefiz himself, though he is a bearer of the ancient ways. The importance given to the priceless stones foreshadows the encounter with the Grail, which is the rarest of stones, embodying, like the mythical phoenix—*new beginnings*. The old, out of necessity, must burn to ashes, out of which the new can arise. It is an essential fact of evolution that it must come to pass, like the change from childhood to adolescence to adulthood to old age. It is the secret of the seasons, of all growth. For humans, too, though the one constant is the individuality, the eternal I that goes from one incarnation into the next, while the rest falls away, perishes, turns to "ash."

It is as if his skin, resembling writing on a parchment, is a script containing the secrets of the past that lead into the future. A script that still needs deciphering. Feirefiz is the embodiment of the polarities, the one needing the other, unified in the Tao. We all carry that script within us, and once decoded will show us the path forward.

Leaving Feirefiz to the admiring attention of the ladies, Arthur proposes to Parzival, Gawain, and Gramoflanz, a festival to be held on the meadow the next morning, saying, "Apply your best thought and energy to enlisting him [Feirefiz] as a fellow member of the Table Round" (p. 384). Again, it is remarkable that they welcome and invite Feirefiz to the Round Table without the slightest prejudice, purely based on his merits as a person. As a modern culture, we are still so far removed from these essential ideals.

Induction to the Table Round

"If you have some power, then your job is to empower somebody else."
~ Toni Morrison

There are similarities to the ceremony that was prepared during Parzival's first induction. Precious cloth is cut in a circular fashion to represent the Table Round, to be spread in the meadow, with no costs spared. The next day the knights approach, all wearing wreaths, to highlight the occasion's theme of unification and rounding out. Knights and ladies are attired in clothes from many countries, each according to the national customs, reflective of the world's diversity. Among all the new inductees to the Table Round, Feirefiz, without doubt, is the mightiest and richest of them all.

Once they have taken their places, a maiden is seen riding up to the Table Round, her richly embellished clothes adorned with turtle doves of gleaming Arabian gold. It is none other than Cundrie, the sorceress. Immediately, she jumps from her palfrey, and kneels before Parzival, and, amidst tears, asks for his pardon. His resentment toward her dissolves and he forgives her, though he refrains from kissing her. She is still as ugly as before, which can serve as a reminder of our own shadowy double—a warning of our potential fall. However, Wolfram uses no animal imagery in describing her this time, but focuses on the precious materials and jewels. She addresses Parzival and welcomes "particoloured Feirefiz for Secundille's sake and for the many high distinctions he has won so gloriously since boyhood days" (p. 387). She continues:

> "O happy man. ... The inscription has been read: you are to be lord of the Gral. Your wife Condwiramurs and your son Loherangrin have both been assigned there with you. When you left the land of Brobarz she had conceived two sons. For his part, Kardeiz will have enough there in Brobarz. Had you known no other good fortune than that your truthful lips are now to address noble, gentle Anfortas and with their Question banish his agony and heal him, who could equal you in bliss?" (p. 387)

As a confirmation, she goes on to name the seven planets in Arabic, starting from Zval (Saturn), the most distant, to Alkamer (Moon), the nearest, calling them the bridal of the firmament, keeping it in balance.[6] By using the Arabic names she embraces Feirefiz and the star knowledge of the East, in which he would have been well versed. Thereby it highlights the merger between the ancient Eastern esoteric traditions and the new Grail impulse. The one fructifies the other and points toward a common spiritual worldview shared by all of humanity. "All that the planets embrace within their orbits, whatever they shed their light on, marks the scope of what it is for you to attain and achieve. Your sorrow is doomed to pass away" (p. 388). At last, he is found worthy and is redeemed. Cundrie, on their first meeting, represented Parzival's unpurified life forces. By mentioning the planets by their Arabic names, Cundrie confirms that Parzival has been able to consciously develop the virtues associated with each of the planets—a purification process. With the help of Gawain and Feirefiz (heart and will), Parzival (thinking) was able to reinforce and transform pride, envy, anger, sloth, greed, gluttony, and lust, into *fidelity, hope, courage, justice, charity, temperance,* and *wisdom*, the seven prerequisites to the selfless and radiating Love of the Grail.

6 Zval (Saturn), Almustri (Jupiter), Almaret (Mars), Samsi (Sun), Alligafir (Venus), Alkiter (Mercury), Alkamer (Moon).

And Parzival is able to admit his culpability, realizing that his own failure led to greater understanding and ultimately to the desired end: his summoning to the Grail. "Nevertheless, if I had not done amiss, you would have spared me your anger on one occasion . . . Then, most assuredly, my luck was not yet in" (p. 388). The news is received with elation, and Orgeluse weeps for joy because Parzival's Question will finally put an end to Anfortas' suffering. Cundrie proceeds to tell Parzival that he is allowed to *choose* one person to accompany him, and without further ado he chooses his brother, Feirefiz. He is his brother's keeper as much as Feirefiz is his.

At the ceremony's end, Feirefiz requests that no one leave on their respective journeys home, but wait *four* days so that he can bring back treasures from his fleet in order to share them out between all those assembled, from minstrels and poor knights, to lords, barons, princes and kings. It is agreed.

Economic life based on *gifts* is the way of the future. Giving and receiving is the bedrock of true fellowship, of brother- and sisterhood, where everybody receives the free gifts according to their respective needs. It is the core of equality, where people can pursue their goals regardless of money, free of commercial manipulation. Every person should be entitled to economic means, like free healthcare, or education. The manifestation of this ideal will rest and depend on the giving of gifts, from one person or institution to another, from the Haves to the Have-Nots. It is based on generosity of soul and compassion for one's sibling, for as humans we are all kindred. Feirefiz epitomizes that ideal. It is a voluntary and independent gesture, which relies on cooperation and collaboration. Feirefiz offers an imagination of how to move into the future in a wholesome way, with no strings attached. All humans should have their basic needs covered. We all have gifts to share, some more, some less. The generous gesture comes near the end of the epic and is part of the sorting-out process, the culmination of social harmony.

After the messengers leave to fetch Feirefiz's treasure, Parzival makes a misleading and ambiguous announcement: he repeats what Trevrizent had told him, declaring that nobody can ever win the Grail by force, except for those who are summoned to the Grail, by God. True, it cannot be found through force, yet Parzival never gave up his quest and "fought" in the name of the Grail. Without that perseverance his name would never have appeared on the Grail. By having the conquered knights go out in search for the Grail, they became *aware* of the Grail, which in turn spread the word. The "impossible" quest raised questions such as: What is the Grail? Where can the Grail be found? Why is it so important? How do I go about tracking it down? Who has it? Parzival's announcement causes many to abandon the Quest for the Grail, which, as Wolfram suggests, is the main reason why it is hidden to this day. This can be seen as his last error before becoming Grail King, though it can also be taken as a necessary statement to discern between those who have the *will* to fight for the Grail, by never giving up—as Parzival did— and those who do not have that existential drive. Wanting the Grail needs to arise *freely* from *within*, it is not something that one is *told* or *forced* to pursue. That so many simply gave up after Parzival's statement spread shows that the need to attain the Grail did not yet live strongly enough in people—and still does not to this day. Those who, like Parzival, have gone through severe travails and multiple failures, often need to find some form of redemption, come what may, which becomes the impetus to quest after something to annul their suffering and sorrow—their personal Grail. Parzival would not have been summoned, and his name would not have appeared on the Grail had he not fought for it, pursued it relentlessly. He put in the time, the effort and work, without which any kind of accomplishment is sheer impossible.

On the third day, Feirefiz's gifts are brought to Joflanze and distributed. "[A]ny king acquainted with a gift from Feirefiz benefited his land for ever after. No man, in terms of what was proper to his rank, had ever been shown such rare gifts. All the ladies had costly gifts from Triande and Nourient" (p. 390). Wolfram seems to imply that these gifts—beyond their material value—are endowed with ancient and spiritual wisdom. After the ceremonial gift-giving, Feirefiz, Parzival, and Cundrie ride away toward Munsalvæsche.

I have long wondered about the meaning of Joflanze, the place where so much of the sorting-out happens, where the four grand armies meet, where three of the last four major jousts take place, and where the best knights are inducted to the Round Table, including Parzival and Feirefiz. And lastly—as a culmination—the summoning of Parzival to Munsalvæsche. It all takes place on the Joflanze plane.

"Flanze" in Joflanze sounds like "Pflanze," indicating a "plant" that is rooted, then sprouts, grows, buds, and flowers. The "Jo" is easily recognized as "I," as in "je" (French), "Yo" (Spanish), or "Jo" (Catalan). Hence, the "I plant," or the individuality that grows selflessly like a plant. Heinz Mosmann also indicates that "vlans" means "Maul," i.e., "mouth," and that "Jo" could also (according to some sources) refer to the old French word "joye," meaning joy or happiness. This could evoke a "joyful and laughing mouth."[7] Mossman also compares the similarity between the names Gramoflanz and Joflanze. "Gram" or "Grimmig" ("grim" or "wrathful") suggest someone who is angry, grumpy, or cantankerous. Gramoflanz, the "angry-mouth," equates to "big-mouth."

Discussion Topics, Questions

- Discuss the power of gift-giving. What gifts are squandered? How could the concept of gift-giving change the socio-economic life for the better?
- "Intimate strangeness": have you ever seen a stranger, where you immediately felt a connection or a kinship, which then proved to be true? What form did it take?
- Give examples of people acting in contradictory ways. Do you recognize it in yourselves?
- What could be the deeper meanings of gemstones described in *Parzival*?

7 Mosmann, p. 346.

- Discuss the power of forgiveness. Parzival forgives Cundrie, Gawain forgives Orgeluse. Orgeluse forgives Gramoflanz.
- Do you ever feel as if your thinking, feeling, and willing are not aligned? Give examples.
- Is everybody entitled to second chances? If yes, in what circumstances? Have you experienced second chances? How about third, fourth, or fifth chances?

Illustrations:

1. The four directions (Magdalen Garrity)
2. Two knights fighting (Torrin Pewtherer)
3. Blackboard from a Parzival block

BOOK SIXTEEN

The Suffering of Anfortas

A wound awoke me,
Opened the lids that lie closed
Over the eyes of the longing
That lives in the sleeping soul
To be whole;

And a word woke me
To reach
Into the wounds of the world –

And the wounds
Became speech.[1]

~ Christy Barnes

---

1 Christy Barnes, *A Wound Awoke Me*, Adonis Press, 1994. It was always a privilege to hear Christy read and recite her poems.

The final chapter starts with Anfortas's plight, and his intensified suffering from which he desperately wants to be released. However, he is kept from death, no matter how much he pleads, by repeatedly exposing himself to the power of the Grail. He wonders for how long he can live in this wretched state, devoid of happiness. "I have paid in full for any disgrace that may have befallen me and which may have been seen by any of you" (p. 391). He has paid his dues, and then some, due to Parzival's failure. Had it not been for the writing that appeared on the Grail and Trevrizent's assurance that release is imminent, they would have let him die. Now, for the second time, they wait for the person to release Anfortas of his infirmity.

We know that release is coming, but Anfortas has to live through the pain of the moment, when the planets, "Mars or Jupiter," are aligned to cause him enhanced suffering, similar to the evening of Parzival's first visit. Wolfram paints a vivid picture of the wound and the Grail King's suffering, describing at length the wound's stench, the herbs and spices applied to alleviate the pain, and the healing properties of noble stones ("*edelen steinen*"). The stench represents the negative forces expelled from Anfortas, his fall into matter through desire—the secretions from the wound, expressive of his deeds. His entire bed is adorned with precious gems that have been inserted on every side, with no equal on this earth. Wolfram lists them all—thirty lines in the text—an allusion to Saturnine qualities, Saturn taking approximately thirty years to revolve around the sun. Each line in the original text mentions two stones.

Estlîcher lêrte hôhen muot
Ze saelde unt ze erzenîe guot
Was dâ maneges steines sunder art.
Vil kraft man an in innen wart
Derz versuochen kund mit listen.[2]

2 Lachmann, XVI, 792, 1-5, p. 372.

Some inspired noble courage,
good medicinally and for the soul,
with several stones of special type,
endowed with great inner strength,
with which they merged knowledge with artfulness.[3]

However, all attempts are futile, for there is only *one stone* in all the world that can truly heal Anfortas, and that is the Grail. The Grail not only contains the cumulative power of all the stones mentioned, found throughout the earth, but contains a new force that goes beyond that. It is a stone that does not only radiate from the outside in, but shines from within each person who has attained that capacity. It is the stone by which we become the vessel if we open ourselves up to its light. And for it to work for Anfortas, something else is needed: The Question.

Parzival Asks the Question

"I was in darkness, but I took three steps and found myself in paradise. The first step was a good thought, the second, a good word; and the third, a good deed." ~ Friedrich Nietzsche

The triad of the two brothers and the Grail Messenger make their way from the level plain of Joflanze to the mountainous and wild Terre de Salvæsche. Close to Munsalvæsche, Templars are ready to attack. Fierefiz is eager to respond, but Cundrie restrains him, grasping his bridle. The protective Grail knights, spotting the manifold turtledoves in Cundrie's precious garments, dismount, remove their helmets, and welcome them with tears of joy.

A short time later, they are greeted by a multitude of people at Munsalvæsche. After receiving identical new robes to wear—expressive of their relatedness and equal standing—and some refreshing drinks served in gold cups, Parzival immediately goes to the ailing Anfortas, who welcomes

3 Loose translation by author.

him, though he requests to be kept from the Grail for seven nights and eight days so that he may die at last, ending the agony, adding, "I dare not prompt you otherwise" (p. 394), regarding the Question. Parzival does not need any prompting, not after his first failure and all those years of suffering and searching for the Grail. He knows what must be done. Not only has he been given a second chance—he's earned it. He has lived and breathed for this moment, battled and wept and bled for it.

He does not rush into asking the Question. He has waited for years for this moment and knows what's at stake. Instead, he inquires to the whereabouts of the Grail, then turns in that direction and genuflects three times, paying homage to the trinity and offering a heartfelt appeal that Anfortas' sorrow be lifted. Only then does he stand upright, face his uncle and ask:

‚œheim, waz wirret dier?'

The Question is translated as "Dear uncle, what ails thee?" (p. 395), or "What is it that troubles you, Anfortas?" They are both right, but the word "wirret" has deeper and more encompassing connotations. "Wirret" indicates confusion, an inner disorder or dishevelment, an element of chaos and soul-spiritual turmoil. The consequence of having succumbed to misplaced desire is what caused the incurable wound in his scrotum. The genital wounding is a piercing of one of the most spiritual regions of the body: the creative, reproductive area that produces new life, but is susceptible to the greatest of urges and desires, which has caused the downfall of many a talented, powerful, and reputable person, including, in this case, the Grail King, Anfortas. In the words of Rudolf Steiner: "The more divine the thing we drag into the mire, the greater the sin."[4] While fighting in the name of love—"amor"—for Orgeluse, Anfortas let himself be led astray, becoming entangled in something bewildering, all of which is embedded in the word "wirret," and also in "wirren," "verwirren," or "verwirrt," connoting lack of control. Furthermore, we have an English cousin in the word "worry," which, like "wirret," includes troubles, unease, anxiety, torment,

4 Rudolf Steiner, *Aus den Inhalten der esoterischen Stunden: Band 1 1904-1909* (Rudolf Steiner Verlag, 1995), GA 266.

and great suffering, to the point of feeling crazed. "Wirret" also implies turbulent movement, preventing clear-headedness, where all thoughts are roiled by agonizing incessant pain. In Anfortas, the death forces of Saturn and the reproductive forces of the moon are not in harmony—where the one polarity "warreth" with the other. Only Parzival, in whom the planets have settled into harmony and a state of calm, can now bestow the needed balance.

Parzival has readied himself for this moment. In his long journey, he has gone through all the planetary stages, uniting their forces within him: the reproductive Moon influence through his mother in his early childhood; the Mercurial through his life and immersion in the nature of Soltane (and elsewhere), coupled with the concept of heaven and Hell (God and the devil); the Venusian influence, particularly through his encounter and betrothal to Condwiramurs; Mars powers through his education as a knight and his becoming the Red Knight; the Sun impact through his finding, losing, and regaining of the Grail; the guidance of Jupiter through his unification with his half-brother Feirefiz, which integrates the polarities of light and darkness in the world; and lastly the Saturnian, conveyed especially through Anfortas and the knowledgeable Trevrizent.[5]

Anfortas had succumbed to the urges and forces of nature, which include decay and death, instead of pursuing the soul's freedom. And he had to pay the price—as do we all in one way or another.

It is the power and supremacy of the Grail that Parzival has invoked and heightened through his genuflections, which brings health and life back into Anfortas, an etheric life-current that overcomes death, comparable to the spiritual vivifying stream that brought the Sylvester bull or Lazarus back to life. Wolfram also mentions that Anfortas' complexion is infused at once with what the French call "fleur." It is akin to a moment of enlightenment, a rebirth and resurrection of sorts. It is death overcome. It comes about through the attention of one person to another—both of whom have known suffering. By the mention of Lazarus, we are witnessing more than

5 Ueli Seiler-Hugova, *Das Grosse Parzival Buch*, p. 300.

the power of life over death, but an *initiation*. An initiation through love, through the "holy lance of love," in contrast to the poisonous lance of the counter-Grail forces.

The question— "What troubles, ails, or bewilders you?"—is seminal to our age and time, supplying an antidote for the social travails of our modern world. It is the love-cure for what *ails* the world, from one person to the other, throughout the respective realms of nature—each grain of sand, plant, or animal. We can all be healers and all is in need of healing. We do not need to be enlightened, or have gone through all the stages of Parzival's development to begin asking the healing Question, each in our own humble way. Anfortas' wound is all around us and within us. May we ask and be asked. The Question becomes an inner attitude. The Question can live in every gesture, movement, smile, look, thought, feeling. And when it does, it radiates out like sunrays, warming and nurturing all. In the face of all the suffering, tragedy, and human travails, we can often feel utterly helpless and powerless. Yet, we can always ask the Question. As long as it is earnest, heartfelt, and truly compassionate, it will have an effect. It is the centerpiece of this entire epic. It cannot be mouthed, but wishes to be filled with the power of the Grail, which means we have to find our own inner Grail, that creative, freeing, nourishing force that we can let stream through us out into the world. Imagine if we all sent our creative light to radiate as love in the world so that it can embrace the hurt, spread balm over the world's multiple wounds—imagine what a difference that could make. We could make the hurt whole, one Grail-lit Question at a time. We might not see the results of our own Compassion-Question, but at least we've done it, thought it, felt it. With trust it will land where it must. A true question goes beyond time. The Grail's power weaves and works through us. Anfortas could not be healed by the Grail alone, though it kept him alive. The healing and resurrective powers had to come through the channel of another human being, through Parzival in this case. We all need to become like Parzival, so that we can internalize the Grail and let it satiate us to have its salutary effects.

Students are deeply stirred, awed, and moved by the power of *compassion* that leads to Anfortas' transformation. It is an *awakening force* that expresses care and interest, and its greatest manifestation—Love. Each care-filled Question is a "holy lance of love." This theme has generated earnest and stimulating discussions during class. The students get it. All sorts of contemporary "troubles," great and small, are mentioned as fitting examples; issues like the border crisis in America, the ongoing wars and conflicts (Afghanistan, the Middle East, Ethiopia, Ukraine, etc.), the suffering that the pandemic has brought on, the opioid crisis, poverty, sex-trafficking, abuse, sexual harassment, racial profiling and inequalities, gender bias, and so forth. Do we take an interest? Do we think deeply enough about these kinds of topics? Do we change our empathy into action?

For years now, I have had the privilege of witnessing where students go after graduating from Waldorf School, and what they choose to make out of their lives. It is heartwarming and humbling to see how many of them sacrifice themselves to ensure that others receive the help they need—going into social work, doing prison outreach, fighting for the rights of incarcerated women, helping immigrants at the border, on and on. The question, "What troubles you?" sits deep within them. Through their activism and commitment, they change the world. It is interesting that the Spanish word for "commitment" is "compromiso." Commitment does require compromise, yet it heals, nourishes, and enriches everybody, the one who asks and the one who receives. The essential ingredient is true compassion, for true compassion, ultimately, is selfless love, a creative radiating force that never runs out of fuel, but generates more love—a never-ending source of healing life. It defies all boundaries and restrictions. It is *the impossible dream* made possible. It is the power of the Grail, the Love Stone.

The transformative power of Parzival's Question is also largely due to the accomplishments of Gawain in the realm of the heart—his victory over Lit marveile, crowned by his steadfastness to Orgeluse, which brought everybody, all four armies and their leaders, together. The transferred capacities gave Parzival the needed heart forces to ask the quintessential Question (just as Gawain received the needed thinking forces to overcome his trials). It has ensured that Parzival's heart is no longer empty of true feeling, but filled with distilled soul capacities, as pure as dew on the grass. Knowledge of head and heart has been brought together, enflamed and directed by the force of will—the worked through and culminating qualities of Parzival, Gawain, and Feirefiz. The heart has to do with the blood. Schooling the heart forces means transforming the blood—refining, purifying, and transmuting the blood, by overcoming the lower forces, so that the distilled spiritual essence can come to the fore. Old blood ties must be overcome so that a new community of the Grail can find itself, born from each person's sacred I, achieved through one's own resources. Each person is a temple, is Munsalvæsche, with the Grail within reach, the Sangreal or "Holy Grail" found in one's own transfigured heart. Throughout the epic we have noticed that all the main characters are connected through blood ties in one way or another. It makes up the Grail community, whose destiny it was to prepare the way for the rest of humanity. As we see, Parzival and his unique path—starting from scratch—has brought something entirely new into the world, a fresh spiritual stream that will have long-lasting and essential effects, especially from our time onward. It has to do with individual striving for the truth, each in their own way.

> Here the remnants of the old blood and family ties, which still had an effect on the Grail community during the time of Anfortas' Grail Kingdom, are finally overcome by the strength of the individuality. Whoever is "lord" of the Grail determines the Grail on the foundation of individual conditions, not those established by succession based on lineage.[6]

It is worth dwelling on this transformation—this miracle, which we can all replicate in our own small way. All threads of the epic lead to this turning point. It is a Sun-moment that puts everything in context—the Sun as the center and balance point between the outer planets (Saturn, Jupiter, and Mars) and the inner planets (Venus, Mercury, and Moon) as they move

6 Mosmann, p. 503 (translated by the author).

through the zodiac. It is the light streaming out of the darkness, through the innermost point to light up the periphery. This transfiguration comes right at the end of the block, where we are trying to wrap things up (often left with very little time). I have found myself consciously restraining myself from rushing ahead, knowing that it is a pivotal moment in this initiation epic. If we can foster and reinforce compassion in the students through this powerful imagination of the decisive, socially crucial, and most humane of Questions, then it truly has been worth our while.

Not only have the rules changed regarding the overcoming of the bloodline, but also the patriarchy. It is not only Parzival who becomes Grail King, but Parzival together with Condwiramurs, the Grail Queen. They become equals—a sovereignty based on equality. They reign over Munsalvæsche as one, sharing the responsibilities, each contributing their special gifts. The same holds true for the upcoming union between Feirefiz and Repanse de Schoye. They will return to the East as one, founding a new realm together. Wolfram highlights the eternal feminine and honors the feminine attributes of the spirit.

Throughout this epic, we have heard how beautiful and handsome Parzival is, beyond all others, not least in the previous two chapters, when he reappeared on the scene after the Gawain chapters. Yet, the very moment after Anfortas' miraculous change we hear that "Parzival's beauty was as nothing beside it" (p. 395), i.e., in comparison to Anfortas' beauty. This healing, this change, this cathartic moment brought about by the interest of one person toward another, is as much an act of love, as it is of beauty. Wolfram adds, "God's power to apply his artistry is undiminished today" (p. 395). I always have a few avowed atheists in class, but they have no problem with the mention of God in this setting because it is a reference to the creative force that we can see displayed around us in nature every day. That makes sense to them, and, paradoxically enough, they usually sense the sacredness of it all.

Parzival is directly recognized as the Grail King, which makes him a sovereign of mighty wealth, emphasized by Wolfram: "If I am a judge of wealth, I would imagine that no one would find a pair of men as rich as

Parzival and Feirefiz in any other place" (p. 395). It refers mainly to inner wealth. The most powerful and influential rulers of East and West are *united* in one place—the inner Munslavæsche. The ideal of uniting these polarities was what their father Gahmuret strove for when he first set out on his adventures, first by serving the Baruch of Baghdad, followed by marrying Belacane. His valiant effort had lacked continuity, which now seems possible through the perseverance and ongoing steadfastness of both his sons. The promise of accomplishing what their father had failed to achieve—the peaceful unity of East and West—is within reach, at least within the realm of possibility. As modern people on our individual path of development, we have to unite the cultural and religious East and West (in contrast to the geographic classification) within us, the polarities, which includes the illimitable diversity of the in-between. It is what is demanded by the Grail sovereignty, the potential of which we all carry in our soul-spiritual interior. This inner evolution based on our self-development cannot be achieved over one lifetime, but lifetimes. However, the journey, stage for stage, is as important as the destination, and the vision of the destination will determine the tenor of the journey. And there are always moments when we do attain the ideal, even if only for a few moments at a time.

Reunions: Trevrizent, Condwiramurs, Sigune

"Darkness cannot drive out darkness. Only light can do that.
Hate cannot drive out hate. Only love can do that." ~ MLK Jr.

On his way to meet Condwiramurs, Parzival makes a quick stop at the hermitage, dwelling place of Trevrizent, where Parzival had spent two life-changing, self-effacing and transformative, blissful weeks. The old hermit is glad that Anfortas has been relieved of his pain, that he does not have to die from the results of the joust, and that he has found his peace through Parzival's Question. He considers it a miracle that Parzival was able to defiantly force God to grant his wish through sheer power of perseverance.

Trevrizent admits that he *lied* to him when he told him that nobody can fight their way to the Grail, that only those who are called by the Grail can find it. Parzival, by not accepting defeat, by persevering—come what may—proved that he *is* worthy of being summoned a second time. Each battle that Parzival fought was a battle of the soul, a battle he fought with himself, similarly to his battle with the dragon-knight Orilus. The fighting itself would not have gained him access to the Grail, but his persistence and his devoted dedication caused his name to appear on the Grail. Had he given up, he would never have attained his goal. He defied the odds and the gods; he listened to his inner voice, even when he was told it was impossible. At the outset of his adventures, he had listened and adhered to misleading advice too much—those of his mother and Gurnemanz, which ended up causing so much pain for him and others. Having found and listened to his *own* voice, Parzival was able to achieve the impossible. When do we listen to other people's advice and when do we adhere to the guiding inner voice?

Trevrizent acknowledges that he wanted to divert Parzival, to save and spare him from more pain and suffering. "I lied as a means to distract you from the Gral and how things stood concerning it," adding a few lines later, "It was never the custom that any should battle his way to the Gral. I wished to divert you from it. Yet your affairs have now taken another turn, and your prize is all the loftier! Now guide your thoughts to humility" (p. 396).

Customs change, time's change, and the rules by which the Grail leads, change. What is right for one age is not necessarily right for another. Customs and traditions can ossify, become hollow and meaningless. Humanity's evolution has illimitable examples of that, yet it's easy to forget. What is right and accepted today is not automatically going to be right for tomorrow. Every year we see new examples of that, expressly over the last few years. The entrenched patriarchal system, or how we think about gender, race, religion, and the numerous inequalities in society—they are all examples of outdated mindsets giving way to new ways of thinking, based on inclusivity and respect for one another. These social shifts, though receiving major pushback, are irreversible. Trevrizent's lie is well meant. It arose out of his care for Parzival, a bit like a parent wanting to spare their child unnecessary harm. But at some point that does not hold anymore, for it belongs to the path that leads to independence and to the irrepressible emergence of the individuality. It is true for the development of humanity as much as for the individual person. We remember Sigune's "good lie" when she pointed Parzival in the wrong direction to avoid him fighting Orilus. It was the first encounter and she saw he was not ready. Nevertheless, he was led to where he was meant to go and eventually the path did lead to Orilus—when he was ready. Trevrizent, in his disclosure, does, however, caution Parzival to remain humble, to consciously practice humility. Achieving one's goal defiantly and against all odds can easily lead to hubris. True to Parzival's name, he needs to "pierce through the middle," and not succumb to the imbalance of the extremes. It is the Buddhist path of the Middle Way—the core of the Buddhistic worldview—and it is attained through the practice of the eight-fold path, which consists of *right view*, *right judgement* or *aspirations, right speech*, *right conduct* or *action*, *right livelihood* or *vocation*, *right effort,* or *habit*, *right mindfulness*, and *right concentration* or *contemplation*. Out of his own resources and effort he brought the eight closed petals to open and into movement, which in turn activated the other eight, so that all sixteen petals could be brought into motion. In one way, Trevrizent was right that one cannot "fight" one's way to the Grail. However, Parzival was able to steer his destiny, which had derailed itself, back on track. It reminds one of the Angels' words spoken at the end of *Faust Part Two*: "Whoever strives with all his power, we are allowed to save"[7] ("*Wer immer strebend sich bemüht, den können wir erlösen*"). Of course, he also says, "man errs as long as he will strive"[8] ("*Es irrt der Mensch, so lang er strebt*"). Both hold true for Parzival. Through honest and sincere striving, one does arrive at some objective *truths*, the unwavering effort drawing it forth from the invisible realms. Parzival never gave up in his striving, his quest for the Grail, though he erred throughout his travels. In the end, however, no matter how much one has striven, it's still a matter of *Grace* whether one gets summoned, though it did need the resolute and unshakable striving.

7 *Faust* p. 493.

8 Ibid., p. 87.

It is a tragic maxim of our modern lives that most people veer off from their destinies, lose sight of their pre-earthly intentions and do not "listen" or heed their inner voice. Anfortas, too, was led astray from what was destined for him as Grail King. Maybe that's why he had to pay the karmic penalty by having to endure prolonged suffering due to Parzival's failure—to rise to the destined occasion. Parzival, from the moment he became aware of his failure, tried to rectify his own destiny, though it entailed a huge detour. Modern life is made up of multiple detours, because we are blind, ignorant, and desensitized to our destinies. By working on the disciplines of the eight-fold path, we can align ourselves with our destinies once more, for the sixteen-petaled lotus flower has to do with the laws of karma, and destiny is subject to its rules. In Book Sixteen, we see the results of his development from dullness, through doubt, into bliss—*Saelde*.

Parzival's eight-fold path is a record of his failures—expressed in every one of the soul qualities that he needed to activate and practice. However, each battle was a stage in self-development. The battles themselves did not earn him the invitation to the Grail. Throughout he was guided by Condwiramurs, her love. His quest for the Grail was always buoyed by the momentum of her love. In essence each battle, was another rung upwards, another opportunity to fight with his love-lance. She was always close, helping him to show compassion, generosity, and freedom to those he conquered, helping him to keep his love for the Grail alive. By the grace of the Grail, he was deemed worthy of the summons. And in that sense, he did "fight" for the Grail. It's a matter of perspective.

Before Parzival's parting he says to Trevrizent, "Of course I wish to have your advice as long as we are both alive: you advised me well in the past when I was in great need" (p. 396), which shows his gratitude, humility, and reverence for the hermit. Moreover, Trevrizent blesses his reunion with Condwiramurs.

⁂

Parzival rides on to meet Condwiramurs, whom he has not seen for over five years. She has been a true guide and conduit of love for him. He remained steadfast and she gave him the inner sustenance to continue his quest for the Grail. She and her entourage are encamped in the very spot where Parzival had stood in a somnambulant state looking down on the three drops of blood. It is early morning when Parzival arrives, met by Kyot of Katelangen (Sigune's father and husband of deceased Schoysiane, sister of Anfortas, Trevrizent, and Herzeloyde),[9] who shows him to Condwiramurs' tent where she is still asleep with her twin sons, Loherangrin and Kardeiz, whom Parzival has never met before. Tactfully, Kyot removes the boys, allowing Condwiramurs and Parzival some time alone to reacquaint themselves and rebirth their love. This renewal of their relationship is important in that it coincides with all the other aspects of rejuvenation, healing, overcoming, and *re-pairing*. Their love has gone through a death process caused by their separation. The pain of her absence that he had felt at that very spot is now made up, resolved. There is no longer any dependency or egotism involved, and Condwiramurs is now able to make amends for the torment he went through on that snowy day. With the students, one can inaugurate a discussion about the different stages of love relationships, and how they are in need of renewal every once in a while. What might that entail, and why is it important? This is true for all relationships, also between friends and within a family.

Now that Parzival has inherited the Grail, Kardeiz is crowned king over his parents' countries and returns to Belrepeire with Kyot and his army. Later, when he is older, he will recapture Waleis and Norgals. After poignant farewells, Parzival, Condwiramurs, and Loherangrin ride to Munsalvæsche with the templars.

---

9 And according to Werner Greub, he is also the mysterious Kyot the Provencal.

On their return to the Grail Castle, Parzival remembers that Sigune must be close by. "Once upon a time in this forest . . . I saw a cell through which ran a swift, clear brook. If you know it, show me the way there" (p. 399). They arrive at the stone hut at dusk, finding that she has died while praying in front of the tomb. They break through the wall, lift the tomb's lid, and discover the embalmed Schionatulander, beautiful and without the slightest sign of decay (in line with the life-giving forces of the Grail, which is close by). Gently, they place Sigune beside him and close the tomb. At last she's freed from inconsolable grief and the two lovers are finally *united.*

Every encounter with Sigune has been decisive, redirecting him toward the next step of his journey and serving as a lesson in self-knowledge. She showed him the way forward—each a nodal point of destiny—indicating another step of his growth. This time, the direction is toward the beyond, the eternal realm, which he has to attain out of himself. She has now joined Schionatulander as Parzival's guide from the beyond, an invisible source always ready to impart needed direction. Her cell turned tomb, not far from Munsalvæsche, can now serve as a reminder that the dead are always with us, willing to help. This, too, as a theme, can be brought up and discussed with the students. Even if they have not yet experienced the death of a loved one, they certainly have thought about it and can express themselves eloquently on the topic.

Sigune served as a link to the Grail, even before he knew about it, before it became his main quest. On their first encounter, she watered his seminal Grail destiny with her tears of grief, a preparation for what was to come. At the second meeting, she woke him up to the reality of his failure, which fueled his need to redeem his wrongdoings, launching his own descent into grief. At the third meeting she facilitated his pivotal meeting with Trevrizent. Now, she shares in Parzival's bliss, blessed by her release from life, as Parzival is released from his suffering and constant wandering. Her mother, Schoysiane, was the Grail bearer until Repanse took over when she married Kyot. It was always Parzival's destiny, as it is for all human beings who strive to know themselves on all levels. Sigune is not gone but will convey her directives from the stars under which they ride back to Munsalvæsche.

Grail Ceremony

> *"It's important to look at yourself and notice how you've been shaped and what your major influences have been."* ~ Sylvie Berquist (student)

A REGAL RECEPTION awaits them, with many candles lighting up the space while all gather round to welcome and kiss the new Queen and King and their young son Loherangrin. Earnest preparations are underway for the Grail ceremony, which is only brought forth on festive occasions. This time, in contrast to the previous doleful event, the Grail procession will not be preceded by the bloody lance but by jubilant hearts and the lifting of all sorrows. The spear denotes Saturn, which in the Middle Ages was "connected with the forces which bring old age and death. This time the Grail is comforting and refreshing."[10] Whereas the first Grail ceremony had a Good Friday quality—with the bloody lance reminding us of the lance that pierced the side of Christ by the Centurion Longinus—this ceremony is connected with the power of resurrection and the rejuvenating currents of life. The formal ritual celebrates the overcoming of the Saturnine death forces.

Once again, the great hall is festively decorated with three fires burning aromatic aloe wood. Forty carpets adorn the floor and more seats are made

---

10 Stein, *The Ninth Century*, p. 268.

available than on the former woeful occasion. A most magnificent seat is set aside for Feirefiz, Anfortas, and Parzival. The ceremony soon begins, and like before, the maidens enter with their respective accoutrements, all twenty-four of them, till Repanse de Schoye, the twenty-fifth, carries in what only she is permitted to carry—the Grail. The Grail will allow no other to be its bearer. Similarly to the twenty-five armies of Feirefiz that represent the nations of the outer world, so the twenty-five ladies signify the world's nations, but inwardly and spiritually united—each person in their own way.

Everybody receives from the Grail the victuals of their choice, depending on personal taste, custom, or need. Feirefiz, however, is left wondering how empty cups are able to fill and refill themselves with mead or wine, for he cannot see the Grail. But what he does see—and it pierces his heart to the core—is Repanse de Schoye, with whom he immediately falls in love, leaving him unhappy amidst the exultant joy surrounding him, to the point that he wishes great Jupiter had never guided him to this place. It is reminiscent of Parzival, who—when he first witnessed the Grail ceremony—was more focused on Repanse than the Grail, thinking only that he was wearing her cloak. At the time, Parzival still lacked the necessary maturity, and now Feirefiz still lacks true in-*sight*, which his love for Repanse will unlock for him.

The love he had cherished for Clauditte, Olympia, and Secundille, suddenly mean nothing to him. Anfortas, who knows the pangs of love all too well, recognizes that Feirefiz is caught in the snares of love and has great empathy for him, divulging that as yet no man has suffered love pangs for Repanse, nor become her servitor, which has been the cause of some anguish on her part. "She has been at my side in great sorrow, and her looks have suffered somewhat for her having had so little pleasure. Your brother is her maternal nephew, he can perhaps help you in this affair" (p. 403). Anfortas suggests that she would welcome his attention.

This sudden change of heart in Feirefiz has disturbed some students over the years, especially since he'd sung Secundille's praises and received so much strength and direction from her during his battles. It was, after all, her powerful motivating force that guided him to the West, and ultimately to Munsalvæsche. What does it say about the major theme of steadfastness? How can it be justified and resolved? What is Wolfram's intention? How can it be understood? It cannot be glossed over.

Feirefiz is set on winning Repanse's love. There is something in her that has inexplicably touched his heart, unfamiliar to any of his previous relationships. Moreover, it is not a love that he can fight for, though he is an expert at the five lance-strokes, which he explains in some detail (which now need to be internalized as inner qualities of a flexible and willing heart). He wishes that the fame he has achieved so far could have been entirely for her. "Of all the days the shield became my shelter, this is my day of deepest affliction" (p. 403). It is a wholly new experience for him, and as with all suffering, it raises consciousness. Initially, it saps him of his usual sense of insouciant sovereignty. A fresh and new will is stirring within him brought on by love, and the pangs are piercing right into the *four* heart chambers of his inner life. He has to freely want to learn to see the Grail, just as we need to want to learn about foreign cultures and the people when we go traveling. There is so much we do not behold, that we do not understand, that we simply cannot see because we are ignorant of the customs and traditions and of all the subtle habits and rituals—especially regarding any of the more spiritual and religious aspects. Anybody who has traveled and sojourned in other countries and cultures will know that full well.

Anfortas notices that Feirefiz cannot see the Grail, confirmed by Feirefiz, which strikes all the knights as mysterious. The bedridden Titurel also hears of it and lets it be known that it is because Feirefiz has not been baptized. Feirefiz responds: "If I were baptized for your sakes, would Baptism help me win love" (p 404?) Love is the driving force and he will do anything to win Repanse, though he does not know what "Baptism" means, just like Parzival did not initially know the meaning of the Grail, yet it spurred his quest. Parzival answers: "If you allow yourself to be given Baptism . . . you will be in a position to seek her love, dear man," adding, "I can now address you familiarly, since our possessions are just about equal, on my side thanks to the Grail" (p. 404). Feirefiz, who does not know what Baptism entails is willing to fight for it. Though the idea amuses Parzival and Anfortas, the notion is not entirely unrelated to Parzival's "fighting" his way to the Grail. It shows that Feirefiz is willing to do whatever it takes to gain Repanse's love. The following words by Parzival, however, tend to disturb our modern sensitivities: "You will have to break with your god Jupiter and give up Secundille" (p. 404). In discussing and thinking about it, we can broaden our perspectives, while endeavoring to reconcile contrary viewpoints. Where, why, and when do we hold on to old notions that were or are sacred to us? These kinds of questions are especially pertinent in our time. What are we reluctant or unwilling to let go of, even when we know it is harmful or wrong? Like writers or journalists—it's hard to "kill your darlings." But if we can overcome ourselves and slough off the old skin, then we open ourselves to something new.

Baptism

The great things of the world are not born in noise and tumult but in intimacy and stillness. ~ (Steiner, The Temple Legend, p. 279)

This matter of the Baptism can initially be a stumbling block to the prevailing attitudes because it appears to unfairly pit one creed against another, favoring the Christians over the "Pagans." Pir Zia Inayat-Khan, for instance, in his book Saracen Chivalry, calls it "wishful embroidery" on the part of Kyot or Wolfram. Nevertheless, it is worthwhile reassessing and viewing it from a contemporary perspective and context without immediately discarding the thought. The epic, after all, though written during the Middle Ages, steeped in Christianity, contains esoteric content that was considered highly heretical, punishable by death, as demonstrated by the cruel and horrific eradication of the Cathars (and the attempt to cancel Wolfram by the Catholic Church). We are called to shift our positions and to open ourselves to broader, more tolerant outlooks even, as in this case, the condition of Baptism can be perceived as an example of dogmatism. Furthermore, Christianity did not begin roughly 2000 years ago. Before the Christ's physical incarnation, there was nevertheless "Pagan Christianity," where the Christ being was known under different names. These mythic and religious beings express a certain aspect of the approaching Sun Being. We see qualities of this mighty Sun Being in Apollo (Greeks), Osiris (Egyptians), Ahura Mazdao (Persians), Vishva Karman (Ancient Indians). Steiner clarifies: "That Christ is a reality has always been known wherever [humans] have steeped themselves in the wisdom of the world, and because He has revealed Himself in so many different ways He has been called by diverse names."[11] In Norse mythology, for instance, the Sun Hero is known as Baldur. "There is a Pagan Christianity, Christianity that is not directly bound up with the actual historical Event of Golgotha."[12] And for the Arthurian western stream, the Cosmic Christ was the Sun Hero, both before and after the Event of Golgotha. Steiner also mentions in the same lecture that the Pagan stream is still present to this day, bearing elements of the Sun Being, the pre-Christian Christ. We know that this holds true for other parts of the world as well, such as the Americas and the more southern parts of Africa, though we cannot assume anything, for much of the secret lore has never been recorded, except for oral transmissions—from mouth to ear through the generations, as the words of Tom Porter demonstrate. Most are still kept secret or have been lost, with a few appearing in legends. The future will undoubtedly reveal more.

Sakokwenionkwas, the Bear Clan Elder of the Mohawk Nation who gave a powerful Opening Address at our school, made a point of calling himself

11 Rudolf Steiner, *The Gospel of Saint Luke*, Lecture Seven, September 21 1909, in Basel, GA 114.

12 Rudolf Steiner, *Karmic Relationships*, Vol. VIII, August 27, 1924, London, (London Rudolf Steiner Press), p. 80.

a Mohawk *Pagan*, repeating it so that we would take it in, after which he spoke in the most beautiful, moving, and elegant terms about the Sun, and how the "Big Man's" sunrays are like hands of the Creator touching each one of us. His words reminded me of the Pharaoh Akhenaton who, in his veneration of the Sun God Aten, has the Sun depicted with hands at the end of the sunrays, caressing the humans they touch. Sakokweniónkwas, or Tom Porter, spoke movingly about how the Sun sees everything that we do during the day, and how, when the sun sinks into darkness, He reports on all the things we have done throughout the day—the good and the bad. He told us that it serves as a reminder to always do our best, for the Big Man sees and notices all. We felt blessed by the sacredness of his words. It reminded me of Steiner's depiction of the greater Guardian of the Threshold.

We recall the weak excuse of Gahmuret in his parting letter to Belacane, where he stated that he would have stayed had she been baptized, when in reality he simply wished to fight, joust, and pursue adventure. Furthermore, Herzeloyde, in love with Gahmuret, insisted he give up Belacane, arguing, "In the sacrament of Baptism there is greater virtue" (p. 57), even though he loved Belacane, ached to be back with her, and did not demand that she get baptized anymore. Besides, Belacane would have consented to Baptism without question, purely for the sake of love. However, because of Gahmuret's fickleness, it never came to pass. Feirefiz, in this concluding final chapter, consents to Baptism, born out of his *love* for Repanse, thus redeeming his father's fault and closing the circle. Titurel, in his wisdom, realized that Feirefiz needed Baptism in order to fully see and recognize Repanse, because she is the Grail bearer. She bears a certain quality within her which makes her worthy of the honor. The Baptism will allow Feirefiz to see that part of Repanse—an essential and profound part of her being. Repanse de Schoye would otherwise never feel fully recognized and seen by Feirefiz if he were unable to understand that part of her. Similarly, if a person is, let's say, an artist, and their partner has no understanding of art or the desire and drive to create and be artistic, then the relationship would be missing an important ingredient. The artist would feel unseen, unrecognized, and unappreciated in that area. One could find countless examples in different areas. The willingness to be baptized shows that Feirefiz is striving to understand and see her whole being, which transcends her earthly embodiment.

It's an interesting question to ask the students: Would you change or give up your religion in order to marry the one you love? The question gives rise to others: Would you expect it from your partner? What does it entail? Does it make a difference to one's inner life, spiritual outlook, or the love relationship? Is one accepted into the other religion? Who should decide? After all, it's a common occurrence and most of us know people who consciously chose to "convert" in order to marry. Often, they take on their new religion with great dedication. Interestingly enough, all the examples that come to mind entail conversions outside of Christianity.

Nor is Baptism solely a Christian ritual, though there are differentiating elements. A form thereof has existed for millennia, and the Jewish ritual called Mikvah preceded the baptism of Jesus by John the Baptist in which the Christ entered in the form of a dove (the essence of the Christian Baptism). Other forms can be found in Hinduism, Buddhism, in some Indigenous American traditions, and in ancient Egypt and the Middle East, to name only a few. These purifications by water represent a cleansing before entering a holy sanctuary. I remember emulating a ritual washing in the stream that runs close the entrance of Delphi before passing across the threshold into the sacred Apollonian site.[13] Something beyond cleanliness enters the soul, clearly perceptible as a sublimated mood. The Sikhs have a baptism they call *amrit*. In Istanbul, when my wife and I visited the various magnificent mosques, we observed the ablutions, which consist of the washing of the face, hands, arms, according to specific rules. Alone, the sound of the water is refreshing and uplifting. Anybody who goes through this *wudhu* ritual can sense how the outer cleansing supports the inner cleansing, making one more receptive to the divine. There is a common expression which states: "Cleanliness is next to Godliness," which is similar to Muhammad's purported words, "Cleanliness invites toward faith, and

13 No longer possible as the cleansing pool and stream has been closed off, much to my disappointment on a recent visit.

faith leads its possessor to Paradise." It is salutary for students to hear of these diverse rituals.

Most importantly, Baptism was a form of initiation, similar to the three-day death, practiced in various Mystery Centers in Egypt, Greece, or Saxon Germany. In some rituals, the people were held under water to the point of losing consciousness (full immersion), where they momentarily left their bodies, with the result that they were endowed with spiritual knowledge from then on (or in a following incarnation). This guided initiation in the Mystery Centers is essentially a union between the macrocosm and the microcosm. It is the union between the stream coming down from cosmic heights (expressed by a triangle pointing downwards) and the stream rising up from the earth (triangle pointing upwards). It has existed in ancient traditions, but now this merger between the earth and the divine is made possible for all human beings—attained out of and through themselves, which constitutes the essential difference between the old and the new forms of initiation. *The upper and lower triangles blending together was considered in the Middle Ages as the symbol of the Holy Grail.* The six-pointed star of the

interlocking triangles is also found in the Star of David (King's Star), preceded by the sacred Seal of Solomon,[14] the sign of the Macrocosm, and the Hindu *Anahata* (connected to the twelve petaled lotus flower of the heart). Baptism is a union. However, each depiction in the mystical tradition has a different quality, according to the evolutionary period of humanity.

This element of cleansing is wonderfully depicted in various statues and reliefs from Ancient Egypt. The words from a museum caption not only highlight the union between the "other world" and the earthly sphere, but also reminds us of Tom Porter's wonderful words regarding the Sun. We can recognize the Grail being in the Sun God before mystically entering and dwelling within the earth sphere.

> *Purification with water*: Upon his arrival from the other world, the Sun God purifies himself in the eastern horizon before his shining in Heaven, where the four gods, "Horus," the Lord of the North, "Seth," the Lord of the South, "Dewen-anwy," the Lord of the East, and "Toth," the Lord of the West, pour the water of life and power over him from the four corners of the universe. This rare statue depicts king Amenhotep II, assimilated with the Sun God in his shining in the moment of his purification on the horizon. (New Kingdom, 18th Dynasty (1550–1295 BC) / Valley of the Kings—Thebes / Alabaster.)[15]

Indeed, the above coincides with Steiner's intermittent referral to the Grail as a being.

With Feirefiz we are dealing with a change of consciousness, a transformation, expressed through Repanse de Schoye and the Baptism. The relationship with Repanse de Schoye is in the mystical tradition of *Minne*, and Repanse, the Grail bearer, is akin to Isis-Sophia and the Queen of Sheba—divine star wisdom, *lost* to humanity through the ages, to be rediscovered within, succinctly expressed in an oft-quoted verse by Rudolf Steiner that reads:

---

14 Sometimes depicted as a pentagram

15 From the statue's plaque, exhibited at the National Museum of Egyptian Civilization.

The stars once spoke to humans.
It is world destiny that they are silent now,
But in their silence, there grows and ripens
What the humans speak to the stars!

The Baptism scene with Feirefiz represents this moment of vital renewal, which transcends the constrictions of institutionalized Christianity. Humanity, during the course of evolution, was no longer able to access the gods of old, and even the Mystery Centers had lost their power and abilities to connect—the hidden reason why Feirefiz is asked to give up his gods. In our age when humans no longer want to be forced to "believe" in something or be commanded, something *new* needs to take the place of the old. Parzival suffered through his years of silence, in order to start *listening to the inner voice*, allowing him to arrive at the point of freely choosing to speak to the stars. Parzival, we know, did not have the inner maturity to ask the Question when he first came to Munsalvæsche. Likewise, Feirefiz does not have the inner capacity to see the Grail—that ever-renewing force. Just as Parzival could not be prompted, Feirefiz cannot be forced into baptism. In both cases it's a matter of freedom—freedom of choice. Feirefiz's source of motivation is Repanse de Schoye, whose love can lead him to speak to the stars from within. Secundille led the way. She was always interested in what and who Feirefiz would *become*. More than Jupiter, it was Secundille who paved the way for Feirefiz, who fired his will. She is the feminine soul force, the Black Madonna—like Belacane—leading from the outside through ancient wisdom to the juncture where Repanse can take over, as the inner guide. In that respect, Repanse can be imagined as the transformed Secundille. Again and again, mention has been made of Secundille's searching and questing, implied by the gifts to Anfortas. She is another form of the phoenix rising out of the ashes. Secundille, as a guiding principle, rising from the ashes as Repanse! Repanse de Schoye as the next Queen of Sheba in the coming. Steiner once referred to the Queen of Sheba as "the soul of humanity,"[16] which in this case could also refer to Repanse de Schoye. Similarly to the Queen of Sheba uniting herself with Hiram, we can see the union between Repanse and Feirefiz as a way of uniting the polarities of fire and water in the proper way, a continuation of "when the calm wisdom is united with the fire of the astral world, with the fire of passion and desire."[17]

In the 11th grade, one can observe the students turning inward, in both dramatic and subtle ways. It is a new experience, which is exciting, but also potentially devastating and painful. They have received outer guidance through their parents, guardians, teachers and friends, but they need even more conscious guidance in this inward journey, but often they do not receive it. One can observe how they suddenly change friends, choose to go into different directions. They are desperately looking for people to emulate, for things in life to give them meaning. *Parzival* creates the space and opportunity to address a multiplicity of existential and essential themes. The road to oneself is not easy. If there is no help in this venture into the interior, then drugs, violence, sex, depression, neuroses, can easily take over, causing people to lose control. A student from our Alkion Center (teacher education program) recently said, "I wish that someone would have said it was okay to *not* be okay while I was a teenager."

When Belacane and Gahmuret found each other, the stark polarities of life equaled themselves out and were briefly brought into harmony. We can also say that fire and water was brought into balance, the one needing the other. Baptism is a water ritual, which moderates the heat of the will, epitomized by Feirefiz—the will forging ahead into the future. We talk of trials by fire and trials by water. To bring these yin-yang opposites into balance belongs to the most noble yet challenging trials of our modern age. Whereas Gahmuret failed in his union with Belacane, Feirefiz can immerse himself in the watery element of Baptism and find happiness—saelde— with the promise of love. Repanse breaks the mold in that she becomes the *fourth* woman in Feirefiz's life—or the third transformed. It also heralds the beginning of a new epoch, with seeds for further expression in another epic or cycle of adventures.

16 *The Temple Legend*, p. 54.

17 Ibid. p. 54.

The Grail ceremony comes to an end, though Wolfram says that it would "make a long tale" if all the details were told. And it is safe to say that it would be even longer if one would or could plumb the depths of all the hidden meanings.

At dawn the next morning Feirefiz is invited into the temple in the presence of the Grail, accompanied by a throng of wise templars, squires, Parzival, and Anfortas. The baptismal font is made of ruby on a jasper pedestal. The precious stones complement one another: the ruby is more aligned to fire, warmth, and vitality, whereas jasper contains the power of renewal, healing, and protection—also known as the bringer of rain by some Indigenous Americans (washing, cleansing). Feirefiz is ready: "Whatever will assure me of winning the maiden shall be done and seen to be done, fully and faithfully" (p. 405). He does not fully understand the breadth of the Baptism, but he does understand the depth of his love for Repanse, which is all he needs, for he trusts it unequivocally. The font is tilted toward the Grail, and it fills with water at once.

For the modern student or reader, the words of the priest during the baptism might be off-putting, especially if they've had negative experiences with the outer conventions of Christianity. Too many people have had to endure the brunt of harsh dogmatism, constricting and restrictive forms of Christianity, not to mention the level of overt hypocrisy. However, the last part is accessible to most:

> "Trees have their sap from water. Water fecundates all things made that are called 'creature'. We see by means of water. Water gives many souls a splendour not to be outshone by the angels" (p. 406).

Though Feirefiz abjures his former gods, it can be seen more as a metamorphosis of those gods. In their old form, they had lost their power on earth, but they emerge in a new form from within. With that he is baptized, able to *see* the Grail and "win" Repanse de Schoye. There is so much that we do not see—where we are kept in the dark of our own loss.

We are blind to the light, or get blinded by the light. We are stuck in the endless shade (an allusion to Amanda Gorman's poem, "The Hill"), but the light, whether we see it or not, is always around us. It reminds me of St. Odilie, who was born blind and remained so for many years, until her eyes were washed open during her baptism. As modern people, we have to wash and cleanse ourselves into seeing. In the great and the small, our eyes need washing, every day a little bit. If we undergo self-reflection, we know that all too often our eyes weren't washed.

Departure and New Beginnings

"We must become bigger than we have been: more courageous, greater in spirit, larger in outlook. We must become members of a new race, overcoming petty prejudice, owing our ultimate allegiance not to nations but to our fellow men within the human community." ~ Haile Selassis

Shortly after Feirefiz's baptism, writing appears on the Grail, declaring

> that any Templar whom God should bestow on a distant people for their lord must forbid them to ask his name or lineage, but must help them to gain their rights. When such a question is put to him the people there cannot keep him any longer. Because gentle Anfortas had remained in bitter agony so long and the Question was withheld from him for such a time, the members of the Gral Company are now forever averse to questioning. They do not wish to be asked about themselves. (p. 406)

It is a perplexing message, a confounded riddle. The overarching theme of questioning is brought into question. It seems contradictory and comes across as a paradox. This last chapter, however, is all about renewal, changes, and transformations, which includes the rules that govern the Grail and Munsalvæsche. Parzival's failure was based entirely on his *not* asking the Question. What do we make of it? Each question, if asked sincerely, is like a key, and the Grail is the living ingredient that unlocks the door to release the answer, different for every person, even if the question appears the same.

The above echoes the last part of Book sixteen when Loherangrin, years later, approaches on a Swan, to marry Elsa, the Duchess in Brabant, on the condition that she never ask who he is (made famous by Richard Wagner's opera, *Lohengrin*).[18] However, she loses him because she *does* ask him who he is, which breaks the pledge. *Doubt* had crept in, planted by the conspirators who had tried to shake her faith in him. Having succumbed to the illusory trickery of the schemers and plotters, she could no longer fully intuit his essence. She had lost her unequivocal knowledge and faith in his being. It reminds one of the old mysteries where the neophytes (meaning "newly planted") were not allowed to ask questions. We remember the Young Man of Sais, who died because he lifted the veil of Isis. Insights were only given when the disciples were deemed ready. In the Middle Ages, the strength and faculties for understanding were not yet fully developed. However, Loherangrin did reveal his heritage to her before he left, accentuating the loss, which causes her to fall lifeless to the ground. Instead of asking about his identity, she should have asked about the strength of spirit that he represents.

Nowadays things need to be questioned. The time for understanding is at hand. Parzival paved the way to the questioning mind. He was a forerunner, a trailblazer. During the Middle Ages, the people were still not quite ready, therefore they needed faith. Through their faith, they could recognize the wisdom of the "master," the initiate. The time was not quite at hand, hence the retreat of Loherangrin. But Parzival's development points to the future. Great spiritual impulses were given during the ninth century, expressed in the Grail legends. This is especially true of Chrétien and Wolfram's Grail epics. We can also safely assume that the unidentified Kyot, like Loherangrin, is a high Initiate, who was carried to the place of need by a metaphorical "Swan."[19] Steiner writes that the messenger of the great Initiate is called a "Swan" in the Middle Ages.

18 Loherangrin is connected to the moon (Teutschmann, p. 182). "Heran" means to "approach."

19 Identified by Werner Greub as Kyot the Provencal.

> His authority may not be doubted. By his words he must be believed, by the truth shining in his countenance he must be recognized. He who has not this faith is incapable of understanding, unworthy to listen. . . . The *Swan* is the *chela* who bears the master.[20]

From the early Renaissance, it became increasingly important to begin asking questions, most clearly depicted in the emerging sciences, but also in the voyages of discovery: What lies beyond the oceans? In our time it is an essential prerequisite. Many of Rudolf Steiner's major contributions to society are due to the questions people asked him. In fact, he was disappointed that people did not ask more questions or show more interest. Interest is a form of questioning, as is love.

Depending on the need, rules change, as they do from one epoch to another. Clearly, in our time it is essential to ask questions. Questions lift veils. There is a growing danger that the biggest questions remain unasked, therefore unresolved, which leads to fear instead of bearing fruit. There is power in the word, and it has healing properties as we witnessed with the recovery of Anfortas. The weakening of the Word can easily result in havoc, especially in the social realm. The very Word is ailing in our age. And when it weakens, it succumbs to lies and illusions, which breeds fear. It is up to each one of us to strengthen the Word so that our speech is meaningful, truthful, and healing.

Some veils, however, should only be lifted when there is a capacity for understanding. And sometimes the situation requires that we "Tell all the Truth but tell it Slant," as Emily Dickinson writes in the prescient poem that ends with the line: "The truth must dazzle gradually / or every man be blind." In our time, the truth must be made available, especially the esoteric knowledge, which has been kept secret for millennia, well-guarded in the mystery centers and by initiates or high priests, shamans and sangomas, the world over. As we go into the future, humanity will not be able to make

20 *The Holy Grail: From the works by Rudolf Steiner*, compiled by Steven Roboz (An Esoteric Cosmology. Lecture 8, June 1906, Paris), (Steiner Book Center, 1984), p. 8.

sense of the intellectual barbed-wire fences erected all around without the spiritual aspect. Science and esoteric science will draw ever closer together, the one shedding light on the other, till reconciliation between the two will transpire, as it must. Still, there are insights for which people are not ready, for which we will have to wait, for which we do not yet have questions. If the questions are authentic, answers will come. The danger comes when answers are given to questions that have not yet ripened in people's souls.

Parzival needed to find the Question within himself, out of himself, before it had the power to heal Anfortas, which points to our time now and beyond. The new law of the Grail, as it appeared immediately after the Baptism, intimated the mindset of the Middle Ages right through to the threshold of our scientific era. Faith was needed to recognize the spiritual source of the other person without having to ask. That, to a certain degree, still holds true today. Anybody who has tried to argue a point with someone who has no understanding where you are coming from, will realize the futility of it all. This holds especially true for esoteric truths. True questions in regard to the spirit rely on authentic receptivity. There are times to be silent. People need some inner readiness to understand some truths. The swan (or chela) will come to those who are ready, wanting, and seeking to receive. Questions cannot be taken lightly, and that is what the message on the Grail was alluding to. Questions must come from the heart, be taken seriously, born out of earnestness. True questions are holy—the "Holy Question." Hence, the proximity of the Baptism to the message. Baptism initiates a new consciousness. Questions, if honestly asked, raise awareness and enlighten. They become keys that unlock the spirit. Intellectual questions, or those raised because of some prejudiced doubt, suspicions, vain curiosity, or any kind of egoism, cannot unlock any doors. Do we ask questions in order to put the other person down, to justify our own points, or do we ask out of an expectant reverent mood of truly wanting to know, where we silence our own judgement and remain open to the answer? True, authentic questions, however, will always be honored by the Grail community. If they come from the Grail center of the heart, they will be heard. That which is Holy needs to be protected from the profanity. That is what essentially is meant by the story with Loherangrin when he comes on a Swan to marry Elsa, as portrayed in Richard Wagner's opera, *Lohengrin*. Loherangrin, and other initiates do not want their time and effort wasted by senseless questions. It's an appeal to *right questioning*. May we be able to distinguish the one from the other.

Feirefiz wants Anfortas to join him on his journey back to the East, but he declines, wishing to live a life of humility, having forfeited his position through arrogance, as he admits. And Condwiramurs won't allow Loherangrin to accompany Feirefiz either. She knows he has a different destiny, specific to the Grail's calling.

Feirefiz stays for eleven days and leaves on the *twelfth*, escorted part of the way by Anfortas. "In the number twelve it is possible to unite all karmic directions of human striving, and thus it provides the broadest possible foundation for a community."[21] Feirefiz and Repanse will have the greatest influence in the "Orient," which included northern Africa (until the mid-twentieth century). In the future the zodiacal number twelve will have its direct influence throughout the entire world, when the earthly and the heavenly will have merged together through the radiance of the Grail.

Parzival and many others could not restrain their sorrow. Arriving at his army, Feirefiz receives the message that Secundille has died. "Only now could Repanse de Schoye be glad of her journey" (p. 408). As the previous Grail bearer, she brings something new to the Orient, just as Secundille's influence helped to bring the ancient wisdom to the West.

Prester John

"Time flies over us but leaves its shadow behind." ~ Nathaniel Hawthorne

In India, Repanse gives birth to a son, Prester John. Through them the Grail knowledge moves South and to the East. The West, in danger of spiri-

21 Lutters, *An Exploration into the Destiny of the Waldorf School Movement*, p. 35.

tual ossification through materialistic culture, will need to be "renewed by forces of Oriental wisdom."[22] Later, when the Grail became invisible and left middle Europe to reside in the Orient, Prester John became Parzival's successor. It foreshadows the next part of the Grail epic that is still waiting to be composed, where the setting will be in the East and beyond. No matter how much the various ethnic groups, tribes, peoples, or countries

squabble and clash about religion and cultural dos and don'ts externally—day consciousness—the Grail impulse works underneath the surface all around the world on a subconscious level.

Over time, *all* the Grail Kings of that Eastern realm became known as Prester John, and the Grail impulse, though still unconscious to most, began to work in the depths of people's souls—into our times and beyond. The fame of Prester John spread throughout many lands and he and his empire reached mythical status. For hundreds of years, people in middle Europe went in search of that mythical realm with its many wonders, where people of different cultures lived in peace with one another. It is another example of what has been mostly forgotten or avoided in the teaching of history. Nowadays, very few people have heard of or know about Prester John, and he is certainly not taught in any schools, including Waldorf Schools—or barely.

22 Steiner, *The Holy Grail*, compiled by Steven Roboz (12th April 1909, Düsseldorf), p. 14.

Even though he is a legendary figure with scant historic evidence, he—i.e., the succession of Prester Johns—has played an essential role in history. It is a little-known fact, but Henry the Navigator's naval explorations initially commenced with the search for Prester John, and not—as it is claimed—to find a sea route to the East in order to exploit and profit materially. History, as we know, is often one-sided, misrepresented, and incorrect—often for socio-political reasons for the benefit of one group or another. But the greatest distortions are because the spiritual dimensions are no longer recognized or sought after. There are, however, hidden reasons behind many impulses that are not so easily unveiled, though they will be with the sweet by and by—once the historians' eyes are washed free of prejudice and the prevalent materialistic confines.

The exact placement of Prester John's realm is uncertain. Though Wolfram says: "Here we call it 'India': there it is Tribalibot" (p. 408), the people in the Middle Ages also considered Ethiopia as India and vice versa—part of the "Orient." Not only was Ethiopia considered by many as India, but "in former times this country [Ethiopia] stood in a sense for the whole of Africa."[23] The Middle Ages and the Renaissance recognized Ethiopia as the land of Prester John and a stronghold of Christianity. Hence, some of the people sent by the Pope and others to find him also went to Africa. Indeed,

23 Rachael Shepherd, "Lalibela: An expression of Prester John," in *Invisible Africa*, Novalis Press, 198, p. 85.

some Rastafarians claim that Haile Selassie (which means "Power of the Trinity") was the thirty third descendent of Prester John, while others claim he was a descendent of King Solomon and the Queen of Sheba, and even of Jesus himself. Nonetheless, his realm has been compared to that of the mythical Prester John, as also alluded to in a poem by Hazel Napier in dedication to Haile Selassie: "This is the conquering lion of Judah, scion of Solomon, Christian Emperor of the golden realms of Prester John!"[24] Ethiopia did become the center of African Christianity in the fourth century, highlighted by the incredible site of Lalibela, which some people have associated with Prester John.

Wolfram's brief mention Prester John heralds and foreshadows a future task, where unity between the races, religions, and cultures is of existential importance, not only for peace but for the nurturing of the highest ideal: Love, which rests on the freedom of all people. All people! The name Prester John only started to appear in Europe around the time Wolfram composed his epic. The name Prester John conjured forth an idyllic realm in contrast to the corruption of the Catholic Church, which had become a temporal power during the late Middle Ages rather than a spiritual sanctuary. The twelfth/thirtienth century is no longer the time of Parzival, which took place in the ninth century. It was another nodal point of humanity's descent into matter, just before the beginning of the Consciousness Soul Age in 1413, which heralded the Renaissance, the emergence of science, and all the subsequent changes. Against this corrupt background, people dreamed of an ideal realm imbued with a natural order based on freedom, love, peace and the salvation of all people. It certainly was not to be found in middle Europe. Thus began the search for Prester John, with thousands of people setting out to find this mythical realm. The ideals they were searching for could not really be found on earth in the way people imagined. It is a dominion that people have to find in themselves and then implement in the world, so that it spreads in freedom, from one individual to the next, until it encompasses all.

24 Hazel Napier: Secretary of the Friends of Abyssinia League, 1935. http://www.rastafari-in-motion.org/haile-selassie-prester-john1.html

Prester John was known under various names in the respective countries, such as Jeliu-Linya in China (according to the Manichean Chinese annals), or "El Avar" in the Middle East (according to the Oriental historian Ibn-el-Atir in his chronicles El-Kamîl, which means "The Perfect One").[25] However, the person most associated with Prester John was King Lalibela of Ethiopia. Rachael Shepherd describes in her article "Lalibela" how the book *The Way of Life*, which tells the story of Lalibela's extraordinary life, was only discovered in the twentieth century. It ranks in importance with other relatively recent findings, including the *Dead Sea Scrolls*, the *Mani Codex*, or the *Voynich Manuscript*. The name "Lalibela" means "he whom the bees love," and his recorded life reads like a legendary mystical initiation.

Similar to Gahmuret, Feirefiz, or Parzival, Lalibela rides on his horse like a medieval knight throughout the Orient, from place to place, from one adventure to another, visiting all the major mystical and holy sites important to human development. He journeys for *forty* years before returning home where, for the ensuing forty years, he builds the ten churches, hewn entirely out of rock, which are a unique architectural wonder. "The number forty is the number of complete transformation and metamorphosis whether of a person, a race, or an idea."[26] He, too, experienced a baptism in the Jordan that sealed his initiation to Christianity. Thousands visit and make pilgrimages to Lalibela, an active holy site to this day. The ten churches can be seen as a unity, an expression of ten-in-one. Christ's words in Saint John's Gospel give voice to this: "Ten Commandments of old must give way to the one New Commandment, that of love."[27] This intimate connection to John is reflected in the name Prester John, which was a name given by the Europeans, as Rachael Shepherd suggests.

Ethiopia was peopled not only by Africans, but included Indians, Arabs and Jews. The "Queen of Sheba, an Arabian Queen . . . was also known as Makedda of Ethiopia. . . . It had also been ruled for some time by some of

---

25 *Elisabeth Leu-Schmidt, Ein Gralsimpuls im Osten* (Rudolf Geering Verlag, Goetheanum, Dornach, 1980), p.15.

26 Rachael Shepherd, p. 86.

27 Ibid., p. 86.

the greatest of Egyptian Pharaohs like Hatshepsut (one of only two confirmed female Pharaohs), Ramses III, and Thutmosis"[28] We see its integral importance to Africa and to the dream of a perfect world order by the Europeans over hundreds of years.

For the modern person, it needs to become a vision to work toward—an ideal turned into reality through inner and outer deeds, starting with self-transformation, step by step, no matter how small and seemingly insignificant. What does it mean to love—to love to such a degree that it transcends race, religion, gender, and any form of blood ties? To love through the recognition of the eternal humanity of the other person. It must also express itself on the practical level when people cease to see each other as rivals, as competitors, which affects hate, greed, destructive, and anti-social forces—the counter-Grail, which will only grow in intensity. Everything external must become internal, but what kind of internal life is needed, is wanted, is good for the earth and its future evolution? "We must round the Cape of Catastrophe in order to find the realm of [Prester] John, the realm of love."[29] The inner realm.

Who Is Titurel?

When Love goes Deeper . . .
Fear Disappears;
Love is the Light,
Fear is Darkness.
~ Osho

Titurel is barely mentioned in the epic, though he holds a significant position, and his presence can be felt throughout the epic. On Parzival's first arrival at the Grail castle, he sees him through the steel door as Repanse de Schoye and the twenty-four maidens remove the Grail and all the

28 Ibid., p. 85.

29 Ibid., p. 89.

accoutrements: "On a sling-bed in a chamber before the doors had been shut behind them, Parzival glimpsed the most handsome old man he had ever seen or heard of" (p. 128). And on Parzival's second visit, it is Titurel who says that Feirefiz cannot see the Grail because he has not been baptized.

Titurel built the first Grail castle in the wilds of Spain in order to give the spiritual Grail, which had come from the East and had hovered in the spiritual world for centuries, a home on earth, guarded by the Templars. Though the Grail is not physical, physical places and objects serve as a threshold or gateway to the spiritual. Titurel, according to Rudolf Steiner, founded the Grail initiation, which is still ongoing today, and will continue far into the future, albeit in different forms. In the six, respectively seven, versions of his lecture on August 27, 1909, Steiner mentions that Titurel belongs to one of the most advanced and sublime initiates, guiding and *guarding* the plans for the evolution of the entire world. However, he does not specifically name the initiate.[30]

Frans Lutters came across an excerpt from the same lecture in the archives of Elisabeth Vreede, where she clearly brings Titurel in connection with Zarathustra (a disciple of the divine Manu): "Titurel is the one who left at the time when Christ descended to earth: the Zarathustra individuality."[31] However, Manfred Schmidt-Brabant writes in the book *Paths of the Christian Mysteries*, "A number of us agree that we have here a reflection of the great Melchizedek—the one who brought the bread and the chalice to Abraham. Now as Titurel he [Melchizedek] prepares the Grail."[32] The two seemingly contradictory versions can be reconciled, for there is truth to both. Melchizedek was the teacher of Zarathustra, and as such he carried within him aspects of this lofty being who was the divine Manu, the sun-initiate of Atlantis (also a teacher of Zarathustra). Schmidt-Brabant cautions us that "we cannot speak here of an incarnation in the way we usually hear it discussed in [Steiner] lectures about karma. It is as if such

30 Rudolf Steiner, *Aus den Inhalten der esoterischen Stunden*, 27 August, 1909, (GA 266/1).

31 Lutters, *An Exploration into the Destiny of the Waldorf School Movement*, p. 138.

32 *Paths of the Christian Mysteries*, pp. 56-57.

beings squeeze into a physical corporeality, but innumerable parts of their existence never appear in the physical world."[33] In the second variation of the above-mentioned Steiner lecture, it is said that Titurel made use of both great spiritual and worldly leaders of humanity. In this way, one could understand how Melchizedek could be instrumental for the Zarathustra-being incarnated as Titurel. To add another layer of complexity to this question, Karl König brings Titurel, the "keeper of primal wisdom," for humankind into connection with Skythianos.[34] Be that as it may, it is clear that Titurel is the legendary representation of one of the greatest initiates of humankind.

Steiner does mention that Titurel inspired Charlemagne in his endeavors, especially in regard to education, bringing to his court teachers from the Celtic north, as well as teachers of high learning from the realm of Harun Al Rashid in the south. The most positive contributions of Charlemagne were inspired by Titurel in regard to renewing cultural impulses (while not discounting the negative aspects of Charlemagne's rule, which cannot be overlooked). In that light, the possible meaning behind the name Titurel as a "tutor" ("tuteur") makes sense. "It is the impulse of Zarathustra [Titurel] which came to fruition in Carolingian times, in a subsequent phase in the evolution of humanity. In our time this was continued in the founding by Emil Molt of the first Waldorf School in Stuttgart."[35] In the lecture of August 17, Steiner refers to Charlemagne as a high adept from India. There are indications by Steiner where he confirms that Emil Molt is the reincarnated Charlemagne: in both incarnations this being inaugurated far-reaching new educational impulses. Thus, we can say that behind Waldorf education is the spirit of Titurel—i.e., Zarathustra, Melchizedek, and the divine Manu[36] of the Sun-Oracle.

33 *Paths of the Chrtistian Mysteries,* p. 57.

34 Karl König, *The Grail and the Development of Conscience* (Floris Books, 2016), p. 79.

35 Lutters, p. 139.

36 Manu means "to know" or "the thinker," and he was called the child of the sun. He is the son of Virag, who is the son of Brahma, the source and originator of the world. Brahma revealed the Sacred Laws to Manu, who taught them to humans as their first king (from the Rig Veda).

In certain respects, it makes one ponder Steiner's statement (see Book Four: "Who is Parzival?") regarding the individuality behind Parzival as being *greater* than Zarathustra. Lievegoed connects the divine Manu to the earthly Mani, thus also to Parzival (as opposed to Brabant who cautions against assuming that they are the same):

> He [Manu] was the founder of the central sun mystery on Atlantis. Hermes and Zarathustra were two of his disciples who were prepared by him to take a leading role in post-Atlantean times. This is in agreement with Rudolf Steiner's words about an individuality who stood higher in his spiritual development than Zarathustra. . . . I have already mentioned Rudolf Steiner's statement that one day the "Divine" Manu will become a "human" Manu. He will then no longer be guided by the hierarchies but develop his insights through his own powers.[37]

Lievegoed is convinced that the "Divine" Manu became the "earthly" Mani, the individuality behind the Youth of Sais, Nain, Mani, and Parzival. I see Titurel (the Zarathustra and Melchizedek being) preparing the way for Parzival, the highest of them all. This does not necessarily contradict Titurel's connection to the "Divine" Manu, since many aspects of this lofty being would never be able to find corporeality in Titurel, nor in Parzival, for that matter. Seen in that light, there is truth to both viewpoints. Either way, it needs further contemplation, study, and intuitive insights.

Charlemagne, who inaugurated schools in the ninth century, and, through his incarnation as Emil Molt, founded the Waldorf school in Stuttgart (together with Rudolf Steiner), was not only inspired by Titurel but also by the exalted individuality behind the legendary "Fleur," of *Fleur and Blanchefleur*—the highly popular tale which appeared in the Middle Ages around 1160 (in old "aristocratic" French), just before the Grail stories were written down.[38] This touching and beautiful legend from the Provence

37 *The Battle for the Soul*, pp. 82-83.

38 This legend fits well into the 6th grade Waldorf curriculum that includes the history of Islam and Christianity.

(translated into many languages even back then), served as a precursor to the Grail stories in that they express what later happens in the Holy Grail. The story shows how the human soul finds its higher self.

> Going back to Charlemagne's grandparents, to Flor and Blancheflor, we can see living in them the Rose and the Lily, which was meant to keep esoteric Christianity pure. . . . One saw in the Rose, in Flor or Flos, the symbol for the human soul, which has absorbed the personality, the ego impulse, allowing the spirit to work out of its individuality. This, in turn, even penetrated the red blood, carrier of the ego impulse. In the Lily, however, one saw the symbol of the soul which can only remain spiritual if the ego remains outside of it, only reaching the boundary. Thus, the Rose and the Lily are polarities. The Rose has self-confidence all within himself, whereas the Lily quite outside of herself. . . . Flor and Blancheflor expresses the finding of the world soul, the world ego through the human soul, the human ego.[39]

This moving story of two lovers of different religions, reminds one of Gahmuret and Belacane, or Repanse de Schoye and Feirefiz. It highlights the impulse to unite the East and the West, the Saracens and the Christians, the races of different colors—in short, it voices the ideal of uniting all of humanity in love.

Charlemagne's mother, Bertrada, also known as Bertha of the Big Foot or "Queen Goose-Foot," who wrote many of the best-known fairy tales (made famous by Charles Perrault and the Brothers Grimm), was greatly inspired by her father Charibert de Laon, the historical figure behind Fleur (or Flor/Flos). Steiner indicates that Charibert was John the Evangelist in a previous life, and that he later incarnated as Christian Rosenkreutz, the founder of Rosicrucianism. "The individuality reincarnated as Hiram Abiff and Lazarus-Johannes [John the Evangelist] was reincarnated and

---

39 Rudolf Steiner, *Wo und wie findet man den Geist? „Die europäischen Mysterien und ihre Eingeweihten,"* (Rudolf Steiner Verlag, 1984) (GA 57) p. 438 (translated by the author).

once again initiated in the thirteenth and fourteenth centuries as Christian Rosenkreutz."[40]

We can now see how intimately Bertha of the Big Foot was influenced by this great initiate, and how the esoteric secrets flowed into the fairytales, which indeed are exemplars of the "separation tales." In that sense, these fairytales, born in the womb of esoteric mystery temples, are highly relevant to our modern age, which is so separated from the spirit as no culture ever before, which includes all people, irrespective of all that divides humanity. Many of the Troubadours, trouvéres, and Trobairitz (women), as well as the bards and Minnesänger of the time were inspired by the contents of these mystery centers, the secrets of which then seeped into their songs and poems, spreading a new worldview, based on a spirit-infused Love that highlights the emergent individuality:

> Where was the center of these rhapsodes [troubadours]? Where had they learned to put such pictures in front of people? They had learned it in the same temples that we have to regard as the schools of the Rosicrucians. They were adherents of the Rosicrucians.[41]

As Waldorf teachers, we hold a huge responsibility to the founding impulse, for the leading spirits of humanity united in order to prepare the world for a way to overcome the discords of our globality through an education that respects each human being, drawing the very best out of them in order for the ideals of the future to come to pass. The solution to overcoming human discord in the world, between people, within communities and especially within ourselves, can be found in the Grail because the most sacred part of our inner life is our Heart Temple, where the light is purified blood, the place we feel most unified with ourselves

---

40 Rudolf Steiner, *Zur Geschichte und aus den Inhalten der erkenntniskultischen Abteilung der Esoterischen Schule: 1904 - 1914* (Rudolf Steiner Verlag 1987) (GA 265), p. 420 (translated by the author).

41 Rudolf Steiner, *Exkurse in das Gebiet des Markus-Evangelium*, Rudolf Steiner Verlag, 1995, Juni 10, 1911, GA 124, p. 207 (translated by the author).

and the world—*not I but the Grail in me*. The Grail throbs and cares only for the essential human being and pays no heed to divisiveness, especially in regard to race, gender, creed, nationality, or lineage. The Sacred Grail is concerned with the eternal "I am" that lives and weaves in every soul. The Grail is the Sun God that shines brighter than all the stars and planets, that radiates as truth and goodness within us, and welcomes, embraces, and accepts all people with the warmth of selfless love. Who is the Grail? It is us at our freest; it is us united with the universe; it is us as a creative force; it is us as a mystical fact; it is us as the crescent moon receiving the light of the sun; it is us as many suns united as one; it is the us within the I of the world; it is you in me; it is the culmination of our striving—the Us as Is—if we're bold enough to become It.

Discussion Topics, Questions

- Do you have a sense of your "inner voice"? Do you hear it?
- Discuss the different stages of a love relationship. Does it need to be renewed intermittently? What form would that renewal take?
- Do you feel a connection to the people who have died?
- Do you try to rectify your failures?
- What could it mean to be Grail King?
- What does the journey into the interior look like? How does it manifest itself?
- Do you recognize when you have been holding on to principles that no longer hold true?
- Would you agree that Parzival is all about self-education?
- Would you change or give up your religion in order to marry the one you love? Would you expect it from your partner? What does it entail?

Illustrations:

1. Aspects of *Parzival*
2. Bird, sword, and hexagram

3. Fired clay knight, painted (Odin Esty)
4. Purification with water, alabaster sculpture (National Museum of Egyptian Civilization)
5. Lalibela, Ethiopia (Photo: Brian Scannell)
6. Lalibela, Ethiopia (Photo: Brian Scannell)

ROUNDING OUT THE CIRCLE

There is a knighthood of the twenty first century
whose riders do not ride through the darkness
of physical forests as of old,
but through the forest of darkened minds.
They are armed with a spiritual armor
and an inner sun makes them radiant.
Out of them shines healing,
healing that flows from the knowledge
of the human being as a spiritual being.
They must create inner order, inner justice,
peace and conviction in the darkness
of our time.[1]
~ Karl König

THE END OF the *Parzival* block always comes too soon, whether we have three or four weeks at our disposal (often less, due to snow days, power outages, or—as witnessed over the last couple of years—the pandemic). Only

1 Karl König, *The Grail and the Development of Conscience* (Floris Books, 2016), p. 12.

a fraction can ever be covered, but one holds the whole within, as best as possible, which allows something more to emanate.

Toward the end of the block, I usually gather the qualities of the diverse women together, which also serves as a review of the unfolding imaginations. The zodiac of *The Eternal Feminine* offers a profound picture of our inner life, and they represents different manifestations of Love. Though we elucidate and examine the respective women as they fit into the developing story, they summarize the stages of human initiation in a reflective and pictorial manner. Some students might choose to write an essay on the topic, or capture their essence in a diagram, where the fundamental qualities are mentioned—elements that the triumvirate of men need to make their own.

Wolfram portrays women in an unusually positive light, contrary to what one might expect from a medieval tale and certainly not the way they are represented in the series *Game of Thrones* or *House of the Dragon* (albeit enjoyed by many 11th graders). In the words of a student who chose to write an independent paper on the women in *Parzival*:

> What do you think when you hear the words "medieval maidens?" Medieval women, especially Arthurian women, are often associated with simply being damsels in distress, meek angels that dictated the Code of Honor, or glamorous but wicked sorceresses. However, in *Parzival* nothing could be further from the truth. Eschenbach's women are independent, strong characters that are crucial catalysts to Parzival's transformation from the pure fool to Grail King."[2]

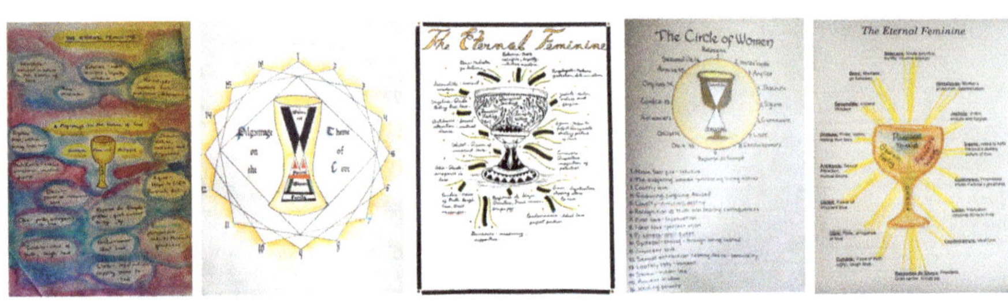

2 Jae-Yeon Yoo, "*Role of Women*," from the *Parzival* Main Lesson book.

Indeed, the surrounding constellation of women is all important to the development of the three heroes: Parzival, Gawain, and Feirefiz, in relation to achieving the Grail's essence. Esoterically speaking, women represent the soul life. But they are also the carriers of mystical knowledge, drawing forth faculties and capacities in the heroes during their respective journeys and initiations.

Coming up with the qualities of the respective groups can be discovered during class discussions or using the structure of the world-café method, where each group can explore one or more of the most prominent women. I ask the students to find the most meaningful keywords or phrases for each woman. The results might be verbalized in the following way:

Belacane: African, noble sacrifice, devoted, intuitive wisdom, Black Madonna. *Herzeloyde*: mother's love, determination, protectiveness, heart suffering. *Jeschute*: victim, sensuous, endurance, forgiveness.

Sigune: Parzival's destiny guide and awakener, pietá image of bridal loyalty and love, steadfastness.

Cunneware: prophetess, prescient recognition of someone's potential, suffering the consequences for expressing an insight and intuitive truth.

Liaze: infatuation, puppy love, stepping stone to love.

Condwiramurs: ideal love, perfect partner, conduit of love.

Repanse de Schoye: Priestess, Grail bearer, bringer of joy.

Cundrie 'La Surziere': Grail messenger, voice of essential truths—whether good, bad, or ugly—tough love.

Obie: shrew, arrogance in love (precursor to Orgeluse), love rejected and accepted, emerging independence.

Obilot: power of innocent love, wisdom of a child.

Antikonie: sexual attraction, consensual love, mutual attraction, object of lust.

Orgeluse: pride, shrew, femme fatal, wronged, bitter, revengeful, hidden nobility of soul, keeping true feelings locked within, testing true love, appearance and reality.

Bene: epitome of goodness, mediator and go-between in the service of love and social relations.

Secundille: ancient wisdom, prescience, soul guide, Eastern mysticism, Black Madonna, Soul of the Orient.

Arnive: healing queen, wise, perceptive crone.

I have called them the *sixteen Manifestations of Love*, which conveniently fits into the number symbolism, but some students suggest we add other women, such as *Ekuba:* empathy, numinous African insights, independence, consolation, herald, self-determination; *Itonje:* intuitive unseen love; *Imane:* healing, rejuvenating potential, vulnerability, faith; *Ampflise:* Lady-knight-servitor prototype. *Guinevere:* supportive, helpful, reassuring.

This circle or womb of women represents *The Eternal Feminine*, a concept introduced and coined by Goethe and exemplified by Margarete in Goethe's *Faust.* However, the idea and experience of the Eternal Feminine has always existed in one form or another, such as in the portrayal of Beatrice in Dante's *Divine Comedy.* These women drew forth essential qualities from the heroes or protagonists and are vital on their pilgrimage toward freedom and creative love. They are more than a muse for them, but a necessity, a life source that transforms deficiencies, weaknesses, flaws, failures, dormant and latent qualities into good. The Eternal Feminine lifts the human toward the spiritual, and the divine toward the human. We see the Eternal Feminine reflected in the respective Madonna embodiments, the Isis Sophia, Mother Nature, Gaia, Prakriti (Hindu), or the Wisdom Goddesses from India as depicted in the *Dasa Maha Vidyas*, amongst many others. Whatever the gender, we all carry the Eternal Feminine within us.

During the final days of the block, I also invite the students to act out different scenes from *Parzival*, if time allows. This inevitably draws forth a great deal of levity. They usually put the scene into a modern context, switch gender roles, and come up with little surprises and twists.

Rather than ending with a final paper or test, I use the available time to the last second. For many years already I have discontinued the practice of ending the block with a "comprehensive exam." I know very well where they stand. Instead, we round out Parzival's circuitous journey, sum up the contents of the epic in various ways through final discussions, questions, the sharing of poems and artwork, skits, and an overall review. Thus, the end is more like a ceremony, and it allows the essence to linger on within the depths of their being.

Though the last day varies depending on the class, I always set some time aside for them to voice their own favorite or most prominent imagination from the epic—the one that touched them the most, or simply the first section that comes to mind. Invariably, an almost sacred and intimate mood descends over the class as we go round, each student revealing their scene of choice. I am often surprised who says what. Not only does it say something about the individual students but also about the class, and it is always revealing and illuminating. This almost festive practice also serves as a review, allowing the scenes to rise up in our imaginations once more. Often, they also voice *why* they chose the specific scene. We become privy to how deeply some of the content has affected them. Indeed, I am convinced that some students have an experience of a past incarnation while studying and living into Parzival. Over the years, some scenes are mentioned more often than others, such as the "three drops of blood," the first "meeting with Cundrie" or the "battle between Parzival and Feirefiz." Every now and then, we have a first: in a recent block, a student mentioned the final meeting between Parzival and Sigune, where she is found dead, kneeling in front of Schionatulander's tomb: "The idea that Sigune, even though she was dead, could still serve as a guide and direct him from the beyond—that stuck with me—as well as Sigune asking him not to forget the world of the dead, the eternal world. . . . After a short pause he smiled, and added, "That moved me." Another imagination that has only been mentioned a few times is Parzival's "encounter with the birds" in Soltane.

Sometimes I have them choose one to three "life questions" from their list of questions that they have accumulated during the block and read them out aloud. That, too, can be a poignant moment. Or I ask them to come to the blackboard on the last day and write down what they consider the most urgent and pressing needs of our time, both for the world and humanity—inner and outer challenges. Once completed, we compare them to the struggles of the various scenes and characters within *Parzival*, how they might be reflected in the epic, and what possible answers are offered to overcome the difficulties. The connections the students make, the discoveries and insights never cease to impress me. And often it takes the whole class to arrive at the parallels and relationships. These points also serve as an appraisal, assessment, and summary of the block. It was especially poignant during the block where we had to start off with an online class (see "Zooming In"). In that instance, I brought up all the thoughts they'd mentioned on the first day and we discussed them, one by one, connecting them—as a group—to the different sections of the book. That certainly rounded out the circle of that main lesson block, surpassing my expectations; unique points were mentioned that I had either not thought about or even considered.

During the last ten to fifteen minutes of the last class, I attempt to round out the block with some closing words that incorporate and reinforce the most archetypal themes of Parzival, especially in regard to human development and the highest ideals of humanity, which includes the human endeavor to bring the outer world into balance with the inner, to harmonize the dualities of life. These concluding future-bearing words—different for every class—are both meant to serve as a metaphorical anchor in their lives and as a seminal thought vessel—a cornucopia filled with food for the developing soul life.

"In the dark part of the moon that we see, we behold the spiritual power of the sun. In the shell with the golden sheen, we see the physical power of the sun, which is reflected as radiant power. The spirit of the sun rests in the shell of the sun's physical power. Thus, the sun spirit actually rests in the moon shell."[3]

~ Rudolf Steiner

Suggested Activities and Assignments

- Write a questioning letter to the spirit of our age.
- Write a poem about a vessel, chalice, or bowl.
- Write an essay on the historical background of *Parzival* or an Introduction, based on what you connected to most during the opening lessons.
- Keep a journal throughout the block.
- Have the students collect "life questions" in their journals. The ideal is to have them come up with at least one question a day or a few for every chapter. As part of the review, they can be read in class. No need to answer them. Just hearing them is profound. They linger on

3 Steiner, *Esoterische Betrachtungen* (GA 149), p. 137 (translated by the author).

and many are answered during the course of the block.
- Lead the students in a "rice bowl" meditation.

- In class writing assignments (at the beginning, middle, or end of the main lesson): examples below.
- Read and recite the original Middle-High-German opening lines of *Parzival* with the class.
- Write about the meaning and "secret" of your name. If you don't know, use your imagination and make something up. Write your name backwards. Share the results in class.
- Write about the theme of light and darkness.
- Write a paragraph or a poem about specific colors (can also be done in pairs or groups).
- What is your relationship to your family background, taking religion, race, language, gender, etc., into consideration? Write an essay on the positive and negative aspects of your "inheritance." What aspects are you proud or ashamed of? Which aspects can you discard? Which ones are a challenge or a privilege? What elements can be useful or transformed.
- Design a crest, emblem, seal, or coat of arms that fits who you are. Write about why you chose the design. Do you have a family crest?
- Write on "The Sense of Belonging." Where do I belong?
- Poem or in-class writing on: What does "home" mean for you?
- Read Amanda Gorman's poem: "The Hill We Climb," (which was read at President Biden's inauguration on Wednesday, January 20, 2021)
- Read Mari Evans' poem: "I Am a Black Woman."

- Sing "Whatever Lola Wants, Lola Gets."
- Write down a significant nightmare. What truth did it reveal or foreshadow?

- Write an essay on Gahmuret, elucidating his positive and negative attributes. Where did he succeed, where did he fail? What does it mean for Parzival?
- Compare and contrast Herzeloyde and Belacane.
- During the review, ask students to read drafts of their essays out loud, or to share the poems that have been written in the class—on a voluntary basis. Often, the content of their work stimulates further discussion.
- The essay topics I ask the students to write are mostly assigned the day after we have covered the material, and once it has been thoroughly reviewed and discussed. Sleeping on the presentations reinforces the content.
- Encourage the students to make some of their drawings on black pastel drawing paper. It captures a very different atmosphere.

- Write a summary of all the encounters Parzival has in Book Three. Focus on the significance of each encounter.
- Sing: "Nature Boy" or "Fool on the Hill" by the Beatles.
- Discuss and/or write on the different types of "Fools" in the world. (In class writing or poem)
- Compare and contrast any two encounters Parzival has in Book Three.
- Intermittently have the students gather in groups to discuss characters, symbology or certain themes, to be followed by oral reports in front of the class. It helps if one person is assigned to be the scribe, notating what each student contributes. Go around to each group, making sure they stay on track and prodding and giving input.
- As part of the review have each student summarize one page from a specific chapter.
- Write an essay on an experience of failure and how it was overcome and redeemed, and what lessons it taught.

- Some chapters take longer to cover than others. It helps to have the students give reports on the Gawain chapters (not necessarily all of them). It shows how well they can read, comprehend, and understand the text.
- Convert certain imaginations into drawings, designs, or even paintings. Often, they are able to convey the mood of a scene better through an illustration than an essay.
- Give essay choices, and ask the students to come up with their own essay suggestions
- Allow students to choose a poetic format instead of an essay if it seems appropriate.

- Offer extra credit for independent work. Thematic content could include: birds, horses, plants, gemstones, planetary influences (astronomy), the role of the women in *Parzival*, color imagery, food, clothing, landscapes, and nature as such. Oftentimes these themes are included in the essays or their creative writing.
- Compare and contrast Parzival and Gawain, or write a paper on a character of your choice.
- Go on a hike or a nature walk where you encourage the students to take note of the nature surrounding them. Have them imagine they are children for part of the walk. On the return journey they can imagine being a shaman, a hermit, or a wise person. Write a poem on the experience.
- Explore the different facets of the hero's journey.
- Always relate the themes and topics to our own time and to the predominant socio-political issues of the moment. Ensure that the contents remain global, inclusive of all cultures. This takes a tremendous amount of extra effort on the part of the teacher.
- If possible, invite a storyteller to come in and present a scene from the epic. Alternatively, invite the students to become storytellers and present a scene. Note and discuss the difference between

telling the story and giving a report on a chapter. Cultivate the art of storytelling. This is one block in the high school where it is appropriate for the teacher to become a storyteller.

- Write poems accompanied by a drawing or painting.
- Write a summary of Parzival's most important encounters throughout his adventures.
- Compare and contrast any two encounters.
- Write your own list of advice for a friend in which you address the needs of the times. Write an advice list for yourself.

- Recite "The Tables Turned," by William Wordsworth.
- Write a paper or poem on ideal love. Refer to the relationship between Condwiramurs and Parzival.
- In class writing: Arranged marriage as opposed to marriage based on romantic love (needs a thorough discussion beforehand).
- Write a ballad based on a section of the book. Review the structure of the ballad. Invite the musical students to compose music to the ballads, which can be performed in class—special moments.
- Singing: "The Twa Corbies." (This ballad is based on one of the oldest extant poems in the English language. The students can use it as a template for their own ballads.)
- In class writing on the importance of dreams.
- Summarize Book Five, based on what you find significant or important.
- Write a paper on Failure and Redemption.
- Write a paper on the theme of "Questions."
- Write about someone who has had a severe setback or a rejection and how they were able to continue.
- Suggest keeping dream diaries, which fosters the ability to remember dreams and get a sense for their revelatory quality.
- Write a poem or an essay on the significance of the three drops of blood.

- If time allows, tell the story of the "The Green Knight and the Loathly Lady." (Dame Ragnell and Gawain). It answers the question: What do women want most?
- Write a poem or essay on "Silence" and "Loneliness."
- Write a poem, paragraph, or essay on "Doubt." Why do we doubt the truth continuously?
- What would your double look like? Do a drawing of your own double, either on paper or on the blackboard, singularly or in a group.
- Assign some of the Gawain chapters to individual students or groups of students to report on, bearing in mind plot, characters, symbolism, and thematic content.
- Have you ever been falsely accused? Write a poem or story or an anecdote on the topic. How did you respond? Have you ever witnessed someone suffering through false accusations? Did you do something about it?
- Write a poem about spurned love, unrequited love, or rejected love.

- Essay choices: write on the relationship between Trevrizent and Parzival.
- Express the essence of Book Nine in poetic form.
- Write a confessional poem.
- Write a contemporary version of Parzival's confessional meeting with the hermit.
- Singing: "The Long and Winding Road" by the Beatles.
- Write a poem exploring the concept "Sanctuary."
- Write poems about larks and swallows.
- Drawing of the Castle of Wonders.
- If you were to design symbols to represent thinking, feeling, and willing respectively—what would they look like?
- Write about the power of questions.
- Write a poem or paragraph on the theme of "wings": what do wings

evoke and symbolize? Take into account different types of wings.

Illustrations:

1. Assortment of Parzival books
2. The Eternal Feminine
3. Notes and diagram from the Blackboard: The Eternal Feminine
4. Parzival Main Lesson Book (Odin Esty)

A note from a student after the 2023 Parzival block:

> *Dear Mr. Müller,*
>
> *I would never have read Parzival on my own, because I had never heard of it. As you have shown me, it is a masterpiece that should be taught everywhere (hopefully it is). I would like to thank you for all of the dedication that you put into this block. The material was presented in such a way that I always felt a part of the discussion, intrigued and entertained. I also (almost) never got distracted (when things go slow, I easily get distracted, not in this main lesson). I am very grateful that you brought this book into my life. Thank you for teaching this wonderful main lesson block.*
>
> *S.D.*

Bibliography

Achenbach, Joel. "The God Particle," *National Geographic* (March 2008).

Ali, Ayaan Hirsi. *Infidel.* Free Press, 2007.

Angelou, Maya. "Keep the Faith." In *Letters to my Daughter.* Random House Trade Paperbacks, 2009.

Bishop, Orland. *The Seventh Shrine: Meditations on the African Spiritual Journey: From the Middle Passage to the Mountaintop.* Lindisfarne Book, 2017.

Chrestien de Troyes. *Perceval.* Aus dem Französischen von Konrad Sandkühler. Verlag Freies Geistesleben, 1977.

De Boron, Robert. *Joseph of Arimathea: A Romance of the Grail.* Translated by Jean Rogers, Rudolf Steiner Press, London, 1990.

Diallo, Yaya and Mitchell Hall. *The Healing Drum: African Wisdom Teachings.* Destiny Books, 1989.

Durrel, Shelley. *Healing the Fisher King: Spiritual Lessons with Parzival, Gump, the Grail, Tao, and Star Wars.* Art Tao Press, Miami, Florida, 2002.

Edusei, Kofi. *Für uns ist Religion die Erde, auf der wir leben: Ein Afrikaner erzählt von der Kultur der Akan.* Urachhaus, 1985.

Emerson, Ralph Waldo. *Emphatically Emerson.* Selected & arranged by Frank Cocitto. Candlepower, New Paltz, NY, 2004.

Fink, Dagmar. *Das Wunder des Lachens.* Verlag Freies Geistes Leben, 2001.

Frei, Joel. "The Unparalleled Experiment," in the "Swiss Review: The Magazine for the Swiss Abroad." 2011.

Göbel Nina. *Julian: Herzeloyde: Tycho Brahe.* Goetheanum. Freie Hochschule für Geisteswissenschaft, 1987.

Goethe, Johann Wolfgang. *Goethe's Faust.* Translated by Walter Kaufmann. Anchor Books, 1961.

Greub, Werner. *Wolfram von Eschenbach und die Wirklichkeit des Grals.* Philosophish-Antroposophisher Verlag, Dornach, Schweiz, 1974.

Gruwez, Christine. *Mani & Rudolf Steiner: Manichaeism, Anthroposophy, and their Meeting in the Future.* Steiner Books, 2014.

Fee, Christopher R. *Arthur: God and Hero in Avalon.* Reaktion Books, 2019.

Hansberry, Lorraine. *A Raisin in the Sun.* A Signet Book (Penguin Group),1988.

Homer. *The Iliad.* Translated by Robert Fitzgerald. Anchor Books, 1975.

Homer. *The Odyssey.* Translated by Robert Fitzgerald. Anchor Books, 1963.

Hutchins, Eileen. *Parzival: An Introduction.* Temple Lodge, 1992.

Ilona Schubert. *Reminiscences of Rudolf Steiner and Marie Steiner-von Sivers.* Temple Lodge Press, 1991.

Inayat-Khan, Pir Zia. *Saracen Chivalry: Counsels on Valor, Generosity and the Mystical Quest.* Suluk Press Omega Publications INC., New Lebanon, New York, 2012.

Kirchner-Brockholt, Margarete, and Erich. *Rudolf Steiner's Mission and Ita Wegman.*

Rudolf Steiner Press, Reprint Edition, 2016.

König, Karl. *The Grail and the Development of Conscience.* Floris Books, 2016.

Kovacs, Charles. *Parsifal and the Search for the Grail.* Floris Books, 2002.

Lievegoed, Bernard. *The Battle for the Soul.* Hawthorne Press, 1994.

Leu-Schmidt, Elisabeth. *Ein Gralsimpuls im Osten.* Rudolf Geering Verlag, Goetheanum, Dornach, 1980.

Lutters Frans. *An Exploration into the Destiny of the Waldorf School Movement.* Translated by Philip Mees. AWSNA, 2011.

Mandela, Nelson Rolihlahla. *Mandela: An Illustrated Autobiography.* Little, Brown and Company, 1994.

Margulies, Julianna. *Sunshine Girl: An Unexpected Life*. Ballantine Books, 2021.

Meyer, Rudolf. *Zum Raum wird hier die Zeit: Die Gralsgeschichte*. Urachhaus, 1980.

Meyer, Rudolf, *The Wisdom of the Fairy Tales*. Translated by Polly Lawson. Floris Books, Anthroposophic Press, 1988.

Mosmann, Heinz. *Der Parzival Wolframs von Eschenbach: Erkenntnis und imaginative Gestaltung des Gralsmysteriums.* Verlag Freier Geistesleben, 2020.

Murad, Nadia. *Last Girl: My Story of Captivity and My Fight against the Islamic State.* Tim Duggan Books, 2017.

Mutwa, Vusamazulu Credo. *Indaba, My Children: African Tribal History, Legends, Customs and Religious Beliefs*. Canongate, 1998. First published in 1964 by Blue Crane Books.

Old Testament. Book of Proverbs, 16:18.

Porter, Tom (Sakokweniónkwas), Bear Clan Elder of the Mohawk Nation. *And Grandma Said…, Iroquois Teachings as passed down through the oral tradition.* Xlibris, 2008.

Querido, René. *The Mystery of the Holy Grail: A Modern Path of Initiation*. Rudolf Steiner College Publication, 1991.

Ravenscroft, Trevor. *The Cup of Destiny: The Quest for the Grail.* Samuel Weiser, 1995.

Reclams Namenbuch. Hrsg. Theo Herrle, Philipp Reclam Jun, Stuttgart, 1981.

Seas, Virginia, and Manfred Schmidt-Brabant. *Paths of the Christian Mysteries: From Compostela to the New World.* Temple Lodge, 2003.

Seiler-Hugova, Ueli. *Das Grosse Parzivalbuch: Wolfram von Eschenbachs Parzival als ein moderner Einweihungsweg, der zur Integration und Individuation führt.* SchneiderEditionen, 2014.

Shepherd, Rachael. "Lalibela: An Expression of Prester John." *Invisible Africa*. Novalis Press, South Africa, 1987.

Smith, Neil J. *On the Ropes.* Austin Macauley, 2020.

Staley, Betty K. *Adolescence: The Sacred Passage: Inspired by the Legend of Parzival.* Rudolf Steiner College Press, 2006.

Steiner, Rudolf. *Aus den Inhalten der esoterischen Stunden Band 1: 1904-1909* Rudolf

Steiner Verlag, 1995 (GA 266).
——. *Zur Geschichte und aus den Inhalten der ersten Abteilung der Esoterischen Schule 1904 – 1914*. Rudolf Steiner Verlag, 1984 (GA 264).
——. *How to Know Higher Worlds: A Modern Path of Initiation*, Anthroposophic Press, 2008.
——. *Der Jahreskreislauf als Atmungsvorgang der Erde und die vier großen Festzeiten*, Rudolf Steiner Verlag, Taschenbuch Ausgabe, 1990 (GA 223).
——. *Esoterische Betrachtungen: Von der Suche nach dem heiligen Gral*, Philosophischer-Antroposophischer Verlag am Goetheanum, 1934 (GA 149).
——. *Esoterische Betrachtungen: Karmische Zusammenhänge* (GA 238).
——. *Zur Geschichte und aus den Inhalten der erkenntniskultischen Abteilung der Esoterischen Schule: 1904 - 1914*, Rudolf Steiner Verlag, 1987 (GA 265).
——. *Die Evolution vom Gesichtspunkte des Wahrhaftigen*. Rudolf Steiner Verlag, Berlin 1987 (GA 132).
——. *The Gospel of Saint Luke*. Rudolf Steiner Press, 1990 (GA 114).
——. *The Holy Grail: From the works by Rudolf Steiner*. Compiled by Steven Roboz. Steiner Book Center, 1984.
——. *Karmische Betrachtungen*, Band IV. Rudolf Steiner Verlag (GA 238).
——. *Karmic Relationships: Esoteric Studies*, Vol. VII. Translated by D.S. Osmond, Rudolf Steiner Press, London, 1973 (GA 239).
——. *Karmic Relationships: Esoteric Studies*, Vol. VIII. Translated by D.S. Osmond, Rudolf Steiner Press, London, 1975 (GA 240).
——. *Das Lukas-Evangelium*. Rudolf Steiner Verlag, 1977 (GA 114).
——. *Man as Symphony of the Creative Word*. Rudolf Steiner Press, 1991 (GA 230).
——. *The Kingdom of Childhood*. Anthroposophic Press, 1995 (GA 311).
——. *Occult Signs and Symbols*, Anthroposophic Press, 1972.
——. *An Outline of Esoteric Science*, Anthroposophic Press, 1997 (CW 13).
——. *Der Orient im Lichte des Okzidents: Die Kinder des Luzifer und die Brüder Christi*. Rudolf Steiner Verlag, Dornach, 1977 (GA 113).
——. *Exkurse in das Gebiet des Markus-Evangeliums*. Rudolf Steiner Verlag, 1995 (GA 124).
——. *Practical Advice to Teachers*. Anthroposophic Press, 2000 (CW 294).
——. *The Temple Legend: Freemasonry & Related Occult Movements: From the Contents of the Esoteric School*, November 11, 1904. Rudolf Steiner Press, Forest Row, 1997. (CW 93).
——. „Die europäischen Mysterien und ihre Eingeweihten." *Wo und wie findet man den Geist?* Rudolf Steiner Verlag, 1984 (GA 57).

Stein, Walter Johannes. *The Death of Merlin: Arthurian Myth and Alchemy.* Floris Books, 1989.

Stein, Walter Johannes, *The Ninth Century: World History in the Light of the Holy Grail.* Temple Lodge Press, London, 1991.

Steindl-Rast, O.S.B., David, with Lebell, Sharon. *The Music of Silence: Entering the Sacred Space of Monastic Experience*. Harper San Francisco, 1995.

Storm, Hyemeyohsts. *Seven Arrows*. Ballantine Books, New York, 1972.

Subin, Anna Della, *Accidental Gods*. Metropolitan Books, 2021.

Sussman, Linda. *Speech of the Grail: A Journey Toward Speaking that Heals and Transforms*. Lindisfarne Press, 1995.

Tutu, Desmond & Mpho. *The Book of Forgiving: The fourfold path for healing ourselves and our world.* William Collins, imprint of Harper Collins Publishers, 2014.

Van der Post, Laurens. "Intuition, Intellect, and the Racial Question." Transcript of a lecture at the Waldorf School, Adelphi University, October 2, 1963.

Von dem Borne Gerhard. *Der Gral in Europa: Wurzeln und Wirkungen*. Urachhaus, 1976.

William Forward and Andrew Wolpert.*The Quest for the Grail: The Golden Blade No. 47*. Floris Books, 1994.

Wolfram von Eschenbach. *Parzival.* Translated by A.T. Hatto. Penguin Books, 1980.

Wolfram von Eschenbach. Hrsg. Karl Lachmann, Fünfte Ausgabe: *Vorrede und Texte: Lieder, Parzival, Titurel, Willehalm.* Druck und Verlag von G Reimer, Berlin, 1891.

Wolfram von Eschenbach. *Parzival: A Romance of the Middle Ages.* Translated by Helen M. Mustard & Charles E. Passage. Vintage Books, 1961.

Wolfram von Eschenbach. *Titurel.* Translation and studies by Charles E. Passage. Frederick Ungar Publishing Co., New York, 1984.

Wunderworte: Mit Novalis durch das Jahr. Hrsg. von Florian Roder. Verlag Freies Geistesleben, 2000.

Acknowledgments

THIS BOOK OWES its existence to many people, long before I considered writing *Why Parzival?* First among these is Francis Edmunds, founder of Emerson College in Sussex, England, who gave a series of inspiring lectures on the Grail and Parzival's quest while I was a student there. It launched my own quest to know more about this mysterious epic. About fifteen years later, my quiet wish to teach *Parzival* availed itself when I started teaching at the Hawthorne Valley Waldorf High School. It is to the students whom I taught over the years that I am most indebted. Heartfelt thanks to all of them! They gave me the opportunity to delve into this epic, year after year. More importantly, their fresh insights, both in writing and during the discussions, greatly enriched and deepened my own understanding of the text. Unfortunately, I do not remember the names of all the students whose contributions can be found in this book in one way or another, and for that I apologize. I trust and hope that they will be happy that their work is included in this book.

Furthermore, I would like to express my sincere gratitude to the following people: to Leif Garbisch for his deep reading of the original manuscript and his poignant, comprehensive, and perceptive comments; to Ella Manor Lapointe for her untiring work on the design and layout, greatly enhancing the book's aesthetics; to Clifford Venho for his meticulous proofreading of the final draft. I would also like to give special thanks to the Fern Hill Fund and the Foundation for Rudolf Steiner Books, which made this publication possible. Finally, I am deeply indebted to my wife, Martina Angela Müller, for the endless discussions we had on all aspects of the project and her insightful suggestions and editorial comments that have enriched *Why Parzival?* on many levels.

About the Author

Eric G. Müller is the director of Teacher Education at the Alkion Center, and a humanities teacher at the Hawthorne Valley Waldorf High School in Harlemville, New York. Born in Durban, South Africa, he studied literature and history at the University of the Witwatersrand, Johannesburg. He continued his studies at Emerson College, England, and the Institute for Waldorf Pedagogy in Witten-Annen, Germany, where he specialized in drama and music education. He was a class teacher in Eugene, Oregon, for eight years before moving across the country to become a high school teacher. He has published numerous books, including novels, children's books, and poetry.

Author at the Hermitage near Arlesheim (Photo: Martina Angela Müller)